New Orleans

Tom Downs
John T Edge

LONELY PLANET PUBLICATIONS
Melbourne · Oakland · London · Paris

New Orleans
2nd edition – January 2000
First published – January 1997

Published by
Lonely Planet Publications Pty Ltd A.C.N. 005 607 983
192 Burwood Rd, Hawthorn, Victoria 3122, Australia

Lonely Planet Offices
Australia PO Box 617, Hawthorn, Victoria 3122
USA 150 Linden St, Oakland, CA 94607
UK 10a Spring Place, London NW5 3BH
France 1 rue du Dahomey, 75011 Paris

Photographs
Richard Cummins; Tom Downs; John Elk III; Mason Florence; Lee
Foster; Rick Gerharter; Michael Girard; Jeffrey Greenberg/The Picture
Cube, Inc; Christian Heeb/Gnass Photo Images, Inc; Rini Keagy;
Dorothea Lange (Southern Media Archive, University of Mississippi);
Adam Lutz; Stephen G Maka/The Picture Cube, Inc; Anthony
Pidgeon; Jim Schwabel/Index Stock Photography; Porché West

Some of the images in this guide are available for licensing from
Lonely Planet Images.
email: lpi@lonelyplanet.com.au

Front cover photograph
French Quarter (Christian Heeb/Gnass Photo Images, Inc)

ISBN 0 86442 782 4

text & maps © Lonely Planet 2000
photos © photographers as indicated 2000

Printed by The Bookmaker Pty Ltd
Printed in China

Contents

INTRODUCTION 11

FACTS ABOUT NEW ORLEANS 13

NEW ORLEANS' MUSICAL HERITAGE 37

FACTS FOR THE VISITOR 48

MARDI GRAS 77

GETTING THERE & AWAY 95

GETTING AROUND 104

The Authors

PHOTO BY JENNIFER MOE

Tom Downs
Growing up, Tom spent a lot of time in buses. To hear him tell it, he 'came of age aboard a Scenicruiser.' On one trip across the country, he got off in New Orleans. He settled into a fleabag hotel on St Charles Ave and accepted work moving used office furniture. It was the steamy month of July. He fell in love with the place. Tom is the author of Lonely Planet's *San Francisco*, and today he lives in that city with his wife, Fawn, and their children, Mai and Lana.

John T Edge
John T is an independent writer of nonfiction based in Oxford, Mississippi. He is coauthor of Lonely Planet's *Deep South* guide and *A Gracious Plenty: Recipes and Recollections from the American South*, recently published by Putnam. John T's writing has appeared in numerous national magazines, including *Cooking Light*, *The New York Times Magazine*, *Saveur*, *Southern Living* and the *Oxford American*, where he is the food writer.

PHOTO BY SARAH TORIAN

FROM THE AUTHORS
Tom Downs Firstly, I'd like to thank my family (especially Maybone, my little Carnival Queen), who are very supportive of my Lonely Planet efforts. Then there's the cast of accomplices in New Orleans, namely Bob Girault, a real demon of knowledge and without whom I'd have only scratched the surface for this book. He put me up and put me down and sort of knocked me around town for two months, and for it I'm grateful. Robert Florence, yet another New Orleanian who seems to know everything, made it his mission to keep me informed and on many occasions he and Helene Florence kept me company. Media-savvy folks like Beverly Gianna and Tara Marine of the NOTCB and Ann Christian often pointed me in the right direction and they introduced me to important and interesting characters in town.

Honestly I never expected to find so many people willing to help out this sorry-looking travel writer, but they seemed to jump out from behind bushes and lampposts all over town. In particular, I'd like to mention the good citizens of the Bywater: Robyn, Carla, Allison, Christopher, Dr Bob, Kermit and the folks at Vaughan's, and, with special fondness, Heidi and Linda, who made sure I was well fed. French Quarter denizen John Heinmann shuttled me around town one day, enabling me to take in four Mardi Gras parades. John T Edge was as sharp and enjoyable to work with as anyone could hope for. Finally, a wink to Ernest and Antoinette K-Doe for their hospitality on a very memorable night.

The 'krewe' in California also deserve a little ink: Mark Carrodus and Chris Harris provided essential reading and music and accompanied me on two trips to New Orleans in the early '90s. Prior to my latest foray to New Orleans, Hayden Foell hepped me to some music I hadn't heard before, and Beca Lafore and John Fadeff each grabbed me by a boot and catapulted me to Louisiana. Greta Schnetzler pulled my coat on contemporary culinary issues. Peter Ivey sold me his '79 Scirocco for $700 and it got me and my luggage to New Orleans and back without breaking down.

At Lonely Planet, Kate Hoffman and Eric Kettunen generously agreed to hire me for this job, and Brigitte Barta was my supportive in-house contact while I was out plowing the field. Maureen Klier, my editor, was on all counts a joy and privilege to collaborate with, as were Laura Harger and Valerie Sinzdak. Patrick Huerta, a mad-scientist and cartographer, also left his indelible stamp on this book, as did artist Hayden Foell and designer Wendy Yanagihara. Good workin' with y'all!

John T Edge Thanks to my friends Charlie Hammond, Matt Konigsmark, Anne Rochelle-Konigsmark, Mike Luster, Dannal Perry and Aimee Schmidt, who shared secrets, advice and tales of the road ahead. Praise and appreciation to the staff at Lonely Planet Publications in Oakland, California, especially my editor for this project, Maureen Klier.

This Book

The 1st edition of *New Orleans* was written by Robert Raburn. Tom Downs wrote this second edition with help from John T Edge, who wrote the Excursions chapter.

FROM THE PUBLISHER

Meanwhile back at Lonely Planet's Oakland office, Maureen Klier had such a great time editing this book that she is considering running away to join a second-line parade or to become a sous chef at K-Pauls (she hears the restaurant's 'Turducken' is tasty as all get-out). In addition to the talents of Tom and John T, others who made this book possible include senior editors Brigitte Barta and Laura Harger, proofer-extraordinaire Valerie Sinzdak, cartographic sharp-shooter Patrick Huerta and senior cartographers Amy Dennis and Tracey Croom. Other cartographers who lended a helping hand include Ivy Feibelman, Chris Gillis, Dion Good, Mary Hagemann, Monica S Lepe, Andy Rebold and Chris Whinihan.

A very special thanks goes to Quark queen Wendy Yanagihara, who designed the book; Beca Lafore, who selected the photos and color scheme; and Hayden Foell, who drew the illustrations. Hugh D'Andrade, John Fadeff, Rini Keagy, Jennifer Steffey, Jim Swanson, and Wendy also contributed illustrations. Rini was the mastermind behind the book's cover, and senior designer Margaret Livingston oversaw the whole production. Ken DellaPenta created the index.

THANKS
Many thanks to the travelers who used the last edition and wrote to us with helpful hints, advice and interesting anecdotes. Your names appear in the back of this book.

Foreword

ABOUT LONELY PLANET GUIDEBOOKS

The story begins with a classic travel adventure: Tony and Maureen Wheeler's 1972 journey across Europe and Asia to Australia. Useful information about the overland trail did not exist at that time, so Tony and Maureen published the first Lonely Planet guidebook to meet a growing need.

From a kitchen table, then from a tiny office in Melbourne (Australia), Lonely Planet has become the largest independent travel publisher in the world, an international company with offices in Melbourne, Oakland (USA), London (UK) and Paris (France).

Today Lonely Planet guidebooks cover the globe. There is an ever-growing list of books, and there's information in a variety of forms and media. Some things haven't changed. The main aim is still to help make it possible for adventurous travelers to get out there – to explore and better understand the world.

At Lonely Planet we believe travelers can make a positive contribution to the countries they visit – if they respect their host communities and spend their money wisely. Since 1986 a percentage of the income from each book has been donated to aid projects and human-rights campaigns.

Updates Lonely Planet thoroughly updates each guidebook as often as possible. This usually means there are around two years between editions, although for more unusual or more stable destinations the gap can be longer. Check the imprint page (following the color map at the beginning of the book) for publication dates.

Between editions, up-to-date information is available in two free newsletters – the paper *Planet Talk* and email *Comet* (to subscribe, contact any Lonely Planet office) – and on our website at www.lonelyplanet.com. The *Upgrades* section on the website covers a number of important and volatile destinations and is regularly updated by Lonely Planet authors. *Scoop* covers news and current affairs relevant to travelers. And, lastly, the *Thorn Tree* bulletin board and *Postcards* section of the site carry unverified, but fascinating, reports from travelers.

Correspondence The process of creating new editions begins with the letters, postcards and emails received from travelers. This correspondence often includes suggestions, criticisms and comments about the current editions. Interesting excerpts are immediately passed on via newsletters and the website, and everything goes to our authors to be verified when they're researching on the road. We're keen to get more feedback from organizations or individuals who represent communities visited by travelers.

Lonely Planet gathers information for everyone who's curious about the planet – and especially for those who explore it first-hand. Through guidebooks, phrasebooks, activity guides, maps, literature, newsletters, image library, TV series and website, we act as an information exchange for a worldwide community of travelers.

Research Authors aim to gather sufficient practical information to enable travelers to make informed choices and to make the mechanics of a journey run smoothly. They also research historical and cultural background to help enrich the travel experience and allow travelers to understand and respond appropriately to cultural and environmental issues.

Authors don't stay in every hotel because that would mean spending a couple of months in each medium-size city and, no, they don't eat at every restaurant because that would mean stretching belts beyond capacity. They do visit hotels and restaurants to check standards and prices, but feedback based on readers' direct experiences can be very helpful.

Many of our authors work undercover; others aren't so secretive. None of them accept freebies in exchange for positive write-ups. And none of our guidebooks contain any advertising.

Production Authors submit their raw manuscripts and maps to offices in Australia, the USA, the UK or France. Editors and cartographers – all experienced travelers themselves – then begin the process of assembling the pieces. When the book finally hits the shops, some things are already out of date, we start getting feedback from readers and the process begins again...

WARNING & REQUEST

Things change – prices go up, schedules change, good places go bad and bad places go bankrupt – nothing stays the same. So, if you find things better or worse, recently opened or long since closed, please tell us and help make the next edition even more accurate and useful. We genuinely value all the feedback we receive. Julie Young coordinates a well-traveled team that reads and acknowledges every letter, postcard and email and ensures that every morsel of information finds its way to the appropriate authors, editors and cartographers for verification.

Everyone who writes to us will find their name in the next edition of the appropriate guidebook. They will also receive the latest issue of *Planet Talk*, our quarterly printed newsletter, or *Comet*, our monthly email newsletter. Subscriptions to both newsletters are free. The very best contributions will be rewarded with a free guidebook.

Excerpts from your correspondence may appear in new editions of Lonely Planet guidebooks, the Lonely Planet website, *Planet Talk* or *Comet*, so please let us know if you *don't* want your letter published or your name acknowledged.

Send all correspondence to the Lonely Planet office closest to you:

Australia: PO Box 617, Hawthorn, Victoria 3122
USA: 150 Linden St, Oakland, CA 94607
UK: 10A Spring Place, London NW5 3BH
France: 1 rue du Dahomey, 75011 Paris

Or email us at: talk2us@lonelyplanet.com.au

For news, views and updates, see our website: www.lonelyplanet.com

HOW TO USE A LONELY PLANET GUIDEBOOK

The best way to use a Lonely Planet guidebook is any way you choose. At Lonely Planet, we believe the most memorable travel experiences are often those that are unexpected, and the finest discoveries are those you make yourself. Guidebooks are not intended to be used as if they provided a detailed set of infallible instructions!

Contents All Lonely Planet guidebooks follow the same format. The Facts about the Country chapters or sections give background information ranging from history to weather. Facts for the Visitor gives practical information on issues like visas and health. Getting There & Away gives a brief starting point for researching travel to and from the destination. Getting Around gives an overview of the transport options available when you arrive.

The peculiar demands of each destination determine how subsequent chapters are broken up, but some things remain constant. We always start with background, then proceed to sights, places to stay, places to eat, entertainment, getting there and away, and getting around information – in that order.

Heading Hierarchy Lonely Planet headings are used in a strict hierarchical structure that can be visualized as a set of Russian dolls. Each heading (and its following text) is encompassed by any preceding heading that is higher on the hierarchical ladder.

Entry Points We do not assume guidebooks will be read from beginning to end, but that people will dip into them. The traditional entry points are the list of contents and the index. In addition, however, some books have a complete list of maps and an index map illustrating map coverage.

There may also be a color map that shows highlights. These highlights are dealt with in greater detail later in the book, along with planning questions and suggested itineraries. Each chapter covering a geographical region usually begins with a locator map and another list of highlights. Once you find something of interest in a list of highlights, turn to the index.

Maps Maps play a crucial role in Lonely Planet guidebooks and include a huge amount of information. A legend is printed on the back page. We seek to have complete consistency between maps and text, and to have every important place in the text captured on a map. Map key numbers usually start in the top left corner.

Although inclusion in a guidebook usually implies a recommendation, we cannot list every good place. Exclusion does not necessarily imply criticism. In fact, there are a number of reasons why we might exclude a place – sometimes it is simply inappropriate to encourage an influx of travelers.

Introduction

New Orleans seduces its visitors. It casts its spell Uptown in the spotted shade of a live oak tree and again downtown within the worn stucco confines of a Creole courtyard, slipping voodoo potions into sweet tasting cocktails, casually dropping anecdotes about its past. It subdues defenseless hearts with a sultry heat that envelops the lacy iron galleries and pealing rusted balustrades in the French Quarter. A moist gust of wind makes fan-like palmettos slap into each other, dime-sized raindrops pelt the leaves of banana trees, and Caribbean colors intensify.

This is merely the beginning. New Orleans – lazily pronounced 'new **or**-luns' by some, more liltingly articulated as 'new **or**-lee-uns' by others – is a psychologically complex city, unlike any other in North America, with an impractical, romantic heart and a defiant, artistic nature. Its very setting, on a waterlogged patch of earth beside a particularly sensuous and ominous curve of the Mississippi River, defies logic. Its tragic flaws only endear the city to those who love it.

New Orleans exists out of time. It has followed an unorthodox and capricious course through the past century, taking side roads and back alleys, exploring the bad neighborhoods of each decade with one hand on the wheel, the other twisting the dial on the radio, seeking comfort in the deeply felt lament of songs recorded long ago. It skulks through time with the cunning of a viper indulging its own peculiar, distrusting sensibilities. It lives it up as though a death sentence hangs over it.

Strangely, this enigmatic municipality has become a major tourist draw, and its decadence has become something of a commodity. Just as sailors once salaciously anticipated shore leaves spent lolling about in Storyville parlors, today enthused travelers and conventioneers come to hedonistic New Orleans with thoughts of stepping out of the routines of their lives. They flood Creole restaurants, Bourbon St bars and French Quarter jazz clubs, they lose themselves for a little while, go a little crazy, and in the morning civic workers come out to hose away the previous night's sins. Although New Orleans remains somewhat secretive and mysterious, it is sincere in welcoming visitors. It throws annual parties and opens up certain rooms in the house, leaving us to wonder what's hidden behind the closed doors. Every once in a while a privileged visitor who has shown enough interest is invited to pass through them.

Still, what less inquisitive visitors are treated to is no cheap sideshow, for New Orleans stamps enough of its own unique character onto everything that happens here. In a town as poor and small as New Orleans (just 500,000 residents – roughly half the number of out-of-towners who visit the city each month), tourist dollars exert a strong influence and could easily convert the city into an amusement park, distilling all that is real and vital and attractive in the Crescent City into an easily digestible, ersatz version of the real thing. In some cases, that has already happened. New Orleans, showing an unsuspected pragmatism, has donated a few of its lesser limbs and organs to tourism, lest out-of-towners try to swallow the city whole. But the indelible spirit of New Orleans will not be denied, and even its tourist traps are, well, distinctly New Orleanian.

Take Bourbon St – if you aren't looking for the real pulse of the city, you just might enjoy yourself there. It's as architecturally charming as any street in the Quarter, but on Bourbon you can drink liquor while walking from one bar to another. You can shout from the top of your lungs and still only amount to another member of the chorus.

A much better example of the New Orleans spirit is Mardi Gras, the grand spectacle that the city has brought to the New World from the Old. It is the pinnacle of the tourist calendar, as hundreds of thousands of people descend on the city to shed their puritanical ways for just a few days. Does it get out of hand? Sometimes, yes. But the spectacle is purely New Orleanian, and it is a beautiful reaffirmation of the city's identity. The city puts its pulsating heart on a platter and parades it down St Charles Ave for all to see. The locals do this purely for themselves, and they look forward to doing it all year long.

Perhaps an even better example of the real New Orleans is the New Orleans Jazz & Heritage Festival, which distills all of the most vital facets of the city's culture into two intense weekends. Musical performances are staged in circus tents rather than in nightclubs, food is served from stalls rather than at restaurants, and thousands come to take part in this celebration of the city's virtues.

What other city can package its culture in this way and still draw enthusiastic crowds? All it takes is a compelling spirit that people can't help but fall in love with. And, of course, it doesn't hurt to posses the guile of a seducer.

When your visit is over and you're back home, alluring dreams of the city stay with you like the lingering sensation of a kiss. Your thoughts continually revolve back to New Orleans and the desire to return.

Facts about New Orleans

HISTORY

Among US cities, New Orleans is in so many ways an anomaly that one can't help but wonder how the city came to be the way it is. Many aspects of New Orleans' culture today suggest a profound influence left behind by the French, who colonized New Orleans for the better part of a century, and by the Spanish, who ruled during a few formative decades. In addition, African culture has always held a stronger sway here than elsewhere in the US, often with Caribbean influences. And of course, being a major capital of the South has determined many events in the city's history and contributes to its character today.

By North American standards, New Orleans is an old city, and the depth of its history is cherished by locals. Visitors can't help but sense the city's palpable past while taking an inquisitive stroll through the Vieux Carré (old quarter), as the French Quarter is commonly called.

Native Americans

While nomadic Paleo-Indians were likely to have spent time in the area more than 10,000 years ago, humidity, shifting river courses and rising sea levels have apparently destroyed most evidence of their stay.

By 5000 BC, Archaic-period Americans were constructing a few earthen mounds, such as those at Avery Island in southern Louisiana. The following Neo-American period, from 2000 to 700 BC, saw the construction of extensive earthwork structures and the first use of pottery.

A simpler culture replaced the Neo-Americans. The Tchefuncte built small scattered settlements with circular shelters made from poles and covered with mud-caked thatch. From their large middens, we know they gathered plants and depended on clams, oysters and wild game. They also employed pottery for cooking and burial.

After 1700, Europeans documented numerous direct contacts with local tribes. Seven small tribes known collectively as the Muskogeans inhabited the parishes north of Lake Pontchartrain and occasionally the banks of the Mississippi River. They spoke Choctaw dialects but were not members of the larger Choctaw nation. One band, the Quinapisa, attacked La Salle's expedition and later settled above New Orleans on the Mississippi River as the tribe fled an epidemic in 1718. Other tribes south of New Orleans inhabited the bayous in Barataria and the lower course of the Mississippi River. Colonists adopted native foods such as maize, beans, wild rice, squash and filé, a thickening agent made from sassafras leaves.

Most groups suffered from European contact. Those who survived the epidemics or avoided capture by slave traders were most likely absorbed by the Houma and Choctaw tribes, who were themselves moving westward in flight from English and Chickasaw slave raids. Until the 1940s, when oil exploration came to the isolated coastal bayous from Terrebonne to Lafourche, the Houma thrived.

Alliances between escaped African slaves and Native Americans were common. Early French settlers also often married Native American women. Today, it is not uncommon to encounter culturally and racially mixed descendants among the nearly 19,000 dispersed Louisianans who identify themselves as American Indian.

European Exploration

Europeans probably first saw the mouth of the Mississippi River as early as 1519, when the Spanish explorer Alonso Alvarez de Pineda is believed to have come upon it. Word of such an entryway to the heart of North America reached Europe, and several explorers attempted to find it. Some of these expeditions did actually reach the Mississippi, only to meet with tragedy. The Spanish conquistador Hernando de Soto is a well-known case in point: His overland expedition from Florida to the Mississippi was a grueling three-year trek through some of the most inhospitable turf in North America. De Soto did eventually reach the river in 1542, only to be buried soon after within its murky depths.

Well over a century passed before anyone else undertook an expedition on the mighty river. In 1682 René Robert Cavelier La Salle headed an expedition of 23 French and 18 Native Americans to probe southward from French outposts on the Great Lakes. Upon reaching the Gulf of Mexico, he staged a ceremony to claim the Mississippi River and all its tributaries for France. This was no modest claim, for it included not only the entire river from Minnesota to the gulf, but a considerable part of North America extending from the Rockies to the Alleghenies. La Salle honored the extravagant King Louis XIV in naming the area Louisiana. His maps inaccurately (or perhaps deliberately) showed the Mississippi River in the vicinity of Matagorda Bay (Texas), suspiciously close to New Spain's silver mines, which would have meant his claim directly challenged Spain's claims there. In fact, upon his later return to the region, La Salle bypassed the Mississippi mouth – whether intentionally is anyone's guess – and he was murdered in Texas in 1687.

The Mississippi delta continued to elude sailors until 1699 when Canadian-born Pierre Le Moyne, Sieur d'Iberville, and his younger brother Jean-Baptiste Le Moyne, Sieur de Bienville, located the muddy outflow. They encamped 40 miles downriver from present-day New Orleans on the eve of Mardi Gras and, knowing their countrymen would be celebrating the French pre-Lenten holiday, christened the small spit of land Pointe du Mardi Gras – a name that would later have special cultural significance for New Orleans. With a Native American guide, the Le Moyne brothers sailed upstream, pausing to note the narrow portage to Lake Pontchartrain along Bayou St John in what would later become New Orleans.

French New Orleans

Iberville died of yellow fever in 1706, leaving Bienville to found Nouvelle Orleans – so named in honor of the Duc d'Orleans – in

1718. Bienville returned to the Bayou St John, which connects to Lake Pontchartrain and thereby offers more direct access to the Gulf of Mexico, and chose a site nearby on the Mississippi. The building of New Orleans was assigned to architect Adrien de Pauger, whose plans from 1722 still outline the French Quarter today. Promotion of the endeavor fell into the hands of the shrewd Scotsman John Law, head of the Company of the West, an important branch of the Company of the Indies, which controlled the world trade of France. Law's task was to populate Louisiana and make a productive commercial port of New Orleans. While Bienville's original group of 30 ex-convicts, six carpenters and four Canadians struggled against flood and yellow fever epidemic, Law busily portrayed Louisiana as heaven on earth to unsuspecting French, Germans and Swiss, who soon enough began arriving in New Orleans by the shipload. To augment these numbers, additional convicts and prostitutes were freed from French jails if they agreed to relocate in Louisiana. This inauspicious start for the colony would no doubt have an indelible impact on the city's character for generations to come.

In just four years, the colony's population ballooned from 400 to 8000. This figure included African slaves, thousands of whom the French landed during New Orleans' first decade. Whites born in New Orleans, mostly of French descent, came to be known as Creoles, and their French-derived culture quickly evolved into one that was unique to New Orleans. German immigrants gallicized their names, began to speak French and blended in. Black and white unions, although legally forbidden, were not uncommon, and several new castes emerged based on the amount of African blood people had – quadroons were one-fourth black, octoroons one-eighth black. These people, too, spoke French and in time also became known as Creoles.

The number of free blacks – *les gens de couleur libre*, or the free people of color – grew in New Orleans. Bienville, for one, owned 27 slaves in 1721, and freed two of them in 1733 after long years of service. Some slaves, after taking on additional work for wages, were permitted to buy their own freedom. And some free persons of color actually owned slaves. In 1724, French Louisianans adopted the Code Noir (Black Code), a document regulating the treatment and rights of slaves and free people of color. Freed slaves still had to carry passes to prove their status and were restricted from voting, holding public office or marrying someone of another race.

Colonial mercantilism was an economic failure, and the harsh realities of life in New Orleans inhibited willful civilian immigration – especially by women. As a result, the colonists created an exchange economy based on smuggling and local trade. When the Ursuline nuns arrived in 1728, they brought with them young, marriageable women, who were instantly known as 'casket girls' because they packed their belongings in casket-shaped boxes. Looking about her, Sister Hachard commented that 'the devil here has a very large empire.'

New Orleans under Spanish Rule

Realizing that Louisiana was a needless drain on the French treasury, French officials negotiated a secret pact with Spanish King Charles III – the 1762 Treaty of Fountainbleu. In return for ceding to Spain the extensive Louisiana territory west of the Mississippi plus New Orleans, France gained an ally in its war against England. On Spain's part, Louisiana represented a buffer between its possessions in New Spain and the English colonies along the Atlantic coast. The 'Frenchness' of New Orleans was little affected throughout Spain's administration.

A reminder of the past

Picayune

Spanish coinage can help define this word, which appears on the masthead of the local newspaper. The Spanish *peseta*, otherwise known as a 'piece of eight,' is the forerunner of the US silver dollar and its fractional divisions. Often the coin was inscribed so that the user could break it into quarters representing two *reales*, or bits, each worth 12$^1/2$¢. Further subdivision of a bit to its smallest possible fraction resulted in the *picayune*. The cost of a *Times-Picayune* was once a little more than a nickel, or 6$^1/4$¢. Hence, a picayune is something exceedingly small.

Not until 1766 did Spain bother to assert its control. By sending only a small garrison and few financial resources with the politically inept Governor Don Antonio de Ulloa, Spain aggravated the locals' bitterness over becoming Spanish subjects. Ulloa only spoke Spanish, and after he attempted to forbid trade with French islands, a rebel force drove him from office in 1768. In response, Spain sent General Alejandro O'Reilly and 2000 troops in 1769. 'Bloody' O'Reilly arrested hundreds and set a stern example by executing five rebels by firing squad.

Also during the onset of Spanish control, in 1755 the British deported thousands of Acadians from Nova Scotia, sending them away on unseaworthy ships after they refused to pledge allegiance to England. Some Acadians spent three decades in the forced migration known as *le grand dérangement*. The largely illiterate and Catholic peasants were unwanted in the American colonies and elsewhere in the Americas. Their French loyalty, however, appealed to the same French officials who had secretly ceded Louisiana to Spain. By transporting the Acadians to New Orleans beginning in 1765, France hoped to advance French interests in Louisiana. However, the Acadians, or Cajuns as they are now called, were not told that they were to become Spanish subjects.

And they were also unwelcome in New Orleans, where the citified Creoles regarded them as country trash. Once again, the Acadians were banished, this time to the upland prairies of Western Louisiana, where they at last were able to resume their lifestyle of raising livestock.

The slave revolt of 1791 in St Domingue abolished slavery in Haiti and established the country as the second independent nation in the Americas. Thousands of former slaves set out for New Orleans as free people of color. They were joined in ideology by partisans of the French Revolution, which had abolished slavery in all French colonies. Wealthy New Orleans planters and merchants, however, rejected notions of equality and denounced efforts to liberate slaves. In siding against France's revolutionary principles, Governor Carondelet deported activists and tried to quarantine the revolutionary contagion. But the seed was planted – even lower-class whites widely supported one failed slave uprising in 1795.

Louisiana Purchase & Antebellum New Orleans

Like the French earlier, Spanish officials were anxious to jettison the financial burden of Louisiana. In addition, Spain feared that it would eventually have to fight the Americans to retain its control. Hence, Spain jumped at Napoleon Bonaparte's offer to retake control of Louisiana in 1800.

Meanwhile, US President Thomas Jefferson clearly envisioned the nation's need to seize the river capital New Orleans, by force if necessary, to proceed on a path of western expansionism. Bonaparte knew that he risked losing New Orleans to the British and preferred that the territory be in American hands rather than under British control. Nevertheless, the US minister in Paris, Robert Livingston, was stunned by the offer to sell the entire Louisiana Territory – an act that would double the US's national domain – at a price of $15 million. On the final day of November 1803, the Spanish flag was quietly replaced by the French flag on the Place d'Armes, which in turn was replaced by the American flag on December 20.

Little cheer arose from the Creole community over the transfer. Americans would arrive in great numbers with their puritanical work ethic. Their Protestant beliefs and support for English common law jarred with the Catholic Creole way of life. In 1808 the territorial legislature sought to preserve Creole culture by adopting elements of Spanish and French laws – especially the Napoleonic Code as it relates to equity, succession and family. Elements of the code persist in Louisiana to the present.

Only one month after Louisiana's admission to the Union as the 18th state in 1812, President James Madison called for war against the British. His unpopular action barely registered with New Orleans residents until a British force assembled in Jamaica. Meanwhile, Louisiana Governor William C Claiborne pursued ridding the state of smugglers like Jean and Pierre Lafitte. These Baratarian pirates conducted an illicit slave trade, among other things (in the USA, the import and export of slaves had been outlawed in 1804). General Andrew Jackson arrived in Louisiana in November 1814, but New Orleanians were suspicious of his intentions when he imposed martial law. The locals' distrust of Jackson changed when word spread that the British intended to free slaves willing to fight against the Americans. Meanwhile, Jackson convinced Lafitte to side with the American forces in exchange for amnesty, thereby gaining the help of the pirate's band of sharpshooters and his considerable arsenal of weapons. Jackson also shocked many whites when he enlisted free black battalions and Choctaws. The Battle of New Orleans at Chalmette, just 4 miles from the French Quarter, was a one-sided victory for the Americans – around 300 British losses versus only 13 US losses – decisively ending the War of 1812.

The city grew quickly as Americans moved into New Orleans to make their fortunes in the increasingly busy port, and soon the city's populace began spilling beyond the borders of the French Quarter. During the 1830s Samuel Jarvis Peters (1801–55), a wholesale merchant born in Quebec, purchased plantation land to build a new community upriver from the French Quarter. Peters helped create a distinctly American residential section, separated by broad Canal St from the Creole French Quarter. He married into a Creole family and epitomized the 'American' entrepreneur operating within the Creole host community. Though Peters and other American and Creole merchants and businessmen were successful with American settlement, they maintained their principal establishments in the French Quarter. Today N Peters St passes through the French Quarter, while S Peters St extends into the American section.

Developers further transformed the 15 riverbank plantations into the ostentatious Uptown residences of Americans. By 1835 the New Orleans & Carrollton Railroad initially provided horse-drawn streetcar access along St Charles Ave to the growing community of Lafayette (not to be confused with the present Louisiana city) and beyond.

In spite of the Napoleonic Code's mandate for Jewish expulsion, and an anti-Semitic Southern Christian culture, trade

Yellow Fever

New Orleans' reputation as an unhealthy place was widespread and well deserved during the 18th and 19th centuries, when its residents were ravaged not so much by wild living but by the horrors of yellow fever. Symptoms of the disease showed themselves suddenly, and death soon followed. The epidemics frequently rose to Biblical proportions. An 1853 epidemic resulted in almost 8000 deaths – about 10% of the residents who had remained in the city after some 30,000 had fled with their lives.

Yellow fever's primary victims were male immigrants, children and laborers, many of whom lived and worked in squalid conditions. Yet no one was immune, and entire families (some of them prominent) were often lost. Numerous orphanages arose to care for children who survived their parents.

Many 'cures' were as harmful as the disease itself. 'Treatments' that hastened death included exorbitant bloodletting and large doses of calomel, a poisonous mercury compound whose horrid effects mortified skin and bone, causing them to slough away. In 1836 one visiting physician commented, 'We have drawn enough blood to float a steamboat and given enough calomel to freight her.'

Morticians were overworked and underpaid during these epidemics. In the rush to entomb those suspected of being contagious, undertakers lost the opportunity to embalm, preserve tissues on ice or even conduct services. Many cemeteries became putrid, fouled by the mass of bodies that could not be interred quickly enough.

Dr Carlos J Finlay, a Cuban, announced in 1881 that mosquitoes *(Aedes aegypti)* were responsible for spreading the disease, an explanation that was further proven by Walter Reed in 1905. The mosquito vector explained why those who were likely to spend a lot of time outdoors were at greatest risk. Health authorities in Louisiana urged people to screen their homes and eliminate mosquito breeding grounds. Apathy and disbelief led to one last New Orleans epidemic in 1905.

practicalities led to tolerance of Jewish merchants. In particular, Alsatian immigrants augmented the small Jewish community in New Orleans – by 1828 they had established a synagogue. Judah Touro, whose estate was valued at $4 million upon his death in 1854, funded orphanages and hospitals that would serve Jews and Christians alike.

Americans took control of the municipal government in 1852, illustrating that the Creole influence in New Orleans had eroded. American commerce had turned New Orleans into one of the world's wealthiest cities, but a political maelstrom had already appeared on the national horizon and would soon bring the city's prosperity to a crashing halt.

Civil War

During the first half of the 19th century, New Orleans' commercial ties to the North and to the rest of the world were much more developed than any other city in the American South, and these connections had been instrumental in the city's rise to prominence. At the dawn of the Civil War, New Orleans was by far the most prosperous city south of the Mason-Dixon line. But Louisiana was a slave state, and New Orleans was a slave city, and it was over this very issue that the nation hurtled towards civil war. Politicians from the North increasingly spoke out against slavery, while Southerners began to clamor for secession from a Union that had grown hostile to their way of life. New Orleans wavered on the issue of secession. The city's merchants and bankers argued that New Orleans was economically tied to the North, but the tide shifted as the election of 1860 neared. Firebrand politicians warned that 'tame submission' to the North would lead to 'widespread ruin.' Abraham Lincoln, an Illinois Republican who was known for making statements like 'I believe this government cannot endure permanently half slave and half free,' was elected president in November 1860, and incendiary newspaper editors responded by pronouncing, 'The Union is dead.' On January 26, 1861, Louisiana became the sixth state to secede from the Union, and on March 21 the state joined the Confederacy.

Fighting began in April at Fort Sumter, South Carolina, and the war didn't reach New Orleans until a year later. The Union readily achieved its objective to control the lower Mississippi River and New Orleans' port in April 1862. Captain David G Farragut led a US Naval fleet up the Mississippi, bombarding Fort Jackson and Fort St Philip, which flanked the river south of New Orleans. The battle that took place there was brief but dramatic – likened to the 'breaking of the universe with the moon' by one particularly rhapsodic eyewitness – and Farragut's ships reached New Orleans a day later. It was the first Confederate city to be captured, and it would be occupied for the duration of the war, which ended in 1865.

New Orleanians, otherwise famous for their hospitality, didn't take too kindly to the occupation forces, who were led by the notorious Major General Benjamin Butler. 'Beast' Butler, as the locals called him, was not intent on winning the hearts of the city's populace, and his presence unified the city in its hatred of him. Soon after the US flag went up in front of the US Mint, a New Orleanian named William Mumford cut it down, and Butler had the man hanged from the very same flagpole. The women of New Orleans, noting that the flag was not to be touched, began instead to insult Butler's troops by spitting on them and yelling insults. Butler's response to this recurring outrage was to enact a measure specifying that women who partook in such unladylike acts would be handled by law enforcement as women 'plying' their 'avocation.' Under Butler's rule, property was confiscated from citizens who refused to pledge loyalty to the Union.

On the other hand, Butler was also credited with giving the French Quarter a much-needed cleanup, building orphanages, improving the school system and putting thousands of unemployed – both white and black – to work. But he didn't stay in New Orleans long enough to implement Lincoln's plans for 'reconstructing' the city. Those plans, blueprints for the Reconstruction of the South that followed the war, went into effect in December 1863, a year after Butler returned to the North.

Reconstruction & Racial Fallout

The 'Free State of Louisiana,' including only occupied parts of the state, was readmitted to the Union a month later (the entire state wasn't readmitted until after the war was over). The new state constitution abolished slavery and granted blacks the right to public education. The right to vote, which was extended to a select few blacks, soon followed. Two years later, a bloody riot erupted over attempts to extend suffrage to all black men, and the exceedingly violent police intervention in the melee led to the deaths of 34 blacks and two whites. It was a grim beginning

Civil Rights in New Orleans

Race relations in New Orleans have taken an up-and-down ride since whites and blacks began cohabiting the city nearly three centuries ago. Under French rule, Louisiana's Napoleonic Code included a Code Noir (Black Code), which addressed some of the needs of slaves and accorded certain privileges to free persons of color. Under the Code Noir, abused slaves could legally sue their masters, and free blacks were permitted to own property and conduct business.

After the US purchased Louisiana, many aspects of this code were dropped from state law, but nevertheless blacks in Louisiana continued to enjoy liberties not seen elsewhere in the South. On Sunday, slaves in the city were permitted to sell their wares at markets such as Congo Square, where some were able to earn enough money to buy their freedom. New Orleans was also unique in that at these markets, blacks were free to celebrate African culture, and African music and spiritual practices continued to thrive here, more so than elsewhere in the US.

But the Civil War and Reconstruction prompted a backlash throughout the South, with devastating repercussions for African Americans. The slaves were free, but between the Civil War and 1954, institutionalized segregation and codified relations – known as Jim Crow laws – limited the movements and actions of all persons of color. For many in New Orleans' black Creole population – the gens libre de couleur, who were accustomed to decent education and relatively comfortable standards of living – this meant that their social status took a dramatic turn for the worse.

With many blacks feeling the loss of their accustomed rights, New Orleans was a natural setting for the early Civil Rights movement. In 1896, a New Orleans man named Homer Plessy, whose one-eighth African lineage subjected him to Jim Crow restrictions, challenged Louisiana's segregation laws in the landmark Plessy v Ferguson case. Although Plessy's case exposed the arbitrariness of Jim Crow, the US Supreme Court interpreted the Constitution as providing for political, not social, equality and ruled to uphold 'separate but equal' statutes. Separate buses, water fountains, bathrooms, eating places and even courtroom Bibles became fixtures of the segregated landscape. Louisiana law made it illegal to serve alcohol to whites and blacks under the same roof – even if the bar had a partition for segregation.

Separate but equal remained the law of the land until Plessy was overturned by Brown v the Board of Education in 1954. Congress finally passed the Civil Rights Act in 1964.

Today, New Orleans is governed by a multiracial council and a popular black mayor, Marc Morial. Additionally, the city's police force has become increasingly mixed. Still, most of the city's elite are white, while the vast majority of the population is comprised of blacks living at or near the poverty line. An uncodified brand of segregation is maintained by this disparity of wealth, and, as in all of the US, racial inequality is hardly a thing of the past.

for the Reconstruction period, foreshadowing an endless series of race-related struggles that would leave the people of New Orleans hardened, embittered and battered. (See the boxed text 'Civil Rights in New Orleans.')

Causing no small amount of resentment among white Southerners, Louisiana's state constitution was redrawn to include full suffrage to blacks but not to former Confederate soldiers and rebel sympathizers. Blacks, attempting to gain further rights, began challenging discrimination laws forbidding them from riding 'white' streetcars, and racial skirmishes regularly flared up around town.

White supremacist groups like the Ku Klux Klan began to appear throughout the South. In New Orleans, organizations called the Knights of the White Camellia and the Crescent City Democratic Club initiated a reign of terror that targeted blacks and claimed several hundred lives during a particularly bloody few weeks. In the 1870s the White League was formed, with the twin purposes of ousting what it considered an 'Africanized' government (elected in part by newly enfranchised black voters) and of ridding the state of 'carpetbaggers' and 'scalawags,' popular terms for the Northerners and Reconstructionists then in government. By all appearances, the White League was arming itself for an all-out war – claiming that a similarly armed 'Black League,' which now is believed to have been conjured up by white propagandists, was organizing for the same purpose – when police and the state militia attempted to block a shipment of guns in 1874. In an ensuing 'battle,' clearly won by the White League, 27 men were killed and scalawag Governor William Pitt Kellogg was ousted from office for a period of five days. Federal troops entered the city to restore order. Although Reconstruction ended in 1877, in New Orleans the dark cloud of a city at war with itself wouldn't lift for many decades. Many of the civil liberties blacks were supposed to have gained through the outcome of the Civil War would be reversed by Jim Crow laws, which reinforced segregation and inequality.

As the 20th century neared, New Orleans got back to business, staging the World's Industrial and Cotton Centennial Exposition of 1884-5 to herald the city's return to life. Although the expo was, by most accounts, a disappointing spectacle with lackluster exhibits (the awkward name was emblematic of muddled planning), it did serve notice to the rest of the world that the city was making a comeback. Manufacturing, shipping, trade and banking all resumed, and soon the city was again bustling with all the vigor and passions of a major port.

20th-Century Adjustments

New Orleans snapped out of the Great Depression as WWII industries created jobs, and continued prosperity in the 1950s led to suburban growth around the city. Meanwhile, desegregation laws finally brought an end to Jim Crow. Many middle-class whites fled the city to live in the suburbs, and poor blacks took their place. In the mid-1970s the Louisiana Superdome opened. The home of the city's NFL team, the Saints, it also has hosted Superbowls and presidential conventions and sparked a major revenue-earner for New Orleans: trade shows. All around the Superdome, new skyscrapers rose in the Central Business District, as oil and chemical companies were drawn to New Orleans by low taxes and lenient environmental restrictions. By the end of the 1980s, however, the local oil boom went bust.

Meanwhile, the French Quarter, which had become a dowdy working-class enclave during the first part of the century, was treated to long overdue restoration efforts, and it emerged primed for mass tourism, which was already one of the city's most lucrative industries.

In 1978 New Orleans elected its first black mayor, Ernest 'Dutch' Morial, marking a major shift in the city's political history. Morial, a Democrat, appointed blacks and women to many city posts during his two terms. During that time, the city once again hosted a world expo, and once again the event was an utter economic failure. However, the 1984 exposition did help to revive a long neglected warehouse district, which soon became a hub for art galleries and studios. Morial's tenure ended in 1986, and

Storyville

Hard as the city tried to keep its mind on business, it still succumbed to every vice known to humankind. As the song goes:

There is a house in New Orleans
They call the Rising Sun
And it's been the ruin of many a poor boy
And God, I know I'm one...

Many such houses – live-work spaces for thousands of lushly limbed gals from every corner of the globe – sprang up all over town, catering to the natural and unnatural needs of men. At the end of the 19th century, prostitution was such a flourishing business that it began to invade even the city's finer neighborhoods, and politicians, having little hope of ending the trade, sought at least a way to contain and control it. A district where prostitution would remain legal was created to the lake-side of the French Quarter, and it quickly gained renown as a modern Gomorrah – a domain of whores, pimps, madames, drug peddlers and a tragic number of wanton street urchins; a district whose very existence rested on its ability to foster and nurture any form of depravity. Some of the district's houses were sordid cribs enlivened by barrelhouse piano men like Jellyroll Morton, a jazz pioneer who was also a journeyman card cheat and pimp, while other estates, capped with Moorish turrets, were genuinely posh. This district was proposed in 1897 by a city official named Sidney Story, and although Story neither owned nor patronized any house of prostitution – in fact, he reputedly lived a squeaky-clean life – he will always be remembered as the man for whom Storyville was unofficially named. Its residents simply called it 'the District.'

WWI spelled the end for Storyville. In 1917, Secretary of the Navy Joseph Daniels, whose nickname was 'Teetotaling' Joseph, ordered the District officially closed, expressing the Navy's fears that legalized prostitution would cause the spread of social diseases among servicemen based at a New Orleans training camp. However, prostitution continued illegally along the same streets until the entire district was razed in the 1940s. A housing project now stands on the site.

in 1994 his son, Marc Morial, was elected mayor and then reelected in 1998.

Like most US cities, New Orleans has benefited from trends toward urban revival at the end of the millennium, and crime has dropped in recent years. And although New Orleans remains largely a poor city with a small tax base to support public schools and social programs, the city retains its uniquely New Orleanian spirit.

GEOGRAPHY

At roughly the same latitude as Cairo and Shanghai, 30° north of the equator, New Orleans occupies the east bank of the Mississippi River, about 90 river miles above where the Mississippi empties into the Gulf of Mexico. The Gulf Coast once reached to Donaldsonville, south of the bluffs occupied by Baton Rouge and now about 80 river miles upstream from New Orleans. Hence, the river has created a broad, featureless coastal plain, with the sediments washed from its upper reaches and deposited as it sluggishly meanders toward the gulf.

Were it not for human intervention, much of New Orleans would now be swampland. The city's elevation averages 2 feet below sea level. Elevated land, formed naturally by the Mississippi River's historic floods, exists near the river levees, which generally serve as the city's crescent-shaped southern boundary.

Local drainage flows northward toward the shallow, saltwater Lake Pontchartrain, which forms the northern edge of New Orleans. By reclaiming low-lying swamps along the lake, engineers have created neighborhoods that depend on massive pumps to carry storm water to the lake to avoid flooding.

New Orleans is literally a fortress guarded by 130 miles of surrounding levees. We can assume that Fats Domino's hit song *Walkin' to New Orleans* refers to travel along the river levees, because no other land connections exist. Motorists heading toward New Orleans on I-10 from either the east or west travel over waterways on elevated freeways.

On the west bank of the Mississippi River, extensive tracts of low-lying swamps and bayous were difficult to travel through, except by shallow-draft boat. Aside from ferryboat service, vehicle access from New Orleans to the west bank did not occur until the 1930s, when the Huey Long Bridge opened 9 miles upriver from downtown. West bank access was further enhanced by construction of the Greater New Orleans Bridge, also called the Crescent City Connection, during the late 1950s. See Orientation in Facts for the Visitor for information on how the lay of the land shaped the city's development.

CLIMATE

New Orleans' climate is influenced by its subtropical latitude and proximity to the Gulf of Mexico. It's hot, wet and sticky for most of the year. The gulf provides plenty of moisture – New Orleans receives about 60 inches of rainfall annually. See the boxed text 'Hurricane Season' for details.

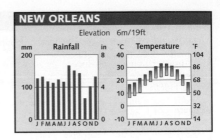

No season is immune from rain. In March, April and May the weather is quite variable, with plenty of rain; but it's warm, with long stretches of sunny, mild days too – perfect for the festivals.

During the summer it's hot and humid. Brief afternoon thundershowers occur almost daily. Technically, the term 'relative humidity' describes how saturated the air is. At 100% relative humidity it rains; near that level it just seems that your perspiration never dries. Because warm air can store more moisture than cold air, summer thundershowers can be quite explosive, as the air mass rids itself of excess moisture amid peals of thunder. On long summer days you can expect about eight or more hours of sunshine out of 14 possible hours. September and October days are the most likely to offer clear, temperate weather.

Winter temperatures average a comfortable 54°F, yet occasional drops in temperature, combined with the damp atmosphere, can chill you to the bone. Snow is rare. During December's short days, fog and rain conspire to allow only 4½ hours of daily sunshine. Localized river fog often forms from December to May.

ECOLOGY & ENVIRONMENT

New Orleans exists in a precarious position, especially when one considers geologic time. Should global warming continue unabated, the resulting rise in sea level will place the city at increased risk of flooding. Equally threatening is the prospect that the Mississippi River will shift its course, as it has done many times over the last millennia, leaving New Orleans surrounded by seawater and without a supply of freshwater.

The latter problem is likely to manifest itself in concurrence with a major flood, which would create a truly cataclysmic disaster. John McPhee brilliantly describes a near disaster and the prospects for such a course shift in his book *The Control of Nature* (1989). He notes:

Southern Louisiana exists in its present form because the Mississippi River has jumped here and there within an arc about two hundred miles wide, like a pianist playing with one hand – frequently and radically changing course, surging over the left or right bank to go off in utterly new directions. Always it is the river's purpose to get to the Gulf by the shortest and steepest gradient.

The likely breech will occur at the Old River Control Auxiliary Structure, more than 200 miles upriver, where the US Army Corps of Engineers operates a navigation lock offering a shortcut to the gulf via the Atchafalaya River. In 1973 the force of the river at flood stage partially undermined this keystone safety valve. A rebuilt and reinforced structure repelled repeated floods in 1983 and 1993, yet none of these events matched the flow seen in 1927. Most observers agree that a so-called 100-year flood would overwhelm the structures.

Part of the solution has been to divert the Mississippi River floodwater before it

Hurricane Season

As it passes through New Orleans, I-10 is flanked by signs informing motorists that the interstate serves as a hurricane evacuation route. Local officials estimate that a full-scale evacuation of the low-lying flood-prone city would take three days. Motorists caught in the typical rush-hour gridlock can imagine that such an evacuation might even be impossible. Anyway, the only people likely to react to early warnings of approaching tropical storms would be visitors who cancel their travel to New Orleans. Just remember that the average elevation here is 2 feet below sea level and all evacuation routes cross open water.

Hurricanes in the Gulf of Mexico occur from June 1 to November 30. They happen with the greatest frequency in late summer and early autumn.

A developing hurricane passes through several stages. In short, a tropical depression is the formative stage. A tropical storm is a strengthened tropical depression, with wind speeds between 39 and 73mph. A Category-1 hurricane brings winds between 74 and 95mph. This can produce a storm surge, or large waves, which can flood coastal roads. The most intense is a Category-5 hurricane, with sustained winds of 156mph or greater.

Fortunately, New Orleans has been spared a direct hurricane hit for more than 30 years. The last occurred when hurricane Betsy crashed ashore in early September 1965, taking 74 lives throughout coastal Mississippi and Louisiana.

Following Betsy, the US Army Corps of Engineers began adding to the height of the 130 miles of levees that protect all of Orleans Parish and some adjacent areas. The engineers' intention was to create a barrier capable of resisting the storm surges generated by winds of up to 130mph. Nevertheless, if a storm like hurricane Andrew (1992), with 170mph winds, had veered directly toward New Orleans, a catastrophic disaster would have ensued.

Hurricanes are sighted well in advance. There are two distinct stages of alert: a Hurricane Watch, issued when a hurricane *may* strike in the area within the next 36 to 48 hours, and a Hurricane Warning, issued when a hurricane is likely to strike the area. This is when you should consider canceling your visit or evacuating. Hotels generally follow evacuation orders and ask guests to leave. Ask at your hotel or hostel for more information as to the logistics of evacuation.

Mississippi River Floods

For the better part of three centuries, people have gone to great lengths to prevent the Mississippi River, the largest river in North America, from spilling over its banks into the city of New Orleans. Upon settling the site in 1718, Jean-Baptiste Le Moyne, Sieur de Bienville, directed construction of a mile-long, 3-foot-high levee to protect the village from floods. With encouragement from Bienville, himself a slaveholder, the French landed African slaves in Louisiana, in part to work on the levees. French prisoners whose sentences were commuted were also deported to work in Louisiana. By 1735 this labor force had extended the levees along both banks by about 30 miles upstream and 12 miles downstream. That year, high water breached or topped much of the system and filled the low areas to the north and northwest of the present French Quarter.

View of the Mississippi River

Continued building extended the levee system to Baton Rouge on the east bank and all the way to the confluence with the Red River on the west bank by 1812. However, the levees deteriorated under American control, particularly during the Civil War.

In the spring of 1927, a 100-year flood – so called because, according to local myth, floods of such size occur only once a century – devastated communities throughout the lower Mississippi River Valley, inspiring a

reaches New Orleans. In 1931, the Bonnet Carré spillway was opened about 30 miles upriver to act as a relief valve by diverting the water into Lake Pontchartrain. Ironically, by that time most of the river's natural tributaries had been plugged by levees meant to contain the flow.

The problem of land subsidence also imperils many of the neighborhoods built on newly reclaimed lands near Lake Pontchartrain. Local flooding was most pronounced on such property during the 1993 flood and again on May 8, 1995, following a storm that dumped 18 inches of rainfall within 24 hours. It will likely get worse. All of New Orleans is sinking, but the recently drained lakeside wetlands are particularly susceptible. Foundation cracks and broken pipelines are common throughout Jefferson Parish, which was drained and developed only during the past

40 years. In some areas a predicted subsidence to 12 feet below sea level will increase the vulnerability to flooding.

Yet another hazard to the population and environment are the toxic emissions and river discharges from the many industrial and petrochemical plants that line the waterway between Baton Rouge and New Orleans. From the air at night, the string of plants resembles a foreboding film noir scene. This section of the 'American Rhur' has also received the sobriquet 'Cancer Alley.' Louisiana leads the nation in toxic emissions, and a faint petroleum smell is often noted in New Orleans.

You needn't worry, however, about the local drinking water – New Orleans' water is surprisingly good. By drawing its supply from below the river's surface north of the city, New Orleans avoids the floating pollu-

Mississippi River Floods

bevy of blues songs, like Blind Lemon Jefferson's 'Rising High Water Blues' and Bessie Smith's 'Muddy Water.' Congress' response to the disaster was less musical, but welcomed – in 1928, it passed the Flood Control Act, allotting funds to raise levees, dredge sediment from the river bottom and build floodways to divert high water into shorter paths to the Gulf of Mexico. The US Army Corps of Engineers, which had previously focused on channel improvements for navigation, then became responsible for flood control. So far, the Corps has been successful. Recent floods have only inundated the same low-lying areas that experienced flooding during Bienville's time. During the early 1990s the Army Corps completed an 8 1/2-mile above-ground floodwall in New Orleans. The giant steel floodgates at the foot of Canal St are normally open to allow traffic to reach the ferry. When closed, they represent a last-ditch defense against the rising water.

But the point of so much defense would become moot if the river were to suddenly change its course – a prospect that appears inevitable if the river's history is any indication. Over many millennia, the Mississippi has shifted its way across the wide flatlands from East Texas to the Florida Panhandle –'like a pianist playing with one hand,' in the words of writer John McPhee – always seeking the shortest path to the gulf. Its current course, past New Orleans, is no longer the most direct, and the nearby Atchafalaya River, to the west, is clearly pointing a shorter way. If the Mississippi were to follow its natural inclinations and join with the Atchafalaya, New Orleans would bite the dust. The city would lose its freshwater source, its harbor and virtually all of its industry.

Upriver from New Orleans, the Army Corps wages an ongoing war against nature in an attempt to keep the Mississippi on course, but human intervention in large-scale hydrologic processes is only a temporary fix in the geologic time frame. The will of the river never diminishes, and nature bides its time.

---

tants and its own waste. Huge settling ponds effectively remove the suspended sediments, while chlorine and other treatments destroy bacteria and improve taste.

While humans cope by applying technological fixes, it's the river and gulf ecosystems that suffer from the pollution. Microbiologists have noted a 'dead-zone' of oxygen depletion extending along the gulf's entire near-shore waters between the mouth of the Mississippi and the Texas state line. Nutrients from plant discharges, agricultural runoff and sewage treatment plants are largely to blame for this threat to fish and bottom-living organisms, including shrimp and oysters.

Perhaps the ultimate force in the efforts to clean up the pollution will come from the state's residents. With the help of people who depend on the heretofore abundant river and gulf resources for their livelihood, economic and political pressure can be focused on the polluters. This assumes that other controls are in place to prevent overexploitation of the natural resources. For instance, the recent craze for blackened redfish led to a rapid decline of the redfish fishery until the Louisiana Department of Wildlife & Fisheries restricted the limit. As Marc Reisner documents in his undercover study of poaching in Louisiana, *Game Wars* (1991), commercial ravishing of selected species can outstrip even productive habitats.

Reisner also documents an environmental problem of epic proportions. Wave erosion cuts away at almost 40 sq miles of coastal marsh each year, allowing brackish seawater to intrude inland. For years humans have cut shallow hunting and fishing paths across the marshlands. Since oil companies initiated large-scale channel cutting for exploration and drilling access, the erosion has accelerated. Dredging of the Mississippi River Gulf Outlet ('MR GO') has also gobbled up much of St Bernard Parish – the canal's up to three times wider than when it was built. Overall, the gulf is advancing northward at a rate of a half mile per year. This represents a tremendous loss of habitat for estuary-dependent species. Already, the lost marsh buffer has exposed fishing villages to direct storm impact. Eventually New Orleans itself will be lost.

FLORA & FAUNA

The distribution of flora and fauna throughout southern Louisiana is largely determined by elevation and the water's degree of salinity. Natural levees represent the area's only natural solid ground. On the river side of the levee crest is the *batture*, a narrow zone of trees, vines and shrubs that slow the flow and cause sediment accumulation. Away from the levee crest, the sands and silts deposited by occasional flood diminish in thickness, as these lands have often been cleared for agricultural uses.

Wetlands adjacent to the levee consist of swamps and marshes. Swamps are permanently waterlogged areas, which often exhibit tree growth. Marshes tend to be poorly drained areas that may be only periodically inundated. Grasses and low shrubs are common marsh plants. Both swamp and marsh soils are primarily peat, organic materials mixed with fine silts and clays.

Bayous are the sluggish freshwater natural canals away from the main river channel. Most often they are abandoned and cut-off portions of the channel. A combination of elevated land (however slight it may be), a rich freshwater environment and removal from the threat of flooding make bayous relatively attractive settlement areas – at least when compared with other wetland environments. Their gradual subsidence without any substantial replenishment of sedimentary deposits dooms the bayou to evolve into a mere ridge, without channel, that may eventually be entirely submersed in swamp or marsh.

Flora

The live oak *(Quercus virginiana)* is the most emblematic tree in New Orleans. Before harvesting for shipbuilding, these magnificent wide-spreading evergreens covered the natural levees. Now they are relegated to the parks and older neighborhood streets. Today, a Formosan termite infestation threatens their domain. A few great specimens, like the famous dueling oaks in City Park, are more than 500 years old; one tree, the John McDonald Oak, first sprouted in about 992 AD!

Spanish moss *(Tillandsia usneoides)* often gracefully drapes the broad oak branches. It is neither a moss (it's actually a relative of the pineapple) nor a parasite (it's an epiphyte). Many Cajuns once harvested Spanish moss with long poles for furniture stuffing. Commercial production peaked in the 1920s, and the last processing plant closed at Labadieville, 9 miles north of Thibodaux, during the 1980s. Also note the aptly named resurrection fern *(Selaginella lepidophylla)*, often seen growing directly on the branches of the live oak. Following a rain, the otherwise brown plant unfurls and turns green.

Another tree species common to the levee soils is the southern magnolia *(Magnolia grandifloria)*, with large, creamy-white springtime blossoms, which figure as the state flower. Linger in the shade of a magnolia and enjoy the fragrance.

In swamp areas the bald cypress *(Taxodium distichum*, the state tree), tupelo gum *(Nyssa aquatica)* and cabbage palm *(Sabal*

JOHN ELK III

Sunrise through Spanish moss

palmetto) form the dominant overstory. The cypress trunks are often laced with trumpet creeper *(Campsis radicans)* – both are eerily bare in winter months. Cypress lumber is extremely durable and resists rotting in the humid climate. The odd-looking cypress 'knees' protrude from the water like many knobby cones around the base of the trunk. Some biologists suggest the cones aerate the roots, while others believe they merely provide a stable base for the tree.

The most common freshwater marsh species are maiden cane *(Panicum hemitomom)*, spike rush *(Eleocharis sp)* and bulltongue *(Sagitarria falaca)*. These offer abundant game food, while tall reeds *(Phragmites sp)* provide an excellent habitat. Where brackish water conditions exist, relatively useless cordgrass predominates.

Fauna

Alligators Thanks to the Endangered Species Protection Act of 1970, alligators *(Alligator mississipiensis)* have made a miraculous comeback from near extinction at the hands of commercial hunters. By the 1970s alligators were hunted out in Louisiana, and the large reptiles were only seen in a few protected refuges. Now New Orleans can brag about having the largest gator population of any city in the USA. The state has even re-established a legal cull. All of those hideous lacquered skulls from 10- to 12-foot gators piled for sale on tables at the French Market were probably taken legally – their hides already sold and their meat consumed.

Official ambivalence about allowing a full repopulation will likely keep the statewide alligator population at about one-half million. Meanwhile, alligator nuisance control, operated by the Louisiana Department of Wildlife & Fisheries, reports the greatest amount of action following floods.

Plenty of guide boats offer circus-like alligator feeding frenzies as the highlight of a 'swamp tour.' To appease the tourist need to see alligators in the winter, when most gators disappear into a muddy nest to hibernate, some operators (including the Audubon Zoo) keep a few gators awake with artificial heat lamps.

STEPHEN G MAKA

Soft and fuzzy reptiles of the swamp

Fish Freshwater species like the bottom-dwelling catfish, named for whisker-like barbels extending from the upper jaw, form a large part of Southern lore. Mark Twain often referred to the blue catfish *(Ictalurus furcatus)*, a giant that can grow to more than 100 pounds, and the predatory flathead *(Ictalurus olivaris)*, a large fish reported to chase dogs. Now protein-rich channel catfish *(Ictalurus punctatus)* are commercially raised in ponds on converted cotton and soybean fields and shipped throughout the US. Warm and nutrient-rich rivers and bayous also encourage rapid growth of bass and sacalait (Cajun for 'bag of milk' and otherwise known as white perch or crappie).

Also lurking in the Mississippi River are ancient species like the paddlefish *(Polyoden spathula)*, a Paleozoic monster that grows up to 6 feet and shares characteristics with both bony fish and cartilaginous sharks. Now protected, the paddlefish population suffered large losses when commercial fishing operations harvested the fish for their roe. Growing to 9 feet with plate-like scales reputed to turn an ax, the alligator gar *(Lepisosteus spatula)* inhabits shallow water, where it captures fish in its ferocious-looking jaws. You can see some of these species at the Aquarium of the Americas.

Birds The naturalist John James Audubon (1785-1851) painted more than 80 of his beautiful folios for the monumental *The Birds of America*, especially volume II (1831-4), during his stay in New Orleans and near St Francisville in 1821 and 1822. Ironically, he occasionally used dead subjects found at the French Market for some of the game bird portraits. On another visit in 1837, he spent most of his time studying in the Barataria swamp. His biographer, Alice Ford, has also assembled a *Handbook of Audubon Prints*, which lists where each was painted.

Numerous migrating species visit New Orleans, located on one of North America's four flyways. During the winter, waterfowl are in the greatest abundance. In April and May more than 70 species of thrushes, warblers, buntings, vireos, grosbeaks and tanagers arrive from South America. Many fly the 600- to 800-mile journey over the Gulf of Mexico in a single night.

Audubon's painting of the mockingbird *(Mimus polyglottos)* shows it aggressively killing a rattlesnake. Atticus Finch in Harper Lee's Southern classic *To Kill a Mockingbird* (1963) warned his children, 'It's a sin to kill a mockingbird.' The mimicking songbird can do no wrong and has won the hearts of many listeners throughout the American South.

As you prepare to cross the river on the ferry, you may be treated to a greeting by brown pelicans *(Pelecanus occidentalis)* swimming and diving in the boat's current. The pelican's massive bill and throat pouch are used to catch fish and separate the prey from the water. With luck, you might see a spectacular diving display. Accumulated pesticides digested by pelicans cause their eggs to be easily broken; hence, the species is endangered.

Glimpses of long-legged wading birds add excitement to wetland forays. Careful study requires binoculars, as most birds take flight at the slightest disturbance. Even casual visitors can distinguish gray-blue Louisiana herons *(Egretta tricolor)* from the pure white plumage of the yellow-billed great egret *(Casmerodius albus)* or black-billed snowy egret *(Egretta thula)*. A variety of ibis, readily identified by their down-curved bills, are somewhat less common. The ibis easily accomplishes what first-time visitors struggle over – it eats crawfish. All are attracted to the abundant fish nurseries that exist in the saltwater marshes and warm freshwater swamps and bayous.

Nutrias This large rodent goes by the name 'coypu' in its native South America and is sometimes called a 'mouse beaver.' An accident during a storm in 1938 allowed nutria *(Myoester coypus)* to escape from cages kept by the McIlhenny family on Avery Island. To the detriment of the indigenous muskrat *(Ondatra zibethica)* and river otter *(Lutra canadensis)*, whose populations have diminished, the nutria has thrived in Louisiana bayous and swamps.

Armadillos The only obvious control on the population of nine-banded armadillos *(Dasypus novemcinctus)* is the motor vehicle – as evidenced by the countless armadillo carcasses you will likely see along Louisiana highways. Nevertheless, the peril of road travel has not stopped the spread of this armor-clad critter's range northward into the US and southward into Patagonia since the 1890s. Armadillos are almost oblivious to humans as they forage for insects with their anteater-like snout. Listen for rustling in the brush near swamps, bayous, river levees and upland plains.

GOVERNMENT & POLITICS

Orleans Parish (as counties are called in Louisiana) is governed by an elected mayor and city council. In the adjacent suburbs of

Jefferson Parish, Kenner is the only incorporated city; Metairie relies on parish government and services. The parish unit originated with the Catholic Church and was adopted by the Spanish provisional governor in 1669. Five of the seven New Orleans council members represent districts of equal population, largely drawn to reflect a particular racial or ethnic community of interest. The other two council members are elected at large. Creoles occupy most council seats and the mayor's office. For visitors unacquainted with local politics, Thursday city council meetings at City Hall, 1300 Perdido St, offer a mildly entertaining alternative to a matinee, though some may argue that the entertainment value is not up to the standard set by state officers.

French governing precepts and a colonial heritage help explain the voters' greater willingness to forsake civil rights in favor of state control. Unlike other state governments, which are based on the common law of England, Louisiana derives its laws from the Napoleonic Code of France. The Code was enacted by the largely French and Spanish populations in 1808 to preserve local customs in the face of a competing Anglo-American culture.

Current mayor Marc H Morial, a Democrat, was elected in 1994 at the age of 35 and was reelected to a second term in 1998. He first rose to power on the coattails of his popular father, Ernest N 'Dutch' Morial, the first black mayor of New Orleans, who served two terms from 1978 to 1986.

Some disturbing political weirdness takes place on the fringes of the Orleans Parish. In 1988 voters from the unincorporated Jefferson Parish suburb of Metairie sent David Duke, the former Grand Wizard of the Ku Klux Klan, to the state capitol as their representative. His race for governor in 1991 gave voters the unenviable choice between the Klansman and Edwin Edwards, who was widely considered a crook. Edwards quipped that 'the only way I won't get reelected is if I get caught in bed with a live boy or a dead woman.' National attention created curious allies for Edwards, whose supporters displayed bumper stickers reading 'Vote for the Crook – It's Important.' Edwards narrowly won, with 34% of the vote to Duke's 32%. Duke unsuccessfully set his sights on the US Senate in 1990 and 1996; check out Tyler Bridges' book *The Rise of David Duke*. For excellent dramatizations of Louisiana politics, see the Film section, later in this chapter.

ECONOMY

New Orleans is reviving its trade with Latin America, resuming a relationship that thrived in the 19th and early 20th centuries. The city lost much of this trade to Miami in the 1960s, but investments in new cold-storage facilities for tropical fruits and coffee-bean silos are paying off. Even grain and steel exports from inland plants are now reaching the Pacific Rim after transshipment from barge to ocean freighter at New Orleans.

Making up an increasing share of the city's economy, tourism has seen steady growth and provides many low-paying service jobs in lodgings, restaurants and museums. Wages in the state, as measured in income per person, lag behind the wages in all other states except the horribly destitute levels found in Mississippi and Arkansas. Even with its white-collar offices and good-paying waterfront trades, New Orleans suffers from declining earnings, and one person in four lives below the poverty level in the city.

Equally bleak are the prospects for energy-based companies. Oil and gas extraction remains an economic bust. From 1972 to 1981 New Orleans enjoyed a booming economy propelled by the manufacture and financing of offshore oil rigs. The economic turmoil of the 1981 oil price crash reverberated throughout the state in the following years. Energy produced 41% of the state's revenues in 1982 but only 13% in 1992.

POPULATION & PEOPLE

The US Bureau of the Census reports a metropolitan population of more than 1.2 million among six widespread parishes. Among these, only Orleans and Jefferson – each with approximately 500,000 people – figure into most visitor's plans. Jefferson Parish contains the middle-class suburb of

Metairie plus Kenner, where the airport is located.

Diversity reigns in New Orleans. African Americans constitute the majority, with 62% of the population, while Anglos comprise about 35%, and Hispanics around 3%. Many of the more recent arrivals have ties to Central America, while Hispanics of Cuban extraction are well established.

Despite its diversity, New Orleans shows signs of geographic segregation, especially for the most recent arrivals from Southeast Asia. By strolling through the French Quarter, one would never suspect that upwards of 12,000 Vietnamese and other Asians live in New Orleans. Nevertheless, the Versailles enclave at the far eastern edge of the city, anchored by Chef Menteur Expressway, is a Vietnamese cultural center.

The gap between the inherited wealth of the upper class and the poverty of the lower class is more pronounced here than in any other large US city. New Orleans is like a banana republic, where class and caste stifle social mobility.

Gays and lesbians have long found acceptance in New Orleans, particularly in the lower French Quarter and Faubourg Marigny.

MASON FLORENCE

Schoolgirls at Jazz Fest

ARTS
Architecture

On the eve of Spanish control, New Orleans was a symmetrical grid of 44 blocks formally centered about the Place d'Armes – a muddy parade ground facing the river and surrounded on three sides by religious and government buildings. At that time a quarter of the blocks were unoccupied, but some residents upgraded earlier wooden structures with red-tiled brick houses. Spanish architecture, with cross ventilation and shaded interior courts, was better suited to the tropical climate and gradually altered the town. Fires in 1788 and again in 1794 wiped out most of the remaining French architecture. New building codes specified brick construction with tile or slate roofs. Houses facing the levee were to be two stories with a gallery in front and residential quarters on the upper floor.

Historic preservation of the vernacular architecture in the French Quarter has led to what some critics regard as a 'Creole Disneyland.' But still, one cannot dismiss the Place d'Armes, now Jackson Square, which qualifies as one of the finest architectural spaces in the country. Nor can one dismiss the accumulated impression from an overwhelming assortment of Creole houses and simple cottages. The familiar houses with overhanging balconies decorated by lacy iron railings are among the most emblematic features of the French Quarter.

Few recognize that efforts to preserve the quaint and distinctive elements of the French Quarter began when the federal government enlisted the efforts of the unemployed during the economic depression of the 1930s to restore the French Market and Pontalba buildings. If the preservation efforts have any notable failings today, they are social. The working-class families have been largely displaced due to high maintenance costs and rents.

Uptown mansions are also worthy of investigation. Wealthy Americans settled the area and adopted Greek Revival architecture as a symbol of staunch classical tastes. The evolution of American designs can be seen on tours that begin in the Lower Garden District (see the Things to See & Do chapter) and continue on to the Garden District proper. Tours of the area around Audubon Park and the Tulane and Loyola campuses also offer much architectural splendor.

French Quarter ('Vieux Carré') balconies

The most renowned of New Orleans architects is Benjamin Henry Latrobe. Latrobe was the noted architect of the Capitol in Washington, DC, and the Baltimore Cathedral. After his arrival in New Orleans in 1819, Latrobe's early commissions included the St Louis Cathedral tower and the construction of the waterworks, with their innovative pumping stations. Before he succumbed to yellow fever, Latrobe designed the Louisiana State Bank building, at 403 Royal St (see French Quarter Walking Tour in the Things to See & Do chapter).

Another well-known architect is James Gallier Sr, father of distinguished architect James Gallier Jr. Gallier Sr is best known for the Greek Revival-style Gallier Hall, 545 St Charles Ave, where Farragut's forces took control of the city in 1862. He also took part in designing the Pontalba Apartments fronting Place d'Armes (renamed Jackson Square after the buildings went up).

Literature

Ever since Samuel Clemens acquired his Mark Twain pseudonym while piloting a steamboat on the Mississippi River, New Orleans has made an impression on American writers. You can pay homage to past greats at the March literary festival celebrating Tennessee Williams (see Special Events in the Facts for the Visitor chapter).

For some authors the impression was negative. George Washington Cable (1844-1925), described by Twain as 'the South's finest literary genius,' abhorred slavery and racism. He touched many Creole nerves with his fictional books *Old Creole Days* and especially *The Grandissimes*, both set in New Orleans. His essays in *The Negro Question* (1885) offer an indictment of the Code Noir and make compelling arguments for civil rights.

Author Kate Chopin (1851-1904) only spent 14 years in New Orleans and southern

Louisiana after marrying a cotton broker. She wrote her evocative accounts of Creoles and Cajuns after returning to St Louis as a widow in 1882. Her second novel, *The Awakening,* was originally condemned for its portrayal of a young woman's adultery, but it was rediscovered in the 1970s as a masterpiece that evokes the region while chronicling a woman's discontent. Also look for her nonfiction books *Bayou Folk* (1894) and *A Night in Acadie* (1897).

In the modern era, the same diverse stimuli that attract visitors to New Orleans provide writers with abundant subjects. The city's cheap rents, ease of mobility sans automobile, and 'slacker' community also appeal to struggling writers.

The Faulkner House, 624 Pirate's Alley, is where William Faulkner, at the onset of his career, briefly stayed with fellow author William Spratling. Novelist Francis Parkinson Keyes' former home at 1113 Chartres St inspired the bestseller *Dinner at Antoine's* (1948).

Robert Penn Warren's fictional novel, *All the King's Men* (1946), captured a Pulitzer for portraying Louisiana politics in the era of the 'Kingfish,' Governor Huey Long. Penn Warren then went on to win more Pulitzer Prizes for *Promises* in 1958 and for *Now and Then* in 1979.

While living at 636 St Peter St, playwright Tennessee Williams (1911-83) wrote *A Streetcar Named Desire* (1947), which won a Pulitzer Prize for its portrayal of Blanche Dubois' descent from an elite family to life in the French Quarter with her sister and low-brow brother-in-law Stanley Kowalski. As Williams himself descended down a path of alcohol and drug abuse, his pathos became increasingly evident in works like *Suddenly Last Summer* (1956), set against a decadent New Orleans background.

Shirley Ann Grau writes fiction about the American South with a sympathetic eye toward African American women. She won a Pulitzer for her Mississippi-based novel *The Keepers of the House* (1965). Among her works set in New Orleans are *The Hard Blue Sky* (1958) and *The House on Coliseum Street* (1961).

Walker Percy's first novel, *The Moviegoer* (1961), captured the National Book Award for his existentialist portrayal of a young New Orleans stockbroker, Binx Bolling, whose despair and relationship with his cousin Kate are revealed against a muted Mardi Gras background.

When a determined Thelma Toole finally pressed Percy to review her son's manuscript after he committed suicide in 1969 at the age of 32, the outcome was quite unexpected. John Kennedy Toole posthumously received a Pulitzer Prize for his on-the-mark portrayal of a laughable hot-dog vendor, Ignatius Reilly, in *A Confederacy of Dunces* (1980). Perhaps no one other book so readily prepares the visitor for the

Tennessee Williams

The ever-cantakerous Ignatius Reilly

hapless and semidysfunctional personalities that abound in all spectrums of New Orleans life.

Romanian-born novelist and poet Andrei Codrescu presents commentary during short weekly NPR broadcasts heard throughout the nation. On one broadcast he critiqued the unfinished Harrah's casino as a 'museum to greed' and a 'massive windowless hulk,' which he suggested would be even uglier had it been finished. A collection of his NPR stories is contained in *Zombification* (1995). He is appropriately decadent: Among his many publications is a 1973 soft-porn novel, *The Repentance of Lorraine*, that he concedes fails 'the porn-novel test of one erection per page.' He offers a collection of essays in *The Muse is Always Half-Dressed in New Orleans* (1993) and sets off from New Orleans on a coast-to-coast road trip in a '59 Cadillac convertible in *Road Scholar* (1993), also available on film. His most recent novel is *The Blood Countess* (1995). Codrescu lives in New Orleans and teaches English at LSU.

Nelson Algren is rightfully claimed by Chicagoans, but one of his most influential novels, *A Walk on the Wild Side* (1956), is set largely in New Orleans' decaying Storyville District. The saga of a Depression-era scamp named Dove Linkhorn, it is surely a definitive Crescent City novel.

New Orleans native Anne Rice established her credentials as a careful researcher and storyteller with *The Feast of All Saints* (1979), a semifictional account of the *gens de couleur libre* in antebellum New Orleans. Her best-selling vampire and witchcraft novels are *Interview with the Vampire* (1976), followed by *The Vampire Lestat* (1985), *The Queen of the Damned* (1988) and *Lasher* (1993), among others. If you yearn for more of her erotica without the gore, look for her pseudonym AN Roquelaure. Rice's success has led to burley bodyguards and multiple mansions in the Garden District – her First St home is the setting for *The Witching Hour* (see Walking Tours in the Things to See & Do chapter, but be forewarned that her private residences are not open for admission). She hosts visiting journalists at her raised cottage during Mardi Gras to offer a respite from what she describes in *Lasher* as 'the ugliness of the parades, the crowds, *and* the garbage littering St Charles Avenue.'

You can't stop reading once you pick up one of James Lee Burke's novels about fictional New Orleans detective Dave Roubicheaux (pronounced rho-bih-**cho**). They include *The Neon Rain* (1987), *Heaven's Prisoners* (1988, released on film in 1996) and *Dixie City Jam* (1994), among others. In *Burning Angel* (1995), Burke breaks away from the detective series to write a fictional account of organized crime and race relations. For yet another story about the mob in New Orleans (this one made into a movie) check out John Grisham's *The Client* (1993).

Native son Elmore Leonard is another prolific detective and mystery novelist who occasionally pens a Western. His 1987 novel *Bandits* is set in New Orleans. In a shift from his regional nonfiction work, Tony Dunbar has also written the New Orleans detective novels *Crooked Man* (1994) and *City of Beads* (1995), featuring the Dubonnet Tubby character.

Anne Rice, aka AN Roquelaure

Film

Motion pictures set in New Orleans have captured the city's cultural peculiarities in addition to its overstated politics, sex, violence and drinking. The musical genre, for which New Orleans once served as a staple location, has faded since 1958, when Elvis Presley starred in *King Creole*. Archives, however, are rich with footage of tap dancer Bill 'Bojangles' Robinson in *Dixiana* (1930) and jazz singer Billie Holiday's only screen appearance in *New Orleans* (1947). Louis Armstrong performed in *Hello Dolly!* (1969).

The highest-grossing film shot locally is director Oliver Stone's controversial *JFK* (1991), which includes numerous French Quarter scenes. Another hit, *Dead Man Walking* (1996) stars Susan Sarandon in a true story about Sister Helen Prejean, a New Orleans resident who devotes time to death-row inmates and inspires discussion about the state's death penalty.

Romanian emigrant Andrei Codrescu's witty *Road Scholar* (1994) begins with his driving lessons in New Orleans before he hurtles across the US in a '59 Cadillac convertible.

Dennis Hopper and Peter Fonda play bikers in *Easy Rider*, the 1969 film classic. The scene of the two smoking pot in St Louis Cemetery No 1 upset the locals, since it introduced legions of youth to the New Orleans party scene.

Former Governor Earl Long's main squeeze, Blaze Star, told her story in an autobiography made into the 1989 movie *Blaze*, starring Paul Newman. Former Governor Huey Long (Earl's brother), the 'Kingfish,' has been fictionalized in the Oscar-winning *All the King's Men* (1949), based on Robert Penn Warren's best-seller, and in *A Lion is in the Streets* (1953).

Hollywood has adapted many of Tennessee Williams' plays for film. His persistent portrayal of sexual repression and sexual obsession often features New Orleans as a suitably decadent setting. In *Suddenly Last Summer* (1959), Katherine Hepburn as Violet Venable plots the forced lobotomy of her niece, played by Elizabeth Taylor, to preserve the reputation of her sexually irrepressible homosexual son. Vivian Leigh won an Oscar for best actress opposite a brutish Marlon Brando in *A Streetcar Named Desire* (1951), which also featured Oscar-winning supporting roles for Kim Hunter and Karl Malden. Filmed in and near the French Quarter, 'Desire' deals with madness and rape. Don't bother looking for the famous streetcar that once ran on Desire St – it no longer exists. One further disappointment: The name only sounds suggestive - it actually honors a woman named Desirée, rather than any particular form of yearning.

Louis Malle filmed *Pretty Baby* (1978), starring Brooke Shields as a pubescent streetwalker, on location at the Columns Hotel (see the Entertainment chapter). Julia Roberts plays a Tulane law student in *The Pelican Brief* (1993), a film adaptation of John Grisham's best-seller. *Interview with the Vampire* (1994) features Tom Cruise and Brad Pitt in the big-screen version of Anne Rice's novel.

Locals note that New Orleans police officers would never use French terms like 'cher,' as portrayed in *The Big Easy*. Its star, Dennis Quaid, also stars in *Undercover Blues* – one of the few local films acknowledged in the Planet Hollywood restaurant's formulaic display. Even devout fans of James Lee Burke's detective novels may flinch at the gratuitous violence in the screen adaptation of *Heaven's Prisoners* (1996), starring Alec Baldwin.

The film *MATA: The Mark Essex Story*, presents a true story about a New Orleans sniper, who killed six people from the roof of the downtown Howard Johnson lodge (now Holiday Inn) in early 1973. The 12-hour siege ended when a Marine sniper in a helicopter shot Essex, a disgruntled young man who was perhaps unfairly discharged from the Navy following racial conflicts. (Local author Walker Percy presaged the sniper incident in his novel *Love in the Ruins*, published in 1971.)

Michael Beaudreaux (pronounced **boo**-dro) stars in *The Louisiana Story* (1945), a semidocumentary about a young Cajun boy who scouted the swamps for oil drillers. The film's point of view – that Cajun culture and livelihoods can coexist with modern technology – is pure propaganda from Standard Oil Company, which helped to fund the production.

Writer-director Jim Jarmusch's *Down by Law* (1986) stars lanky avant-garde jazzman John Lurie, grizzled crooner Tom Waits and the crowned prince of Italian slapstick, Roberto Benigni (now an Oscar winner), as three down-and-outs at Orleans Parish Prison. The repartee between the three is the stuff of comic legend. The black-and-white film also features songs by Waits and background music by Lurie.

Other Hollywood films set in New Orleans, such as *Candyman II* and *Zombie vs Mardi Gras*, had short runs at the box office. Nevertheless, *Zombie* has become something of a cult classic.

SOCIETY & CONDUCT

In all, there is no other US city like New Orleans. Just try to appreciate and enjoy the unique cultural experience. Visitors are treated cordially, even if they are never quite admitted to the club; you need to have a few generations under your belt before you may be accepted. However, conversation flows easily between perfect strangers, whether in a bar, at a restaurant or while in line at the grocery store.

You will find that if you participate, pleasantries abound: The use of 'no, thank you,' 'yes, please,' 'ma'am,' 'sir,' 'How are you today?' might get you a better room, a faster drink, a good table and at least, generally, a smile. Merchants are liable to offer friendly visitors a little something extra, or *lagniappe* – it's like getting a baker's dozen.

RELIGION

Roman Catholics predominate in New Orleans and the Cajun country of southern Louisiana, creating an anachronism amid the Protestant 'Bible Belt,' which shapes much of the South. The French and Spanish heritage, along with a later influx of Irish among others, accounts for the Catholic pre-eminence. Slaveholders were required by Bienville's 1724 Code Noir to baptize and instruct their slaves in the Catholic faith – an edict not rigidly followed. Nevertheless, Catholicism is not uncommon among blacks today. A visit to the St Louis Cathedral during midnight mass, when crowds of visitors overflow its tremendous capacity, suggests that the New Orleans Archdiocese might be the nation's second most important, after that in New York City.

New Orleans' signature celebration – Mardi Gras – is rooted in Catholic beliefs. Carnival begins on 'Twelfth Night,' January 6 (the twelfth night following Christmas), and continues to Mardi Gras, or 'Fat Tuesday,' which is the day before Ash Wednesday. Catholics traditionally feast (hence in 'Carnival' the Latin root 'carne' or meat) before Ash Wednesday, the beginning of Lent and a period of penitence that continues until Easter. (See Special Events in the Facts for the Visitor chapter.)

Slaves and immigrants from Haiti also perpetuated their own belief systems brought from West Africa. Afrocentric American voodoo is centered on New Orleans and reflects beliefs brought to the New World – particularly to Brazil, the Caribbean and the American South. Central African women of the Fon and Yoruba tribes were especially influential on the plantation estates and at gatherings at Congo Square – now Armstrong Park. Much conjecture about voodoo focuses on its mystery and on ceremonies where worshipers enter a trance. Small temples like the Voodoo Spiritual Temple, 828 N Rampart St, continue to serve worshipers.

Protestant Americans settled in the Uptown area and built the great churches that line St Charles Ave. A few of those churches now cater to immigrants – particularly the Asians.

LANGUAGE

Visitors expecting to hear French will be greatly disappointed. Nor should you expect to find a preponderance of the familiar Southern drawl. Instead, the dialect is most like that heard in the northeastern cities of Baltimore or Brooklyn. It reflects the same Irish, Italian and German influences, with some interesting Creole influences.

Many words have a unique meaning in New Orleans. When ordering a po' boy (equivalent to a hero or submarine sandwich in other parts of the US), you may be asked: 'You want it dressed?' An affirmative nod will get you lettuce, tomato and dressing (often mayonnaise). Check the Glossary for other locally employed terminology.

Local idioms abound. One may hear residents comment that they are going to 'make' groceries, meaning they are going shopping. People also 'save' clothes, dishes or files, meaning they are going to put these items away.

Sentence tags like 'hear,' 'yeah,' 'no,' 'him' or 'her' were once commonly heard on the street. Cable's *The Grandissimes* contained the following example: 'I think Louisiana is a paradize-me!' More recent examples appear in Toole's *Confederacy of Dunces*, such as when the underpaid character in The Night of Joy bar proclaims, 'I bet you give some color baby one-year-old a broom in he han', he star sweeping his ass off. Whoa!'

A possibly Southern trait found in the dialect at any level of society is the dropping of the final 'g' in words ending in 'ing.' For example: 'I was drivin' over to the Voo Carray to get a swimmin' suit.'

'Voo Carray' is an example of the local pronunciation of French. Its actual spelling is Vieux Carré.

New Orleans'
Musical Heritage

As the hometown of an extraordinary number of early jazz stars, New Orleans holds a special place in the heart of all lovers of jazz music, and over the years a variety of monikers has been bestowed upon the city to express this affection. Music historians no longer get away with calling New Orleans the 'birthplace of jazz,' as any notion that the music was born here – or in any one place – has been decisively shot down. However, in its infancy jazz was certainly rocked and burped here, which has led many music lovers to describe New Orleans as the 'cradle of jazz.' Jelly Roll Morton, King Oliver, Louis Armstrong, Sidney Bechet and many others strengthened their chops while suckling on the Crescent City's ample bosom.

New Orleans wouldn't be such an important place for music if music weren't so important to New Orleans. This is a celebratory city – surely more parades are staged here than anywhere else in the US – and in New Orleans no celebration is complete without music. Second-line parades, funerals, parties, brunches, festivals, fireworks, steamboat rides down the Mississippi – all are accompanied by music. As many a visitor to the city has observed, New Orleanians use music the same way they do a good pepper sauce – they pour it over everything.

The city has always been that way. The French and their descendants, the Creoles, were mad about ballroom dancing and opera – New Orleans boasted two opera companies before any other US city had even one – and slaves and free persons of color preserved African music and dance at public markets like Congo Square. French-speaking black Creoles, who prided themselves on their musicianship and training, often found they could rouse black audiences by livening up a tune with African rhythms.

A proliferation of brass instruments after the Civil War led to a brass-band craze that spread throughout the South and the Midwest, and many musicians of that generation of musicians learned how to play without learning how to read. These musicians 'faked' their way through a tune, playing by ear and by memory, often deviating from the written melody. Soon, improvisation, as it became known when practiced effectively, became another way to breathe extra life into musical arrangements. The stage was set for jazz.

Jazz Pioneers
Buddy Bolden

One of the most problematic figures in jazz history is Charles 'Buddy' Bolden (1877-1931), New Orleans' first 'King of Jazz.' Very little is known about the cornetist's life or music, and no recordings survive. The details of his legend paint an attractive, larger-than-life picture, indicating that he made a huge impression on those who saw him play. Some said he 'broke his heart' when he performed, while others mused that he would 'blow his brains out' by playing so loud. One eyewitness account confirmed that his cornet once exploded as he played it.

But the exaggeration veiling the actual truth about Bolden does not undermine the fact that for roughly a decade, between 1895 to 1906, he

Inset: Artwork, Jackson Square (photograph by Richard Cummins)

Right: New Orleans' first 'King of Jazz,' Buddy Bolden led a too-short, cloudy life.

dominated a town loaded with stellar musicians. Bolden's playing was so dynamic and full of feeling and energy that he lured audiences to his stage – audiences were often said to migrate from the halls where rival dance bands were performing when word spread that Bolden was playing somewhere in town. Naturally, all the young musicians of New Orleans wanted to be just like him.

Bolden's rapid decline was brought on by insanity. Some say he lived life too hard and drank too much, and that the pressures of being 'King of Jazz' were too great for the minimally trained cornetist to handle. In any case, Bolden, at the top of his game, rapidly lost his mind. He was institutionalized for 25 years, oblivious to the fact that jazz was becoming popular worldwide and evolving into swing. When Bolden died, he was already long forgotten. He is buried in an unmarked grave in Holt Cemetery.

King Oliver

After Bolden, New Orleans enjoyed a series of cornet-playing kings, including Freddie Keppard, Bunk Johnson and Joe 'King' Oliver. While Keppard's star passed over like a comet and Bunk languished in obscurity until he was rediscovered by 'trad jazz' enthusiasts in the 1940s, Oliver (1885-1938) made a break for Chicago, where his Creole Jazz Band reached a much larger audience. Those who followed Oliver's career say his sudden fame was deserved but that he was past his prime when he reached Chicago. He was soon overshadowed by his protégé, Louis Armstrong, whom Oliver summoned from New Orleans in 1922. Together with Baby Dodds, Johnny Dodds and Lil Hardin (Armstrong's wife), Oliver and Armstrong made many seminal jazz recordings, including 'Dippermouth Blues.' By the late '20s, Oliver had lost his chops – and his teeth – and his career quickly went south. He hocked his horn, and ended up supporting himself as a fruit vendor in Savannah, Georgia, where he died in 1938.

Louis Armstrong

Although sometimes referred to as 'King Louie,' in the world of jazz Louis Armstrong (1901-71) is really beyond royal sobriquets. The self-deprecating Armstrong preferred to go by the nickname 'Satchmo,' and that's the handle by which New Orleans' most famous and best-loved native son will always be remembered.

Armstrong made his greatest contributions to music during the 1920s, when he began to modify the New Orleans sound. New Orleans jazz had always emphasized ensemble playing, but to better utilize his own gifts for improvisation, Armstrong assembled his Hot Five (including Kid Ory on trombone and Johnny Dodds on clarinet) and shaped his arrangements specifically to support his own driving improvised solos. With his cornet riding above the ensemble, songs like 'Muskrat Ramble' and 'Yes! I'm in the Barrel' had an intensity not heard before – if the music sounds all too familiar today, it's because Armstrong's influence was so far-reaching. As his popularity mounted, he became the consummate showman, singing, jiving and mugging for his audience. Even during the '40s and '50s, when jazz changed without him, demand for Armstrong only seemed to increase. His tours of Europe helped spread the popularity of jazz worldwide.

All of this, incredibly, was accomplished by the son of a prostitute. Armstrong grew up on the outskirts of New Orleans' notorious Storyville district, where he and his fellow street urchins would sing on the streets for pennies. While residing in the Waifs' Home for troubled youth, he began to play the trumpet, and, obviously, he was a natural talent because he was soon playing professionally. Armstrong's big break came in 1922, when King Oliver hired him to play in his band in Chicago, and Satchmo never looked back. He only returned to New Orleans to play the occasional gig and, in 1949, to assume the role of Zulu on Mardi Gras.

Depth of the Talent Pool

The story line from Bolden to Oliver to Armstrong neatly illustrates the evolution of jazz in New Orleans, but it unfortunately leaves out many key players. At heart, New Orleans will always value the beauty of the ensemble; indeed, to consider all of the great musicians who played jazz early on in New Orleans is to regard a rare and wonderful collection of talent. Many musicians left New Orleans, but they carried the imprint of the city with them.

Their ranks included one who preferred to stand alone. Pianist **Jelly Roll Morton** was a controversial character – he claimed to have 'invented' jazz while performing in a Storyville bordello in 1902 – but he had uncommon talents in composition and arrangement. **Kid Ory**, who hailed from nearby La Place, Louisiana, was also important in the development of jazz. His expressive 'tailgate' style on the trombone accompanied many of the first jazz stars, including Louis Armstrong, and when Ory moved his band to Los Angeles in 1919, he introduced jazz to the West Coast. **Sidney Bechet** was the first jazz musician to make his mark on the soprano saxophone, an instrument he played with vibrato and deep, often moody

Left: Storyville son Louis Armstrong, jazz virtuoso and musical pioneer

feeling. For 14 years clarinetist **Barney Bigard** was a key member of the Duke Ellington Orchestra.

The Barbarin family is legendary in New Orleans for producing some of the city's best-loved musicians, including drummer **Paul Barbarin** and his nephew, banjo and guitar player **Danny Barker**. Barker also wrote many popular tunes for his wife, singer **Blue Lu Barker**. Members of the Barbarin family are still playing in New Orleans today. **Louis Prima** also hailed from New Orleans, and although the Italian trumpet maestro (composer of 'Sing Sing Sing' and 'Just a Gigolo') is more often associated with the highly esteemed Las Vegas music scene, he was laid to rest in his home town at Metairie Cemetery.

It should go without saying that this brief overview merely scrapes the surface.

Rhythm & Blues

Despite its proximity to the Mississippi Delta, where the blues began, New Orleans never became a blues capital the way Chicago did. The blues have always been the domain of guitarists and harp players, and New Orleans has always been primarily a brass and ivory city. But it has never lacked great blues artists. Asked to name the king of New Orleans blues, a local musician will likely name trumpeter Louis Armstrong, whose blues-based solos of the 1920s and '30s were equal in expression and original-ity to those of any Delta guitarist of his day.

New Orleans has also been home to a few great blues guitarists, begin-ning with Mississippi native Eddie Jones, who preferred to be known as **Guitar Slim**. By the 1950s, Guitar Slim was based in New Orleans, where he packed patrons into nightclubs like the Dew Drop Inn. He wooed audi-ences with unparalleled flamboyance (his hair dyes and sartorial style defied color coordination), and he knocked them out with his anguished vocal style and agitated guitar licks. His biggest hit – a gift from the devil, he said – was 'The Things I Used to Do,' which sold a million copies. Other New Orleans blues guitarists include living legends **Earl King**, whose 'Trick Bag' and 'Come on Baby' are essentials in the New Orleans canon, and blind guitarist **Snooks Eaglin**, whose singing and playing are characterized by a unique expressiveness.

Although New Orleans is still widely regarded as a jazz city – as it should be – it is as much an R&B and soul city. Since the 1950s and '60s, the city has been churning out singers, drummers and piano players in truly mind-boggling numbers.

New Orleans owes its solid reputation as a breeding ground for piano players to a man named Henry Roeland Byrd – otherwise known as **Professor Longhair**. His

Right: The flamboyant key-board wizard Professor Longhair

rhythmic rhumba and boogie-woogie style of playing propelled him to local success with tunes like 'Tipitina' (for which the legendary nightclub is named) and 'Go to the Mardi Gras.' He did not tour, though, and his name soon faded away. His style of playing, however, lived on in younger pianists like **Huey 'Piano' Smith** ('Rockin' Pneumonia and the Boogie Woogie Flu') and the eye-patched genius **James Booker**. In 1970, Professor Longhair was barely making a living sweeping floors when promoter Quint Davis tracked him down and booked him for that spring's Jazz Fest. That performance launched a decade of long-overdue recognition for one of New Orleans' great performers. He died a peaceful death in 1980.

While Professor Longhair was still mired in obscurity, some very unforgettable tunes came out of the Crescent City to rock the nation. 'Lawdy Miss Clawdy' was the inspired creation of New Orleanian **Lloyd Price**. His backup band included **Dave Bartholomew** and **Fats Domino**, the duo credited with shaping the New Orleans sound. Bartholomew's trademark arrangements, built on soulful horns and a solid backbeat (laid down by drummer Earl Palmer), can be heard on many of the big hits of the '50s, including some of Little Richard's early recordings. In collaboration with Bartholomew, Domino would go on to become one of the city's most successful musicians, recording a string of hit singles including 'I'm Walkin',' 'Blueberry Hill,' 'My Blue Heaven' and 'Ain't that a Shame.'

If you've ever wondered where the expression 'See you later, alligator' originated – by now you're probably guessing it was in New Orleans – it all began with a catchy tune by that name, recorded by **Bobby Charles** in 1955. The often-covered 'Ooh Poo Pah Doo' is also a local creation, first delivered by singer **Jessie Hill**. Other stars to emerge from the Crescent City during this period were the late, great **Johnny Adams**, who wooed the city with smooth, gut-wrenching ballads, and the dynamic pop duo **Shirley & Lee**, who put the local standard 'Let the Good Times Roll' on radio playlists nationwide.

By this time it was the 1960s, a decade marked by the guiding hand of **Allen Toussaint**, a talented producer, songwriter and musician whose legion of hits is legendary. As the producer and talent developer at Minit Records, he exhibited a remarkable adaptability in molding songs to suit the talents of many of New Orleans' diverse young artists. The formula worked for **Ernie K-Doe**, who hit pay dirt with the disgruntled but catchy 'Mother In Law,' a chart-topper in 1961, and the coy 'A Certain Girl.' (See the boxed text in the Entertainment chapter for an update on the life and times of K-Doe.) Toussaint also wrote and produced the **Lee Dorsey** hit 'Working in the Coal Mine,' which couldn't have been more different from the K-Doe songs.

CHRISTIAN HEEB

Irma Thomas also frequently collaborated with Toussaint. The former waitress was discovered in a talent show and was soon recording hits like the just-you-wait-and-see anthem 'Time is on My Side' (later covered by the Rolling

Left: Irma Thomas, the Soul Queen of New Orleans

Stones) and the touching, autobiographical 'Wish Someone Would Care.' A number of Toussaint-penned ballads, including 'It's Raining' and 'Ruler of My Heart,' lent definition to her body of work. These melancholic songs of resigned waiting and diminished expectations, supported by the cool inner strength conveyed in Irma's voice, draw a character portrait of the singer, who certainly experienced her share of ups and downs. She's one of New Orleans' most compelling artists – her 'title,' the 'Soul Queen of New Orleans,' is well deserved. Irma still performs regularly in town, sometimes at her own bar, The Lion's Den (see the Entertainment chapter).

Toussaint's most enduring and successful partnership was with the Neville Brothers, who have reigned as the first family of New Orleans music for four decades. **Aaron Neville**, whose soulful falsetto and inflections are hallmarks of one of the most instantly recognizable voices in pop music, began working with Tou-

ssaint in 1960, when his first hit single, the menacing but pretty 'Over You,' was recorded. The association later yielded the gorgeous 'Let's Live.' But 'Tell It Like It Is' (1967), recorded without Toussaint, is the biggest national hit of Aaron's career.

Art Neville, a piano player from the Professor Longhair school, began performing with a group called the Hawkettes in

the late-'50s. In the late '60s, he formed the group Art Neville and the New Orleans Sound with guitarist Leo Nocentelli, bassist George Porter and drummer Zigaboo Modeliste, a group that would soon change its name to the **Meters** and define New Orleans funk music. The Meters later joined forces with George Landry, who as Big Chief Jolly was head of the Wild Tchoupitoulas Mardi Gras Indian gang (see the Mardi Gras section of

this book); Landry also happened to be uncle of the Nevilles. When **Wild Tchoupitoulas** began performing funk- and reggae-based Indian anthems ('Meet de Boys on de Battlefront') in the mid-'70s, it marked the first time the four Neville brothers performed together – Charles and Cyrille rounded out the quartet. The Meters disbanded, and Landry passed away, but the brothers continue to perform together to this day, as do **Cyrille Neville & the Uptown Allstars**.

The Meters and Allen Toussaint also contributed to the success of **Dr John**, who recorded his best-selling album *Right Place Wrong Time* with their support in 1973. Dr John

Top right: Art Neville of the Professor Longhair school of piano

Bottom right: Charles Neville performs with brother Cyrille's Uptown Allstars

MASON FLORENCE

began life as Mac Rebennack. He played guitar as a sideman for many New Orleans artists during the late '50s, but he switched to piano after his left index finger was shot off and sewn back on. He moved to Los Angeles and toured with Sonny and Cher in the mid-'60s before developing his voodoo priest persona, based on the historic New Orleans conjurer, by the end of the decade (see the boxed text 'Yesterday's Voodoo' in the Things to See & Do chapter for more on the original Dr John). His psychoactive soul and voodoo rock have earned him a loyal cult following that is still going strong.

Rebirth of Brass

PORCHÉ WEST

It could reasonably be argued that modern New Orleans music began with marching brass bands. Mobile brass outfits parading through the city's back streets for funerals and benevolent society 'second-line' parades during the late 19th century pretty much set the tone for things to come – Buddy Bolden, Freddie Keppard and even Louis Armstrong grew up idolizing the horn players who frequently played along the streets where these future jazz innovators lived. While early-20th-century ensembles like the Excelsior, Onward and Olympia brass bands never became nationally recognized, their tradition did not die. Many brass bands today, including the current generation of the Onward, Olympia and the Tremé brass bands, still play very traditional New Orleans music, though surely they're jazzier than pre-20th-century bands were.

The brass band scene received a welcome infusion of new blood in the late 1970s with the emergence of the **Dirty Dozen Brass Band**. The Dirty Dozen were anything but traditional, fusing diverse styles of music from 'trad jazz' to funk to R&B to modern jazz, much as Charles Mingus had been doing since the 1950s. No longer a marching band, the Dirty

JOHN ELK III

Top left: A Grand Marshall leads a jazz funeral procession in the Tremé District

Bottom left: Young New Orleans street musician

Dozen continue to perform in clubs around town and tour frequently. They paved the way for the much funkier and streetwise **Rebirth Brass Band**, formed in 1983. Original members of Rebirth, including trumpeter Kermit Ruffins, have moved on, but a younger crew of musicians has kept the band alive, and it remains one of the most popular groups in New Orleans, where Rebirth performs regular club gigs. In recent years, brass music has continued to evolve in New Orleans, sometimes fusing with reggae music and even hip hop. Rappin' trombone player **Coolbone** is at the forefront of what he terms the 'brasshop' movement.

Jazz Resurgence

When **Wynton Marsalis** released his first album in 1982, he was only 19 years old – and yet music critics proclaimed him a genius. Not since Louis Armstrong had a New Orleans musician been so well received on the national scene. It was the start of good things to come. Soon, Wynton's older brother **Branford Marsalis** was also making waves, and other young musicians who were studying with Winton and Branford's father, **Ellis Marsalis**, at the New Orleans Center for the Creative Arts, formed the nucleus of a New Orleans jazz revival. These included pianist **Harry Connick Jr** and trumpeter **Roy Hargrove**.

MASON FLORENCE

This wasn't another resuscitation of 'trad jazz,' though. The young turks of the '80s were clearly coming out of the post-Miles Davis and John Coltrane world. Since their beginnings in New Orleans, they have all relocated to other parts of the country, where media exposure and greater amounts of money tend to be available.

The flow of talent from New Orleans hasn't ceased, and in recent years more rising stars have elected to stay at home, rather than seek the spotlight of New York or Los Angeles. The concentration of jazz artists in New Orleans is an obvious inspiration – this is an exciting time to be a musician or a fan of music in the Crescent City. **Henry Butler**, a blind pianist with extraordinarily quick hands, moved to California, but then returned to New Orleans, where he plays several nights a week in local clubs. He's been able to pursue several musical paths, from straight jazz to blues to funk and Latin. Trumpeter **Nicholas Payton** began his career recording classic New Orleans standards with a modern musical approach. He also joined forces with the ancient legend Buck Clayton in a Grammy-winning performance of 'Stardust.'

Right: Louisiana accordion sensation Rosie Ledet at Jazz Fest

Trumpeter **Kermit Ruffins** may not have Payton's chops, but he's got more heart and is one of the most entertaining musicians in town. His shows often attract other musicians, who come for the chance to play with Kermit's band, the Barbecue Swingers – clearly a sign of a healthy music scene.

Top left: Kermit Ruffins and his Barbecue Swingers

Bottom left: Street musicians on Chartres St, French Quarter

Another trumpet player to watch is **Irvin Mayfield**, whose popular outfit, Los Hombres Calientes, includes yet another Marsalis brother, drummer **Jason Marsalis**, and the relative elder statesman, the legendary percussionist **Bill Sumners**. They've got a good thing going, an intense concoction of wildly expressive and percussive Latin jazz, and they put on a great live show.

Yet another trumpet player, **James Andrews**, has been gaining notice since the release of his album *Satchmo of the Ghetto*, on which Dr John (tinkling the ivories) and Allan Toussaint (producing) lend support. Andrews, who heads up an illustrious family of young musicians (**Trombone Shorty**, a local celebrity since he was around eight years old, is his younger brother), lays down some catchy, Toussaint-flavored licks on the album, but the

album's title only perplexes (wasn't the original Satchmo also from the ghetto?). Additional musicians to check out include **Davell Crawford** (grandson of Sugarboy Crawford, of 'Jockamo' fame), a funk-driven tour de force on piano and Hammond B-3, and **Donald Harrison Jr** (namesake son of the late Mardi Gras Indian chief), an inspired contemporary jazz innovator.

When in New Orleans, you'll have to make some difficult but enviable decisions, because on many nights several of these talented musicians will be performing at the same time in clubs around town.

Recommended Listening

To get up to speed on New Orleans music, from the 1920s to the present, here's a highly subjective list (in roughly chronological order) of 10 great CDs, all widely available.

Louis Armstrong, *1925-26* (Chronological Classics) – definitive early jazz recordings

Jelly Roll Morton, *1939-40* (Chronological Classics) – the sound of Storyville

Sidney Bechet, *Best of Sidney Bechet* (Blue Note, 1940s) – some sultry playing by a soprano sax maestro

Professor Longhair, *Collector's Choice* (Rounder, 1950s) – a good introduction to one of New Orleans' most important R&B artists

Irma Thomas, *Time Is On My Side* (Kent Soul, 1960s) – essential selections from the Soul Queen's songbook

The Meters, *The Very Best of the Meters* (Rhino, 1970s) – steady, funky instrumental grooves

Dr John, *In the Right Place* (Atlantic, 1973) – psychoactive soul with an Allan Toussaint groove

Wild Tchoupitoulas, *Wild Tchoupitoulas*, (Island, 1976) – a remarkable collaboration, bringing together Mardi Gras Indians, the Meters and the Neville Brothers

Dirty Dozen Brass Band, *Voodoo* (Columbia, 1989) – the second line meets modern jazz

Wynton Marsalis, *Standard Time, Vol 3* (Columbia, 1990) – jazz standards by Wynton and his father, Ellis Marsalis

Nicholas Payton, *Gumbo Nouveau* (Verve, 1996) – modern treatments of New Orleans classics

Los Hombres Calientes, *Los Hombres Calientes* (Basin Street, 1998) – hip, modern, Latin sounds

Also, for a great overview of R&B, blues and soul of New Orleans, check out *Crescent City Soul: The Sound of New Orleans 1947-1974*, which was issued as the 'official CD collection of the 1996 New Orleans Jazz and Heritage Festival.' It includes everyone from Professor Longhair to Dr John.

That was more than 10 selections, wasn't it? You didn't expect to go away without a little lagniappe, did you?

Facts for the Visitor

WHEN TO GO

From February through April the climate in New Orleans is most agreeable, coinciding with the city's two most spectacular events – Carnival and Jazz Fest. May heat begins intensifying, readying residents for summer. June marks the official beginning of the hurricane threat, which can last through October and sometimes into November. The oppressive heat and humidity during the summer months cause many residents to flee to the Gulf Coast in Mississippi. August is simply stifling. If you're visiting in summer, prepare for the 'oven' effect of walking out of chilly 70°F air-conditioning into overwhelming tropical 95°F heat by wearing light clothes and bringing a sweater along for restaurants and theaters (not for most bars, however). September and October are months with agreeable humidity and temperatures for visitors. Christmas is an off-peak period with discounted accommodations and holiday food and decorations. Although winter temperatures during the large New Year's Eve celebration and the Sugar Bowl can be chilly, they are balmy in comparison with those in the Midwestern US and Canada.

ORIENTATION

New Orleans is wedged between the meandering Mississippi River to the south and Lake Pontchartrain to the north. The original and most compact portion of the city parallels the river.

Within the city, the earliest settlements evolved first on the relatively high ground along the river levee. Bienville's surveyor, Adrien de Pauger, plotted a rectangular grid plan for Nouvelle Orleans around a central square, Place d'Armes, following the 'Laws of the Indies' precepts widely used by colonial powers in planting new cities. This became the Vieux Carré, or French Quarter. Colonial developers formed two additional municipalities bordering the Quarter, Faubourg Marigny and Faubourg Tremé.

Upriver from the town square, riverside plantations extended from the levee toward the lake in long, narrow rectangular plots. Their typical depth of 40 arpents (just under an acre) roughly coincides with Claiborne Ave, which therefore parallels the river, while St Charles Ave was intended to split the properties at the 20-arpent line. Anglo Americans subsequently subdivided and settled this area, generally referred to as Uptown.

One further feature had an impact on the city form. A subtle ridge of high ground near Bayou St John served as an early portage route between the river and the lake. Such so-called ridges were actually low natural levees. It attracted early plantation houses and other substantial homes and became known as Esplanade Ridge, part of the City Park and Fair Grounds area, as it's noted in this guide. Other bayou ridges include the suburb of Metairie (pronounced **met**-ar-ee) and Gentilly.

Today, an important thing to note about getting around on New Orleans' streets is that 'avenues' are generally four-lane major thoroughfares and 'streets' are one or two lanes. Street numbering between the river and lake typically starts at the river. On routes that parallel the river, street numbers begin at Canal St. Due to the vagaries of the river, Uptown streets are labeled 'south' and downtown streets are 'north.'

The Mississippi River is the 'main street' and historical focal point for New Orleans. Directions, up- or downriver, are relative to the water flow, which bends to all points of the compass: 'The Convention Center is upriver from (or above) the French Quarter,' even though a compass would show that the Convention Center is south-southwest.

In addition, the river and Lake Pontchartrain serve as landmarks in 'river side' or 'lake side' directions: 'You'll find Louis Armstrong Park on the lake side of the French Quarter – head toward the lake and you'll find it,' and 'Preservation Hall is on St Peter St toward the river from Bourbon St.'

The broad Canal St divides Uptown from Downtown. However, as added confusion, a large part of the city, from the Garden District to the Riverbend, is commonly referred to as Uptown.

People of different wealth, race and ethnicity create a checkerboard of neighborhoods in the compact city. It's often only a few steps from a ghetto to endowed estates. Note that the following overview is best accompanied by a look at a map.

Neighborhoods

The French Quarter (often shortened to 'the Quarter' and also known as the Vieux Carré) originally consisted of 44 blocks (it's now 80 blocks) centered on Place d'Armes (now Jackson Square) next to the river levee. The touristy 'upper Quarter' is bounded by Canal St, where one finds most large convention-style hotels; Canal St separates the lower Quarter and the CBD (Central Business District). The lower Quarter, at the French Quarter's downriver boundary, meets the Faubourg Marigny at Esplanade Ave, and both of these areas harbor the gay district. Below the Faubourg Marigny is the transitional Bywater, fast becoming a burgeoning artists' neighborhood.

Beyond the Quarter's lakeside boundary at N Rampart St (named for the historic fortification that once surrounded the city) begins the African American Tremé District. Away from the Quarter, lakefront City Park and the Fair Grounds (site of the Jazz Fest) are reached by Esplanade Ave.

On the river-side periphery of the CBD is the Warehouse District, a zone from Poydras Ave to Howard Ave, bounded by the river and St Charles Ave. The city encourages upscale galleries and developers to reuse the old warehouse spaces. On the river-side boundary of the Warehouse District, you'll find the Convention Center and Riverwalk Mall. Downriver past the Canal St Ferry are Woldenberg Park, the Aquarium of the Americas and the Moonwalk. This general area is known as the Riverfront, and the

Moonwalk along the Mississippi River

Riverfront Streetcar Line traverses it before skirting the Quarter.

St Charles Ave, the main Uptown corridor and streetcar route from Canal St, travels upriver past the Lower Garden District and the Garden District to S Carrollton Ave in the Riverbend area.

MAPS

Good-quality maps of New Orleans are available from most bookstores, but free maps from a variety of sources are generally adequate for most visitors. Rental-car agencies have heaps of maps, but the best is the excellent *New Orleans Street Map & Visitor Guide*, available from tourist offices. It depicts Regional Transit Authority (RTA) bus routes and also includes a street index. Most tourist offices also offer free copies of the *African American Heritage Map*, which shows points of historical interest in New Orleans along with contemporary enterprises.

Most of the commercial mapping companies insist on disorienting the visitor by not placing north at the top of their downtown inset maps. Rand McNally's *New Orleans City Map* offers an up-to-date depiction of all streets in the city and also contains a street index. American Automobile Association members using AAA's *New Orleans & Vicinity Map* will appreciate the detailed 'Metropolitan' coverage of the CBD and French Quarter, but the greatly simplified map of the city is disappointing.

De Ville Books (Map 4; ☎ 525-1846, 344 Carondelet St) stocks maps and guidebooks for New Orleans. A good selection of historical maps and prints is available from The Centuries (☎ 568-9491, 517 St Louis St).

TOURIST OFFICES
Local Tourist Offices

Right next to popular Jackson Square in the heart of the French Quarter, the New Orleans Welcome Center (Map 2; ☎ 566-5031, 529 St Ann St), in the lower Pontalba Building, offers maps, up-to-date pocket guidebooks, listings of upcoming events, a variety of brochures and discount RTA passes. The helpful staff can help you find accommodations in a pinch, answer ques-

Jackson Square in the rain

tions and offer advice about New Orleans. However, relatively little information is available for the non-English speaker. It is open 9 am to 5 pm daily.

Small information kiosks scattered through the main tourist areas offer most of the same brochures as the Welcome Center, but their staff tend to not be as knowledgeable.

Jean Lafitte National Park maintains an NPS Visitor Center (Map 2; ☎ 589-2636, 419 Decatur St) in the French Quarter. The Park Service's mission here is to interpret the history of the Mississippi Delta and New Orleans (the French Quarter and the Garden District are National Historic Districts), and it offers a variety of ranger-led programs, including talks and walks.

Tourist Offices Abroad

The USA does not have a well-developed overseas tourist-office system. Contact your local US diplomatic office (see Embassies & Consulates, below) concerning information from the United States Travel & Tourism Administration (USTTA). Information on Louisiana tourism can be obtained by mail from the Louisiana Office of Tourism (☎ 342-8119, 800-414-8626, PO Box 94291, Baton Rouge, LA 70804). In the UK, contact the New Orleans & Louisiana Tourist Office (☎ 020-8760-0377); there are no walk-in facilities. French visitors should contact Claude Teboul of France Louisiane de la Nouvelle Orléans (☎ 01 45 77 09 68, 28 Boulevard de Strasbourg, 75010 Paris).

The best way to request that local information be sent by mail is by calling the New Orleans Welcome Center (☎ 566-5031) day or night. The New Orleans Metropolitan Convention & Visitors Bureau (☎ 566-5011, www.neworleanscvb.com/) and the Greater New Orleans Multicultural Tourism Network (☎ 523-5652, www.soulofneworleans.com) are only open on weekdays and share an address near the Superdome at 1520 Sugar Bowl Drive, New Orleans, LA 70112. The Multicultural Tourism Network publishes a free visitor guide geared toward African Americans, *The Soul of New Orleans*.

The *Times-Picayune* has a Destination New Orleans site on the World Wide Web (www.neworleans.net) with current events listings and other information for travelers. Check out the 'Carnival Central' section for maps of all the parades.

DOCUMENTS

With the exception of Canadians, who need only proper proof of Canadian citizenship, all foreign visitors to the USA must have a valid passport, and most visitors must also have a US visa. It's a good idea to keep photocopies of these documents; in case of theft, they'll be a lot easier to replace.

Your passport should be valid for at least six months longer than your intended stay in the USA. Documents of financial stability and/or guarantees from a US resident are sometimes required, particularly for visitors from Third World countries.

Visas

A reciprocal visa-waiver program applies to citizens of certain countries who may enter the USA for stays of 90 days or less without having to obtain a visa. Currently these

HIV/AIDS & Entering the USA

Anyone entering the USA who is not a US citizen is subject to the authority of the Immigration & Naturalization Service (INS). The INS can keep people from entering or staying in the USA by excluding or deporting them. This is especially relevant to travelers with HIV (human immunodeficiency virus) or AIDS (acquired immune deficiency syndrome). Though being HIV-positive is not a ground for deportation, it is a 'ground for exclusion,' meaning that the INS can invoke this rule and refuse to admit an HIV-positive visitor to the country.

Although INS officers don't test people for HIV or AIDS at the point of entry into the USA, they may try to exclude anyone who answers 'yes' to this question on the non-immigrant visa application form: 'Have you ever been afflicted with a communicable disease of public health significance?' An INS officer may also stop someone who seems sick, is carrying AIDS/HIV medicine or appears to be from a 'high-risk group' (ie, gay), though sexual orientation itself is not legally a ground for exclusion. Visitors may be deported if the INS later finds that they are HIV-positive but did not declare it. Being HIV-positive is not a 'ground for deportation,' but failing to provide correct information on the visa application is.

If you can prove to consular officials that you are the spouse, parent or child of a US citizen or legal permanent resident (green-card holder), you are exempt from the exclusionary law, even if you are HIV-positive or have AIDS.

Immigrants and visitors who may face exclusion should discuss their rights and options with a trained immigration advocate within the USA before applying for a visa. For legal immigration information and referrals to immigration advocates, contact the National Immigration Project of the National Lawyers Guild (☎ 617-227-9727), 14 Beacon St, Suite 506, Boston, MA 02108, or the Immigrant HIV Assistance Project, Bar Association of San Francisco (☎ 415-782-8995), 465 California St, Suite 1100, San Francisco, CA 94104.

Embassies & Consulates

US Embassies
US diplomatic offices abroad include the following:

Australia
(☎ 2-6270-5000)
21 Moonah Place
Yarralumla, ACT 2600

Austria
(☎ 1-313-39)
Boltzmanngasse 16, A-1091
Vienna

Belgium
(☎ 2 513 38 30)
Blvd du Régent 27, B-1000
Brussels

Canada
(☎ 613-238-5335)
100 Wellington St
Ottawa, Ontario 1P 5T1

Denmark
(☎ 31 42 31 44)
Dag Hammarskjolds Allé 24
Copenhagen

Finland
(☎ 0-171-931)
Itainen Puistotie 14A
Helsinki

France
(☎ 01 42 96 12 02)
2 rue Saint Florentin
75001 Paris

Germany
(☎ 228-33-91)
Deichmanns Aue 29
53179 Bonn

Greece
(☎ 1-721-2951)
Leoforos Vasilissis Sofias 91
115 21 Athens

India
(☎ 11-60-0651)
Shanti Path, Chanakyapuri
110021, New Delhi

Indonesia
(☎ 21-360-360)
Medan Merdeka Selatan 5
Jakarta

Ireland
(☎ 668-8777)
42 Elgin Rd, Ballsbridge
Dublin

Israel
(☎ 3-519-7575)
71 Hayarkon St, Tel Aviv

Italy
(☎ 6 46 741)
Via Vittorio Veneto 119a-
121, Rome

Japan
(☎ 3-224-5000)
1-10-5 Akasaka Chome
Minato-ku, Tokyo

Korea
(☎ 2-397-4114)
82 Sejong-Ro, Chongro-ku
Seoul

Malaysia
(☎ 3-248-9011)
376 Jalan Tun Razak
50400 Kuala Lumpur

Mexico
(☎ 5-211-00-42)
Paseo de la Reforma 305
Cuauhtémoc, 06500
Mexico City

Netherlands
(☎ 70-310-9209)
Lange Voorhout 102
2514 EJ, The Hague

New Zealand
(☎ 4-722-068)
29 Fitzherbert Terrace
Thorndon, Wellington

Norway
(☎ 22-44-85-50)
Drammensvein 18, Oslo

Philippines
(☎ 2-521-7116)
1201 Roxas Blvd, Ermita
Manila 1000

Russia
(☎ 095-252-2451)
Novinskiy Bul'var 19/23
Moscow

Singapore
(☎ 338-0251)
30 Hill St, Singapore 0617

South Africa
(☎ 12-342-1048)
877 Pretorius St, Box 9536
Pretoria 0001

Spain
(☎ 1 577 4000)
Calle Serrano 75, 28006
Madrid

Sweden
(☎ 8-783-5300)
Strandvagen 101, S-115 89
Stockholm

Switzerland
(☎ 31-357-70-11)
Jubilaumsstrasse 93
3005 Berne

Thailand
(☎ 2-252-5040)
95 Wireless Rd, Bangkok

UK
(☎ 020-7499-9000)
24 Grosvenor St
London W1

Embassies & Consulates

Consulates in New Orleans

Check the White Pages phone book (business listings) under 'Consulates' for diplomatic representation. Canada does not have a consulate in New Orleans; the nearest is in Miami. Other consulates include the following:

Denmark
Consulate of Denmark
(☎ 586-8300)
321 St Charles Ave

Dominican Republic
Consulate-General of the
Dominican Republic
(☎ 522-1843)
2 Canal St

Finland
Consulate of Finland
(☎ 523-6451)
1100 Poydras Ave

France
Consulate-General of
France
(☎ 523-5772)
300 Poydras Ave

Germany
Honorary Consulate of FRG
(☎ 576-4289)
639 Loyola Ave

India
Honorary Consulate of India
(☎ 582-8000)
201 St Charles Ave

Japan
Consulate-General of Japan
(☎ 529-2101)
639 Loyola Ave

Korea
Honorary Consulate of
Korea
(☎ 524-0757)
321 St Charles Ave

Mexico
Consulate-General of
Mexico
(☎ 522-3596)
2 Canal St

Netherlands
Consulate of the Netherlands
(☎ 596-2838)
643 Magazine St

Spain
Consulate-General of Spain
(☎ 525-4951)
2 Canal St

Sweden
Consul of Sweden
(☎ 827-8600)
2640 Canal St

Switzerland
Honorary Consulate of
Switzerland
(☎ 897-6510)
1620 8th St

Thailand
Consulate of Thailand
(☎ 522-3400)
335 Julia St

UK
Honorary Consulate of
Great Britain
(☎ 524-4180)
321 St Charles Ave

Your Own Embassy

As a tourist, it's important to realize what your own embassy – the embassy of the country of which you are a citizen – can and can't do.

Generally speaking, it won't be much help in emergencies if the trouble you're in is remotely your own fault. Remember that you are bound by the laws of the country you are in. Your embassy will not be sympathetic if you end up in jail after committing a crime locally, even if such actions are legal in your own country.

In genuine emergencies you might get some assistance, but only if other channels have been exhausted. For example, if you need to get home urgently, a free ticket home is exceedingly unlikely – the embassy would expect you to have insurance. If you have all your money and documents stolen, it might assist in getting a new passport, but a loan for onward travel is out of the question.

Embassies used to keep letters for travelers or have a small reading room with home newspapers, but these days the mail-holding service has been stopped and even newspapers tend to be out of date.

countries are Andorra, Austria, Belgium, Brunei, Denmark, Finland, France, Germany, Iceland, Italy, Japan, Liechtenstein, Luxembourg, Monaco, the Netherlands, New Zealand, Norway, San Marino, Spain, Sweden, Switzerland and the UK. Under this program you must have a roundtrip ticket on an airline participating in the visa-waiver program; you must have proof of financial solvency and sign a form waiving the right to a hearing of deportation; and you will not be allowed to extend your stay beyond 90 days. Consult with your travel agent or contact the airlines directly for more information.

Other travelers will need to obtain a visa from a US consulate or embassy. In most countries the process can be done by mail.

Visa applicants may be required to 'demonstrate binding obligations' that will insure their return home. Because of this requirement, those planning to travel through other countries before arriving in the USA are generally better off applying for their US visa while they are still in their home country, rather than while on the road.

The most common visa is a Non-Immigrant Visitors Visa, B1 for business purposes, B2 for tourism or visiting friends and relatives. A visitor's visa is good for one or five years with multiple entries, and it specifically prohibits the visitor from taking paid employment in the USA. The validity period for US visitor visas depends on what country you're from. The length of time you'll be allowed to stay in the USA is ultimately determined by US immigration authorities at the port of entry.

Visa Extensions Tourist visitors are usually granted a six-month stay on first arrival. If you try to extend that time, the first assumption will be that you are working illegally, so come prepared with concrete evidence that you've been traveling extensively and will continue to be a model tourist. A wad of traveler's checks looks much better than a solid and unmoving bank account. Extensions are handled by the US Justice Department's Immigration & Naturalization Service (INS; ☎ 589-6533), in the main post office at 701 Loyola Ave, room T8011. Callers wishing to speak to an information officer must call between 8 and 11 am.

Other Documents

Bring your driver's license if you intend to rent a car; visitors from some countries may find it wise to back up their national license with an International Driving Permit, available from their local auto club. You'll also need a picture ID that shows your date of birth in order to buy alcohol (you must be 21 years old) or to enter bars and clubs. Make sure your driver's license has a photo on it, or bring some other form of ID.

A comprehensive travel or health insurance policy is very important for overseas visitors, and if you're coming from abroad, you should carry a membership card or documentation.

CUSTOMS

US Customs allows each person over the age of 21 to bring 1 liter of liquor and 200 cigarettes duty-free into the USA. Non-US citizens are allowed to enter the US with $100 worth of gifts from abroad. There are restrictions on bringing fresh fruit and flowers into the country and a strict quarantine on animals. Should you be carrying more than $10,000 in US and foreign cash, traveler's checks, money orders or the like, you need to declare the excess amount. There is no legal restriction on the amount that may be imported, but undeclared sums in excess of $10,000 may be subject to confiscation.

MONEY

There are three straightforward ways to handle money in the US: cash, US-dollar traveler's checks and credit or bank cards, which can be used to withdraw cash from the many automatic teller machines (ATMs) across the country.

Currency

US dollars are the only accepted currency in New Orleans. The dollar is divided into 100 cents (¢) with coins of 1¢ (penny), 5¢ (nickel), 10¢ (dime), 25¢ (quarter) and the relatively rare 50¢ (half dollar). Quarters are the most commonly used coins in vending

Origin of $

New Orleans played a role in the origin of the US dollar sign during the Spanish colonial period of the late 1700s. Oliver Pollack, a wealthy Irish merchant engaged in Mississippi River trade, made notations for 'peso' in his ledger that evolved from a separate 'P' and 'S' to an overlapping symbol by 1778. Further shorthand reduced the 'P' to a single slash.

machines and parking meters, so it's handy to have a stash of them. Bills can be confusing to the foreign visitor, as they're all the same size and color. Bills come in denominations of $1, $2, $5, $10, $20, $50 and $100 – $2 bills are rare but perfectly legal. There are also two different $1 coins that the government has tried unsuccessfully to bring into mass circulation. You may receive the Susan B Anthony silver dollar occasionally as change from a machine; be aware that it looks similar to a quarter.

Exchange Rates
The Travel section in the Sunday edition of the main New Orleans newspaper, the *Times-Picayune*, publishes current exchange rates as provided by American Express. At press time exchange rates were as follows:

country	unit		dollars
Australia	A$1	=	US$0.66
Canada	C$1	=	US$0.68
euro	€1	=	US$1.04
France	FF10	=	US$1.60
Germany	DM1	=	US$0.53
Hong Kong	HK$10	=	US$1.28
Japan	¥100	=	US$0.84
New Zealand	NZ$1	=	US$0.53
UK	UK£1	=	US$1.57

Exchanging Money
Most major currencies and leading brands of traveler's checks are easily exchanged in New Orleans. You will also find various independent exchange bureaus. When you first arrive at the airport terminal, you can change money at Travelex (☎ 465-9647), open daily from 6 am to 7 pm, or at Whitney National Bank (☎ 838-6492), which will not charge the $5 service fee if you show a copy of the *New Orleans Street Map*, available free from all information booths. Since the exchanges are only feet apart, get quotes from both.

Better exchange rates are generally available at banks in the CBD, typically open 10 am to 5 pm Monday to Thursday, 10 am to 6 pm Friday and 10 am to 1 pm Saturday. American Express (☎ 586-8201, 201 St Charles Ave) buys and sells foreign currency, as do the main offices of banks such as First NBC (☎ 623-1371, 210 Baronne St) and Hibernia (☎ 533-5712, 313 Carondelet St). Remember to show your street map for a fee waiver at Whitney National Bank's main office (☎ 586-7272, 228 St Charles Ave) or the Vieux Carré branch (☎ 586-7502, 430 Chartres St).

The AAA office in the suburb of Metairie (☎ 838-7500, 3445 N Causeway Blvd) will also exchange foreign currency.

Cash US law permits you to bring in, or take out, as much as US$10,000 in American or foreign currency (including traveler's checks) without formality. Larger amounts must be declared to customs.

Traveler's Checks Traveler's checks are virtually as good as cash in the USA; you do not have to go to a bank to cash a traveler's check, as most establishments accept the checks just like cash. The major advantage of traveler's checks over cash is that they can be replaced if lost or stolen. Both American Express and Thomas Cook, two well-known issuers of traveler's checks, have efficient replacement policies. Keeping a record of the check numbers is vital when it comes to replacing lost checks. Put this record in a safe place, separate from the checks themselves.

You'll save yourself trouble and expense if you buy traveler's checks in US dollars. Exchanging traveler's checks denominated in a foreign currency is much easier than it used to be but is rarely convenient or economical. Purchase traveler's checks in large denominations like US$100. Having to change US$10 or US$20 checks is inconvenient, especially as you may be charged service fees when cashing the checks at banks.

ATMs With a Visa or MasterCard and a PIN (personal identification number), you can easily obtain cash from bank ATMs all over greater New Orleans. The advantage of using ATMs is that you do not need to buy traveler's checks in advance, you do not have to pay the usual 1% commission on the checks, and if you're from a foreign country, you receive a better exchange rate. The disadvantage is that you are charged interest on the withdrawal until you pay it back. In most cases you are also charged a fee for each withdrawal.

With the increasing interstate and international linking of bank cards, you can often withdraw money straight from your bank account at home. However, there is typically a terminal fee of $2 or more, and in some cases your bank back home will charge you an additional fee. Most ATMs in the area accept bank cards from the Plus and Cirrus systems, the two largest ATM networks in the USA.

First NBC Bank contributed to producing the free *New Orleans Street Map*, and naturally the map indicates the locations of First NBC banks and ATMs.

Credit & Debit Cards Major credit cards are widely accepted by car-rental agencies and most hotels, restaurants, gas stations, shops and larger grocery stores. Many recreational and tourist activities can also be paid for by credit card. The most commonly accepted cards are Visa, MasterCard and American Express. However, Discover and Diners Club cards are also accepted by a fair number of businesses.

In fact, you'll find it hard to perform certain transactions without a credit card. Ticket buying services, for example, won't reserve tickets over the phone unless you offer a credit card number, and it's virtually impossible to rent a car without a credit card. Even if you loathe credit cards and prefer to rely on traveler's checks and ATMs, it's a good idea to carry one for emergencies. (Visa and MasterCard are your best bets.)

American Express card holders can obtain cash advances from the main American Express Travel Services office (☎ 586-8201, 201 St Charles Ave).

If your bank debit card is affiliated with a major credit card company, businesses will accept it as they do a credit card. Unlike a credit card, a debit card deducts payment directly from your checking account. At some establishments (like supermarkets, drugstores and gas stations), you can receive additional cash back when you use your debit card.

Costs

How much money you need for visiting New Orleans depends on your traveling style and the season when you visit. During the sweltering summer months, the same room that might cost $300 during Mardi Gras may go begging for under $50. Even restaurant menu prices fluctuate between the peak and off seasons – but not nearly so much as lodging prices. New Orleans' famed top-end

The Dixie

The word 'Dixie,' synonymous with the South, traveled a peculiar road. Prior to the Civil War, the Citizen's Bank of New Orleans printed $10 banknotes. On the back of these bills appeared the French word *dix* (10). Southerners handling these bills came to refer to them as 'dixies.' A minstrel song, 'Dixie's Land,' by Daniel D Emmett, popularized the use of the word, and during the Civil War the Confederate States became affectionately known as Dixie. The phrase 'whistling Dixie' refers to the custom of Confederate soldiers to whistle the optimistic tune. No doubt the meaning of the expression – to entertain fantasies – was contrived by victorious Northerners.

restaurants will always test your credit card limit. Alternatively, you can stay cheap outside the French Quarter, live on po' boys and soul food and hit all the happy-hour drink specials.

Getting to New Orleans may take the biggest bite out of your budget. Car rental typically starts at around $40 a day. Parking a car in the French Quarter can be an expensive headache, particularly during busy tourist periods. If you're sticking close to the Quarter and along the St Charles Ave axis, you can save yourself that expense by riding the streetcar ($1 a ride) and walking. New Orleans has decent bus service. For excursions, organized tours may be available at less cost and hassle than renting a car. Nevertheless, if you plan much traveling in southern Louisiana, a car may be essential.

Tipping

Tipping is a US institution that can be a little confusing for foreign visitors. Tipping is not really optional; the service has to be absolutely appalling before you should consider not tipping. In bars and restaurants, the waitstaff are paid minimal wages and rely upon tips for their livelihoods. Tip at least 15% of the bill or 20% if the service is great. You needn't tip at fast-food restaurants or self-serve cafeterias.

Taxi drivers expect a 10% tip. If you stay at a top-end hotel, tipping is so common you might get tennis elbow reaching for your wallet. Hotel porters who carry bags a long way expect $3 to $5, or $1 per bag; smaller services (holding the taxi door open for you) might justify only $1. Valet parking is worth about $2, to be given when your car is returned to you.

Bargaining

Almost everything at the Flea Market (Map 2) is negotiable. Sometimes, you will automatically get a discount of about 10% if you're buying a quantity of books or recordings. When you shop also has a lot to do with the amount of bargaining that a seller will allow. If the shop or service is open during the off-peak season and keeps regular hours, it is a sign of desperation. Most tour guides

and shopkeepers prefer to spend the hot-wet-and-sticky months at a seaside cottage.

Taxes & Refunds

New Orleans' 9% sales tax is tacked onto virtually everything, including meals, groceries and car rentals. For accommodations, room and occupancy taxes, add 11% to your bill plus $1 per person.

International visitors to Louisiana can receive refunds on sales taxes (up to 10%) from more than 1000 Louisiana Tax Free Shopping (LTFS) stores. Look for the 'Tax Free' sign in store windows. Foreign visitors must show participating LTFS merchants a valid passport (Canadians may substitute a birth certificate or driver's license) to receive a tax refund voucher. To get your refund at the LTFS refund center at the New Orleans International Airport, you must present the following: voucher(s) with associated sales receipt(s), passport and roundtrip international ticket for less than 90 days' stay. Refunds under $500 are made in cash; otherwise, a check is mailed to the visitor's home address.

A complete listing of LTFS merchants is included in the *New Orleans Visitor Guide*, available free from the New Orleans Tourist and Convention Bureau (☎ 566-5005). The guide includes instructions printed in French, German, Italian, Japanese, Portuguese and Spanish. Also included is a useful description of each store, including its address, hours and telephone number, which credit cards the store accepts and which languages the store's staff speaks.

POST & COMMUNICATIONS

The main New Orleans post office (Map 4; ☎ 589-1135, 701 Loyola Ave) is near City Hall. There are smaller branches throughout the city, including the Airport Mail Center (☎ 589-1296, in the passenger terminal); the World Trade Center (Map 4; ☎ 524-0033, 2 Canal St); the Vieux Carré (Map 2; ☎ 524-0072, 1022 Iberville St); and in the CBD at Lafayette Square (Map 4; ☎ 524-0491, 610 S Maestri Place). Post offices are generally open weekdays 8:30 am to 4:30 pm and Saturday 8:30 am to noon.

In the French Quarter, there are independent postal shops, including Royal Mail Service (Map 2; ☎ 522-8523, 828 Royal St) and the French Quarter Postal Emporium (Map 2; ☎ 525-6651, 940 Royal St). These shops will send letters and packages at the same rates as the post office.

Postal Rates

Postal rates frequently increase, but at the time of writing, the rates were 33¢ for 1st-class mail within the USA for letters up to 1oz (22¢ for each additional ounce) and 20¢ for postcards.

International airmail rates are 60¢ for a half-ounce letter, $1 for a 1oz letter and 55¢ for a postcard to any foreign country with the exception of Canada (48¢ for a half-ounce letter and 45¢ for a postcard) and Mexico (40¢ for a half-ounce letter and 40¢ for a postcard). Aerogrammes are 60¢.

The US Postal Service (☎ 800-222-1811, www.usps.gov) also offers Priority Mail service, which delivers your letter or package anywhere in the USA in two days or less. The cost is $3.20 for 2lb or less and $6.50 for 5lb. For heavier items, rates differ according to the distance mailed.

If you need to send it in a hurry, overnight Express Mail starts at $11.75. The Postal Service will even pick up your Express or Priority Mail packages for $8.25 per pickup.

Sending Mail

If you have the correct postage, you can drop your mail into any blue mailbox. However, to send a package that weighs 1lb or more, you must bring it to a post office. You can buy stamps and weigh your packages at all post office branches.

Receiving Mail

If you don't want to receive mail at your hotel, you can have mail sent to you at the main post office, marked c/o General Delivery, New Orleans, LA 70112. General Delivery is the US terminology for what is known as *poste restante* internationally. General Delivery mail is only held for 30 days, and it's not advisable to try to have mail sent to other post offices in New Orleans.

Telephone

New Orleans telephones are run by Bell-South. The Yellow Pages directory offers comprehensive business listings, organized alphabetically by subject. The New Orleans area code is ☎ 504 – it includes Thibodaux and the rest of southeastern Louisiana. Baton Rouge and its surrounding area, including St Francisville, use area code ☎ 225. Area code ☎ 318 applies to the western part of the state.

When dialing another area code, you must dial ☎ 1 before the area code. For example, to call a Baton Rouge number from New Orleans, begin by dialing ☎ 1-225. At pay phones, local calls start at 35¢, but long-distance charges apply to 'non-local' calls even within the same area code – to Thibodaux, for example – and costs rapidly increase once you dial another area code. Hotel telephones often have heavy surcharges.

Toll-free numbers start with 1-800 or 1-888 and allow you to call free within the USA; they're commonly offered by car-rental operators, hotels and the like. Dial ☎ 411 for local directory assistance; dial ☎ 1 + area code + 555-1212 for long-distance directory information; dial ☎ 1-800-555-1212 for toll-free number information. Dial ☎ 0 for the operator.

International Calls If you're calling from abroad, the international country code for the USA (and Canada) is ☎ 1.

To dial an international call direct from New Orleans, dial ☎ 011 + country code + area code (dropping the leading 0) + number. For calls to Canada, there's no need to dial the international access code, ☎ 011. For international operator assistance, dial ☎ 00.

As a general rule, it's cheaper to make international calls at night, but this varies with the country that you are calling. The exact cost for making an overseas call from a pay phone depends on the long-distance company and the country in question. For calls to Australia and Europe, typically the cost should be about $1.50 for the first minute and $1 for each subsequent minute. Calls to other continents usually cost about twice as much.

To avoid having to keep feeding coins into a pay phone while on a long-distance call, you should use a credit card, subscribe to a long-distance carrier or purchase a phone debit card. Long-distance debit cards allow purchasers to pay in advance and then access their account through a toll-free 800 number.

Phone Cards There's a wide range of local and international phonecards. Lonely Planet's eKno Communication Card (see the insert at the back of this book) is aimed specifically at travelers and provides cheap international calls, a range of messaging services and free email. For local calls, you're usually better off with a local card.

You can join by phone from New Orleans by dialing ☎ 800-707-0031, or join online at www.ekno.lonelyplanet.com. Once you have signed up, dial ☎ 800-706 1333 to use eKno from the US.

Fax

Fax machines are easy to find in the USA – at shipping outlets like Mail Boxes, Etc, photocopy services and hotel business service centers – but be prepared to pay high prices (over $1 a page).

Aside from hotel fax machines, fax services in the French Quarter include Mule-Durel Office Supplies (☎ 529-7484, fax 529-7345, 241 Dauphine St), at Bienville St; French Quarter Postal Emporium (Map 2; ☎ 525-6651, fax 525-6652, 940 Royal St), at St Philip St; and On Dumaine Printing (☎/fax 528-9122, 515 Dumaine St).

Kinko's Copy Centers are open 24 hours in the CBD (Map 4; ☎ 581-2541, fax 525-6272, 762 St Charles Ave) and in the Riverbend area (Map 7; ☎ 861-8016, fax 866-0502, 1140 S Carrollton Ave).

Email & Internet Access

New Orleans continues to lag behind other cities in terms of online availability, but a few services for traveling techies are available. Your best bet is to have a widespread Internet Service Provider like AOL and use a local New Orleans dial-up number. Carry your own laptop to log on or send email. When making hotel reservations, be sure to ask if your room is equipped with a modem line.

Terminals in the New Orleans Public Library (Map 4; ☎ 529-7323, 219 Loyola Ave, www.gnofn.org/~nopl) offer Web browsing and access to chat groups, though they're not equipped for sending or receiving email. For $10 an hour, you can browse the Web and access chat groups at Hula Mae's Laundry (Map 2; ☎ 522-1336, 840 N Rampart St). Kaldi's Coffeehouse (Map 2; ☎ 586-8989, 941 Decatur St) qualifies as a cybercafé, since it has added a smattering of terminals on its mezzanine.

INTERNET RESOURCES

The World Wide Web is a rich resource for travelers. You can research your trip, hunt down bargain airfares, book hotels, check on weather conditions or chat with locals and other travelers about the best places to visit (or avoid!).

There's no better place to start your Web explorations than the Lonely Planet website (www.lonelyplanet.com). Here you'll find succinct summaries on traveling to most places on earth, postcards from other travelers and the Thorn Tree bulletin board, where you can ask questions before you go or dispense advice when you get back. You can also find travel news and updates to many of our most popular guidebooks, and the sub-WWWay section links you to the most useful travel resources elsewhere on the Web.

Useful websites, many of which serve as gateways to an infinite number of interesting links, include the following:

General

New Orleans Online
  neworleansonline.com
Times-Picayune
  www.nolalive.com

Entertainment

Offbeat Magazine
  www.offbeat.com
WWOZ Radio (great links)
  www.wwoz.or
Nitebeat: The Guide to Nightlife
  nitebeat.com

Cemeteries

Save Our Cemeteries
  home.gnofn.org/~soc

Music

Jazz Festival
  www.insideneworleans.com/entertainment/
  nojazzfest
Louisiana Music Factory
  www.louisianamusicfactory.com
Dr John (official site)
  www.drjohn.com
Neville Brothers (official site)
  www.nevilles.com

Mardi Gras

Mardi Gras Link Extravaganza
  www.neworleansonline.com/mg-links
Mardi Gras Indians
  www.mardigrasindians.com

BOOKS

If you're interested in finding out more about the city, the many local bookstores discussed in the Shopping chapter are excellent resources for information. In the CBD, De Ville Books (Map 4) offers friendly help and a good selection of maps and local guidebooks. In the French Quarter, Russell Desmond helps French and English speakers select new and used titles at his Arcadian Books & Art Prints (Map 2).

Most books are published in different editions by different publishers in different countries. As a result, a book might be a hardcover rarity in one country while it's readily available in paperback in another. Fortunately, local bookstores and libraries can search by title or author, so these are the best places to find out about the availability of the following recommendations.

Lonely Planet

If you're exploring Louisiana, Mississippi, Alabama and the music capitals of Memphis and Nashville, Tennessee, pick up a copy of Lonely Planet's *Deep South*. It's the perfect complement to this book. If you're traveling with children, it just so happens that LP publishes the book *Travel with Children*, by Maureen Wheeler. The book contains numerous stories by parents who have overcome the challenge of toting the tots along on difficult trips.

Guidebooks

Specialized guidebooks can really enhance your visit. Foodies will appreciate the pithy, no-nonsense review of more than 430 restaurants in Zagat's *New Orleans Restaurants*. New Orleans' rich diversity is naturally intriguing, but as with gumbo, it's difficult to identify the ingredients. For a real sense of place, read *Ethnic New Orleans* (1995), which uses maps and text to describe how the ethnic neighborhoods evolved. You can devise your own historical architecture tours using Leonard V Huber's *Landmarks of New Orleans* (Louisiana Landmarks Society, 1991). Special note should be taken of the architectural walking tours assembled more than 50 years ago by Stanley Clisby Arthur; numerous reprints of his *Old New Orleans* (1995) have received the careful attention of researchers at the Historic New Orleans Collection. You might have to ride to a few second-hand bookstores to find a copy of Louis Alvarez's excellent *The New Orleans Bicycle Book* (Little Nemo Press, 1984).

If you're planning on going afield, the Sierra Club's rough-hewn *Trail Guide to the Delta Country* (1992), edited by John P Sevenair, stands alone in offering hiking, bicycling and canoe outings geared to the outdoor crowd. The guide can be difficult to find, so you might need to phone or write the Sierra Club (☎ 482-9566, 5534 Canal Blvd, New Orleans, LA 70124). No visitor should venture into either the plains or wetland Cajun areas west of New Orleans without a copy of Macon Fry and Julie Posner's *Cajun Country Guide* (1993).

For out-of-town excursions, also pick up the free *Louisiana Tour Guide* – it's hard to beat for short uncritical descriptions of attractions, accommodations and restaurants throughout Louisiana. It's available from the Louisiana Office of Tourism (☎ 800-633-6970). Members of the American Automobile Association (AAA) can pick up the *Alabama, Louisiana, Mississippi Tourbook* for a list of mid- to top-end restaurants and lodgings.

Royal Street architecture, French Quarter

History

Pre-Columbian settlement is briefly treated in Robert W Neuman and Nancy W Hawkins' *Louisiana Prehistory* (1982). In *The Historic Indian Tribes of Louisiana* (1987), Fred B Kniffen and his fellow authors provide an excellent introductory review of history from 1542 to the present.

Gwendolyn Midlo Hall documents the development of an Afro-Creole culture during the 18th century in *Africans in Colonial Louisiana* (1992). Mary Gehman's slender monograph, *The Free People of Color of New Orleans* (Margaret Media, 1994), offers a brief, nonacademic survey of Creole culture up to the present day. Her work is based on the unpublished work of Marcus Christian, who headed the 1930s New Orleans Black Writers Project of the WPA.

Congo Square in New Orleans (1995), by Jerah Johnson, is a great little history (just 55 pages) about the important gathering place for slaves and free men of color during the

18th and 19th centuries. Published by the Louisiana Landmarks Society, it's available in most good bookstores in New Orleans.

The evolution of New Orleans' unique Franco- and Afro-Creole culture is further explored in *Creole New Orleans* (1992), a collection of six essays edited by Arnold R Hirsch and Joseph Logsdon. They make the point that it was no accident that the major challenge to discrimination came from a New Orleans resident, Homer Plessy, the man who took his case to the US Supreme Court in 1896 (see the History section in the Facts about New Orleans chapter). For additional reading on the Civil Rights struggle in Louisiana, check out Adam Fairclough's *Race & Democracy* (1995). Stetson Kennedy's *Jim Crow Guide* (1959; reprint 1990) offers an eye-opening survey of the Jim Crow South.

Marshall Sprague re-creates the greatest land acquisition in US history – the Louisiana Purchase – in his book, *So Vast So Beautiful a Land* (1974).

General histories dealing with New Orleans are not up to the standards of the above specialized works. Charles L DuFour wrote an archetypal chronology, *Ten Flags in the Wind: The Story of Louisiana* (1967). Cartooist John Churchill Chase offers a witty lay history of New Orleans in *Frenchmen, Desire, Good Children & Other Streets of New Orleans* (1979).

Probably no other historical resource offers so much information on so many topics as the *Historical Atlas of Louisiana* (1995), by Charles Robert Goins and John Michael Caldwell. In addition to statewide maps that encompass Orleans Parish, it includes the routes of Native American migration and colonial exploration, along with eight pages of maps and text specific to New Orleans.

Geography, Environment & Natural History

Southern Louisiana served as one of John James Audubon's prime areas for collecting and painting wildlife in the 1820s. Audubon's stature as one of the foremost artist-naturalists of his time came with the publication of his monumental *Birds of America* (1827-38). Most of his written chronicles about New

Orleans are captured in the widely available second volume of *Audubon and His Journals*, edited by Maria R Audubon (1897; reprint 1986).

The Mississippi River has attracted the attention of many authors. *The Lower Mississippi* (1942), Hodding Carter's contribution to the Rivers of America series, remains a classic.

Wildlife lovers should also see *Louisiana Birds* (1955) and *The Mammals of Louisiana* (1974), both written by George H Lowery Jr and published by the Louisiana State University Press.

Mardi Gras

You can learn so much about the city of New Orleans by researching the topic of Mardi Gras – and you can start with any of a great number of books. Henri Schindler's *Mardi Gras New Orleans* (1997) is a fond remembrance of the days when the old-line krewes Comus, Momus and Proteus ruled the day. These are the krewes that stopped parading when antidiscrimination measures aimed to add color to their all-white membership, so in that respect outsiders might not sympathize with Schindler's sentiment. He is, however, one of the preeminent historians on the subject, and this is a thoroughly researched and beautifully illustrated book. (Expensive, too, at $50 a pop.)

The alternative, more critical view is expressed in James Gill's fiery *Lords of Misrule: Mardi Gras and the Politics of Race in New Orleans* (1997). This is also the much cheaper way to go.

Carol Flake captures the physical and cultural decay of the city in her chronicle of the Carnival season, *New Orleans: Behind the Masks of America's Most Exotic City* (1994). Unfortunately, Flake's return to New Orleans coincided with the vicious controversy over the integration of Mardi Gras krewes. She paints a bleak picture of social collapse rather than a rosy scene of healthy evolution.

Anything about the Mardi Gras Indians is bound to be a fascinating read, and Michael P Smith's *Mardi Gras Indians* (1994) reflects the author-photographer's remarkable access to a fairly closed society.

Music

In Search of Buddy Bolden (1978), by Donald Marquis, is essential reading if you're interested in the origins of jazz. *Remembering Song* (1982), by Frederick Turner, is another very good book portraying the lives of a selection of New Orleans' key jazz originals. This title may be hard to find, however, since it's out of print.

You could read half a dozen books about Louis Armstrong. His autobiography, *Satchmo* (1954), is a classic – a thoroughly engaging read and a fascinating depiction of old New Orleans. Later, academic historians actually refuted some of Armstrong's history – but the great jazzman can certainly be forgiven if he improvised a little.

Miscellaneous

Folk tales of Louisiana told by Louisianans were recorded in the late 1930s by the Federal Writers Program of the WPA and compiled by Lyle Saxon, Edward Dreyer and Robert Tallant in *Gumbo Ya Ya* (1945; reprint 1991). Within that volume, Robert McKinney's story 'Kings, Baby Dolls, Zulus & Queens' is almost worth the book price alone for its description of black Mardi Gras celebrations during an era of segregation. Other stories by Creole writers refer to the ostracism that resulted from any trace of 'café au lait' among white Creoles. The unique aspects of New Orleans cemeteries also get special attention.

New Orleans probably has more books about its cemeteries than any other city in the world. The best is Robert Florence's *New Orleans Cemeteries: Life in the Cities of the Dead* (1997). Florence is a self-proclaimed cemetery hound who has dug up some of the more fascinating stories about the USA's most fascinating resting places. The book is beautifully illustrated, with photographs by Mason Florence.

The ultimate political race from hell featured Edwin Edwards (the crook), David Duke (the Klan) and Governor Buddy Roemer (tainted incumbent) in 1991. John Maginnis follows the antics of the three unpopular candidates in *Cross to Bear* (Darkhorse Press, 1992).

If you must have access to all the facts, try lugging the enormous *Encyclopedia of Southern Culture* (1989) up a flight of stairs. Edited by Charles Reagan Wilson and William Ferris, it offers comprehensive coverage of everything from agriculture (page 1) to women's life (page 1515).

NEWSPAPERS & MAGAZINES

Locals sometimes complain about New Orleans' only daily newspaper, the *Times-Picayune*. Nevertheless, with approximately a quarter of a million readers, it has the largest circulation of any newspaper in Louisiana. For 50¢ daily or $1.50 Sunday – a few 'bits' more than when a *picayune* represented a fair exchange – it offers visitors a daily entertainment calendar and a glimpse of local society in the Living section. Don't miss the Friday *Lagniappe* entertainment guide. The *Times-Picayune* is perhaps the only US newspaper that includes occasional editorials on French issues. Although the paper traditionally supports the Democratic party, in the 1995 governor's race between African American Congressman Cleo Fields and GOP front-runner Mike Foster, the *Times-Picayune* did not endorse either candidate. Don't be surprised to see plenty of front-page murder stories in New Orleans, which has a higher-than-average crime rate.

The *Louisiana Weekly*, published in New Orleans since 1925, offers an African American perspective on local and regional politics and events. Billing itself as 'the people's paper,' the *New Orleans Data News Weekly* focuses on local news. The monthly newspaper *La Prensa* features bilingual articles for Hispanic readers.

For alternative news and entertainment listings, pick up a copy of the free weekly newspaper *Gambit*. Its sporadic distribution makes it somewhat difficult to find; it's surprisingly scarce in coffee shops. The monthly *Offbeat* magazine provides a complete music and entertainment calendar with good reviews of local performances. It's available free at record stores and coffee shops.

At least three magazines focus on New Orleans. The monthly *New Orleans Magazine* is a glossy, tourist-oriented advertisement that offers better-quality writing about the city than you might expect from most city magazines. A bit more risqué and youth-oriented is the monthly *Tribe*, which deals with 'style, culture and ideas.' *Where New Orleans* is a monthly that offers maps of attractions; it's strictly for visitors.

A few magazines about the South deserve mention. Foremost is *Southern Exposure*, a bimonthly journal that carries on the muck-raking tradition of Stetson Kennedy's 1946 book by the same name. Many of its articles on social issues, politics, the economy and regional culture are cited by other researchers. *Reckon*, a glossy quarterly magazine about Southern culture, always includes a 'Down South' listing of new books and notable events. The bimonthly *Oxford American*, published in William Faulkner's hometown of Oxford, Mississippi, preserves the literary tradition of the South.

See Gay & Lesbian Travelers, later in this chapter, for more information on alternative media.

RADIO

Community radio station WWOZ-FM 90.7 offers the most jazz, with a mix of blues, R&B and Cajun and an odd assortment of ethnic music. Its mission is to promote the music of Southern Louisiana, and the more you listen to the station, the more you realize just what an incredibly musical place this is. You're really keeping an ear to the ground when you tune in – the deejays keep you posted on all the comings and goings of the city's homegrown talent.

Station WWNO-FM 89.9 broadcasts a predominantly classical format but plays jazz from 10:30 pm to 1 am. It's the city's only National Public Radio affiliate, offering morning and evening news programs. KLGZ-FM 106.7 plays what the station refers to as 'smooth jazz.'

News and lengthy literary programming is broadcast by WRVH-FM 88.3. Newscasters read the entire local paper – including Ann Landers – on air for 'the blind and print-handicapped' (a boring exercise, but useful for those who have blurred vision after a night on Bourbon St). A lewd counterpoint is the nightly 'passion show' or 'love phones' program on WEZB-FM 97.1; its sexual decadence befits the city.

A zydeco music show is hosted by Kateri Yager every Sunday from 4 to 6 pm on WSLA 1560 AM.

PHOTOGRAPHY & VIDEO

New Orleans is a city where details tell the story, so if you're photographing any significant others, make sure they're not entirely obscuring the ornate cast iron that inspired you to shoot the picture. ('Uh, honey, scoot on over jest a little.')

For professional photo processing and services near the downtown area, there's Primary Color (☎ 581-3444, 1116 Magnolia St), at Calliope. It's in a sketchy neighborhood near the Superdome and only worth going to if you can drive there. More convenient is Liberty Camera Center (Map 4; ☎ 523-6252, 337 Carondelet St). Downtown Fast Foto (☎ 525-2598, 327 St Charles Ave) offers quick color print and E-6 slide processing.

In the Riverbend area is the Camera Shop (Map 7; ☎ 861-0277, 7505 Maple St). Opposite Delgado Community College, Moldaner's Camera (Map 9; ☎ 486-5811, 622 City Park Ave) provides reliable photo finishing services.

For camera repairs and used gear, check out Alfredo's Cameras (☎ 523-2421, 916 Gravier St).

Overseas visitors who are thinking of purchasing videos should remember that the USA uses the National Television System Committee (NTSC) color TV standard, which is not compatible with other standards like Phas Alternative Line (PAL). Unless you find worthwhile PAL-format videos (available in some Canal St shops), it's best to avoid those seemingly cheap movie purchases until you get home.

TIME

New Orleans is on Central Standard Time, one hour behind the East Coast's Eastern Standard Time and six hours behind Greenwich Mean Time (GMT). In early April, all US clocks move ahead one hour for Daylight Saving Time (which roughly corresponds to British Summer Time); clocks move back one hour in October. When it's noon in New Orleans, the time elsewhere is as follows:

Chicago	noon
New York	1 pm
London	6 pm
Tokyo	6 am next day
Sydney	7 am next day
Auckland	9 am next day

ELECTRICITY

Electric current in the USA is 110-115V, 60Hz AC. Outlets may be suited for flat two-prong or three-prong grounded plugs. If your appliance is made for another electrical system, you will need a transformer or adapter; if you didn't bring one along, buy one at Radio Shack (several locations) or another consumer electronics store.

WEIGHTS & MEASURES

Like most Americans, New Orleans residents resist the metric system. Draft beer is commonly offered by the pint. Dry weights are in ounces (oz), pounds (lb) and tons, but liquid measures differ from dry measures. One pint equals 16 fluid oz; 2 pints equal 1 quart, a common measure for liquids like milk, which is also sold in half gallons (2 quarts) and gallons (4 quarts). Gasoline is measured in the US gallon, which is about 20% smaller than the imperial gallon and equivalent to 3.79 liters. Distances are in feet, yards and miles. Three feet equal 1 yard (.914 meters); 1760 yards, or 5280 feet, equal 1 mile. Temperatures are in degrees Fahrenheit, whereby 32°F is freezing. There is a conversion chart on the inside back cover of this book.

LAUNDRY

Drinkers and pool players will appreciate the many New Orleans bars that offer self-service laundry facilities. Most of these are operated by the Igor's chain – with locations Uptown along St Charles and Magazine St and downtown on Esplanade. See the Entertainment chapter for more information. Hula Mae's Laundry (Map 2; ☎ 522-1336,

840 N Rampart St) offers pick-up and delivery services. Additional laundries appear on the maps in this book.

TOILETS

A recording by Benny Grunch, 'Ain't No Place to Pee on Mardi Gras Day,' summarizes the situation in the French Quarter. While tour guides delight in describing the unsanitary waste disposal practices of a bygone era, the stench arising from back alleys is actually far more recent in origin.

You'd think New Orleans would commemorate 300 years of French influence (as the city did in 1999) by adopting the French *pissolr* – or in any case do *something* for the hordes of visitors guzzling 29oz Hurricanes in French Quarter streets. But the only public toilets open in the evening are in the Jackson Brewery mall at 620 Decatur St (Map 2). Another public toilet is available in the French Market (Map 2).

RECYCLING

Return your cans, bottles and other recyclables at the local recycling buy-back center (☎ 826-1791, 2829 Elysian Fields Ave), lakeside from I-10. A few supermarkets offer drop-off bins for aluminum, glass and newspaper.

HEALTH

New Orleans is a typical First World destination when it comes to health. For most foreign visitors no immunizations are required for entry, though cholera and yellow fever vaccinations may be required of travelers from areas with a history of those diseases. There are no unexpected health dangers, excellent medical attention is readily available, and the only real health concern is that a collision with the medical system can cause severe injuries to your financial state.

Should you require emergency treatment while in Orleans Parish, you can request an ambulance by calling ☎ 911. Or have someone take you to the emergency room (ER) at a major hospital with a well-staffed trauma center. Charity Hospital (Map 4; ☎ 568-2311, 1532 Tulane Ave) offers free services to those who qualify and assesses fees on a sliding scale for others.

Nonprescription medications, as well as contraceptives, can be purchased in the pharmacy section of drugstores like Walgreens, with two 24-hour locations within a short drive of the French Quarter: 3311 Canal St at Jefferson Davis Pkwy (☎ 822-8073) and 1100 Elysian Fields Ave near St Claude St (☎ 943-9788). The Walgreens at 900 Canal St (☎ 568-9544) is not a 24-hour store. Many outlying Rite-Aid stores are open 24 hours; the closest to the French Quarter is at 3401 St Charles Ave at Louisiana Ave (☎ 896-4575).

WOMEN TRAVELERS

Intoxicated bands of young men in the French Quarter and along parade routes are a particular nuisance for women. Otherwise respectable students and businessmen are transformed by New Orleans – they expect to drink and carouse in a manner that is not acceptable in their home towns. Women in almost any attire are liable to receive lewd comments. More provocative outfits will lead to a continuous barrage of requests to 'show your tits.' This occurs on any Friday or Saturday night, not just during Mardi Gras. Many men assume that any woman wearing impressive strands of beads has acquired them by displaying herself on the street.

Conducting yourself in a common-sense manner will help you to avoid most problems. For example, you're more vulnerable if you've been drinking or using drugs than if you're sober; you're more vulnerable alone than if you're with company; and you're more vulnerable in a high-crime urban area than in a 'better' district. Of course, any serious problems you encounter (including assault or rape) should be reported to the police (☎ 911). The YWCA offers a Rape Crisis Hotline (☎ 483-8888) and a Battered Women's Hotline (☎ 486-0377).

The Women's Center (☎ 464-8700, 200 Esplanade Ave) offers counseling and obstetrics and gynecology services. The New Orleans branch of Planned Parenthood (☎ 897-9200, 4018 Magazine St) provides health care services for women, including pregnancy testing and birth-control counseling.

GAY & LESBIAN TRAVELERS

The gay community in New Orleans revolves around the lower French Quarter, below St Ann St, and the adjacent Faubourg Marigny. While many businesses in the area are gay-owned and -oriented, and most residents are gay, many of the clubs cater to a mixed crowd.

The Lesbian & Gay Community Center (☎ 522-1103, 2114 Decatur St) is a great resource where you can pick up all of the numerous free rags available in New Orleans. The people working there often have time to tell you what they personally think of just about any bar, club, restaurant or cabaret performer in the city.

The Faubourg Marigny Book Store (Map 3; ☎ 943-9875, 600 Frenchman St) is the South's oldest gay bookstore and is a good place to learn about the local scene. While you're there, pick up a copy of *The Weekly Guide*, a free pamphlet that's chock-full of information about gay and lesbian businesses, entertainment venues, hotels and guesthouses. It features a bar guide pull-out section.

For nightlife ideas, gay and lesbian readers should also check out the free biweekly tabloids *Impact* and *Ambush Magazine*. Both are published in New Orleans on alternating Fridays and offer adult entertainment suggestions throughout the Gulf South, although *Ambush* tends to do a better job of covering the gay scene beyond New Orleans.

The NO/AIDS task force hotline is at ☎ 945-4000.

DISABLED TRAVELERS

Thanks to the federal Americans with Disabilities Act, more and more lodgings and transit agencies are meeting the needs of disabled people. Even older hotels are obligated to provide wheelchair access, although accessible bathroom accommodations are primarily found only at newer properties. Wheelchair ramps and/or elevators are available at the ferry crossings. A few of the RTA buses offer lift service. For information about paratransit service (alternate transportation for those who can't ride regular buses), call the RTA (☎ 827-7433). The Riverfront Street-car Line features Braille kiosks, platform ramps and wide doors that allow anyone to board easily. Unfortunately, the St Charles Ave Streetcar Line has not been modified for wheelchair passengers.

The French Quarter is especially difficult for disabled travelers. Beware that rough masonry sidewalks hinder wheelchair travel and can be equally challenging for near-sighted individuals. Few of the picturesque galleries projecting over the Quarter's streets are accessible to wheelchairs.

Of course, most federal facilities and parks – including Lafitte National Historic Park – offer access for the disabled. Another popular destination is the platform trail over the swamp at the Louisiana Nature Center. See the Things to See & Do chapter for more information on attractions.

SENIOR TRAVELERS

Though the age at which senior benefits begin varies, travelers aged 50 years and older (though more commonly 65 and up) can expect to receive discount rates at such places as hotels, museums and restaurants. Some national advocacy groups that can help seniors in planning their travels are the American Association of Retired Persons (AARP; ☎ 202-434-2277, 601 E St NW, Washington, DC 20049), representing Americans 50 years or older; Elderhostel (☎ 617-426-8056, 75 Federal St, Boston, MA 02110-1941), for people 55 and older; and the National Council of Senior Citizens (☎ 202-347-8800, 1331 F St NW, Washington, DC 20004).

NEW ORLEANS FOR CHILDREN

With the exceptions of the Audubon Zoo and the Aquarium of the Americas, most activities for children are set apart from the city's major attractions for adults. For specially scheduled children's activities, check out the brief 'kid stuff' listing that appears in the *Times-Picayune's* Living section each Monday. See the Things to See & Do chapter for more detailed listings on the following places.

In eastern New Orleans, the Louisiana Nature Center Museum (☎ 246-5672, 5601 Read Blvd), in Joe W Brown Memorial Park, enthralls kids with exhibits of reptiles, amphibians and birds.

The Louisiana Children's Museum (Map 4; ☎ 523-1357, 420 Julia St), in the Warehouse District, caters to kids from ages one to 12.

The Old US Mint (Map 2; ☎ 568-6968, 400 Esplanade Ave) offers occasional free mask-making workshops on Saturdays before Mardi Gras for children aged six to 13.

Look for the classic stories that you loved as a child at Old Children's Books (☎ 525-3655, 734 Royal St). The Maple Street Book Shop – renowned for its 'Eracism' bumper stickers – operates the adjacent Children's Book Shop (Map 7; ☎ 861-2105, 7529 Maple St). Cozy readings take place here.

Accent on Children's Arrangements (☎ 524-1227, 938 Lafayette St) is a service that takes the kids off your hands and engages them in organized activities. Some of the bigger, more expensive hotels also provide child care services.

For general information (and encouragement), see Lonely Planet's *Travel with Children*, by Maureen Wheeler (1995).

USEFUL ORGANIZATIONS

With more than 5500 Louisiana members, the nonprofit Nature Conservancy (☎ 338-1040, PO Box 4125, Baton Rouge, LA 70821) is an influential force in preserving plants, animals and natural communities by protecting the lands and waters they need to survive. Call or write to find out about scheduled hikes, canoe trips and other field trips.

The Sierra Club advocates for environmental protection throughout the USA. The New Orleans Group of the Delta Chapter (☎ 482-9566, 5534 Canal Blvd, New Orleans, LA 70124) is active in promoting low-impact visits to natural sites in southern Louisiana.

The headquarters for the local American Automobile Association (AAA; ☎ 838-7500, 3445 N Causeway Blvd, Metairie) provides members with maps, accommodations suggestions and travel planning services. AAA also offers emergency road and towing services for members (☎ 800-222-4357).

Hostelling International (HI), the new name of the International Youth Hostel Federation and American Youth Hostels,

Mmm...yellowtail; viewing the non-menu items at the Aquarium of the Americas

CHRISTIAN HEEB

has its local office at the Marquette House Hostel (Map 5; ☎ 523-3014, 2253 Carondelet St). Membership costs $25 and entitles you to some of the lowest bed rates in the US for an entire year.

LIBRARIES

If you're interested in finding out more about the city, the Louisiana Room (☎ 596-2610), on the 3rd floor of the New Orleans Public Library main library (Map 4; ☎ 529-7323, www.gnofn.org/~nop, 1219 Loyola Ave), is an excellent resource for books, newspapers and maps. You can search the library catalog with an online connection to NOPLine (☎ 595-8930).

UNIVERSITIES

New Orleans' foremost private universities are Tulane and Loyola, nestled next to each other Uptown on St Charles Ave opposite Audubon Park. Both are architecturally impressive.

In response to the cholera and yellow fever epidemics, seven physicians founded Tulane University (Map 6; ☎ 865-5000, 6823 St Charles Ave) in 1834. It now boasts 12,000 students in 11 colleges and schools, including a law school and school of medicine. Among Tulane's most noted graduates are the Premier of France, Jacques Chirac, who wrote a thesis on the port of New Orleans, and former US Speaker of the House of Representatives Newt Gingrich, who opposed university censorship of the student newspaper in 1968. The Amistad Research Center, the world's largest African American archive, and the WR Hogan Jazz Archives are two of Tulane's attractions; both are discussed in the Things to See & Do chapter.

Operated by the Jesuits since 1917, Loyola University (Map 6; ☎ 865-2011, 6363 St Charles Ave) is best known for its College of Music, School of Business and Department of Communications.

The historically black, private campuses of Dillard and Xavier Universities are well known for excellence. Founded in 1869, Dillard University (☎ 283-8822, 2601 Gentilly Blvd) was an important meeting site for civil rights leaders. The oldest building on the

present campus is the 1934 library building, but the stately Avenue of the Oaks is Dillard's most attractive feature. Established in 1915, Xavier University (☎ 486-7411, 7325 Palmetto St) is the only historically black Roman Catholic university in the USA. Xavier boasts a fine College of Pharmacy.

The public Southern University at New Orleans (SUNO; ☎ 286-5000, 6400 Press Drive) is a relative newcomer, founded in 1959. Its Center for African and African American Studies and Fine Arts boasts a large collection of African art. SUNO is the first major college in the US to be headed by a black woman, Chancellor Dr Dolores Spikes.

The largest public campus in New Orleans is the University of New Orleans (UNO; ☎ 280-6000), on the Lakefront, where 16,000 students study on a site that formerly housed a coast guard station. The history department is gaining a reputation for its cutting-edge approach to Louisiana history. The Keifer Arena attracts thousands for large concert events.

CULTURAL CENTERS

Visitors from France are often surprised to discover that the French language is rarely spoken in New Orleans. The odd truth is that from 1916 until 1968, the Louisiana Board of Education actually forbade classroom instruction in the French language. Pride in Louisiana's French-speaking heritage re-emerged in 1968 when Representative James Domengeaux founded CODOFIL (le Counseil pour le Développement du Français en Louisiane). The University of New Orleans offers assistance through the Council for International Visitors (☎ 280-7266). Alliance Française (☎ 568-0770, 1519 Jackson Ave), near Prytania St, offers a French-language curriculum.

The Amistad Research Center (Map 7; ☎ 865-5535), on the Tulane campus, specializes in African American history. See Tulane University in the Things to See & Do chapter.

The National Park Service (NPS) operates the nearby Isleño Center in St Bernard Parish.

The diversity of New Orleans is evidenced by the many organizations that meet regularly. Local social organizations include the following:

American Italian Museum	☎ 891-1904
Asocación de Guatemala en Louisiana	☎ 733-5070
Club Social Nicaraguense	☎ 524-1329
Deutsches Haus	☎ 522-8014
Honduran Association of Louisiana	☎ 456-0900
Irish Cultural Society	☎ 861-3746
Japan Club	☎ 589-6893
Japan Society	☎ 283-4890
Jewish Community Center	☎ 897-0143

DANGERS & ANNOYANCES
Safety

Even savvy travelers should respect the serious crime problem that many areas of the city present. Tremendous income disparities often manifest themselves in abrupt shifts from pleasant neighborhoods to frightening enclaves of destitute people whose most valuable possession is a gun. In 1995 the city recorded one murder a day on average, but of course the vast majority of these were related to domestic and personal disputes among locals. While recent years have seen a perceptible drop in the murder rate, it will be a long time before New Orleans can be considered a city where you can safely walk anywhere, anytime.

For the tourist, getting mugged is a very real threat, even in areas you'd think are safe (like the Garden District). Naturally, solo pedestrians are targeted more often than people walking in groups, and daytime is a better time to be out on foot than night. If you must travel alone, avoid entering desolate areas like the cemeteries and Louis Armstrong Park. Avoid wandering into the Quarter's unfrequented residential areas late at night or straying across N Rampart St toward the lake at any time. For instance, plenty of group tours go to St Louis Cemetery No 1, and even if you don't care to join the tours, it might be a good idea to wait for them and thereby avoid walking alone on the grounds.

No area is absolutely safe. Large crowds typically make the French Quarter a secure around-the-clock realm for the visitor. However, if your hotel or vehicle is on the margins of the Quarter, you should take a taxi back at night.

The CBD has plenty of activity during weekdays, but it's relatively deserted at night and on weekends. On Canal St the throngs of visitors, local shoppers and transit patrons do not generally represent a threat. The seedy rescue missions in the Warehouse District should not deter a visit to the neighborhood's trendy galleries unless you don't like requests for spare change. The Sunday parking enforcement in the area is a more bothersome problem for many.

You can feel somewhat secure at Audubon Park, but stay out of the dimly lit park and the nearby campus areas at night. Ditto for City Park and the lakeshore. The clubs near S Carrollton Ave in the Riverbend are generally problem free. Not so for the Fair Grounds neighborhood, where you can enjoy Jazz Fest without problems, but you should not stray from the recommended activity centers after the crowds disperse. Esplanade

Ave represents a brave attempt at historic preservation and renewal that cuts through some dangerous areas.

Until you are familiar with the terrain, you should confine your Uptown pedestrian wanderings to the corridor between St Charles Ave and Magazine St that includes the Garden District. Even this area is not entirely safe. Unless you are surveying urban blight, don't get off the St Charles streetcar and go strolling in the lake-side direction from St Charles Ave below Louisiana Ave. With a few exceptions, the Irish Channel area river-side from Magazine St is not recommended for the visitor.

Aggressive Drivers

One might presume that a city that encourages people to walk about with drinks in hand would offer them a little protection from motorists. Wrong! Pedestrians do not have the right of way and motorists (unless they are from out of state) do not yield. The resulting injuries and fatalities are significant but do not get the sensational media attention given to other violent crimes. The fact that so many pedestrians in the French Quarter are intoxicated does not help matters.

Whether you are on foot or in a car, be wary before entering an intersection, as New Orleans drivers are notorious for running yellow lights and even red lights. Most local drivers pause and look both ways after their light turns green.

Rip-Offs

Numerous street hustlers employ the following scam when encountering visitors:

The bet: I bet I can tell you where you got them shoes (shake and bet $10).

The answer: You got them on your feet on Bourbon St in New Orleans.

The police warn visitors not to talk to street hustlers, or shake hands or bet, or let anyone shine their shoes. You should simply walk away.

Another fairly common rip-off meant to take advantage of tourists is short-changing. Be aware that just about anywhere, especially in bars, cashiers might have a tendency to 'assume' a tip. Keep tabs on prices and the amount of the bills you hand over, then count your change! If you're in a better establishment, alert the manager if you feel you've been cheated.

LEGAL MATTERS

Although it may seem that anything goes, even New Orleans has its limits. Anyone under the age of 18 on the streets after 11 pm is violating the city's curfew. During Mardi Gras in 1996, more than 2500 people found themselves behind bars. Women who flash their breasts may get the attention of the police (and many others) but are not typically arrested unless they expose themselves repeatedly. For the most part, the police are interested in crowd control; it's only when things begin to get out of hand that they intervene.

The police are less lenient about a few other matters: Dropping your pants, grabbing or groping another person and urinating in public can all land you in jail. Don't join those who come on vacation and leave on probation.

If you are arrested, you're allowed to remain silent. There is no legal reason to speak to a police officer if you don't wish, but never walk away from an officer until given permission. All persons who are arrested are legally allowed to make one phone call. If you don't have a lawyer or family member to help you, call your embassy. The police will give you the number upon request.

The headquarters for the New Orleans Police Department (☎ 911 for emergencies, 821-2222 for nonemergencies) is at 715 S Broad St.

Alcohol

The legal drinking age for the city is 21, despite efforts to push it back to 18. You can be arrested for carrying open glass or metal containers on the street – grab a plastic 'go cup' when leaving a bar.

Drinking and driving can get you in big trouble. Driving while intoxicated (DWI) is a serious crime; you are considered legally drunk when your blood alcohol level reaches .10 – about two drinks. In addition, motorists are prohibited from carrying open containers of alcohol in vehicles.

Gambling

The legal age for gambling is also 21, and businesses with gaming devices (usually video poker machines) out in the open are closed to minors. Even cafés with gaming devices are off-limits to minors, unless the games are contained within private rooms or booths.

BUSINESS HOURS

While New Orleans is a true 24-hour center of activity, businesses tend to be incredibly lax about operating hours. It's the Big Easy! Some businesses never remove signs stating, 'Come in! We're open.' The proprietors of small shops are notorious for getting up late, closing early, stepping out for extended periods, locking the doors to hide from creditors or ignoring a ringing phone.

In any case, stated business hours are usually 9 am to 5 pm. Note that some stores lock their doors during slow periods for safety reasons; look for a bell to ring for entry. Liquor stores are open until 9 pm, and there's always the corner drugstore, usually open until midnight (if not 24 hours), which sells everything from snacks to nail polish to cough medicine.

PUBLIC HOLIDAYS & SPECIAL EVENTS

Any excuse to celebrate – those are words that New Orleanians live by, and the locals are so good at celebrating, they hardly need national holidays. In fact, what's known as 'the holidays' throughout the rest of the USA – meaning the season from Thanksgiving through New Year's – seems more like a warm-up in New Orleans, for on the heels of 'the holidays' comes Mardi Gras, the king of all celebrations in New Orleans. The Christmas lights and house decorations go down, and the Mardi Gras fringe and masks go up. Mardi Gras season lasts about six to eight weeks.

The city's other great festival, Jazz Fest, is a concentrated dose of good music – but good music, in lesser concentrations, is a commodity that New Orleans enjoys year-round.

New Orleans also celebrates New Year's Eve, St Patrick's Day and Halloween with characteristically whole-hearted and flamboyant style.

Note that when national holidays fall on a weekend, they are often celebrated on the nearest Friday or Monday to make a three-day weekend.

January

New Year's Day
January 1 is a national holiday.

Sugar Bowl
This NCAA football game between two of the nation's top-ranked college teams takes place on or around New Year's Day. It originated in 1935 and fills the Superdome to capacity; call ☎ 525-8573 for information.

Twelfth Night
The Carnival season kicks in on January 6 – 12 nights after Christmas – as the Phunny Phorty Phellows dust off their costumes and assemble at the Willow St car barn prior to an evening ride on the St Charles Ave streetcars.

Battle of New Orleans Celebration
On the weekend closest to January 8, volunteers stage a re-creation of the decisive victory over the British in the War of 1812 at the original battleground in Chalmette National Historical Park (☎ 589-4430). A noontime commemoration on Sunday in Jackson Square features a military color guard in period dress.

Martin Luther King Jr Day
On the third Monday in January, a charming midday parade, replete with brass bands, makes its way from the Bywater to the Tremé District down St Claude Ave.

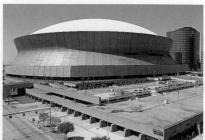

Louisiana Superdome: home of the Sugar Bowl

Mardi Gras Parades

Early Carnival parades in January or February tend to be the most outlandish. In 1996 the Krewe du Vieux celebrated its 'decade-ence' followed by its 10th annual ball. In the Warehouse District, the Krewe of Funky Butts, named after an early jazz hall, presents a jazz and art parade staged by the Contemporary Arts Center (☎ 528-3800).

February

Mardi Gras Parades

The greatest free show on earth really heats up during the three weeks before Mardi Gras, culminating with multiple parades each day. Routes vary, but the largest krewes stage massive parades with elaborate floats and marching bands that run along portions of St Charles Ave and Canal St. None enter the French Quarter.

Mardi Gras Day

In February or early March, the outrageous activity reaches a crescendo as the French Quarter nearly bursts with costumed celebrants. It all ends at midnight with the beginning of Lenten penitence.

Presidents' Day

The third Monday in February is a national holiday.

March

Black Heritage Festival

On the second weekend in March, the city celebrates African American contributions to food, music and the arts at the Audubon Zoo (☎ 861-2537).

St Patrick's Day

Just when you thought the city would calm down, the festivities pick up again on March 17. On the actual day, a major Irish pub crawl

New Orleans Jazz & Heritage Festival

'Jazz Fest,' as New Orleans' second-biggest festival is more commonly known, started as a celebration of the city's 250th anniversary in 1968, attracting jazz musicians Louis Armstrong, Dave Brubeck, Duke Ellington, Woody Herman, Ramsey Lewis and Pete Fountain. After struggling with poor attendance, 'Jazz Fest' moved to the Fair Grounds in 1972 and expanded to two weekends in late April and early May. The organizers also began to showcase a variety of musical forms besides jazz and experienced success.

Jazz Fest offers something for just about everyone's musical tastes. You can hear headliners, cult favorites and relative unknowns on more than 10 stages. At one stage you can listen to zydeco, while others might offer R&B, rock, gospel, bluegrass, reggae, Latin and, of course, jazz.

The 'heritage' part of the festival refers to Louisiana and local arts, crafts and food. This continues downtown at Armstrong Park's Congo Square, where African food and crafts are emphasized.

It's highly recommended to arrive at the Fair Grounds hungry – the plethora of eating options is staggering, and prices are reasonable. But you'll have to decide what you're hungry for: a plate of boiled crawfish (it's peak season!), shrimp étouffée, catfish or oyster po' boys, a heaping helping of jambalaya or red beans and rice, soft-shell crab (also in season), the tastiest crawfish pie, zesty gumbo, crawfish Monica, barbecued anything, crab-stuffed mushrooms, even cherry 'snowballs' and strawberry shortcake, plus cuisine from other cultures (gyros, Cuban sandwiches, fried plantains), and the list goes on and on, with over 60 vendors to choose from. This is an excellent place to get your culinary bearings. And for some reason everything at Jazz Fest tastes more delicious than it might elsewhere!

In addition, plan for heat and sun at the Fair Grounds – bring sunscreen and a brimmed hat and wear light-colored clothing. Keep yourself well hydrated – and though it may be the perfect thirst-quencher, not with beer! Only a few tents at Jazz Fest are ventilated (hardly

through the French Quarter follows a parade through the Irish Channel, starting at Race and Annunciation Sts (☎ 565-7080). The prior weekend (if the 17th falls on a weekday) also features a motley parade, beginning at Molly's at the Market (☎ 525-5169), where a boisterous group tosses cabbage to the lasses in exchange for kisses.

Tennessee Williams Literary Festival
The end of March features five days dedicated to the great American playwright, with plays (by Williams and others), lectures (on such subject as humor and the art of storytelling), literary and gay heritage walking tours, nostalgic panels starring Williams' surviving chums and – natch! – a cocktail party. The festival runs through the last weekend of the month, with events held at Le Petit Théâtre du Vieux Carré and elsewhere in the French Quarter. For information, call ☎ 486-7096.

Easter
Although that big bunny makes his rounds, Easter isn't nearly as much fun as Mardi Gras. The Christian holiday falls on the 1st Sunday after a full moon in March or April.

Isleños Arts & Crafts
The Canary Islanders who settled in St Bernard Parish celebrate their folklife (a culture based on natural resources) during the last week of March. They stage demonstrations and host a crawfish-eating contest at the Isleño Center (☎ 682-0862), 7 miles south of Chalmette and 1½ miles east of Poydras on Hwy 46.

April

Spring Fiesta
Since 1935, locals have donned antebellum outfits to host visitors in historic homes normally closed to the public. Tours are given over a five-day period in April or May beginning on the

New Orleans Jazz & Heritage Festival

air-conditioned, but at least shaded). Most stages are open-air, and you'll end up standing for long periods of time. It's a good idea to bring a blanket or ground cover for resting between concerts, and a rain poncho just in case.

You can check the schedules as early as January (they're not available earlier) and should make reservations as soon as possible to save money and assure that you get your favored weekend dates. Daily passes cost $10 in advance or $15 at the gate. The Fair Grounds are open daily from 11 am to 7 pm, and there are many nightly performances at other sites throughout New Orleans. For information, call or write the New Orleans Jazz & Heritage Festival (☎ 522-4786, 2200 Royal St, New Orleans, LA 70117, www.insideneworleans.com/entertainment/nojazzfest). Tickets are available through Ticketmaster (☎ 522-5555).

Getting There & Away
Ditch your car, as you cannot count on getting one of the few $10 parking spaces near the Fair Grounds. The RTA (☎ 569-2700) operates their regularly scheduled No 82 Esplanade bus from the French Quarter. Special shuttles are available from the New Orleans

Buckwheat Zydeco

Jazz & Heritage Festival at an additional cost. Air-conditioned shuttle buses run back and forth from major hotels on Canal St. Tickets include Jazz Fest entrance for around $17. If you can find a taxi, the special event price from the Quarter is $3 per person.

first Friday after Easter. Fees vary, but you can find out the details by contacting the Spring Festival Association (☎ 581-1367, 826 St Ann St, New Orleans, LA 70116).

Crescent City Classic

Runners from all over the globe compete in a 10K race from the Jackson Brewery to Audubon Park on the first Saturday of the month. Contact the *Times-Picayune* (☎ 861-8686) for details.

French Quarter Festival

Twelve stages throughout the French Quarter showcase New Orleans music, plus the local lifestyles, during the second weekend of April.

Jazz Fest

The Fair Grounds Race Track (and, at night, the whole town) reverberates with good sounds, plus food and crafts, through two weekends in the latter part of April and early May. See the boxed text 'New Orleans Jazz & Heritage Festival' for details.

May

Tomato Festival

In Chalmette, Our Lady of Prompt Succor Church (☎ 271-3441, 2320 Paris Rd), features a pre-Miss Louisiana beauty pageant along with musical performances on the first weekend of the month.

Memorial Day

The last Monday in May is a national holiday.

Greek Festival

On Memorial Day weekend, the Greek community offers food and the entertaining Hellenic Dancers. The festival is held on the grounds of the Greek Orthodox Cathedral of the Holy Trinity Church (☎ 282-0259, 1200 Robert E Lee Blvd), near Bayou St John.

June

French Market Tomato Festival

During the first weekend of the month, you'll find food and entertainment in the French Market (☎ 522-2621).

Grand Prix du New Orleans

If you thought crossing the street in New Orleans was dangerous before, check out what happens when it really becomes a racetrack on the second weekend of June.

Carnival Latino

On the last weekend in June, the Riverfront comes alive with the sounds and flavors of Latin America. For information, contact the New Orleans Hispanic Heritage Foundation (☎ 522-9927).

July

Independence Day

Since the Civil War, folks in these parts have regarded July 4, with evident disdain, as a 'Yank' holiday. Nevertheless, New Orleanians are not known to pass up a good time. Food stalls and entertainment stages are set up on the Riverfront and fireworks light up the night sky.

Essence Festival

On Independence Day weekend, *Essence Magazine* sponsors star-studded musical performances at the Superdome. Started in 1995, the event has featured Stevie Wonder and other renowned black recording artists. Call ☎ 941-5100 for details.

Wine & Food Experience

Find out what wine to drink with your catfish during a four-day foodie event in July (☎ 529-9463). Sometimes the event takes place in late June.

August

Blessing of the Shrimp Fleet

It's an Isleño tradition to parade decorated boats, then party. Festivities annually alternate between the fishing villages at Delacroix Island or Yscloskey in St Bernard Parish. Contact the Isleño Center (☎ 682-0862) for information.

September

Labor Day

The first Monday in September is a national holiday.

October

Swamp Festival

For four days in early October, the Audubon Institute (☎ 861-2537) releases swamp critters into the hands of visitors at both the Audubon Zoo and Woldenberg Riverfront Park. Both locations feature Cajun food, music and crafts.

Columbus Day

The second Monday in October is a national holiday.

Halloween

On October 31, Halloween is not taken lightly in New Orleans. Most of the fun is the giant costume party throughout the French Quarter. In addition, the New Orleans Metropolitan Convention and Visitors Bureau (☎ 566-5055) coordinates a parade, plus a monster bash and Anne Rice Vampire Lestat Extravaganza at the Convention Center.

'Celebration in the Oaks' sounds more organic than it looks.

November

All Saints Day
On November 1, many residents honor the dead by sprucing up the local cemeteries.

Mirliton Festival
The first weekend marks the celebration of the pear-shaped edible fruit at the Mickey Markey Playground in the historic Bywater neighborhood (☎ 948-7330).

Veterans Day
November 11 is a national holiday.

Celebration in the Oaks
If unnatural holiday decorations turn you on, you might check out the colorful constellations of light at City Park (☎ 482-4888). It's a uniquely New Orleanian take on the spirit of Christmas in America – a little bit Vegas, a little bit Disneyland, right in the middle of the oak trees (ah, of course!). As a clincher, you can view it in its entirety from your car only (turn off those headlamps); bicyclists are not allowed, and pedestrians will gain only limited access to the displays by sneaking past the checkpoints. The huge power cord (imagine Dad reaching for it beneath the Christmas tree) is plugged into the socket every night after dark, from the last week of November through the first week in January. Admission for motor vehicles is $7.

Thanksgiving
A national holiday observed on the fourth Thursday in November, this is the day that Americans stuff themselves with turkey dinners. (Picture Grandma chomping on that turkey leg.)

Bayou Classic
Southern University and Grambling University play their traditional end-of-the-season football game at the Superdome (☎ 523-5652) on the last weekend of November.

December

New Orleans Christmas
During the month of December, St Charles Ave is a festival of light, as many of New Orleans' poshest homes are lavishly decorated and illuminated for the holidays. This is also a great time to tour historic homes. The lobby of the Fairmont Hotel in the CBD is transformed into a gaudy but charming Christmas grotto, its walls and ceiling concealed by shredded cotton. And of course, the Celebration in the Oaks continues all through the month (see November, above). On Christmas Eve, St Louis Cathedral attracts a tremendous crowd for its midnight choral mass. Many restaurants offer *réveillon* dinners on Christmas Eve. Contact French Quarter Festivals (☎ 522-5730, 100 Conti St, New Orleans, LA 70130) for a complete schedule of events, open homes and réveillon menus.

Feux de Joie

Fires of joy light the way along the Mississippi River levees above Orleans Parish and below Baton Rouge on Christmas Eve. To reach the giant bonfires, you must either endure incredible traffic along the narrow River Rd or spend almost $100 to see the fires from a riverboat (☎ 524-0814). Another option is to take I-10 to La Place (27 miles) or even Burnside (50 miles) to see the spectacle.

New Year's Eve

Revelers – mostly drunk tourists – pack the French Quarter, especially around Jackson Brewery, where the Baby New Year is dropped from the roof at midnight. Adding to the frenzy are thousands of college football fans, in town for the annual Sugar Bowl, which takes place on New Year's Day (see January, above).

WORK

It perhaps goes without saying that New Orleans is not a magnet for migrating professionals. Tourism puts butter on most people's bread in this town, and passers-through who have a way with people can usually find work in related businesses. Many of the city's bars and restaurants hire seasonal labor, and some get downright desperate for reliable help during Carnival and Jazz Fest.

If you're really hard up for cash, or want to gain greater insight into the character of Ignatius Reilly (of John Kennedy Toole's novel *A Confederacy of Dunces*), you might enlist with the folks at Lucky Dog (☎ 523-9260, 517 Gravier St).

Mardi Gras

Carnival is New Orleans' leviathan holiday, a beautiful, undulating, snakelike festival that first rears its head on January 6 (the Feast of the Epiphany) and, weeks later, unfolds in all its startling, fire-breathing glory – to terrify and delight the millions who worship it.

Sounds pretty fanciful, doesn't it? You have to delve deep into the imagination to describe these sorts of things. In New Orleans, Mardi Gras operates on the subconscious. It's the flame that burns in the city's soul, the elaborate overture that tells us what the city is all about. It's a baroque fantasy, a vibrant flower, a circus, a nightmare, a temptation from the devil.

One telling little fact, offering a glimpse of how deeply ingrained Mardi Gras is in New Orleans' culture, is that in 1699 on Lundi Gras (Mardi Gras Eve), Pierre Le Moyne d'Iberville took possession of the Louisiana territory and named his first encampment Pointe de Mardi Gras. He was just a little ways downriver from the future site of New Orleans. It may be a stretch to say that New Orleans was founded on Mardi Gras – in fact, it was founded 19 years after d'Iberville claimed the territory – but locals can truthfully claim their Mardi Gras tradition dates back three centuries. Over that time, Mardi Gras has evolved into one of the greatest spectacles in the world.

Each year, on the day before Mardi Gras, the mayor of New Orleans steps down so that Rex, the King of Carnival, may rule the city for 24 hours. It may be a symbolic gesture – but it's quite a statement nevertheless.

Although many New Orleanians have lost their taste for Mardi Gras and prefer to observe the holiday on ski slopes in Colorado, those who remain in the city willingly endure the inconvenience wrought by a festival taking over the city. Entire sections of the city – the French Quarter and major thoroughfares like Canal St and St Charles Ave – are tied up in knots. Public transportation comes to a halt, schools are closed and the postal service stops delivering the mail.

RICK GERHARTER

Inset: Detail of an intricately hand-beaded apron worn by a Mardi Gras Indian (photograph by Porché West)

Left: French Quarter merriment

Mardi Gras permeates all levels of New Orleans society. Some of the city's wealthiest citizens, masked and costumed like visitors from the spirit world, tossing trinkets from their arabesque floats. Families of all classes and colors come out beforehand, in anticipation of the parades. All over the city imaginative people create theatrical costumes for seasonal masquerade parties. These events, when characterized by the peculiar local brand of perfectionism, become fantastic flights from time and place. Meanwhile, some of the city's most impoverished inhabitants are among its most passionate celebrants on Mardi Gras. For the Mardi Gras Indians, who hail from some of the poorest, most crime-ridden neighborhoods in the country, the day goes way beyond celebration. The day marks a re-affirmation of their unique cultural identity.

RICK GERHARTER

Above all, Mardi Gras is a hell of a party, and New Orleans, in its characteristic generosity, welcomes travelers from around the world to join in the revelry.

HISTORY

To understand and appreciate Mardi Gras, it is helpful to first become familiar with the history, for many of the traditions that shape the holiday today actually acquired their significance centuries ago. New Orleans is the rare American city where people take care to preserve the spirit of ancient rites like Carnival.

Pagan Rites

As the modern *krewes'* (a variation of 'crews') endless references to classic literature and mythology suggest, Mardi Gras is far older than New Orleans. It can be traced all the way back to the ancient Greeks, who held pre-spring festivals in which people sought purification through flogging. These rites were passed down to the Romans, whose Lupercalia (as they called it) was celebrated in an atmosphere of characteristic debauchery. During Lupercalia, all social order broke down. Citizens and slaves and men and women cavorted in masks and costumes – cross-dressing was common – and behaved, free of guilt, in a totally

Right: A French Quarter facade, all dressed up for Mardi Gras

lawless and licentious manner. Sadism, masochism and prostitution were the order of the day, followed by a period of recovery and introspection. An ox was sacrificed, and its blood was believed to wash away the sins of the people. Similar pagan rites were practiced by Druid priests in France, culminating in the sacrifice of a bull.

CHRISTIAN HEEB

Top: Who *are* those masked gals in the French Quarter?

The early Catholic Church failed to appreciate this tradition, but after trying unsuccessfully to suppress it, the church eventually co-opted the spring rite and fitted it, along with the Feast of the Epiphany, Ash Wednesday, Lent and Easter, into the Christian calendar. In Rome, it came to be called *carnevale* ('farewell to the flesh') referring to the fasting that began on Ash Wednesday. For many centuries the celebration, lasting several days, continued to be characterized by chaos and public lewdness, with a pervading sense of violence in the air – vendettas were frequently carried out on Shrove Tuesday (the day before Ash Wednesday).

But by the 17th century in Venice, a sophisticated theatrical sensibility had turned Carnival into a baroque masquerade in which citizens transformed themselves into characters of the *commedia dell'arte* and frolicked on the city's streets. The festival continued to thumb its nose at social conventions (cross-dressing remained popular), and its former paganistic decadence was hinted at menacingly (satyr costumes were also prevalent), but animal sacrifice and the utter flouting of accepted morals were beginning to fade. This theatrical form of Carnival became the custom in France, and from there it spread to French outposts in the New World.

Creole Carnival

In New Orleans, Carnival took some time to develop into the full-blown spectacle the city would eventually become famous for. Early generations of Creoles loved to dance, and they celebrated the season with balls and a full calendar of music and theater. The Creoles also had a penchant for masking, and on Mardi Gras the people of the city would emerge from their homes wearing grotesque, sometimes diabolical, disguises and masks.

From the beginning, the spirit of Carnival appears to have crossed race lines and permeated every level of society. Early on, Creoles of color held Carnival balls, to which slaves were sometimes invited. The popularity of masking among blacks was made evident by an ordinance, passed during Spanish rule, which prohibited blacks from masking. The fear was that blacks, effectively disguising their color, might easily invade elite white balls. Several times, masking was altogether outlawed by authorities who distrusted the way in which masks undermined the established social order. On Mardi Gras, the citizenry tended to blend into an unruly, desegregated mob, and inhibitions were left at home. The practice of masking continued privately at the city's growing number of masquerade balls, and laws forbidding masking didn't last.

Meanwhile, whites freely joined in the black balls. These mixed balls made one thing perfectly clear: White Creole men desired the company of black Creole women. Quadroons, women of mixed race having (at least in theory) one-quarter African blood and three-quarters Caucasian blood, were especially attractive to white Creoles. Soon, quadroon balls, to which quadroon women and white men were exclusively invited, were among the most fashionable entertainment in the Carnival season, and these events led to the development of an unusual local tradition, the *placage*. In a placage arrangement, a white man would keep a quadroon mistress, set her up in a small cottage and provide for any resulting children, who would become a relatively privileged class of people of color. Quadroon balls were an important part of the Carnival season for half a century.

Carnival remained primarily a Creole celebration for several decades after the Louisiana Purchase made New Orleans a US city, and Creoles continued to elaborate on the festivities. By the 1830s, exuberant parades replete with ornamented carriages, musicians and masked equestrians had become an important part of the Mardi Gras celebration. But the public splendor was short-lived, and by the middle of the 19th century, Creole Carnival revelers had begun withdrawing into their ballrooms. Many Creoles lamented that New Orleans had become too American, too practical-minded, to sustain such a fanciful holiday as Mardi Gras.

Carnival's 'Golden Age'

Ironically, Mardi Gras was saved not by Creoles, but by a secretive group of wealthy Americans who resided in the Garden District. Calling themselves the Mistick Krewe of Comus, these men made their first public appearance after dark, their floats illuminated by *flambeaux* (torches), on Mardi Gras in 1857. On that night, the tone was set for decades of Carnivals to come – indeed, for the Carnival we know today.

Carnival became much more organized than it had ever been before. New clubs modeled themselves on Comus, called themselves 'krewes' (which was supposed to be the Old English spelling of 'crew') and veiled their activities in secrecy. Rex first appeared in 1872, Momus a year later and Proteus in 1882. Pompous parades, presided over by a king, coursed through the streets at night, delighting audiences with elaborately decorated, torchlit floats fashioned from horse-drawn carriages. Mythological and sometimes satirical themes defined the parades, making these processions coherent theatrical works on wheels. The parades would end at a theater or the opera house, where exclusive tableau balls would close out the evening. (In tableau balls, which still take place, krewe members and their guests are entertained by a series of scenes staged to represent the theme chosen by the krewe for that Carnival season.)

Right: Playing with *flambeaux*

TOM DOWNS

Rex – as the name suggests – anointed himself 'King of Carnival,' a title he still holds (although in reality the more mysterious Comus is accorded an even higher status). His krewe also contributed several lasting traditions. He contributed the official colors of Carnival – purple, green and gold, which New Orleanians continue to work into their Mardi Gras attire – and the anthem of Carnival, a sentimental tune called 'If I Ever Cease to Love.' Additionally, the Rex parade featured a *boeuf gras* float, a tradition borrowed (in altered form) from the French Carnival, and floats that depict biting political satire, which would become a recurring motif shared by other krewes.

Also in the late 19th century, another krewe, the Twelfth Night Revelers, introduced several practices that would outlive the krewe's parading days. The first Carnival 'throws,' trinkets tossed from a float to spectators, were proffered in a Revelers' parade as early as 1871. Throws would not become standard parade practice until much later.

Carnival rose to new heights during the years that followed the Civil War, and as New Orleans coped with the hardship and insult of 'carpetbag' rule (see Reconstruction in the Facts About New Orleans chapter), the importance of Mardi Gras as the cultural focal point of the year was cemented. At times, the seriousness with which Carnival was regarded in New Orleans was exhibited in rather extreme ways. In 1890, two parades, those of Comus and Proteus, reached the edge of the French Quarter at the same time. In a heated dispute over which krewe would enter the Quarter first, several krewe members appeared ready to draw swords, but the confrontation was resolved without violence.

Black Carnival

Very little has been written to document early black Carnival, but it seems unlikely that blacks ever ignored the most festive holiday in New Orleans. Parades and musical processions surely took place in the area around Congo Square, and black Creole balls were held even before the Louisiana Purchase. In 1885 one of the most significant and enduring traditions of black Carnival was born as a Mardi Gras Indian gang, calling itself the Creole Wild West, made its first appearance. Eventually, an untold number of black Indian gangs – the Wild Tchoupitoulas, Yellow Pocohontas and Golden Eagles,

TOM DOWNS

among many others – would enter the city's back streets on Mardi Gras, dressed in elaborately beaded and feathered suits and headdresses. A canon of Indian songs was passed down from generation to generation, with lyrics often fusing English, Creole French, Choctaw and African words until their meaning was obscure.

From the beginning, 'masking Indian' was a serious proposition. Tribes became organized fighting units headed by a Big Chief, with Spy Boys, Flag Boys and Wild Men carrying out carefully defined roles. Tremendous pride was evident in the costly and expertly sewn suits, and

Left: Mr Big Shot of Zulu, a spoof on the Carnival traditions of the elitist white krewes

when two gangs crossed paths, an intense confrontation would ensue as members of each tribe sized each other up. Often violence would break out. As is the case with many of Mardi Gras' strongest traditions, this was no mere amusement.

Other black traditions emerged around the turn of the 20th century. The skull-and-bones gangs (influenced, some think, by Mexican Day of the Dead artwork) were men dressed up like skeletons who chased frightened little kids around black neighborhoods on Mardi Gras morning. Their purported 'purpose' was to put a little tear in the youngsters in order to make the kids behave. A group of prostitutes, calling themselves the Baby Dolls, also began masking on Mardi Gras. Dressed in bloomers and bonnets, they danced from bar to bar, turning tricks along the way.

The black krewe of Zulu first appeared in 1909, with members initially calling themselves the Tramps and parading on foot. By 1916, when the Zulu Social Aid & Pleasure Club was incorporated, the krewe had floats, and its antics deliberately spoofed the pomposity of elite white krewes – Rex in particular. Zulu members paraded in black face, and their dress was a wickedly comical interpretation of African tribal culture. Krewe hierarchy included a witch doctor, a mayor, the absurdly uppity Mr Big Shot and a phalanx of tribal warriors bearing shields and wearing grass skirts. It was an obvious commentary on popular 'Jim Crow' depictions of blacks (see the Facts About New Orleans chapter for more about Jim Crow laws). In time, Zulu's members would include some of the city's more prominent black citizens. Jazz star Louis Armstrong reigned as King Zulu in 1949, and although his float broke into pieces during the parade (fortunately, in front of a bar), he had no complaints. As he summed up the experience, 'I always been a Zulu, but King, man, this is the stuff.'

Top right: Float of the Zulu Queen

Bottom right: Mardi Gras Indian procession

Mardi Gras Indians

Perhaps the most amazing part of Mardi Gras is the tradition of the black Indian gangs, otherwise known as the Mardi Gras Indians. Black Indians are a curious expression of 19th-century cross-culturalism (escaped slaves and persecuted Native Americans often united in the dense, tangled forests of Louisiana) and a dazzling example of authentic, unsanctioned inner-city artistry.

Indian gangs began appearing on Mardi Gras in the 1880s, when a group calling itself the Creole Wild West masked in the feathered finery of Plains Indians. Since then, many gangs have come and gone, like the Wild Tchoupitoulas, Yellow Pocahontas and Wild Magnolias, led by now-legendary 'big chiefs' like Big Chief Jolly, Tootie Montana and Bo Dollis.

TOM DOWNS

Over the years, Black Indian suits seem to have grown more extravagant. Although the Indians generally hail from the poorest, most crime-ridden parts of town, they devote extraordinary amounts of time and money toward the creation of their suits. Sewing, a point of pride among Indians, is done by hand, and it is an interesting sight to see tough, street-wise young men perusing the aisles in stores dealing in sewing supplies, sequins and brightly colored feathers. Layers of meaningful mosaics are designed and created in patterns of neatly stitched sequins. Multilayered feathered head-dresses – particularly those of the big chiefs – are more elaborate and flamboyant than the headgear worn by Las Vegas show performers. The making of a new suit can take the better part of a year, and in the course of this arduous work, trickles of blood frequently seep into the suit's fabric as needles prick the sewer's nimble fingers.

On Mardi Gras, many suits are still unfinished. They are closer to completion by the time Indian gangs march the city's back streets again weeks later, on St Joseph's night (roughly midway through the Lenten season), and have usually reached their full splendor by Super Sunday (which usually takes place sometime in April), when the gangs reappear to show off to crowds of admirers. Photographers are not completely welcome at these events, but they show up nonetheless and those most bent on getting quality shots usually only get in the way of an otherwise spine-tingling spectacle. (The best photos are taken by friends of the Indians, who naturally have the greatest access.) Visitors are not advised to go looking for Indians unless they are comfortable with the risks involved in entering crime-ridden neighborhoods. (Claiborne Ave, to the lake-side of the Tremé District, is a frequent stomping ground on Mardi Gras.) Indian music groups can be seen at Jazz Fest and year-round at some clubs.

Modern Carnival

The 20th century has seen the coming and going of dozens of krewes, each adding to the diversity and interest of Carnival. Iris, a women's krewe, was formed in 1917 and began parading in 1959. Gay krewes began forming in the late '50s, with Petronius, the oldest gay krewe still in existence, staging its first ball in 1962. (Petronius is not a parading krewe.)

Today's 'superkrewes' began forming in the 1960s. Endymion debuted as a modest neighborhood parade in 1967; now its parades and floats are the largest, with nearly 2000 riders and one of its immense floats measuring 240 feet in length. Endymion is so big, its ball is held in the Louisiana Superdome. But while Endymion was still fledgling, Bacchus, which began in 1969, shaped the bigger things to come. From its start, Bacchus deliberately set out to break Carnival tradition, wowing its audiences by anointing celebrity monarchs (including Bob Hope, Jackie Gleason, Kirk Douglas and William Shatner) and opening its balls, which old-line krewes had always carried out with carefully tended mystery, to the paid public. Orpheus, a superkrewe founded by musician Harry Connick Jr, first appeared in the mid-1990s.

Tradition was dealt another blow when the old-line krewes Comus, Proteus and Momus stopped parading in the early 1990s. When city council member Dorothy Mae Taylor challenged these all-white krewes to integrate, they elected to retreat from the streets, continuing their elite Carnival traditions in private; Comus and Momus stopped parading in 1992, Proteus a year later.

Despite many changes, and although rambunctious tourists generally outnumber rowdy locals during Mardi Gras, the holiday continues to mark the zenith of New Orleans' festive annual calendar. And despite the grayish ooze of trash, spilled beer, piss and vomit that's ground into the city's gutters by a seemingly mindless shuffle, a hearty spirit manages to shine through, somehow linking today's Carnival to those of 18th-century France and even to the Lupercalia of ancient Rome. The masking tradition, carried out primarily in the French Quarter and the Faubourg Marigny, upholds an ancient and enchanting Mardi Gras

Right: An Orpheus float terrorizes Gallier Hall

TOM DOWNS

Mardi Gras Rhythm & Blues

The official 'anthem' of Carnival is a corny ditty called 'If Ever I Cease to Love,' with swooning lyrics that include the lines 'May cows lay eggs and fish get legs/If I ever cease to love.' (Needless to say, the instrumental version of the song is more popular.) However, hundreds of songs have been written since Rex introduced 'If I Ever Cease to Love' in 1871, and many of them better reflect the spirit of Mardi Gras in New Orleans. Some R&B Mardi Gras tunes are flat-out great songs that get ample play on local radio – especially on WWOZ – during Carnival season.

Classic R&B favorites include Professor Longhair's 'Mardi Gras in New Orleans,' with Fess' infectious, exuberant whistling; Art Neville's catchy 'Mardi Gras Mambo,' which he recorded way back in 1955, long before the Meters or the Neville Brothers reached national stardom; James 'Sugar Boy' Crawford's cryptic 'Jock-A-Mo,' a song built on Mardi Gras Indian chants; and Al Johnson's 'Carnival Time,' which serves as a litmus test of sorts, because if this tune doesn't draw the Carnival spirit out of you, then you just don't have it.

---

aesthetic. Night parades continue to haunt St Charles Ave and Canal St with surreal and terrifying floats, Mephisphelean masked riders and infernal flambeaux. The skull and bones gangs and black Indians continue to carry out their spontaneous rituals. When it comes right down to it, the good, the bad and the ugly are all parts of Mardi Gras tradition.

EXPERIENCING CARNIVAL

Carnival begins slowly, with related events, parties and parades becoming more frequent as Mardi Gras nears. (Mardi Gras, translating as 'Fat Tuesday,' is used here specifically to refer to the actual day, rather than to the entire season; Carnival refers to the season from January 6 to Fat Tuesday.) During the final, culminating weekend, particularly on Lundi Gras and Mardi Gras, many things are scheduled to occur simultaneously, and you will have to make some decisions. Preplanning and prioritizing are definitely in order, as getting around town grows more difficult with each passing day (renting a bicycle will grant you the greatest mobility). Be prepared also to improvise a little.

Twelfth Night

The beginning of Carnival is signaled early in the evening of January 6, as a rowdy band calling itself the Phunny Phorty Phellows parades down St Charles Ave aboard a streetcar. If you happen to be in town on this night, you may catch some of the season's first throws (see the Throws section, later in this chapter). Later in the evening, Twelfth Night masquerade parties are held around town. While many of these are private affairs, some clubs have revelries to ring in the season. Mid-City Rock & Bowl has held Twelfth Night parties open to the public. You may want to ask around at various clubs in town to see if anything's doing.

Parades

The parade season is a 12-day period beginning two Fridays before Fat Tuesday. Most of the early parades are charming, almost neighborly processions that whet your appetite and warm you up for the later parades, which increase in size and grandeur each day, until the awesome spectacles of the superkrewes emerge during the final weekend.

There are two primary Carnival parade routes in Orleans Parish. The Uptown route typically follows St Charles Ave from Napoleon St to Canal St (where these parades actually begin and end can vary widely, but this stretch is fairly constant). The Zulu parade departs from this course by rolling down Jackson Ave until it reaches St Charles Ave, at which point it follows the standard Uptown route toward Canal St. The Mid-City parade route begins near City Park and follows Orleans Ave to Carrollton Ave to Canal St, down toward the French Quarter, hooking into the Central Business District (CBD) in order to pass the grandstands at Gallier Hall.

These lengthy routes, which can take several hours for some of the larger krewes to traverse, obviously afford many vantage points from which to see the parades. But your choice is fairly straightforward: Either head away from the crowded Quarter to get a more 'neighborhood' feel, or stick close to the corner of Canal St and St Charles Ave, where the crowds are heavier and a raucous, sometimes bawdy party atmosphere prevails. Grandstands (with paid admission) are set up along St Charles Ave in the area between Lee Circle and Gallier Hall, and parading krewe members tend to unload beads like crazy through this corridor.

If catching throws is of highest priority, here's a tip: Near the end of parade routes, krewe members often discover they've been too conservative along the parade route, and they tend to let loose. However, the excitement level of the parade may already have passed its crescendo. (Some krewe members start to look tired after a while – and they still have their Carnival balls to attend.)

Bottom: Highly covetable Carnival booty

King Cakes

Mardi Gras has its idiosyncrasies, which New Orleanians, out of their love for the holiday, tolerate, make excuses for and even cherish. None is more kitschy than the king cake. Every year, on Twelfth Night (January 6), the first king cakes emerge from bakeries all over New Orleans and soon appear in offices – including the mayor's – and at Twelfth Night parties throughout the city.

Just what is this regal pastry, you ask?

It just so happens that this gaudy dessert may be the closest thing to a culinary embarrassment offered in New Orleans. It's an oval, spongy Danish pastry with gooey icing and purple, green and gold sugar on top. More importantly, it always contains an inedible, peanut-size plastic baby somewhere inside. The baby is key – it's what perpetuates the king cake tradition. The rule is, whoever is served the piece of cake with the baby inside (careful – don't swallow that baby!) has to buy the next cake. That would be tomorrow, next week or next year, depending on the cycle the group agrees on. If you work in an office, this could mean that from Twelfth Night until the last day of work before Mardi Gras you have to eat king cake five days a week.

The king cake originated in 1870, when the Twelfth Night Revelers used it to select a queen for the 'Lord of Misrule' and a Carnival tradition was born. Early king cakes contained an uncooked golden bean instead of a baby, and the recipient of the bean was crowned king or queen of a Carnival krewe. That ritual is still maintained by some krewes, but such important matters are no longer left to chance. The bean, or baby, is always planted in the piece of cake served to a preselected king or queen. It seems the king cake has lost some of its clout.

Nevertheless, king cakes have become big business. One local bakery chain claims to sell 30,000 king cakes *a day*. According to local statisticians, 750,000 king cakes are consumed annually in the New Orleans metropolitan area.

On Twelfth Night, the **Phunny Phorty Phellows**, trundling down St Charles Ave on the streetcar, qualifies as the first 'parade' of Carnival. It's a very small spectacle, easily missed even by people driving their cars down St Charles Ave at the time.

A more popular preseason night procession, usually held three Saturdays before Fat Tuesday, is that of the **Krewe du Vieux**. By parading before the official parade season and forgoing motorized floats (nearly all krewe members are afoot), Krewe du Vieux is permitted to pass through the Quarter. It's a throwback to the old days, before floats and crowds grew too large, when parading krewes typically traversed the Quarter while onlookers packed the sidewalks and balconies. But the themes of this notoriously bawdy and satirical krewe are not always traditional, in the puritanical American sense. Depending on your religious views, you may find some of the content downright sinful.

A lovely night parade presented by the predominantly black krewe of **Oshun** (named for a West African goddess) has been rolling very early in the season on the Mid-City route. Other krewes that traditionally parade during the first weekend are **Pontchartrain**, with a Mid-City promenade known for its marching band contests; **Sparta**, with an Uptown night parade that features traditional touches like flambeau carriers and a mule-drawn float; and **Carrollton**, a 75-year-old krewe that rolls down St Charles Ave on Sunday afternoon.

In some years, parades are held every night of the subsequent week, getting larger as the weekend gets near. Toward the end of the week, the highly secretive **Knights of Babylon** present their attractive traditional parade, replete with flambeaux and riding lieutenants; it follows the Uptown route but continues toward the lake on Canal St and down Basin St for a few blocks. On Friday night before Mardi Gras, Uptown is the domain of **Hermes**, the oldest and most traditional extant night parade; it's a beautiful spectacle that has maintained the aloof mystery of 19th-century Carnival processions. Hermes is followed directly by **Le Krewe d'Etat**, whose name is a clever, satirical pun: It follows that d'Etat is not headed by a King, as the old-line krewes are, but instead by a dictator. However menacing this modern krewe may be, d'Etat's floats and costumes nevertheless reflect fairly traditional standards of beauty, and in recent years its glowing skull-and-crossbones krewe necklaces have been among the best throws of Carnival.

Mardi Gras weekend is lit up by the entrance of the superkrewes, with their monstrous floats and endless processions of celebrities, marching bands, Shriner buggies, military units and police officers. Unlike the traditional krewes, the superkrewes, following a 'more is better' mentality, are as flashy as a Vegas revue. The crowds of spectators also grow larger by the day, and that comfortable corner you'd staked out for yourself earlier in the week is now likely overrun by tourists. All of these considerations aside, if you've been in town all week, you'll be ready for something bigger by this time. (A few non-superkrewes parade during the weekend as well.)

On Saturday afternoon, the all-women's krewe, **Iris**, parades down St Charles Ave with more than 30 floats and 750 krewe members. It's followed by **Tucks**, an irreverent krewe with the uninspired motto of 'Booze, Beer, Bourbon, Broads' and a giant toilet-seat float, which spectators are encouraged to throw unwanted beads into. It's probably obvious, but Tucks was founded by party-minded college students in 1969.

TOM DOWNS

On Saturday night, the megakrewe **Endymion** stages its spectacular parade and Extravaganza, as it calls its ball in the Superdome. With 1900 riders on nearly 30 enormous, luminescent floats rolling down Canal St from Mid-City, the Endymion parade is one of the season's most electrifying events. In 1999, the krewe debuted its massive, 240-foot steamboat float – by far the biggest float in the history of Mardi Gras.

Sunday is a full day of parade-watching. A daytime highlight is the unique parade put on by the krewe called Mid-City, with dazzling tinfoil-decorated floats twinkling down Canal St in the afternoon sun. At night, **Bacchus** wows an enraptured crowd along St Charles Ave with its celebrity monarch and a gorgeous fleet of crowd-pleasing floats.

In recent years, Monday night has been parade night for **Orpheus**, a spirited and stylish superkrewe founded by singer-pianist Harry Connick Jr (who hails from New Orleans). Connick rides annually and he always enlists a handful of movie stars and musicians to join his 1000-member krewe. Orpheus, riding directly behind the much less impressive Krewe of Bards, often gets off to a late start, and its ranks are usually swollen by so many accessory marching units that you may have to wait several hours before seeing the famous, 140-foot Leviathan float. It's a spectacular float, and most people are glad they waited.

On Mardi Gras morning, **Zulu** rolls its loosely themed and slightly rundown floats along Jackson Ave, where the atmosphere is very different from the standard parade routes. Folks set up their barbecues on the sidewalk and krewe members, ironically made up in black face and chomping on plastic cigars, distribute painted coconuts to a lucky few in the crowd. As Zulu reaches St Charles Ave, it follows the Uptown route toward Gallier Hall for a spell before ending up on Orleans St and the Tremé district. Zulu typically runs blithely behind schedule while the King of Carnival, **Rex**, waits farther Uptown for clearance on St Charles Ave.

Left: Be-masked bequeathers of beads

The contrast between these two venerable krewes couldn't be more apparent. Rex's parade is, naturally, a much more restrained and haughty affair, with the monarch himself looking like he's been plucked from a deck of cards, as he smiles benignly upon his subjects – who, on this unusual day, include the mayor of the city. His floats are beautifully constructed and handpainted, and his elegant procession is reminiscent of the late-19th-century parades that remain fixed in the imaginations of the city's more nostalgic Carnival enthusiasts. But in terms of throws, many a loot-hungry spectator has noted Rex's shocking stinginess.

On Mardi Gras afternoon you can continue to watch parades. The populist spirit of the **truck parades**, haphazardly decorated semis loaded up with people line-dancing and throwing beads, is sociologically interesting but minimally entertaining, as is Mayor Marc Morial's anticlimactic **Krewe of America**, whose ranks are, in theory, supplied by tourists from the 50 states. If you've been in town all weekend you'll be paraded out by this time anyway.

Throws   Parading Carnival krewes don't just aim to entertain – they also give things to people. The custom of throwing trinkets from Carnival floats didn't really start to catch on until the 1920s, but today some spectators evaluate parades solely on the basis of the krewes' generosity. Most beads are mass produced in China (glass beads imported from Czechoslovakia went out of fashion in the early 1970s), but regardless of how cheaply they are made, people want 'em. You have to want them and work to get them, and the more you get, the more you'll want. The traditional holler of 'Throw me something, Mister!' is not as effective as it once was, since women have started participating in parades in greater numbers these days.

Quantity isn't the only issue. Creative throws, like Zulu's famous painted coconuts, are more prized than generic beads, which can be bought at the Flea Market. Medallion beads (or krewe beads) bearing a plastic emblem representing the krewe seem to get bigger with each Carnival

JEFFREY GREENBERG

season, as krewes strive to satisfy their fans' increasing hunger for bigger, better and badder booty. The smaller, common plastic beads that all spectators once hoped to receive from a Carnival float have come to be called 'tree beads,' for their ignominious fate is to be tossed into the branches of the live oaks along St Charles Ave (where some actually hang on long enough to see the following year's Carnival). Doubloons, minted aluminum coins bearing krewe insignia and themes, are also popular collector's items. Other things you may acquire along a parade route range from plastic cups to bags of potato chips.

Right: Begging for throws along St Charles and Canal Sts

The Law of Mardi Gras

New Orleans has fostered a reputation as a permissive city, and Mardi Gras is obviously a time of unbridled debauchery. But don't come expecting utter lawlessness. Overall, the New Orleans Police Department does a commendable job maintaining order, despite immense, spirited crowds consuming unbelievable quantities of liquor. Along parade routes and in the French Quarter, cops are everywhere. If their ranks appear to have swelled, it's because the entire force is working long shifts, with little time for rest in between.

Surprisingly, the presence of so many overworked cops does not interfere with the general merriment of Carnival. The attitude of the police during Carnival is to let people have their fun, but officers draw the line at potentially dangerous behavior. If a cop tells you to watch what you're doing, don't try to argue. If you start with the 'Aw, but ossiffer...' routine, you're likely to end up in the slammer – and you probably won't be released until Mardi Gras is over.

Many special laws go into effect during Carnival. Here are a few that visitors ought to bear in mind:

- Do not park your car along a parade route within two hours of the start of a parade – you are guaranteed to be towed.
- Do not cross police barriers unless permitted to do so by an officer.
- During parades, do not cross the street if it means stepping between members of marching bands or in front of moving floats.
- It is against the law to throw anything at the floats.
- Police tend to look the other way (figuratively, anyway) while women expose their breasts in the French Quarter; don't expect the same tolerance elsewhere, or with other body parts.
- It isn't true that it's okay to have sex in public.

A word of caution: When a throw lands on the street, claim it by stepping on it, then pick it up. If you try to pick it up without first stepping on it, someone else will surely step on your fingers – and then insist that the object is by rights theirs!

Walking Clubs & Foot Parades

In addition to the major parades, Zulu and Rex, that take place on Mardi Gras, there are many 'unofficial' walking parades that are worth seeking out and, in some cases, even joining.

The **Jefferson City Buzzards**, a walking club that has been moseying from bar to bar on Mardi Gras morn since 1890, starts out at 6:45 am at Laurel St near Audubon Park. If you're into drinking early, you may run into them at any drinking establishment between there and the Quarter. Since 1961, jazzman Pete Fountain's **Half-Fast Walking Club** has been making similar barhopping rounds, starting out from Commander's Palace at around 8 am.

Downtown has its own morning activities, the biggest event being the parade of the **Society of St Anne**. This is a gloriously creative costume pageant – krewe members, clad in elaborate hats, capes, makeup and masks or, in some cases, in very little at all, march through the Bywater, Faubourg Marigny and French Quarter to the jazzy rhythms of the Storyville Stompers. The parade starts around 10 am in the Bywater, and the colorful procession, which strives to re-create scenes from 19th-century oil paintings of French Mardi Gras, flows down Royal St all the way to Canal St, where it sometimes arrives in time to run into the Rex Parade.

Another costume-oriented downtown walking parade is that of the **Krewe of Cosmic Debris**, which convenes at around noon in front of the Dream Palace in the Faubourg Marigny. Masked walk-ins are welcome to join the Krewe of Cosmic Debris provided they are costumed – freeloaders in street clothes don't add anything to the visual spectacle. The krewe's wandering musical voyage through the French Quarter is largely determined by which bars it elects to patronize along the way.

Costume Contests

Mardi Gras is meant to be a citywide costume party, and while New Orleanians generally maintain a 'the more the merrier' attitude towards travelers, many rightfully take a dim view of visitors who crash their party without a costume. The true spirit of Mardi Gras – going all the way back to its origins – is to turn the world on its ear, to break form, to be someone or something else for a day.

On Fat Tuesday, imaginatively garbed alter egos wander the Quarter aimlessly, delighting while an uncoordinated pageant unfolds. As exquisitely attired maskers, human beasts and exhibitionists mingle, a spirit unique to Mardi Gras animates the streets; you may want to leave the kids at home.

This unbound creativity is distilled into two costume contests – a highproof one for adults and a watered-down one for the entire family. The notorious **Bourbon St Awards**, attracting a large number of gay contestants, is staged not on Bourbon St (as it once was) but in front of the Rawhide Bar at Burgundy and St Anne Sts; it begins at noon. The cleaner **Mardi Gras Maskathon** is held in front of the Meridien Hotel on Canal St, after the Rex parade concludes.

Right: Cleverly costumed contestants

K GERHARTER

Future Mardi Gras Dates

Mardi Gras can occur on any Tuesday between February 3 and March 9, depending on the date of Easter. Here are the dates for the next several years:

2000	March 7
2001	February 27
2002	February 12
2003	March 4
2004	February 24
2005	February 8
2006	February 28
2007	February 20
2008	February 5
2009	February 24

RICHARD CUMMINS

Balls

You can't expect to roll into town on Friday night and on Tuesday gain admittance to one of the invitation-only society functions that typify the Carnival ball season. You can, however, buy your way into a party put on by one of the more modern krewes, including Orpheus (☎ 822-7211), Tucks (☎ 288-2481), Bacchus and Endymion. Gay krewes include Petronius (☎ 525-4498) and the Lords of Leather (☎ 347-0659).

Information

A glossy magazine, *Arthur Hardy's Mardi Gras Guide*, is an indispensable source of information and a worthwhile souvenir. Published by Carnival aficionado Arthur Hardy, the annual publication appears in bookstores each year before Twelfth Night. In addition to sharing fascinating Mardi Gras trivia, it details parade schedules and includes parade route maps. Similar information is offered by the *Gambit Weekly's* monthly publication, the *Natives' Guide to New Orleans*, which publishes a Carnival edition during February or March, depending on the date of Mardi Gras. *OffBeat*, a music magazine, offers invaluable information on Mardi Gras-related events.

Getting There & Away

AIR

The area is served by one main airport, New Orleans International Airport (MSY). About 98% of the flights that pass through here are domestic – the only 'international' flights are with other North and Central American countries. New Orleans is a medium-size air traffic hub, overshadowed by major hubs at Dallas-Fort Worth, Houston and Atlanta.

Airline phone numbers are listed under Airline Offices, later in this chapter. See the Getting Around chapter for options on getting from the airport to your lodging.

Departure Tax

A standard airport departure tax of $24 is charged to passengers traveling between the USA and foreign cities. If you purchased your ticket to New Orleans in the USA, the tax will normally be included in the ticket price. Tickets purchased abroad may not include this tax. In addition to the airport departure tax, visitors arriving from a foreign country will be charged a $6.50 North American Free Trade Agreement (NAFTA) tax, which also may be included in the price of your ticket, depending on where the ticket was purchased.

Other Parts of the USA

New Orleans International Airport's proximity to major hubs at Dallas-Fort Worth, Houston and Atlanta make it easy to find a convenient flight or connection to and from just about anywhere in North America. A good place to begin your search for the cheapest and/or most convenient flight is the Sunday Travel section of the *Times-Picayune* newspaper, as well as similar sections in *The New York Times*, *Chicago Tribune* and *Los Angeles Times*, in which you'll find any number of travel agents' ads. The Friday travel page of the *Wall Street Journal* offers many useful tips for business travelers. The New Orleans office of Council Travel is a good place to go for competitive fares and

WARNING

The information in this chapter is particularly vulnerable to change: Prices for international travel are volatile, routes are introduced and canceled, schedules change, special deals come and go, and rules and visa requirements are amended. Airlines and governments seem to take a perverse pleasure in making price structures and regulations as complicated as possible. You should check directly with the airline or travel agent to make sure you understand how a fare (and any ticket you may buy) works. In addition, the travel industry is highly competitive, and there are many lures and perks.

The upshot of this is that you should get opinions, quotes and advice from as many airlines and travel agents as possible before you part with your hard-earned cash. The details given in the chapter should be regarded as pointers and are not a substitute for your own careful, up-to-date research.

air travel information. Council Travel also has offices in major cities nationwide (see Travel Agents, later).

Regional airlines (those serving fewer destinations than the intercontinental biggies) may also be a good bet on short or heavily traveled routes, as they require neither a roundtrip purchase nor a Saturday night's stay to get an economical fare. Southwest Airlines covers the western USA fairly completely, with frequently scheduled flights from its hub in Houston. Southwest also offers service to Florida, so you can expect airfares there to remain reasonable. Southwest often offers rates undercutting major airlines and runs specials, such as 'companion fares' that allow two people to travel for the price of one. Delta Air Lines sometimes offers discount flights to compete with Southwest.

Most large domestic airlines dominate a major hub airport, with radiating 'spokes' connecting to other cities. If you book a flight through a carrier's hub, your ticket will typically be cheaper, and you can select from more frequent flights than if you demand nonstop service. Also, by doing a little research on such airline systems, you can figure out why your favorite airline in one travel corridor may be a costly and inconvenient choice in another.

Fares change often, but nearly all of the best fares require an advance purchase of seven to 21 days. Low roundtrip fares to either Dallas-Fort Worth, Atlanta or Memphis typically cost $150, while those to Houston run about $125. Fares to the East Coast fluctuate the most, with New York roundtrips ranging from $150 to $350 during a recent 30-day period. Roundtrip fares to the West Coast typically cost around $300, while a roundtrip fare to Chicago hovers around $150. A comparable roundtrip fare will get you to Orlando, Florida, where you can lunch with Disney characters.

Latin America

New Orleans has long-standing business ties with Caribbean sugar and Central American fruit and coffee plantations, so there is decent service to and from Latin America. Cancún's beaches are less than two hours away aboard daily Aeroméxico or Lacsa flights; economy roundtrip tickets average $250. Aeroméxico continues to Mexico City via Cancún. Flights to San Juan, Puerto Rico, typically cost $325 on American Airlines. TACA International provides daily flights to Belize and El Salvador. Lacsa serves Costa Rica, Honduras and Panama. Many other flights to/from Central and South America go via Miami, Houston, Dallas-Fort Worth or Los Angeles. Most countries' major airlines, as well as US airlines such as United and American, serve these destinations. Continental has flights between New Orleans and about 20 cities in Mexico, Central America and the Caribbean via Houston.

Canada

Despite the tremendous influx of Canadian visitors during winter months, no airlines currently offer direct flights from Canada to

LEE FOSTER

Ferry passenger viewing the New Orleans skyline

New Orleans. Travelers must typically make connections at US gateways, though US-Canadian airline partnership agreements do offer 'through ticketing.' Northwest Airlines offers extensive Canadian service, but you may find lower fares on other airlines.

Availability and cost of through-ticketed flights vary depending upon the time of year, the distance traveled and the whim of the industry. Some typical economy round-trip fares for Canada include Montreal and Quebec (C$450), Winnipeg (C$700), Edmonton (C$800) and Vancouver (C$750). To save money, catch a ride to a US gateway to take advantage of competitive domestic US fares. Call a travel agent or check the newspapers for specifics.

The UK & Continental Europe

British Airways arrives in the USA at many gateways, with connecting service on US Airways or American Airlines domestic flights. Cheaper flights to New Orleans from London may involve landing in New York City. You should also consider traveling to either Atlanta, Orlando, Houston or Dallas-Fort Worth, depending on international fares, and taking a low-fare domestic connecting flight. Westbound passengers usually depart London in mid-morning and, after making a domestic connection, arrive about 12 hours later in New Orleans during the evening. Eastbound flights go overnight with a travel time of 11 hours.

A straightforward economy roundtrip ticket is around £600, and a business class roundtrip ticket costs about £3000. Cheaper fares vary with the season; summer (June through August) and Christmas are the peak periods, and weekends may also be more expensive. Economy or APEX tickets, which usually must be purchased 21 days in advance and involve cancellation penalties if you change your plans, cost from £300 to £1000 roundtrip. Bargain fares around £200 can be found using one of the less popular international airlines from London to New York and continuing on a US domestic flight. Charter flights typically cost around £400 roundtrip. The business of discounting tickets is so well developed in Britain that

you can get heavily discounted 1st-class and business-class tickets as well as cheaper economy tickets.

The weekly London magazine *Time Out*, the *Evening Standard* and the various give-away travel papers are all good sources of ads for cheaper fares. Good agents for low-priced tickets in London include the following:

Campus Travel
  (☎ 020-7938-2188)
  174 Kensington High St, London W8
  (☎ 020-7437-7767)
  28A Poland St, London W1
STA
  (☎ 020-7937-9962)
  86 Old Brompton Rd, London SW7;
  117 Euston Rd, London NW1
Trailfinders
  (☎ 020-7937-5400)
  194 Kensington High St, London W8
Travel Cuts
  (☎ 020-7637-3161)
  295A Regent St, London W1

London generally offers the best values for crossing the Atlantic; however, direct flights from Paris on Delta take about 12 hours and typically cost 3700FF roundtrip. From Amsterdam, KLM offers direct service with Northwest Airlines for about 1300 guilders roundtrip. Lufthansa makes connections with United between Frankfurt and New Orleans for approximately DM1200. Continental offers direct flights to Houston from most European cities. Ditto for American Airlines to Dallas-Fort Worth, Delta to Atlanta and Northwest to Detroit and Memphis.

Asia

None of the many Asian carriers currently offers direct flights to New Orleans – most serve the Los Angeles or San Francisco gateways. American Airlines flies nonstop from Tokyo to Dallas-Fort Worth (economy roundtrip fares cost ¥150,000). Eastbound flights from Tokyo to Dallas-Fort Worth leave in the early evening and arrive in the early evening after traveling for 11½ hours. Add another 1½ hours to the westbound travel time. United and Northwest airlines also fly Asia routes and offer connecting

Air Travel Glossary

Baggage Allowance This will be written on your ticket and usually includes one 45lb item to go in the hold plus one item of hand luggage.

Bucket Shops These are unbonded travel agencies specializing in discounted airline tickets.

Bumped Just because you have a confirmed seat doesn't mean you're going to get on the plane (see Overbooking).

Cancellation Penalties If you have to cancel or change a discounted ticket, there are often heavy penalties involved; insurance can sometimes be taken out against these penalties. Some airlines impose penalties on regular tickets as well, particularly against 'no-show' passengers.

Check-In Airlines ask you to check in a certain time ahead of the flight departure (usually one to two hours on international flights). If you fail to check in on time and the flight is overbooked, the airline can cancel your booking and give your seat to somebody else.

Confirmation Having a ticket written out with the flight and date you want doesn't mean you have a seat until the agent has checked with the airline that your status is 'OK' or confirmed. Meanwhile you could just be 'on request.'

Courier Fares Businesses often need to send urgent documents or freight securely and quickly. Courier companies hire people to accompany the package through customs and, in return, offer a discount ticket that is sometimes a phenomenal bargain. In effect, what the companies do is ship their freight as your luggage on regular commercial flights. This is a legitimate operation, but there are two shortcomings – the short turnaround time of the ticket (usually not longer than a month) and the limitation on your luggage allowance. You may have to surrender your entire allowance and take only carry-on luggage.

ITX An 'independent inclusive tour excursion' (ITX) is often available on tickets to popular holiday destinations. Officially it's a package deal combined with hotel accommodations, but many agents will sell you one of these for the flight only and give you phony hotel vouchers in the unlikely event that you're challenged at the airport.

Lost Tickets If you lose your airline ticket, an airline will usually treat it like a traveler's check and, after inquiries, issue you another one. Legally, however, an airline is entitled to treat it like cash; if you lose it, then it's gone forever. Take good care of your tickets.

MCO A 'miscellaneous charge order' (MCO) is a voucher that looks like an airline ticket but carries no destination or date. It can be exchanged through any International Association of Travel Agents (IATA) airline for a ticket on a specific flight. It's a useful alternative to an onward ticket in those countries that demand one, and it's more flexible than an ordinary ticket if you're unsure of your route.

Air Travel Glossary

No-Shows These are passengers who fail to show up for their flight. Full-fare passengers who fail to turn up are sometimes entitled to travel on a later flight. The rest are penalized (see Cancellation Penalties).

On Request This is an unconfirmed booking for a flight.

Onward Tickets An entry requirement for many countries is that you have a ticket out of the country. If you're unsure of your next move, the easiest solution is to buy the cheapest onward ticket to a neighboring country or a ticket from a reliable airline that can later be refunded if you do not use it.

Open-Jaw Tickets These are return tickets that allow you to fly to one place but return from another. If available, these can save you backtracking to your arrival point.

Overbooking Airlines hate to fly with empty seats, and since every flight has some passengers who fail to show up, airlines often book more passengers than they have seats for. Usually excess passengers make up for the no-shows, but occasionally somebody gets bumped. Guess who it is most likely to be? The passengers who check in late.

Point-to-Point Tickets These are discount tickets that can be bought on some routes in return for passengers waiving their rights to a stopover.

Reconfirmation At least 72 hours prior to departure time of an onward or return flight, you must contact the airline and reconfirm that you intend to be on the flight. If you don't do this, the airline can delete your name from the passenger list and you could lose your seat.

Restrictions Discounted tickets often have various restrictions on them – such as advance payment, minimum and maximum periods you must be away (eg, a minimum of two weeks or a maximum of one year), and penalties for changing the tickets.

Round-the-World Tickets RTW tickets give you a limited period (usually a year) in which to circumnavigate the globe. You can go anywhere the carrying airlines go, as long as you don't backtrack. The number of stopovers or total number of separate flights is decided before you set off, and they usually cost a bit more than a basic return flight.

Standby This is a discounted ticket that allows you to fly only if there is a seat free at the last moment. Standby fares are usually available only on domestic routes.

Travel Periods Ticket prices vary with the time of year. There is a low (off-peak) season and a high (peak) season, and often a low-shoulder season and a high-shoulder season as well. Usually the fare depends on your outward flight – if you depart in the high season and return in the low season, you pay the high-season fare.

flights from West Coast gateways. Ticket consolidators purchase blocks of tickets and typically offer them at a discount from the airlines' prices – don't be shy about asking your travel agent about ticket consolidator deals.

Australia & New Zealand

Neither Air New Zealand nor Qantas currently fly directly to New Orleans. They fly to Los Angeles and offer service to New Orleans on a connecting domestic flight, sometimes on a code-sharing flight designed to make you think it's all the same airline. United Airlines does have convenient connecting flights to New Orleans from both Sydney and Auckland. With the advent of long-range 747-400 aircraft, most services now overfly Hawaii, so at least the Pacific is covered in one mighty leap. From Auckland to Los Angeles, it takes 12 to 13 hours and from Sydney to Los Angeles, 13$^{1}/_{2}$ to 14$^{1}/_{2}$ hours. Typical economy roundtrip fares from the Australian east coast range from A$1400 to A$1800; fares from New Zealand cost NZ$1800 to NZ$2000.

Weekend travel sections in major city newspapers in Australia and New Zealand have ads for travel agents specializing in cheap fares. In Australia, Flight Centre and STA travel agencies have competitively priced tickets. STA also operates in New Zealand.

Airports

New Orleans International Airport (Map 1; ☎ 464-0831) ranks 40th in the USA in passenger volume on account of its being a destination rather than a transfer airport. A single terminal is connected to four concourses. Luggage lockers are available in each concourse, immediately past the security area. There is no need for gigantic tramways or moving walkways here – even passengers fresh from Bourbon St are not likely to get lost. Baggage and ground transportation are on the lower level.

Information The main information booth, at the A & B concourse, is open 8 am to 9 pm daily. Be sure to pick up a free copy of the

---

The Meaning Behind MSY

If New Orleans International Airport's code name, MSY, doesn't appear to have any connection to the airport's current name, that's because it doesn't. MSY dates back to before 1962, when the airport was known as Moisant Field, in honor of the daredevil pilot John Bevins Moisant (1873-1910). Moisant's credentials didn't exactly make him a likely candidate for being memorialized in the name of a commercial airport. In his final stunt, a race pitting his aircraft against an automobile, Moisant crashed and died. Needless to say, his story isn't a comforting one for nervous airline passengers arriving in New Orleans.

---

excellent *New Orleans Street Map*. Brochures are available in Spanish, French, German, Italian, Portuguese and Japanese. A nearby Travelers' Aid information booth (☎ 528-9026, 525-8726) on the upper level operates 9 am to 9 pm daily. New Orleans airport has a post office near Concourse C next to Whitney National Bank.

Money A Whitney National Bank branch (☎ 838-6432) and ATM are in the terminal near Concourse C. Whitney charges a flat $5 foreign exchange service fee, which is waived if you present a *New Orleans Street Map* (available free from the nearby information booth). It's open 10 am to 5 pm weekdays. Exchange rates at Travelex (☎ 465-9647), operated by Mutual of Omaha, are posted. Travelex charges a sliding service fee ($2 for amounts greater than $50, $4 for those less than $50). You may be inclined to comparison shop, but the best bet is to wait until you get downtown on a weekday for the best currency exchange.

Telephones White courtesy phones and a free phone connection to various airport services are scattered through the terminal. Pay phones that accept credit cards are widely available.

Smoking Don't light up inside the terminal. However, some gates have designated smoking areas.

Airline Offices

A few airlines have offices in the Central Business District (CBD). American Airlines is quartered in the Fairmont Hotel, 123 Baronne St, and Delta Air Lines (☎ 529-2431) is at 237 O'Keefe St, near Gravier St. Airlines with ticket counters at the New Orleans International Airport include the following:

Aeroméxico
   ☎ 524-1245, 800-237-6639

AirTran
   ☎ 800-825-8538

American Airlines
   ☎ 800-433-7300

British Airways
   ☎ 800-247-9297

Comair (Delta)
   ☎ 354-9822

Continental Airlines
   ☎ 523-9739, 800-732-6887 domestic,
   ☎ 800-231-0856 international

Delta Air Lines
   ☎ 800-221-1212 domestic,
   ☎ 800-241-4141 international

Lacsa
   ☎ 800-225-2272

Lufthansa
   ☎ 800-645-3880

KLM
   ☎ 800-374-7747

Northwest Airlines
   ☎ 800-225-2525 domestic,
   ☎ 800-447-4747 international

Southwest Airlines
   ☎ 464-9240, 800-435-9792

TACA
   ☎ 800-535-8780

TWA
   ☎ 529-2585, 800-221-2000 domestic,
   ☎ 800-892-4141 international

United Airlines
   ☎ 800-241-6522 domestic,
   ☎ 800-631-1500 international

US Airways
   ☎ 800-428-4322

BUS

As is typical throughout the South, you can rely on good bus service to New Orleans. Greyhound (☎ 800-231-2222, 800-531-5332 for Spanish-language service) is the only regular long-distance bus company serving the city. All trains and Greyhound buses share the New Orleans Union Passenger Terminal (Union Station; Map 4), 1001 Loyola Ave, seven blocks upriver from Canal St. The terminal includes a Travelers' Aid counter (☎ 525-8726, 528-9026 for the airport counter) and an inexpensive cafeteria, which offers red beans and rice for under $3. Note the murals by Conrad Albrizio, created for the terminal dedication in 1954, depicting New Orleans' history from early exploration to the modern age.

From New Orleans, there are two morning, three afternoon and four evening Greyhound buses to Baton Rouge. Travel time is under two hours, and the roundtrip fare is $26. Other frequent departures and roundtrip fares include the following:

Chicago	$198
Houston	$70
Jackson or Memphis	$65
Lafayette	$38
Mobile	$48

Bicycles must be boxed (boxes are not available from Greyhound) and cost an additional $10 each way.

Trains & buses come & go from here

TRAIN

Three Amtrak trains (☎ 800-872-7245) serve New Orleans at the Union Passenger Terminal (Map 4; ☎ 528-1610, 1001 Loyola Ave).

The *City of New Orleans* runs to Memphis, Jackson and Chicago, departing New Orleans at 2:10 pm Thursday to Monday and arriving in Chicago the following morning.

Another train originating in New Orleans is the *Crescent Route*, serving Birmingham, Atlanta, Washington, DC, and New York City. It departs at 7:05 am on Monday, Thursday and Saturday and arrives in Atlanta in time for dinner. There's a one-night layover; trains travel daily between Atlanta and New York.

New Orleans is on the *Sunset Limited* route between Los Angeles and Miami. Eastbound trains are scheduled to arrive on Tuesday, Thursday and Sunday at 7:35 pm and depart at 10:55 pm, but they are notorious for being late. Westbound trains arrive on Monday, Wednesday and Saturday at 10:10 am and depart at 12:45 pm. Again, because of poor performance, don't count on a guaranteed 2¹/₂-hour layover.

All three trains offer both coach seating and different levels of sleeping-car accommodations. Amtrak Thruway Bus Connections allow coordinated service with guaranteed connections between New Orleans and Baton Rouge on one through ticket. Bicycles are accepted on all trains when packed in large, roomy boxes provided at the station for $7 – you will only need to remove the pedals, loosen the post to drop the seat and loosen the neck to turn the handlebars sideways.

CAR & MOTORCYCLE

Call Auto Driveaway Co (☎ 737-0266, 7809 Airline Hwy), in Kenner, if your travel plans are flexible and you are willing to follow a time constraint that does not allow for sightseeing side-trips. Your chances of getting a drive-away car are better if you offer to travel to regions rather than specific destinations. Drive-away companies typically request a substantial deposit, valid driver's license and proof of liability insurance coverage.

As if to emphasize that New Orleans is an isolated piece of high ground, all freeway approaches to the city travel over lakes and bayous and are designated as hurricane evacuation routes away from the city. Interstate 10 is the nation's major east-west route along the southern boundary, linking Jacksonville with Los Angeles via Mobile and Houston. Baton Rouge and Lafayette are also on I-10 west of New Orleans. If you're heading for a destination beyond New Orleans, you can skirt downtown congestion by exiting I-10 and taking the I-610 shortcut. Alternatively, you can completely avoid the metro area by following the north shore of Lake Pontchartrain on I-12 between Slidell and Baton Rouge.

The north-south routes I-55 (to Chicago) and I-59 (to Chattanooga) meet I-10 to the west and east of New Orleans on either side of Lake Pontchartrain.

On the east bank of the Mississippi River, Hwy 61, the infamous Airline Hwy of ill repute, offers an alternate route from New Orleans to Baton Rouge. Another older route, Hwy 90, crosses the Huey P Long Bridge as it follows a southerly course between Mobile and the Cajun bayous south of Lafayette. Both Hwy 90 and the short I-310 connect New Orleans with the West Bank plantations upriver along the so-called 'River Road' (Hwy 61).

BICYCLE

Bicycling is a great way to explore the state. Louisiana gives bicyclists the same rights and responsibilities as motorists; however, the interstate freeways and highway bridges near New Orleans are closed to bicyclists. Instead, use Hwy 90 or Hwy 61. All of New Orleans' free state-operated ferries crossing the Mississippi River offer bicycle transport. Outside of the city, the crossings cost $1.

For information and maps of cross-country touring routes, contact Adventure Cycling (☎ 406-721-1776), PO Box 8308-QO, Missoula, MT 59807. The company's suggested east-west trek across Louisiana crosses the Mississippi River about 100 miles north of New Orleans at St Francisville (see the Excursions chapter).

HITCHHIKING

Travelers hoping to thumb their way around Louisiana may be in for an unpleasant surprise. On the whole, hitching is much less common in the US than elsewhere in the world, and for good reason. With true horror stories and urban myths to deter people from sharing their rides, thumb-mode travel is now almost nonexistent. As hitching is never entirely safe, travelers who decide to do it should understand that they are taking a potentially serious risk.

That said, for people who do choose to hitch, the advice that follows should help to make the journey as fast and safe as possible. Officially, hitchhiking is legal in Louisiana, but it *is* frowned upon by police and the highway patrol and you can expect a hassle. Local laws may be more stringent. As signs at the on ramps will tell you, pedestrians are not allowed on major highways. Try to travel in pairs and always let someone know where you are planning to go.

RIVERBOAT

Visitors to New Orleans during Mark Twain's time arrived by boat via the Mississippi River. This once common mode of travel continues to be offered by a few paddle wheel riverboats and ocean-going cruise ships. Costs are high compared to other travel modes – the era of steerage passage is over. River travel is now typically offered as a package tour or excursion that includes top-end food and lodging.

Headquartered in New Orleans, the Delta Queen Steamboat Company (☎ 800-543-1949) offers occasional paddle wheel riverboat travel to and from ports on the Mississippi River, including St Paul (14 nights), St Louis (seven nights) and Memphis (five nights). It also connects New Orleans with riverboat ports on Mississippi River tributaries such as Little Rock (10 nights), Pittsburgh (12 nights), Nashville (nine nights) and Chattanooga (10 nights); all times are for downriver travel – add at least one day for each five days to head upriver. In addition, voyages on the *Delta Queen* occasionally ply the Intracoastal Waterway between New Orleans and Galveston (six nights).

Paddleboat on the Mississippi

RICK GERHARTER

Riverboat fares typically start at $150 per person per night for a simple double occupancy berth and include all meals and entertainment, but they do not include the $49 port and departure tax. Of the three paddle wheel riverboats operated by the company, two are modern diesel engine vessels, while the handsomely restored *Delta Queen* – originally launched in 1927 – follows the steam-powered tradition.

TRAVEL AGENCIES

The *Times-Picayune* Sunday Travel section is a good place to search for discount travel deals. Local agencies that advertise discounted airline tickets include Omega World Travel (☎ 525-8900, 201 St Charles Ave) and Deviney's Associated Travel (☎ 837-9907, 2305 Veterans Memorial Pkwy) in Metairie.

A few full-service travel agencies offer more than just cheap airline seats. Student and budget travelers can pick up Eurail passes and other tickets from Council Travel (☎ 866-1767, 6363 St Charles Ave) at the Loyola University Student Center. In the French Quarter, Get Me Outta Here Travel (Map 2; ☎ 523-9006, 800-944-9006, 816 Burgundy St) is a personable agency that will hunt and peck to find the best fares and flight schedules. The Four Corners Travel Agency (☎ 822-6244, 1000 N Broad St) emerged in the 1960s to help minorities enjoy newfound equal access to public facilities.

AAA Travel Agency (☎ 838-7500, 800-452-7198, 3445 N Causeway Blvd), Metairie, offers complete travel planning for non-members and free maps and assistance for members. American Express (☎ 586-8201, 158 Baronne St) operates a full-service travel office and currency exchange.

Getting Around

The compact and level nature of the French Quarter and downtown riverfront areas make walking and bicycling the preferred ways to get around for most visitors. As in cities throughout the USA, public transit in New Orleans has deteriorated as transportation funds have been diverted to subsidize motorists. Nevertheless, visitors will find that the buses, streetcars and ferries generally serve the most popular attractions (with the glaring exception of Union Passenger Terminal). In fact, riding the streetcars or ferries is an exciting attraction in itself.

TO/FROM THE AIRPORT
New Orleans International Airport (Map 1) is in Kenner, 11 miles west of the city center.

Shuttle
Most visitors take the Airport Shuttle (☎ 522-3500) to and from the airport. It offers frequent service between the airport and downtown hotels for $10 per passenger each way. It's a cheap and courteous introduction to the city, though it can be time-consuming, especially if you are the last to be dropped off. At the airport, purchase tickets from agents in the baggage area below the arrival gates. You can purchase a return ticket at your hotel or just pay the driver. Be sure to call a day ahead to arrange for a departure pickup, which is typically two hours prior to your flight.

Bus
If your baggage is not too unwieldy, the Louisiana Transit Company (☎ 737-9611) offers the cheapest ride to downtown aboard its Jefferson Transit Airport Express, route E2, for $1.10. Passengers can exit at stops along Airline Hwy (US 61) and along Tulane Ave, but must flag the bus to board in most locations. The bus makes two regular stops: opposite door No 5 on the upper level of the airport's main terminal and downtown on Tulane Ave at Elks Place opposite the public library.

From 6 am to 6:30 pm, buses run every 10 minutes during peak weekday morning and evening hours and at 23-minute intervals midday. On weekends, buses run about every half hour. From 6:30 pm to midnight, buses only operate between the airport and Carrollton Ave, where you can continue to downtown on the Regional Transit Authority's No 39 Tulane bus for $1. There is room for two bikes on the bus' front rack.

Car
The quickest way to drive between the airport and downtown is to take I-10. If you're coming from downtown on I-10, take exit 223 for the airport; going to downtown, take exit 234, as the Superdome looms before you. An alternative route is Airline Hwy (US 61), a surface street with an endless series of stoplights.

Taxi
Taxi service to downtown costs $21 for one or two people, or $8 per passenger for three or more people. Note that if you have two people in your party, taking a taxi to town is only $1 more than the shuttle bus. More than four passengers are not allowed. Taxi stands are on the lower level, immediately outside the baggage claim area.

TO/FROM THE TRAIN STATION
New Orleans provides few options for arriving bus and train passengers. Although it's tempting to walk the short distance to the French Quarter, you should be wary of going solo through the deserted CBD (Central Business District) at night. Cab fare to the corner of Bourbon and Canal Sts costs about $3.50.

As incredible as it may seem, local buses do not directly serve Union Passenger Terminal. In front of the station, arriving passengers must search for the sheltered stop across broad Loyola Ave at Howard Ave. The No 17 S Claiborne Ave bus goes to the edge of the French Quarter at Canal and Rampart Sts ($1 fare plus 10¢ for a transfer).

During the weeks preceding Mardi Gras, a sign directs passengers to board one block down Loyola Ave at Julia St.

Although Union Passenger Terminal provides neither bicycle lockers nor secure racks, Amtrak is obligated to offer a baggage check service to passengers. You can check a bike as stored baggage by paying $1.50 per day.

BUS

The Regional Transit Authority (RTA) offers decent bus and streetcar service (see Streetcar, below). Call the RTA Rideline (☎ 248-3900) for bus route information. The only sure way to get bus schedules is to visit the RTA office, 101 Dauphine St, 4th floor.

Fares cost $1 and transfers are 10¢ extra, except on express buses, which charge a $1.25 fare. All buses require exact change. Consider purchasing an RTA Visitor Pass, good for unlimited travel on buses and streetcars. A one-day pass costs $4; a three-day pass is $8. Visitor passes are available from most hotels (ask the concierge) and at the RTA office.

From the French Quarter, most destinations are served by buses that stop at the intersection of Basin and Canal Sts. All stops have signs noting the route name and number – you may have to explore all four corners of an intersection to find the stop you want. The free *New Orleans Street Map*, available from information booths at the airport and downtown, shows most route numbers and lists the route names you can expect to see displayed on the front of the bus.

The Louisiana Transit Company (☎ 737-9611) operates Jefferson Transit buses, which serve the airport and Metairie, in Jefferson Parish. The Causeway Blvd route E5 carries bikes and connects Jefferson Hwy near the river with W Esplanade near the lake. The fare is $1.10.

You can cross the Greater New Orleans Bridge aboard the buses operated by Westside Transit (☎ 367-7433). Board the Lapalco Blvd bus in New Orleans at the corner of Loyola and Tulane Aves to cross to the Gretna terminal on the West Bank. Up to two bikes can be carried. The fare is $1.50.

STREETCAR

Streetcars are making a comeback in New Orleans. The two existing lines, described below, will soon be linked by a Canal St line. And rumor had it that the famous streetcar named *Desire*, which once provided Blanche Dubois with a ride and Tennessee Williams with a title, may return to action sometime in the foreseeable future. For decades that line, traveling from the French Quarter through the Faubourg Marigny and the Bywater, has been served by a bus.

St Charles Avenue Line

When the St Charles Ave Streetcar route opened as the New Orleans & Carrollton Railroad in 1835, it was the nation's second horse-drawn streetcar line. The line was also among the first systems in the nation to be electrified when New Orleans adopted electric traction in 1893.

Now it is one of the few streetcars to have survived the automobile era – it continues to serve local passengers and introduce visitors to the preferred commuter mode of the early 20th century, when fares cost a nickel. There is no need to worry about breakdowns when you hear the intermittent thunka-thunka sound – it's just the air compressor. The streetcars' brakes, doors and even the fare box operate on compressed air.

Check out the streetcar-era suburbs, with their Georgian architecture and ornate churches that evolved along the tracks extending from Canal St uptown to S Carrollton Ave (see the St Charles Avenue Streetcar Tour in the Things to See & Do

Streetcar: faster than a speeding crawfish

chapter). Of course, you can get off and explore along the way, as the line serves many of the attractions and walking tours listed in this book.

The fare is now $1 each way (exact change required), and a transfer to RTA buses costs 10¢. Both the one- and three-day Visitor Passes (see Bus, above) are valid on the streetcar. The 13-mile roundtrip from the corner of Canal and Carondelet Sts takes 1¹/2 hours. Although the St Charles streetcar operates 24 hours, with frequent peak-hour service, it only runs hourly from midnight to 4 am. Unfortunately, the streetcars are not wheelchair accessible.

Riverfront Line

In 1988 the wheelchair-accessible Riverfront Streetcar Line began operating vintage red cars on the old dockside rail corridor wedged between the levee and flood wall. The 2-mile route runs between the Old US Mint, in the lower end of the French Quarter near the Faubourg Marigny, and the upriver Convention Center, crossing Canal St on the way. The fare costs $1.25 (an additional quarter is required if you use an RTA transfer or Visitor Pass). It operates from 6 am to midnight.

CAR & MOTORCYCLE

Bringing a car to downtown New Orleans is a costly proposition that may actually hinder your visit and create headaches when dealing with the traffic and parking congestion. The narrow one-way streets and crowds in the French Quarter are definitely not conducive to driving, and hotels often charge extra for parking. The CBD is also crowded – many small lots use lifts to make room for more cars. Of course, a vehicle is essential if you are not staying in the downtown area or if you wish to take excursions not accessible by transit.

See Orientation in the Facts for the Visitor chapter for information on getting around on the streets of New Orleans.

Parking

Downtown on-street parking is typically for short-term use. Parking meters offer 12 minutes for a quarter, with a two-hour limit, from

CHRISTIAN HEEB

Those annoying backseat drivers

8 am to 6 pm Monday to Friday. Exceptions are numerous, so be sure to read all posted restrictions to avoid citations or towing. Enforcement is particularly efficient in areas where motorists are deemed capable of paying –for instance, the Warehouse District's premier restaurant and gallery area along Julia St supports two or three parking patrols.

Although free parking on the street is often available in the lower end of the French Quarter (try along Esplanade Ave), it's generally a better idea to pay to park. The Dixie Parking Garage (☎ 522-5975, 716 Iberville St), near the upper end of Bourbon St, charges $4 for the first hour or $11 for 24 hours. Other garages concentrated in the upper area of the Quarter charge similar rates.

The sound of car alarms from illegally parked vehicles being towed is frequently heard in the Quarter. If you park your car in a driveway, within 20 feet of a corner or crosswalk, within 15 feet of a fire hydrant or on a street-sweeping day, you will need about $75 (cash or credit card) plus cab fare (do not walk) to retrieve your car from the Auto Pound (☎ 565-7450, 401 N Claiborne Ave).

Rental

All the big rental companies can be found in New Orleans, particularly at the airport, along with a host of smaller or local operators. If you are staying downtown and only visiting the French Quarter – where hotel parking charges, parking fines and congested traffic make cars an encumbrance – you do not need a car. An option for visitors planning on taking an excursion is to pick up a rental car downtown when checking out of your hotel, then drop it off at the airport when you leave. Companies like Agency, Avis and Hertz have offices downtown, in addition to airport locations. In any case, airport rates are generally better than city ones.

Rates go up and availability lessens during special events or large conventions. It's always worth phoning around to see what's available. Booking ahead usually ensures the best rate. A compact car typically costs $30 to $40 a day or $150 to $200 a week. On top of that, there is a 13.75% tax and an optional $9 to $15 a day loss/damage-waiver or LDW (insurance). Some credit cards pick up the insurance tab, but check with your credit-card company to make sure. Also, your own automobile insurance policy may automatically cover your rental vehicle. If so, it's wise to carry a copy of your insurance policy. Basic liability insurance, which will cover damage you may cause to another vehicle, is required by law and is included with the price of renting a car. This is sometimes called third-party coverage. Most rates include unlimited mileage; if a rate looks like a real bargain, it may be because you're going to get hit for a mileage charge.

Most companies require that you be at least 25 years of age and have a major credit card as well as a valid license. A few agencies will accept a hefty cash deposit in lieu of a credit card. Some will also rent to those younger than 25, though younger drivers may have to pay extra.

Some of the larger agencies with outlets in or near the downtown area include the following:

Avis
   (☎ 523-4317, 800-831-2847) 2024 Canal St
Budget
   (Map 2; ☎ 467-2277, 800-527-0700) 1317 Canal St
Enterprise
   (☎ 522-7900, 800-325-8007) 1939 Canal St
Hertz
   (Map 4; ☎ 568-1645, 800-654-3131) 901 Convention Center Blvd

The lowest rates are available by renting older cars for local travel from Econo-Cars (Map 8; ☎ 827-0187, 4417 Earhart Blvd). The agency offers three-day minimum rentals at $55 or a week for $120.

TAXI

Except when parades are blocking streets and when peak events are taking place, hailing a cab is easy in downtown New Orleans. Taxi stands are located in front of most hotels, and cabs queue like predators to intercept late-night revelers on streets adjacent to Bourbon St.

One downside to staying Uptown or visiting the nightclubs is the difficulty in hailing a cab. You will usually need to call. Also, it's best to give an address and cross streets rather than just cross streets.

Telephoned requests for a taxi are typically quickly met, yet none of the taxi services can be recommended as being completely reliable (see Warning, below). White Fleet Cabs (☎ 948-6605) and United Cabs (☎ 522-9771) will pick up passengers at the airport or anywhere within New Orleans. Metairie Cab (☎ 835-4242) specifically serves the outlying suburbs. Rules are made to be broken, but don't plan on taking a taxi with a crowd of more than four people. Fares in New Orleans cost $2.10 for the flag drop plus about $1 per mile. A 15% tip should be added to the fare.

Warning

As some stranded travelers have discovered, it can sometimes be pointless to call ahead for a taxi pickup, especially during Mardi

Gras or Jazz Fest. Drivers are choosy and may actually decline to pick up a passenger if the destination is a bit out of the way. During Carnival parades, when travel is especially difficult, many drivers refuse to travel beyond the downtown area after being hailed on the street.

Another problem is the restricted service area of the cab companies. One passenger reported calling ahead to United Cab to schedule an early-morning ride from a rental car return lot in Kenner to the airport terminal. No cab was waiting at the prescribed time. After the passenger had made two additional calls and missed the flight, the dispatcher explained that United Cabs do not serve Kenner – except for pickups at the airport.

MISSISSIPPI RIVER FERRIES

The cheapest way to cruise the Mississippi River is aboard one of the state-run ferries. Ferries operate daily between Canal St and the West Bank community of Algiers and between Jackson Ave and Gretna, another West Bank suburb. Another ferry travels between Chalmette, where the battlefield is, and lower Algiers. All begin service at either 5:45 or 6 am and continue to 9 or 9:15 pm, except the Canal St Ferry, which operates until 11:45 pm or midnight. In the vicinity of New Orleans, the ferries are free; farther afield (see the Excursions chapter), the toll is $1. Boats leave the terminals at the following times:

Canal St – on the hour and half hour

Algiers – on the quarter hour and three-quarters hour

Jackson St – on the hour and half hour

Gretna – on the quarter hour and three-quarters hour

Chalmette – every quarter hour

BICYCLE

On the positive side of the ledger, New Orleans is flat and relatively compact. On the negative side are the heavy traffic and potholes, which make fat tires a near necessity. Oppressive summer heat and humidity also discourage some bicyclists.

Routes

Residents typically follow either Burgundy or Dauphine Sts to traverse the French Quarter between the CBD and Faubourg Marigny, where the bicycle is the mode of choice. Esplanade Ave is somewhat busy, but the cars can go around you as you pedal from the French Quarter to the Fair Grounds or City Park. At City Park you should avoid Weisner Blvd where it crosses I-610 and instead travel through the western side of the park to Lakeshore Dr. Roads and paths along the lake are typically bicycle friendly. Racers favor workouts in City Park on the Roosevelt Mall oval and along Lakeshore Dr.

Many visitors travel from the French Quarter through the Warehouse District on Magazine St. Prytania St is a good choice for crossing through the Lower Garden District. The rest of Uptown is readily traversed, from Jackson Ave to Audubon Park, on quiet residential streets such as Camp and Chestnut Sts. A complete circuit of town can be completed from Uptown by following either Napoleon Ave to Octavia St, or State St to the neutral ground (median) bike path on Jeff Davis Parkway leading to Bayou St John. Return to the French Quarter on Esplanade Ave. It's a good idea to have a bike light if you plan to return in the evening (especially during the short winter daylight hours).

From S Carrollton Ave, the River Levee offers a continuous off-road bicycle route upriver to near the airport.

Bicycling on the West Bank is a breeze. You can take the Canal St Ferry to Algiers, follow the levee downriver on Patterson Rd and detour around the US Navy Hospital before returning to Patterson Rd via Odean St. Continue to the Chalmette Ferry, but beware that returning on the St Bernard Hwy is not for beginners – you might want to go back in the same direction.

Rental

Bicycles can be rented for around $15 to $20 a day. Joe's Bike Shop (Map 8; ☎ 821-2350, 2501 Tulane Ave), next to the Dixie Brewery, offers used bikes for $13 a day. Rental bikes are also available from French Quarter

Bicycles (Map 2; ☎ 529-3136, 522 Dumaine St) and nearby in the Faubourg Marigny from Bicycle Michael's (Map 3; ☎ 945-9505, 618 Frenchmen St). In the Riverbend, try GNO Cyclery (Map 7; ☎ 861-0023, 1426 S Carrollton Ave), at Willow St.

See Organized Tours, below, for information on tours offered to cyclists.

Public Transport

You can readily transcend the river barrier by incorporating the ferry service into your rides. All state-operated ferries offer free transportation for bikes. Bicyclists board ahead of cars by walking down the left lane of the ramp to the swinging gate. You must, however, wait for the cars to exit before leaving.

Unfortunately, the RTA does not allow bikes on buses and streetcars. In Jefferson Parish, three bus routes offer fold-down racks, which carry up to two bikes on the front of the bus: Louisiana Transit's Airport Express route E2 and Causeway Blvd route E5 (call ☎ 737-7433 for information) and Westside Transit's Lapalco Blvd route between Gretna and New Orleans (call ☎ 367-7433 for information).

WALKING & JOGGING

The compact French Quarter and adjacent downtown hotels are ideally suited to the pedestrian. In fact, there is no better way to participate in the action along Bourbon St or to appreciate the local architecture than on foot. Aside from the French Quarter, some of the other areas that are best toured on foot include the Warehouse District galleries around Julia St; anywhere along the river levee; and the Faubourg Marigny, wedged between Esplanade and Elysian Fields Aves below the French Quarter. Should a sudden thundershower catch you without an umbrella, many shops offer plastic ponchos for less than $1.

To walk through the Garden District or Audubon Park, ride the St Charles Ave streetcar from downtown. To leave the frenzy and noise behind, consider taking the Canal St Ferry to Algiers for a stroll through quiet neighborhoods or along the West Bank levee, which offers vistas of New Orleans and river shipping.

The best uninterrupted jogging paths are along either the levee above Audubon Park or the West Bank levee. Joggers have also worn pathways between the St Charles Ave streetcar tracks. Be sure to run facing the approaching streetcar so you will be aware of its approach and be able to step aside while it passes. Many joggers also circle the Superdome on the plaza level – each lap is slightly more than a quarter mile.

Safety

Beware that pedestrians do not have the right-of-way and will find their lives in danger should they attempt to challenge motorists. Local motorists consider it a courtesy to honk at pedestrians in the street before speeding by – only out-of-state drivers are inclined to slow down or stop.

See Dangers & Annoyances in the Facts for the Visitor chapter for more on pedestrian safety.

ORGANIZED TOURS

Few cities offer the variety of worthwhile organized tours available to New Orleans visitors. Although independent travelers sometimes scoff at being herded about, group tours can be an entertaining crash course on local history and architecture and can serve to orient new visitors to potentially unsafe areas.

If you do decide to take a tour, choosing one after perusing the tour companies' ubiquitous handbills may call for the eenie-meenie-mynie-moe method. Some people habitually let a hotel concierge make a decision for them, but before you do that, be warned that concierges don't generally spend their free time taking walking tours, and some of them may actually receive kickbacks for recommending a particular company's tours. This not only can add to the price for you, but it also unfairly limits your choices. In some of the larger hotels, tour companies like Grayline actually set up 'information' desks where you can be certain you won't receive honest advice about competing companies.

JOHN ELK III

Mule-drawn carriage

For swamp and plantation tours, see the Excursions chapter.

Walking Tours

Knowledgeable volunteers affiliated with the nonprofit Friends of the Cabildo (☎ 523-3939) lead daily two-hour French Quarter walks emphasizing history, architecture and folklore. Tours cost $10 for adults, $8 for seniors and children over 12. As a bonus, the price includes admission to two of the four Louisiana State Museums: the Cabildo, the Presbytere, the Old US Mint or the 1850 House. Tours start at the 1850 House Museum Store (523 St Ann St) at 10 am and 1:30 pm Tuesday to Sunday and at 1:30 pm Monday.

Historic New Orleans Walking Tours (☎ 947-2120) has a variety of tours that are dense with information. The company was founded by author Robert Florence, one of the city's leading authorities on cemeteries, and his two-hour cemetery/voodoo tour

($15/13), which includes a visit to St Louis Cemetery No 1 and Miriam Chamani's Voodoo Spiritual Temple, is highly recommended. The company also offers a Garden District tour ($14/12), including Lafayette Cemetery No 1, and a French Quarter Mystique tour ($12/10) that delves into the facts and myths of the Vieux Carré.

Historical accuracy is foremost for volunteer guides from the nonprofit Save Our Cemeteries (☎ 588-9357, 888-721-7493, PO Box 68105, New Orleans, LA 70158). The only drawback is that tours are not scheduled every day. The group offers one-hour tours of St Louis Cemetery No 1 on Sunday at 10 am for $12/10 (call for a reservation – essential! – and meeting location). Unreservable tours of the Uptown Lafayette No 1 cemetery cost $6 and meet at the Washington St gate, between Prytania and Coliseum Sts, on Monday, Wednesday and Friday at 10:30 am. Proceeds are used to restore decaying crypts.

Robert Batson's well-regarded Gay Heritage Tour (☎ 945-6789) gets high marks for its humor and historical insight. The 2½-hour walk through the French Quarter is chockfull of colorful anecdotes about local characters, including Tennessee Williams, Ellen DeGeneres and Clay Shaw. Everyone is more than welcome to come along, regardless of sexual orientation. Tours depart from the Alternatives shop (909 Bourbon St) on Saturday at 2 pm and cost $15 per person.

Carriage Rides

Tour guides offering mule-drawn carriage rides through the French Quarter are certified by the city – which means that they have at least a modest understanding of the Quarter's history. However, you should beware that Mark Twain's admonition, 'Get your facts first, then you can distort them all you please,' certainly applies to the carriage-guide business. Historical embellishment is commonplace.

Carriages depart day and night, until midnight, from Jackson Square. You will not be disappointed if you consider the tours to be fun orientation rides. Half-hour tours for up to four people cost $40.

African American Heritage Tours

This company (☎ 504-288-3478) offers three-hour city-wide van tours that explore the African-American heritage of New Orleans, the USA's most African city. The company also gives van tours of a French-speaking Cajun village, with an emphasis on zydeco music, and plantation tours. The van will swing by to pick you up at your hotel. Tickets cost $30 for the city tour, $45 for the Cajun tour and $50 for the plantation tour ($75 with lunch included).

Riverboat Cruises

Take a paddle wheel cruise downriver aboard the *Creole Queen* and visit the 1815 Battle of New Orleans site at Chalmette, a unit of Jean Lafitte National Historic Park (☎ 589-4430; see the Things to See & Do chapter). A brief walking tour of the battlegrounds and Beauregard House is included in the 2¹/₂-hour excursion. Cruises leave daily at 10:30 am and 2 pm from the Spanish Plaza at the foot of Canal St. Tours cost $14 for adults and $7 for children ages three to 12. Another, more mundane boat, the *Cajun Queen*, offers three daily 90-minute sightseeing cruises downriver, departing from the Aquarium Dock at 11 am, 1:15 and 3:30 pm. Tickets cost $12 for adults and $6 for children.

Reservations and information about either cruise are available from New Orleans Tours (☎ 592-0560, 524-0814). Tickets may be purchased at the Aquarium Dock, the Spanish Plaza Dock and selected hotels.

Discordant calliope sounds announce the boarding of the *Natchez*, a 1975 steam-powered paddle wheeler, which departs for two-hour harbor cruises from a dock behind the Jackson Brewery at 11:30 am and 2:30 pm daily. Tickets cost $14.75 for adults and $7.25 for children between six and 12 years old. Tickets are sold at the dock by the New Orleans Steamboat Company (☎ 586-8777).

Things to See & Do

New Orleans is wedged between the Mississippi River and Lake Pontchartrain – only about 5 miles separates the river from the lake. The primary area of interest for the visitor hugs the river from the Faubourg Marigny, through the French Quarter, the Uptown area to the Riverbend, hooking inland to City Park and the Fair Grounds. Most attractions are concentrated within the French Quarter, plus a few areas along easily traveled corridors served by public transit.

HIGHLIGHTS

No city in the US offers such an extensive district of historic architecture as the **French Quarter**. At its heart is the French and Spanish colonial heritage of **Jackson Square**, offering age-old architectural symmetry and modern cultural chaos. The formal garden is a pleasant rest stop. It's easy to spend a day here acquainting yourself with New Orleans' history at the Louisiana State Museums, catch the ever-changing street scene from a sidewalk bench or café or enjoy a cool breeze while watching ships from the river levee.

Within the upper Quarter are the signature tourist areas that the whole world equates with New Orleans. The bright lights and noisy bars along **Bourbon St** are in stark contrast to **Royal St** and its premier antique shops and galleries. Both streets offer some of the finest old-line Creole restaurants in the city. Along Bourbon St, continuous nighttime musical entertainment and strip-tease acts define the Quarter's bawdy character. If the haughty shops along Royal St are too regal for your tastes, try the **French Market**, which houses the Farmer's Market and Flea Market, offering inexpensive goods from Louisiana and around the world (see the Shopping chapter).

Blowin' on the River

The **Mississippi River** holds a magnetic attraction for most visitors. Take the free ferry from the foot of Canal St to Algiers and back for a panoramic perspective of New Orleans from the river. Most visitors are amazed by the tremendous traffic of oceangoing ships and barges that ply the muddy water.

In contrast to the French Quarter's crowded architecture are the elegant mansions of **Uptown**. The earliest settlement was established immediately above downtown in what is now referred to as the **Lower Garden District**. For most visitors, however, the emblematic portion of the American sector is the **Garden District**. As they segregated themselves from Creole society, the wealthy Americans who had profited from the antebellum plantation system made their imprint on the city by building ostentatious mansions. Like the French Quarter, the Garden District has been deemed a National Historic Landmark worthy of preservation by the National Park Service (NPS). An Uptown jaunt almost always calls for a ride aboard the historic and picturesque **St Charles Ave streetcar**.

The eerie mystique of Anne Rice's novels has its origins in New Orleans, her hometown, where live oaks shrouded in Spanish moss shade beautiful and ancient **cemeteries**, which are open to visitors who appreciate the elegance of decay. Numerous **voodoo museums** and temples also bear witness to the Crescent City's exotic otherworldliness.

Early maps show swamps immediately beyond the French Quarter walls. One reminder of this earlier era is **Bayou St John**, which cuts through a historic residential area near **City Park**. Alternatively, the Cajun swamp exhibit at the **Audubon Zoo** offers a glimpse of both the wetlands Cajun culture and the natural wildlife of the bayou. Farther afield, but accessible by public transit, is the small swamp preserve within the city limits at the **Louisiana Nature Center**. Other excursion highlights are detailed in the Excursions chapter.

Jazz music draws legions of musical pilgrims to the city's museums, where **jazz exhibits** detail the history of New Orleans' greatest export. For live performances, the visitor can haunt any of a bevy of nightclubs

(see the Entertainment chapter), or plan a trip to the annual New Orleans Jazz & Heritage Festival (see the Facts for the Visitor chapter).

Of course, **food** is also a highlight of any visit to New Orleans – see Places to Eat for details.

FRENCH QUARTER & TREMÉ DISTRICT (MAP 2)

Founded by and named for the French, the Quarter is surprisingly not notable for its French architecture. With the exception of the Ursuline Convent (1745), the oldest building in New Orleans, French-designed buildings all burned down during a pair of fires that swept through the district. The first of these, in 1788, reduced more than 800 buildings to ashes, including all businesses, mansions, the Cabildo and the church. After a second fire in 1794, the Cabildo (or Spanish Council chamber) mandated use of fire-resistant materials for multistory buildings. Brick, or *briquette entre poteaux* (bricks between posts), covered with plaster became the signature architectural style in the Quarter. While a few building designs retained some French influences, a distinctly Spanish character emerged in the rebuilt city. Among the most readily identified Spanish elements are the broad window openings crowned by graceful arches. Above many entrances, you will note handsome, fan-shaped transoms.

During the last 50 years, preservation edicts have maintained much of the historic building stock throughout the Quarter, but the preservationists also brought about social change. A failure to preserve the Quarter's social character has led some to charge that historic preservation, with its emphasis on buildings not people, has created a Creole Disneyland. In part, they are right. Since 1937, when the French Quarter acquired historic-district status, the population in the Quarter has plummeted from more than 12,000 to about 5000 today. There has been an even greater decline in the proportion of blacks and children in the population mix.

Walking Tour
Obviously, architecture has a lot to do with the beauty of the French Quarter, and an

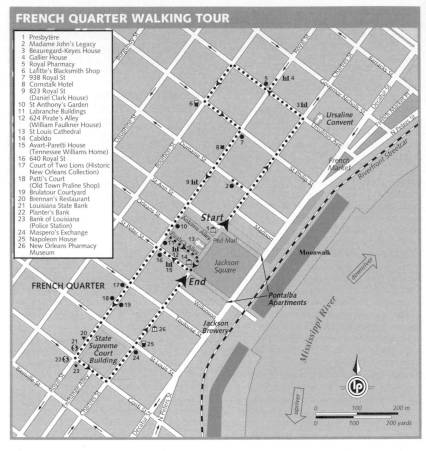

FRENCH QUARTER WALKING TOUR

1 Presbytère
2 Madame John's Legacy
3 Beauregard-Keyes House
4 Gallier House
5 Royal Pharmacy
6 Lafitte's Blacksmith Shop
7 938 Royal St
8 Cornstalk Hotel
9 823 Royal St
   (Daniel Clark House)
10 St Anthony's Garden
11 Labranche Buildings
12 624 Pirate's Alley
   (William Faulkner House)
13 St Louis Cathedral
14 Cabildo
15 Avart-Peretti House
   (Tennessee Williams Home)
16 640 Royal St
17 Court of Two Lions (Historic
   New Orleans Collection)
18 Patti's Court
   (Old Town Praline Shop)
19 Brulatour Courtyard
20 Brennan's Restaurant
21 Louisiana State Bank
22 Planter's Bank
23 Bank of Louisiana
   (Police Station)
24 Maspero's Exchange
25 Napoleon House
26 New Orleans Pharmacy
   Museum

initial walk through its narrow streets and passageways is primarily an appreciation of the buildings. But the French Quarter also has more mysterious charms. Intriguing stories can be sensed, if not always seen, and this certainly enhances the Quarter's lure. After following the course outlined in this tour, you are strongly encouraged to wander through other areas of the Quarter. Some sights given just a cursory description here are examined in greater detail later in this chapter.

Begin your walk at the Presbytère on Jackson Square and head down Chartres St.

At the corner of Dumaine St, go left. Halfway up the block stands **Madame John's Legacy**, 632 Dumaine St, run by the Louisiana State Museum. This French colonial house was built in 1788 and acquired its name when George Washington Cable used it as the setting in his story 'Tite Poullette.' Its raised basement of briquette entre poteaux construction offered protection from floods. An iron gate set in the brick wall across the street is graced by **devil's pitchforks**, a common motif in the Quarter that continues to keep trespassers and evil spirits at bay.

Return to Chartres St. At the corner of Ursulines St, the **Ursuline Convent**, 1114 Chartres St, is partly obstructed from view by a wall surrounding its grounds. Built in 1745-50, it's the oldest structure in the French Quarter and the only French colonial building still standing in New Orleans. (See separate heading for more on the convent.) Directly across Chartres St, the **Beauregard-Keyes House**, 1113 Chartres St, dates to 1826 and combines Creole- and American-style design. Civil War General PGT Beauregard rented rooms here after his wife died, and author Francis Parkinson Keyes lived here from 1944 to 1970.

Walk along Ursulines St to Royal St and turn right. Halfway up the block, the **Gallier House**, 1118 Royal St, is a Greek Revival town house, built in 1857 by architect James Gallier Jr for his family. The house is now a museum (see separate heading, later, for more information). Cross Royal St and back-track to the corner of Ursulines St to take a quick peek inside the **Royal Pharmacy**, 1101 Royal St. The soda fountain, a perfectly preserved relic from the USA's halcyon malt shop days, is no longer in use. The owners of the pharmacy feel it's just too beautiful to pull out.

Turn right on Ursulines St and then left on Bourbon St. The ramshackle one-story structure on the corner of St Philip St is a great little tavern called **Lafitte's Blacksmith Shop**, 941 Bourbon St. Believe it or not, this is a National Historic Landmark, and although stories connecting it with the pirate Jean Lafitte are probably not true (legend has it he ran a blacksmith shop here with his brother), the little cottage stands out for its exposed brick-between-post construction. It is believed that the building dates to the end of the 18th century. Have a drink and then walk down St Philip to Royal St.

When it comes to classic New Orleans postcard images, Royal St takes the cake, and what makes the street so picturesque is that many of its structures are graced by beautiful cast-iron galleries. As you walk along Royal St, keep an eye on the second- and third-floor galleries, where a variety of lush plants hang from ornate cast-iron.

At the corner of Royal and St Philip Sts, the rusty cast-iron galleries at **938 Royal St** were added in 1858 to the three-story brick apartments. This attractive building stands out among its neighbors, as it has yet to be restored in the quaint manner of many French Quarter structures. Half a century ago, most buildings in the French Quarter had a similar weathered, if not dilapidated, look. Half a block up, on the other side of the street, stands the **Cornstalk Hotel**, 915 Royal St. It's one of the most frequently photographed structures in New Orleans – or at least the cornstalk-decorated cast-iron fence in front is (see the Places to Sleep chapter for details on staying here).

The house at **823 Royal St** belonged to Daniel Clark, an Irish-born merchant who aided Thomas Jefferson in negotiating the Louisiana Purchase. His lasting notoriety came when he wounded Governor Claiborne in a duel brought about by charges that he was involved in the Aaron Burr conspiracy. Continue on Royal St to Orleans St, where lush tropical plants fill **St Anthony's Garden**, behind **St Louis Cathedral**. Vistas of the cathedral's steeple are available from anywhere along Orleans Ave, which divides the French Quarter in half.

Alongside the garden, **Pirate's Alley** is an inviting, shaded walkway that calls for a little detour. The name is a purely romantic one, as the little alleyway never harbored pirate activity – Jean Lafitte and his gang were long gone when the passageway was first opened in 1831. The first buildings to the right, 622-624 Pirate's Alley, are just a few of the

Iron pitchforks keep out

Labranche Buildings, which wrap around Royal St to St Peter St. Note the original wrought-iron balconies, which date to the 1840s. Continue on Pirate's Alley, and later you'll catch another look at the Labranche buildings around the block. In 1925, William Faulkner lived at **624 Pirate's Alley** (then called Orleans Alley). The small but charming **Faulkner House** bookstore opened here in 1990 and very quickly became a focal point in New Orleans literary circles. Poet Andrei Codrescu and novelist Richard Ford frequently drop in to visit owner Joe DeSalvo.

Continue down Pirate's Alley, skirting the cathedral and circumventing the **Cabildo**. (These sites require more time than a walking tour allows, and they're covered in detail with other Jackson Square sites later.) Head up St Peter St back toward Royal St. At 632 St Peter, the **Avart-Peretti House** is where Tennessee Williams lived in 1946-7, when he was writing his most famous play, *A Streetcar Named Desire*. On the opposite side of the street there are more of the impressive **Labranche Buildings**, at 621-639 St Peter St

and 700-712 Royal St. On these facades, the original wrought-iron balconies were replaced with ornate cast iron in the 1850s.

While on the corner of Royal and St Peter Sts, also take note of New Orleans' first 'skyscraper,' at **640 Royal St**. Begun in 1795, the structure grew to three stories tall by 1811 (a fourth floor was added in 1876). The building's 1811 owner, Dr Yves LeMonnier, left his initials in the wrought-iron balcony that overlooks the street corner. Until that time, building in New Orleans was generally limited to two floors, for fear that taller buildings couldn't be supported on 'swampy' soil.

Continue on Royal St. From the solid line of facades built to the sidewalk, or *banquette*, it's hard to imagine that this block offers significant open space to merchants and residents. However, large interior courtyards are hidden behind many entryways. Many of these courtyards are open to the public and are worth venturing into, as the Creole custom was to orient a home toward the rear, with more personal style accorded to interiors where families spent most of

Pirate's Alley

their time; by contrast, facades were relatively unostentatious and deliberately unrevealing. During business hours, the Old Town Praline Shop, 627 Royal St, affords entry to **Patti's Court** for a behind-the-scenes peek. Some courtyards are now poster shops, but you can go in without buying anything. You can also enjoy a pleasant coffee or a meal in an alfresco courtyard setting at the Royal Blend Café or the Court of Two Sisters restaurant (see the Places to Eat chapter).

At the corner of Toulouse St, the **Court of Two Lions**, 541 Royal St, was built by Jean François Merieult in 1798. The Toulouse St side is flanked by marble lions atop the entry posts. Merieult built the neighboring house at 527-533 Royal St in 1792 – it is a rare survivor of the 1794 fire. Now it's home to the **Historic New Orleans Collection**. Organized tours of the house and adjacent structures are available (see the Getting Around chapter). You can also enter the distinctive **Brulatour Courtyard**, 520 Royal St, which was built by Bordeaux native François Seignouret after he fought in the Battle of New Orleans. It served his wine importing and fine furniture manufacturing businesses. The courtyard's name came from merchant Pierre Brulatour, who purchased the house in 1870.

Many scenes from the movie *JFK* were filmed at the massive **State Supreme Court Building**. Opened in 1909, the white marble and terra-cotta facade is out of character with the rest of the Quarter's design and scale. Across the street, the famed **Brennan's Restaurant**, 417 Royal St, has occupied this spot since 1955. Vincent Rillieux, the great-grandfather of artist Edgar Degas, owned the property and may have commissioned the 1802 construction. The building housed the Banque de la Louisiane, the first bank established after the Louisiana Purchase, and in 1841 became home to boy wonder chess champ Paul Morphy. At Royal and Conti Sts, **Louisiana State Bank**, 401 Royal St, was designed by nationally acclaimed architect Benjamin Henry Latrobe in 1820, shortly before his death from yellow fever.

Directly across Conti St, the **Planters Bank**, 343 Royal St, is another former bank built by Rillieux shortly after the great fire

of 1794. Its wrought-iron balconies and knee braces are notable examples of Spanish colonial design. The Waldorn antique shop has been on the premises since 1881. Across the street, take a peek at the interior of the Greek Revival-style **Bank of Louisiana**, 332 Royal St, built in 1826. The building has served in many capacities since the bank was liquidated in 1867, including a stint as the State Capitol. Now it houses a police station and a visitor center.

Head down Conti St to Chartres St and turn left. A block up, **Maspero's Exchange**, 440 Chartres St, is a restaurant formerly known as La Bourse de Maspero, the slave-trading house and coffee shop of Pierre Maspero. (See separate heading for more information.) Across St Louis St, **Napoleon House**, 500 Chartres St, is an ancient bar whose crumbling stucco walls would have some intriguing stories to tell – despite their silence, one great story about the building has become part of French Quarter lore. At the beginning of the 19th century, the building's owner, former Mayor Nicholas Girod, plotted to rescue Napoleon Bonaparte from his prison on St Helena and to keep the deposed emperor in an apartment above the bar. The emperor unfortunately died before the plan was carried out.

Another half block up Chartres St, you'll see a sign for La Pharmacie Francaise, which in 1823 was run by the USA's first licensed pharmacist. New Orleans is very proud of its pharmaceutical heritage, and the shop is now the **Pharmacy Museum**, 514 Chartres St (see separate heading).

From here it's just a block or so back to Jackson Square, where you can find a bench and watch free entertainment almost any time of day.

Jackson Square

Jackson Square stands out as the loveliest public space in the USA. The park itself is well-groomed and pleasant enough, but the surrounding architecture is what makes Jackson Square visually spectacular. A striking symmetry is created by the two Pontalba Buildings flanking the square and the nearly identical Cabildo and Presbytere structures

LEE FOSTER

Jackson Square

on either side of St Louis Cathedral, which makes a perfect centerpiece.

Jackson Square thrives as the central, and most important, *entrepôt* (trading place) for visitors to the French Quarter, as it was meant to when Audrien de Pauger laid out the city in 1721. A host of street musicians, artists, tarot card readers and mimes compete for the attention of tourists milling about the banquette. This cultural scene, while not necessarily representative of the best entertainment the city has to offer, does present a constantly changing visual stimulus.

Beneath the mansard roofs of the Cabildo and Presbytère are the major collections of the **Louisiana State Museum**. In the lower Pontalba Building, the Louisiana State Museum (www.crt.state.la.us/crt/museum/lsmnet3.htm) offers tours of a restored 1850 household.

Admission to each Louisiana State Museum is $5 for adults, $4 for seniors and students, free for children under 12. You can readily overdose on museums by buying a combination ticket to all the Louisiana State Museum properties, including the Presbytère, Cabildo, 1850 House, Old US Mint (nearby on Esplanade Ave at Decatur St) and Madame John's Legacy for $10, or $7.50 for students and seniors.

Cabildo The first Cabildo was a single-story structure destroyed by the Good Friday fire of 1788. Reconstruction was delayed by the city's more pressing needs for a prison, cathedral, and police and fire stations. It's a good thing that architect Don Gilberto Guillemard, who was busy with the St Louis Cathedral, did not hurry the reconstruction. The December 1794 fire would likely have destroyed a new Cabildo and the almost completed cathedral as well. Tenants in the rebuilt Cabildo, dedicated in 1799, included the Spanish Council (for which the building is named), the City Hall government from 1803 to 1853, the Louisiana Supreme Court from 1853 to 1910 and the Louisiana State Museum from 1911 to present.

Three floors of exhibits emphasize the significance of New Orleans in a regional, national and even international context. It is a challenge to see it all in part of a day. You might try to quickly survey the lower floor, paying attention to the pre-Columbian Indian artifacts and the colonial exhibits that most interest you. You can overlook Jackson Square from the Sala Capitular (Spanish Council room) on the 2nd floor. This is where the Louisiana Purchase documents were signed, transferring the extensive territory from Napoleonic France to the US. Other displays depict the Battle of New Orleans, including the role of free blacks and members of the Choctaw tribe in Major General Andrew Jackson's force, which decisively defeated General Packenham's British troops in 1814. The 3rd-floor exhibits of racial and ethnic groups from the American period are among the most interesting, with artifacts and shocking depictions of African slaves next to Civil War military displays that show free people of color in support of the Confederacy.

The Cabildo (☎ 568-6968, 701 Chartres St) is open Tuesday through Sunday from 9 am to 5 pm.

Presbytère Although architect Gilberto Guillemard originally designed the Presbytère to be a rectory for the St Louis Cathedral in 1791, the building was never directly used by the church after it was completed in 1813. Instead, the cathedral administrators rented the building to the city for use as a courthouse before selling it to them in 1853. Ownership was transferred to the Louisiana State Museum in 1911.

In contrast to the Cabildo's collection (which signifies the external impact of New Orleans), the Presbytère primarily showcases the internal history of the city and its citizens. In addition, the museum includes local art and furniture treasures. One display showcases the locally produced Newcomb pottery, which was part of the influential Arts & Crafts movement of the early 20th century. The work features decorations based on Southern flora and fauna. Photographs and maps of the great flood of 1927 follow maritime exhibits on riverboat commerce. Somewhat out of place and disorganized is the exhibit on Louisiana native son Zachary Taylor, a plantation slave owner from Baton Rouge and a Whig party politician who was elected as the 12th US president in 1848.

The Presbytère (☎ 568-6968, 751 Chartres St) is open Tuesday through Sunday from 9 am until 5 pm.

St Louis Cathedral During the Christmas midnight mass, the Cathedral of St Louis, King of France, is the most popular spot in the city. In 1722, a hurricane destroyed the first of three churches built here by the St Louis Parish, established in 1720. Architect Gilberto Guillemard dedicated the present cathedral on Christmas Eve in 1794, only weeks after it was saved from a devastating fire by a combination of shifting winds and the firebreak provided by the empty lot where the Cabildo burned in 1788. Extensive remodeling from 1849 to 1851 was designed by French-trained architect JNB DePouilly. In 1850, the cathedral was designated as the metropolitan church of the Archdiocese of New Orleans. Pope Paul VI awarded it the rank of minor basilica in 1964.

Buried in the cathedral is its Spanish benefactor, Don Andrés Almonaster y Roxas, who also financed the Cabildo and the initial construction of the Presbytère – not bad for a minor official who arrived in New Orleans as a poor Spanish notary. He gained his wealth from rents after he acquired real estate facing the Place d'Armes. His daughter, Madame Pontalba, later built the Pontalba Buildings to complete Jackson Square (see the boxed text 'Madame Pontalba').

For information about daily masses, contact the Oblates of Mary Immaculate (☎ 525-9585, 615 Père Antoine Alley). The cathedral is open for tours 9 am to 5 pm daily, 1 to 5 pm Sunday. Donations are accepted.

1850 House The 1850 House is one of the apartments in the lower Pontalba Building. Madame Micaëla Pontalba, daughter of Don Andrés Almonaster y Roxas, continued her father's improvements around Jackson Square by building the long rows of red-brick apartments flanking the upper and lower portions of the square. She was also responsible for renaming the once barren

Interior of St Louis Cathedral

RICHARD CUMMINS

parade grounds, the Place d'Armes, after her friend Andrew Jackson. Initial plans for the apartments were drawn by the noted architect James Gallier Sr (see the Gallier House Museum section). In 1927, the lower Pontalba Building was bequeathed by William Ratcliffe Irby to the Louisiana State Museum.

(In 1930, the city acquired the upper Pontalba Building, where Micaëla once lived.)

Now, knowledgeable volunteers from the Friends of the Cabildo give tours of the apartment, which includes a central court and servants' quarters with period furnishings throughout. Innovations include the use of

Madame Pontalba

The woman behind the Pontalba Buildings on Jackson Square, Madame Micaëla Pontalba, is one of New Orleans' more remarkable historic characters. She is often mistakenly referred to as a baroness – a title she distinctly rejected when she divorced her husband before he inherited the title of baron from his father. Her wealth and power have caused many writers to make the presumption of nobility, and that the present American Embassy in Paris was originally built as her private home only adds to her aristocratic mystique. In reality, she attained her great status by fusing the wealth of the two richest families in Louisiana (Almonaster and Pontalba) through her own shrewd dealings after an ill-fated attempt on her life by her father-in-law.

Micaëla was born in 1795, when her father, Don Almonaster y Roxas, was 71 years old. Almonaster had arrived in Louisiana a penniless Spanish notary in 1769 and amassed a fortune through land transfers and rental income. In fact, Almonaster's contribution to the beautification of Jackson Square far exceeded his daughter's later additions, for it was Almonaster who commissioned the Cabildo, St Louis Cathedral and the Presbytère. But Micaëla led the more interesting life.

At 16, Micaëla married her cousin, Joseph Xavier Célestin Delfau de Pontalba and moved to Paris to live with his family. It was an arranged marriage, and although the couple had three children together, they seem to have developed no affection for one another. Before their first son was born, Célestin asked Micaëla to sign over her fortune to him – apparently he was afraid she might die in childbirth – and she refused. In 1834, they were separated.

Micaëla, however, was unwilling to give up her share of the Almonaster riches. Angered by her demands, her husband's father, Baron Joseph Xavier de Pontalba, shot her while she was visiting in France. Thinking that she was dead, the Baron turned the gun on himself and committed suicide. Though seriously injured, she survived and left Paris with two of her three sons for her native New Orleans in 1848, sans title but with her wealth intact. After commissioning – some say even designing – the upper and lower Pontalba Buildings and making Jackson Square the most elegant public square in the USA, Madame Pontalba returned to Paris, where she died in 1874.

brick imported from the East Coast, extended porches to create covered walkways, and the upstairs galleries, with cast-iron railings in place of wrought iron. Repeated along the railings are the initials AP, signifying the union of the Almonaster and Pontalba wealth.

The 1850 House (☎ 568-6968, 523 St Ann St) is open for self-guided tours Tuesday to Sunday from 9 am to 5 pm. Volunteer guides are available Tuesday through Friday 11 am to noon and 1 to 2 pm, and Saturday from 11 am to noon.

Jackson Monument Following Madame Pontalba's transformation of muddy parade grounds into the beautiful Jackson Square, Clark Mills sculpted the centerpiece equestrian statue honoring General Andrew Jackson, Battle of New Orleans hero and US president from 1829 to 1837. Citizens unveiled the 10-ton bronze statue in 1856 – replicas later appeared in Washington, DC, and Nashville, Tennessee. The inscription, 'The Union Must and Shall be Preserved,' was an added – and locally unwelcome – sentiment from General Benjamin Butler, the Yankee commander of occupying forces in 1862.

Old US Mint

Even if you wouldn't give a nickel to see where coins were once minted, the Old US Mint's foremost exhibits on New Orleans jazz and the city's Carnival history should get your attention. After serving as a US Mint, federal prison and US Coast Guard office, the building was transferred to the Louisiana State Museum, which created the three exhibits in the 1980s.

The Old US Mint (☎ 568-6968, 400 Esplanade Ave) is open Tuesday through Sunday from 9 am to 5 pm. Two gift shops offer a good selection of jazz recordings and an array of coins and Confederate currency minted in New Orleans.

New Orleans Mint On this site once guarded by Fort St Charles, the US government established a branch of the US Mint. The unremarkable Greek Revival building appears out of place among the Quarter's

Creole buildings and predates the Mint's arrival in 1835. From 1838 to 1861 and again from 1879 to 1910, the Mint struck US coinage bearing the 'O' mint mark. The Confederate States of America briefly produced coins after seizing the mint in 1861. Following the fall of New Orleans to federal troops in 1862, General Benjamin Butler had William Mumford hanged in front of the Mint for merely lowering the US flag – without a constitutional flag protection amendment, no less! Exhibits about the Old US Mint are extremely meager – disappointed numismatic collectors will want to visit the gift shop.

New Orleans Jazz Exhibit Upstairs from the Mint exhibit are Tony Green's three murals of Storyville, the historic red-light district (redeveloped into the Civic Center), where many jazz musicians, including Louis Armstrong, began their careers. More sublime is the touching childhood letter from budding pianist Harry Connick Jr to his idol, Armand Hug.

Visitors can spend hours in the comfortable, air-conditioned exhibit examining excellent displays that impart a clear sense of how jazz evolved – from its roots in the rhythms brought by African slaves to recent Jazz Fest performances. Of course, New Orleans artists and their instruments are featured throughout.

Mardi Gras Museum Visitors to the wing displaying Carnival memorabilia are greeted by a mannequin in an elaborate satin gown with a museum plaque proclaiming 'Gay Balls.' The kitschy traditions of Carnival are otherwise taken seriously in this collection of costumes, floats, masquerade gowns and mementos. Early photographs of Carnival confirm that drunkenness, debauchery and silliness are not recent inventions.

Historic New Orleans Collection

Bow ties abound in the academic environs of the Historic New Orleans Collection (☎ 523-4662, www.hnoc.org, 533 Royal St). Beginning in 1070, the complex of historic buildings, anchored by the Merieult House, have displayed private collections of art and historical documents that attract visitors, local researchers and foreign scholars. The collection was founded by Lila and Kemper Williams. In 1996, the research facilities were moved to their own handsome home nearby, the Williams Research Center (☎ 523-4662, 410 Chartres St), in a beautifully refurbished police station. Since the move, the original site, which includes the Williams Gallery and Merieult House, is better suited for the casual visitor. A gift shop offers historical postcards, new and used books and collectibles.

Williams Gallery Rotating exhibits provide visitors with an opportunity to gain an understanding of different aspects of local history. By way of example, a past exhibit featured historical photographs, videos and oral histories to document the changes that mechanization brought to southern Louisiana's rural sugarcane-growing areas. Admission is free. It's open Tuesday through Saturday 10 am to 4:45 pm.

Merieult History Tour Unlike the undocumented anecdotes fed to tourists by carriage guides, the Historic New Orleans Collection's introductions to Louisiana's past are meticulously researched. The many handsome gallery displays are housed in the landmark Merieult House, built in 1792. Showcased are the original transfer documents of the Louisiana Purchase of 1803. If the guide leaves something out, you can pick up a handy listing of each room's contents to find out more on your own. It's a bit fast paced, especially if you want to inspect the many early maps showing the city's evolution or such things as an 1849 broadside advertising '24 Head of Slaves' (individual children for $500 or entire families for $2400). Nevertheless, no better short introduction to the history of the city is available.

The Merieult House, a rare survivor of the 1794 fire, is an almost overlooked part of the tour. It was extensively remodeled in 1832, reflecting the American influence of the period. In one room, sections of plaster are removed to expose the traditional brick-and-post construction, and another room is sheathed with barge boards from river barges dismantled at the end of a down-river trip.

Tours cost $2 and are given Tuesday through Saturday at 10 and 11 am, 2 and 3 pm.

Williams Research Center You can take specific queries about almost any New Orleans property to the staff at this research center. The archives contain more than 300,000 images and a comprehensive block-by-block survey of the French Quarter. Ink pens are not permitted inside. It's open Tuesday through Saturday 10 am to 4:30 pm.

Pharmacy Museum

The Pharmacy Museum (☎ 565-8027, 514 Chartres St) occupies a shop established in 1823 by the nation's first licensed pharmacist, Louis J Dufilho Jr. Dufilho dispensed gold-coated pills to the rich and opium, alcohol and cannabis to those who really needed to feel better. Admission costs $2 (no free samples!). It's open Tuesday through Sunday 10 am to 5 pm.

St Louis Cemetery No 1

New Orleans' oldest cemetery, St Louis Cemetery No 1 dates to 1789. It was originally just outside the city ramparts – still marked by Rampart St – but during the 19th century, the growing city quickly engulfed it. This cemetery has a rare beauty, enhanced by natural decay wrought by time, and if you visit just one cemetery, this one near the French Quarter is certainly a good choice. Time and a willingness to explore the grounds are key – wandering at your leisure, you can appreciate the statuary and ornate ironwork and stumble on many historic tombs.

It's fitting that in death, as in life, mystery surrounds voodoo queen **Marie Laveau**, who purportedly rests here. A family tomb not far from the entrance has the names Glapion, Laveau and Paris – all branches of Laveau's family – etched in its marble front, and a commemorative plaque identifies it as Laveau's 'reputed' resting site. Debates concerning *which* Marie Laveau – mother or daughter, if either – was actually buried here will never be resolved, but popular consensus has designated this as Laveau's memorial (see the boxed text 'Yesterday's Voodoo' for details). People come to scratch an 'x' in the tomb's plaster, presumably to pay their 'respects' to the voodoo queen. However, living members of the Glapion family consider this practice vandalism – there is no spiritual significance to these chicken scratches, particularly when applied for kicks by tourists, and visitors are strongly discouraged from desecrating this or any other tomb.

In the adjacent family tomb rests **Ernest 'Dutch' Morial,** New Orleans' first black mayor. Morial was mayor from 1980 to 1988, and he died in 1989. His son, Marc Morial, was elected mayor in 1992.

Civil Rights figure **Homer Plessy** also rests here (for more on Plessy, see the boxed text 'Civil Rights in New Orleans' in the Facts about New Orleans chapter), as do real-estate speculator **Bernard de Marigny,** architect **Henry Latrobe** and countless others.

The **Italian Mutual Benevolent Society Tomb** is the tallest monument in the cemetery. Like a lot of immigrant groups in New Orleans, the Italians formed a benevolent association to pool funds and assist in covering burial costs. The tomb is large enough to contain the remains of thousands. In 1969, a notorious psychedelic rape scene in the movie *Easy Rider* was filmed in St Louis Cemetery No 1 to the obvious shock of families who own tombs here. Note the headless statue called 'Charity' on the Italian Society tomb – urban myth maintains that actor Dennis Hopper was responsible for tearing the head off.

The cemetery gates are open from 8 am to 3 pm, and you are free to wander around on your own. It can be hard to find all of the noteworthy sights, and a good walking tour will help you see all of them (see Organized Tours in the Getting Around chapter). Even if you aren't interested in taking a tour, it's a good idea to coincide your visit with a tour group's in order to ensure that you are not alone within the cemetery walls. Vandalism

Hounded by rumors, the headless 'Charity' statue remains tight-lipped.

and statuary theft are the most common crimes here, but visitors ought to be mindful of their own safety as well.

Mortuary Chapel

An unfounded fear of yellow fever contagion led the city to forbid funerals for fever victims at the St Louis Cathedral. Built in 1826 near St Louis Cemetery No 1, the Mortuary Chapel (401 N Rampart St) offered hasty services to victims, as its bell tolled constantly during epidemics. In 1931, it was renamed Our Lady of Guadeloupe Church. Inside the chapel, you'll see a statue of Saint Jude, patron saint of impossible cases, and a curious statue of Saint Expedite, a saint who probably never existed – on the plaque there are quotation marks around his name.

Voodoo Spiritual Temple

At the Voodoo Spiritual Temple (☎ 522-9627, 828 N Rampart St), Priestess Miriam Chamani primarily practices spiritual healing rituals, based on Afrocentric American voodooism. Her temple features neither white nor black magic but instead focuses on 'true spiritual power for friendly people.' Drop by the small storefront temple to chat, pick up books on the occult or about the

Yesterday's Voodoo

Voodoo has in no small way contributed to New Orleans' reputation as the 'least American city in America.' It is perceived as both a colorful spectacle and a frightening glimpse of the supernatural, and this has proved to be an irresistible combination. Scores of shops selling voodoo dolls, gris-gris (amulets) and other exotic items attest to the fact that visitors to New Orleans can't help but buy into the mystique of voodoo. But all the hype aside, voodoo has remained a vital form of spiritual expression for thousands of practitioners.

It came to the New World via Haiti, aboard slave ships from West Africa. A hybrid American form of voodoo developed as people from many different tribal communities contributed various spiritual practices – including animism, snake worship, ancestor worship and making sacrifices to deities, called *loas*.

In Haiti, voodoo played an integral role in the slave rebellions that led to Haitian independence at the end of the 18th century. (Haiti is, in fact, the second-oldest nation in the Americas, having gained its independence just 28 years after the USA.) Haitian *vodoun* cults became military units as vodoun priests urged their followers to fight for freedom, and the bravery of the rebels was probably abetted by vodoun charms carried for protection. Haitian landowners fled the island, many settling with their slaves in New Orleans. Liberated black Haitians also migrated to New Orleans, and this influx hastened the spread of voodoo.

In New Orleans, voodoo fused with Catholic beliefs as saints and deities became interchangeable for followers of both religions. And it grew extremely popular as more people turned to voodoo conjurers for advice, fortune telling, herbal medicine, love charms and revenge against their enemies. These conjurers became increasingly influential in the community, and some of the more successful were wealthy and often controversial. Little is known about the famous 19th-century diviners with spectacular names like Doctor John, Doctor Yah Yah and Sanité Dédé. Even the known facts about the life of Marie Laveau, the most famous voodoo queen, continue to baffle historians. Half a century or more after their deaths, their biographies were committed to writing by historians who relied solely on hearsay and scant newspaper clippings. But no matter how true or false, their stories are fascinating.

Inside a voodoo temple

Yesterday's Voodoo

Doctor John

By all accounts, Doctor John was an impressive sight to behold. Born in Africa and raised a slave in Cuba, he had scars on his face, was immense in stature and could conjure up a look so terrifying that he intimidated his master into granting him his freedom (or so legend has it). After traveling the world as a sailor, he settled in New Orleans, where he established himself as the most influential voodoo king of his day.

The evidence suggests he was a flim-flam artist. An army of spies worked for him – household servants in the employ of prominent families – and he used information gleaned from them to bribe people and determine the course of events. At the time of his greatest influence, in the 1840s, Doctor John reputedly had 15 wives, and clients in every stratum of society on both sides of the color line.

Despite Doctor John's nefarious dealings, he had a profound effect on New Orleans voodoo. He popularized the religion, introduced whites to its periphery and is sometimes credited with developing the voodoo-Catholic hybrid. Above all else, however, he made voodoo profitable, and this aspect of the religion has stuck.

Marie Laveau

In many peoples' minds, voodoo means one person: Marie Laveau. She is remembered as a tremendously beautiful, charismatic and shrewd woman who had become one of the most powerful people in New Orleans by the mid-19th century. She was a consummate showperson, and her fame grew as she presided over spectacular rituals at Congo Square, where people of all colors paid to watch. She popularized voodoo like never before or since.

Interestingly, there were actually two Marie Laveaus, a mother and daughter, and it is unclear where the influence of one gave over to the other. This confusion may have been encouraged by these powerful voodoo queens, as they would certainly have known that the illusion of one woman blessed with eternal youth added to her mystique.

Throughout her life, the elder Marie Laveau (also called the Widow Paris) remained a Catholic, and she insisted that her voodoo followers, too, were observing the Catholic faith. Her healing methods often involved prayer in St Louis Cathedral.

But there was an underhanded side to Laveau's brand of voodoo. Like Doctor John, she had many tricks up her sleeve. She started out as a hairdresser, and entering the homes of upper-class white women as a coiffeuse gave her an inside view of the ruling class. She used her knowledge to her advantage. By the time she was a voodoo queen, she had spies in upper-class homes throughout New Orleans.

Reports on Laveau's activities suggest that there was much more to her practice than nonpractitioners were permitted to witness. Only devoted followers were admitted to the rituals she presided over at her house on St Ann St and in the bayous around New Orleans. Sensational accounts, related after her death, portray her followers dancing naked around a fire, drinking blood and slithering on the ground like snakes before engaging in all-out orgies. As the first Marie Laveau grew older, her daughter began to assume leadership of the cult. The second Marie Laveau, apparently unable to maintain the success of her mother, ultimately resorted to running a quadroon whorehouse for the pleasure of wealthy white men.

One of these two women is believed to be buried in St Louis Cemetery No 1 – but no one can say for certain which Marie Laveau it is.

Modern Voodoo

Voodoo is alive and well in the modern world. You can see it in Priestess Miriam Chamani's eyes, and you can see it in the demeanor of her snake. The sageness and evident integrity of this woman suggests that voodoo, with its reputation for trickery and dishonesty, has gotten a bum rap.

When Priestess Miriam raises the snake above her head, she looks transfixed. Hers is a countenance of total concentration, and the snake appears to stretch out and contort its body according to her will. When the snake is safely back in its vivarium, the expression is gone from Miriam's face. She looks a little peaked.

Priestess Miriam founded the **Voodoo Spiritual Temple** (see separate entry) in 1990. The site she chose is a converted storefront next door to a laundry, just a few blocks from Congo Square, where Marie Laveau is said to have performed her theatrical public rituals. In Miriam's dimly lit temple, altars to many deities are endowed with such worldly offerings as cigarettes, liquor, money, candles, toys, photographs and statuettes, and the walls are covered with colorfully patterned cloths. In an adjacent shop she does a modest trade in books, postcards, votive candles and other voodoo artifacts.

TOM DOWNS

Priestess Miriam Chamani

To neophyte eyes (all are welcome to visit the Voodoo Spiritual Temple), the temple is exotic and thrilling. Miriam, herself, is an impressive presence with her face beaming proudly and her hair radiating upward. It is everything you'd expect from the world of voodoo. But Miriam is unconcerned that her shop or her dramatic handling of her snake readily accommodate prevailing misconceptions about voodoo. She often seems dismissive of literal perceptions.

'It's okay that people should have a false opinion of voodoo, because all conceptions are initially false. Ideas progress toward the truth. Every thought is a misconception until something in it touches the thinker in some way. That's what voodoo is like. It is silent. It is an energy that vibrates into our minds.'

Miriam's own attraction to voodoo followed a similar pattern. She was born in rural Mississippi, raised a Baptist and, like many Mississippians, migrated to Chicago. As a child, she says, she was stirred by a Baptist minister's sermon: 'He gave birth to an idea in my soul, a vibration, and I've carried it with me ever since.' But finding that kind of intense experience rare within the context of organized religion, she drifted from the church. Years later, in Chicago's South Side, she consulted a psychic about a problem in her relationship, and he introduced her to the Spiritual Temple. 'It was a voodoo church,' she says,' but in those days, if you called it voodoo the police would come and shut you down.'

Her face radiant, Miriam says she found what she was looking for – and the snake is an integral part of it. 'The serpent is a symbol for stability, swiftness, quietness of time and elusiveness of self, and it has the elements to stir issues and quietness. It is the wisdom of all things. It teaches us to see the clear path before us.'

small collection of arts and artifacts from around the world. Donations are accepted. Priestess Miriam welcomes visitors who are curious about voodoo.

Historic Voodoo Museum

This humble museum has an intricately arrayed collection of voodoo artifacts and is worth visiting. Just make certain that a guided tour is available before you pay admission – otherwise, there is little to explain the exhibited arcana.

Admission to the voodoo museum (☎ 523-7685, 724 Dumaine St) costs $5.25 for a half-hour tour.

Ursuline Convent

After a five-month voyage from Rouen, France, 12 Ursuline nuns arrived in New Orleans to care for the French garrison's miserable little hospital and to educate the young girls of the colony. They were the first nuns in the New World. The French Colonial Army planned and built the existing convent and girls' school between 1745 and 1752, making it the oldest structure in the French Quarter and the Mississippi Valley. It is also one of the few surviving examples of French colonial architecture in New Orleans. The nuns moved Uptown in 1824.

Guided tours of the fully restored convent include a visit to the Chapel of Archbishops, built in 1845. The chapel's stained-glass windows pay tribute to the Battle of New Orleans (Andrew Jackson credited his victory to the Ursulines' prayers for divine intervention) and to the Sisters of the Holy Family, the black Creole nuns established in 1842 by Archbishop Antoine Blanc. Tours of the Ursuline Convent (☎ 529-3040, 1114 Chartres St) are offered Tuesday to Friday at 10 and 11 am and 1, 2 and 3 pm; and Saturday and Sunday at 11:15 am and 1 and 2 pm. Admission is $5/4/2 for adults/seniors/children.

Beauregard-Keyes House

Greek Revival structures such as this house, built in 1826, with slave quarters and a rear courtyard, are uncommon in the French Quarter. After the war, it was the home of Confederate General PGT Beauregard, who made his mark on US history when he gave the order to Confederate forces to fire upon Fort Sumter in Charleston, South Carolina, thus beginning the Civil War.

Historic House Tours

New Orleans offers a tremendous array of houses that are open for tours – a 'cottage' industry of sorts. Rather than wandering through a random sampling of homes, moving back and forth on the time scale, you can observe the evolution of style and technology by following a chronological sequence.

A few aspects of house design and layout are worth noting. The simplicity of French colonial designs and furnishings contrasts with the later Spanish and particularly the American period homes. Slave quarters were common components of antebellum homes. Fire hazards and heat caused most early kitchens to be located outside the main house. Cisterns that collected water from the rooftops allowed indoor plumbing or, when fed from the river, permitted the muddy river sediment to settle.

The following list includes a few of the more significant New Orleans homes open for tours, their neighborhoods and dates of construction. The two earliest homes on the list represent French colonial city and plantation houses.

- Merieult House, French Quarter (1792/1832)
- Pitot House, Fair Grounds (1799)
- Beauregard-Keyes House, French Quarter (1826)
- Hermann-Grima House, French Quarter (1831)
- 1850 House (lower Pontalba), French Quarter (1850)
- Gallier House, French Quarter (1857)
- Longue Vue House, Metairie (1942)

The house's other illustrious resident was the author Francis Parkinson Keyes, who lived here from 1944 until her death in 1970. Beginning in 1926, she became well known for her serialized travel correspondence in *Good Housekeeping* – much of her success came from her incredible ability with foreign languages. She published 51 novels, including many that were set locally, such as *Crescent Carnival* (1942), the bestseller *Dinner at Antoine's* (1948) and *Steamboat Gothic* (1952). Her novel *Madame Castel's Lodger* (1962) is set in this house, which belonged to General Beauregard at the time.

Tours of the Beauregard-Keyes House (☎ 523-7257, 1113 Chartres St) are not as interesting as the individuals who lived there. A gift shop offers most of Francis Parkinson Keyes' books. The house is open Monday to Saturday 10 am to 3 pm. Admission is $4/3/1.50 for adults/seniors/children.

Gallier House Museum

New Orleans owes much of its architectural heritage to James Gallier Sr and James Gallier Jr. They are both renowned for their Greek Revival designs. In 1857 Gallier Jr began work on this impressive French Quarter town house, incorporating numerous innovations – like interior plumbing, skylights and ceiling vents – into the design. A cistern provided fresh water to the kitchen, which in turn provided hot water to the upstairs bath. It is carefully furnished with period pieces. Access to the cast-iron gallery overlooking Royal St and other handsome homes is an added highlight of the worthwhile tour.

The Gallier House Museum (☎ 525-5661, 1118 Royal St) is open weekdays 10 am to 4 pm. Admission is $5/4/3 for adults/seniors/children.

Hermann-Grima House

Samuel Hermann, a Jewish merchant who married a Catholic, introduced the unique American-style Federal design to the Quarter in 1831. Hermann sold the house in 1844 to Judge Grima, a slaveholder, after he reportedly lost $2 million during the na-

---

Galliers' Greek Revival

James Gallier Sr (1798-1866), an Irish architect, and his English wife immigrated to the US following the birth of James Gallier Jr (1827-68). In 1834, Gallier Sr proceeded to New Orleans, where he designed St Patrick's Church (perhaps the first Greek Revival building in the US) and Gallier Hall. Today, Gallier Hall is a prominent municipal building, which stands out near Lafayette Square; it's on the St Charles streetcar Uptown route.

Gallier Jr worked in his father's office before taking over the practice in 1849. Gallier Jr's grand French Opera House of 1859 (it burned in 1919) was his greatest achievement. Perhaps the Galliers' most lasting impact was to make the Greek Revival style locally fashionable.

---

tional financial panic of 1837. Cooking demonstrations in the authentic open-hearth kitchen are a special treat on Thursday from October through May.

Tours of the Hermann-Grima House (☎ 525-5661, 818 St Louis St) are offered Monday to Saturday 10 am to 3:30 pm. Admission is $5/3 for adults/children.

Faulkner House

Considered one of the greatest American novelists, William Faulkner (1897-1962) briefly rented an apartment in a town house on Pirate's Alley at the onset of his career. (At the time, the narrow passageway was called Orleans Alley.) In 1925, he moved to New Orleans from Mississippi, worked as a journalist at the *Times-Picayune* and met Sherwood Anderson, who helped him publish his first novel, *Soldier's Pay* (1926). He also contributed to the *Double Dealer*, a literary magazine published in New Orleans. The site of Faulkner's New Orleans stay is now home to Joe DeSalvo, who runs a bookstore, Faulkner House Books (☎ 524-2940, 624 Pirate's Alley) in the front rooms. It is open daily 10 am to 6 pm.

French Market

This area really consists of three types of market: a collection of air-conditioned stores, an open-air Farmer's Market with produce stands and New Orleans cookery booths, and an open-air Flea Market where the wares of Louisiana and other parts of the world are sold. See the Shopping chapter for details.

Custom House

The fortresslike US Custom House (423 Canal St) covers a square block. Construction on it was started in 1849 and supervised by Lieutenant PGT Beauregard, who later commanded Confederate forces. During the Reconstruction period after the Civil War, it served as headquarters for African Americans in Abraham Lincoln's Republican party. Blacks held a majority in the Louisiana legislature, and two African Americans filled the office of lieutenant governor: Oscar J Dunn and Pickney Benton Stewart Pinchback. Meetings took place in the enormous 'Marble Hall' on the 2nd floor.

The building's construction is also interesting. A cofferdam surrounded the excavation while the foundation was under construction; cotton bales used to seal the dam gave rise to stories that the building was founded on bales of cotton. Despite a mat of cypress timbers, the foundation has settled about three feet under the weight of the brick and granite structure. All four sides of the building are identical.

Maspero's Exchange

Pierre Maspero operated La Bourse de Maspero, a coffeehouse and one of many slave-trading houses in New Orleans. He was a tenant in the building that now houses the restaurant Maspero's Exchange (440 Chartres St – not to be confused with Café Maspero on Decatur St). Regular markets for the unfortunate trade in human chattel occurred on Exchange Alley (now Exchange Place), between Conti and Canal Sts, and at the market beyond the Quarter's wall, now Louis Armstrong Park across Rampart St. Following the Good Friday fire of 1788, Don Juan Paillet built the structure, later to become the scene of slave trading, with an *entresol* (a mezzanine floor with a low ceiling

Joe DeSalvo, proprietor of Faulker House

that was visible from the exterior through the arched windows). This cramped room, then only reached by a ceiling door from the bottom floor, is where the African slaves are said to have been imprisoned. It is now a dining room – a rather discomfiting and tasteless use of the space.

One other historical note about Maspero's is worth mentioning: With British troops approaching in 1814, this building served as the headquarters for the local Committee of Public Safety, charged with marshaling citizens to fight under General Andrew Jackson.

Tremé District
Immediately to the lake-side of the French Quarter's early walls (now N Rampart St) grew New Orleans' first suburb, the Tremé District, an area traditionally populated by black Creoles. The celebrated architect who virtually rebuilt the St Louis Cathedral in 1849-51, JNB DePouilly, designed **St Augustine's Church** (☎ 525-5934, 1210 Governor Nichols St). It opened in 1842 and is the second oldest African American Catholic church in the country. One of its stained-glass panels depicts the Sisters of the Holy Family, the order of black Creole nuns founded in 1842 by Henriette Delille. Today, the small congregation works to provide food for the needy and to maintain the **Tomb of the Unknown Slave**.

FAUBOURG MARIGNY & BYWATER (MAP 3)
If you're heading downriver out of the French Quarter, by crossing Esplanade Ave you enter the Faubourg Marigny, which was developed by the colorful plantation owner Bernard Xavier Philippe de Marigny de Mandeville in the mid-19th century. Originally a Creole suburb, the Marigny today is one of New Orleans' gay hubs, and the neighborhood supports a vibrant bohemian scene as well. Some of the city's hottest music clubs line Frenchman St (see Entertainment for listings).

The Marigny is certainly worthy of an afternoon stroll to observe the rustic elegance of its buildings, most of which are private residences. **Washington Square**, at the heart of the neighborhood, is a peaceful and well-shaded park where you can escape the touristy French Quarter and rest your boots in peace.

TOM DOWNS

Arthur Raymond Smith, local artist

Marigny's Craps

Faubourg Marigny, which begins just across Esplanade Ave from the French Quarter, gets its name from the Creole plantation owner Bernard Xavier Philippe de Marigny de Mandeville, whose colorful sense of humor and love of a good time left an unforgettable impression on downtown New Orleans – and, indeed, on bars, social clubs and sidewalks throughout the US.

In 1800, young Marigny was sent to study in London, where he learned English and a game of dice the English called 'hazard,' which hadn't yet been introduced to America. When he returned to New Orleans, he brought with him a pair of dice and commenced to teach the Creoles of New Orleans the new game, which came to be known in local parlance as 'craps.'

The word 'craps' is another of those remarkable stories behind New Orleans' substantial and lasting contributions to the American idiom. Early Americans in New Orleans, following the British custom of referring to the French as 'frogs,' called their Creole neighbors 'Johnny Crapauds,' using the French term for frog. It thus followed that the Creoles' game of dice came to be called craps, an abbreviation of crapaud.

Unfortunately, Bernard Marigny was unsuccessful at his own game and he forfeited much of his wealth losing at craps. An urgent need for cash forced him to subdivide his vast estate into the Faubourg Marigny. In naming the streets of his new development, Marigny continued to exhibit the romantic and fanciful sensibility that had no doubt contributed to his inability to manage his own finances. Among the names he applied to the streets of Faubourg Marigny were Poets, Music, Love, Good Children – and Craps!

Ironically, Rue de Craps became the site of no fewer than three churches, which is why the street's name was eventually changed to Burgundy. The game of craps, meanwhile, went on to become a national pastime.

Bernard Marigny lived to the ripe old age of 83, but an endless series of unsavvy business deals cost him the remainder of his fortune and he died penniless in 1868. Nevertheless, local historians maintain that he never lost his sense of humor.

If you wonder about the furnishings of many of the Quarter's interior courtyards, stop by and check out the cherubs and nymphs at **American Aquatic Gardens** (☎ 944-0410, 621 Elysian Fields Ave).

As rents in the Marigny rise, greater numbers of poor, creative types have been moving farther downriver to the careworn but up-and-coming Bywater. There are few sights of interest to tourists, but the Bywater is a decent and inexpensive part of town to stay, eat and drink in. See the Places to Stay, Places to Eat and Entertainment chapters.

St Roch Cemetery

Just a few blocks from the Faubourg Marigny (driving is recommended), St Roch cemetery qualifies as one of New Orleans' most intriguing resting places. That's no small feat! It is named after an obscure saint, a French native, whose prayers are said to have protected Rome from the Black Plague. During New Orleans' bouts with yellow fever, Catholics who prayed to St Roch (pronounced 'St Rock') are believed to have been spared, and the small chapel within the cemetery grounds was raised in his honor.

Entering this walled necropolis, you pass through an elegant wrought-iron fence, and the grounds' paved paths are lined with family and society tombs, some magnificent, some decrepit. But the real fascination here is within the chapel itself.

The small gated chamber to the right is filled with ex-votos, testaments to the healing power of St Roch. It is a strange collection of ceramic body parts (healed ankles, heads, breasts), prosthetics, leg braces and

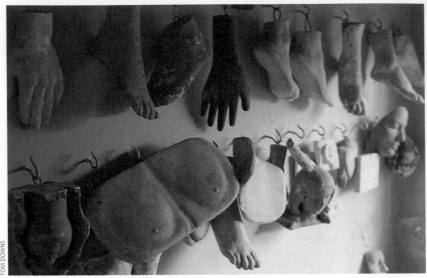

TOM DOWNS

Ex-votos at St Roch's Cemetery

crutches, even false teeth. Marble floor tiles are inscribed with the words 'thanks' and 'merci.'

St Roch Cemetery is on St Roch Ave at N Roman St. It is open daily 9 am to 4 pm.

CBD & WAREHOUSE DISTRICT (MAP 4)

On the other side of Canal St from the French Quarter, the CBD (Central Business District) and the Warehouse District comprise the American commercial sector that was established after the Louisiana Purchase in 1803. Merchants, brokers and manufacturers from New England descended on New Orleans and industriously began making it into a bustling port. Then called the Faubourg St Mary, the American sector developed into a nexus of offices, banks, warehouses and government buildings, with Lafayette Square at its core.

Canal St was the division between the French and American parts of town, and it still represents the boundary between Uptown and Downtown. That's no hollow distinction, as some citizens of New Orleans, set in their Uptown or Downtown ways, never seem to find any reason to cross Canal St. The wide median down the middle of Canal St was part of neither the French nor American sector and was therefore called the 'neutral ground' – in time, all medians in New Orleans would be referred to by that idiosyncratic term. Lee Circle marks the area's downtown boundary.

Toward the lake is the modern Civic Center, the Louisiana Superdome and new office buildings. Most of this modern area was the former red-light district of Storyville, which declined after 1919, when the Navy made it off-limits to sailors.

The Warehouse District faded in its importance as the port shrank in size, but the 1984 Louisiana World Exposition focused attention on the area, as former warehouses were converted into live/work lofts and exhibit spaces for artists. A number of shops, restaurants and music clubs now make it an exciting part of town. The district is defined by Poydras St, Magazine St, Howard Ave, and the river. The change in emphasis from water and rail transportation to highways has led to an industrial decline along the riverfront, and the area was redeveloped with a Convention Center and a shopping mall.

Most of the sights in the CBD and Warehouse District are a good walk from the French Quarter, and with the exceptions of both streetcar lines and the No 11 Magazine bus, public transportation here isn't the best. Wear good walking shoes if you plan to explore thoroughly.

Historic Buildings

At the corner of Carondelet and Gravier Sts (on the St Charles Ave Streetcar Line) the lighted colonnade of the **Hibernia National Bank Building**, built in 1920, once rose above all of New Orleans. Its neighbor, the **New Orleans Cotton Exchange**, and the cornucopia of tropical produce gracing the entrance to the **United Fruit Company** building at 321 St Charles Ave hint at the industries upon which New Orleans was built. **Factors Row**, on Perdido St at Carondelet St, was the site where Degas painted *The Cotton Market in New Orleans* while visiting his uncle's office in 1873. The 13 identical red-brick houses lining **Julia Row**, between Camp and St Charles Sts, were built in 1832. The fan transoms above the doorways are indicative of the Row's aristocratic appeal – also note the servant's wings that project from the rear. The **lighthouse** at 743 Camp St was built in 1922 to house the Lighthouse for the Blind, and is now home to a glass store. Across the street, **St Patrick's Church**, 724 Camp St, was built during the 1830s by Irish immigrants making a break from the French-speaking Catholic parishes of New Orleans.

Canal St Ferry

A short ferry ride from the foot of Canal St to Algiers is the best way to get out on the water and admire New Orleans from the traditional river approach. Ride on the lower deck next to the water, and you're likely to see the state bird, the brown pelican. The state-run ferry is free and runs between 6 am and midnight, leaving Canal St on the hour and half-hour, returning from Algiers on the quarter-hour.

Woldenberg Park

Upriver from the Riverwalk along the riverfront, Woldenberg Park offers a promenade with seating and a grassy strip, where civic events and concerts are occasionally staged. It's a comfortable place to eat a po' boy while watching passersby and river traffic. The park ends at the aquarium and the Spanish Plaza, which continues to the entrance for the Riverwalk Mall (see separate heading).

Aquarium of the Americas

At the Aquarium of the Americas, operated by the Audubon Institute, you can go eye-to-eye with giant tropical creatures like the Amazon's arapaima *(Arapaima gigas)*, see spotted moray eels *(Gymnothorax moringa)* and hawksbill turtles *(Etetmochelys imbricata)* in a walk-through Caribbean reef tube, or watch incredible specimens of gulf species through 14-foot-high windows. Mr Bill, the 40-year-old sawfish, shares the giant gulf tank with an oil platform that doesn't leak. Of course, the Mississippi River and Delta Wetlands environments are also displayed. The 'Americas' also includes the farthest reaches of Arctic environments.

The air-conditioned aquarium (☎ 861-2537) is at the foot of Canal St, adjacent to Woldenberg Park and next to the Canal St Ferry. Use the Riverfront streetcar if you don't want to walk from the French Quarter. Be sure to pick up a program listing times for special presentations such as the penguin feed and diver shows. The gift shop is a good place to pick up books on Louisiana's natural history.

It's open daily at 9:30 am; closing hours vary from 5 to 7 pm. Admission costs $9.75 for adults, $7.50 for seniors and $5 for children two to 12. Discounts on admission are continually offered in tourist magazines like *Where*. In addition, the Zoo Cruise docks here, and you can get a variety of combination tickets that include the Audubon Zoo, the aquarium and the cruise. For the best prices, double-check coupon offers against such combinations. Other combination tickets good for the aquarium and adjacent IMAX theater offer a savings of about 15%

Top of the Mart

The World Trade Center, 2 Canal St, formerly known as the Trade Mart, was briefly the tallest building in New Orleans when its 33rd floor was completed in 1968. Special pumping and foundation technology had to be developed to keep such high-rises from sinking into the mud. Top of the Mart is also a member of the revolving observation deck club, which consists of some 87 buildings in North America. The slowly revolving Top of the Mart Lounge (☎ 522-9795) offers spectacular views for the price of a mixed drink – an Original Doubloon costs less than $6. Also check out the stained-glass murals created by Milton Pounds to depict the history of the city.

Another option for a more limited high-rise view of the city is to ride the glass elevator, open 9 am to 5 pm, for $2/1 for adults/children.

Riverwalk

For nearly half a mile above the Canal St Ferry, the Riverwalk Mall borders the Mississippi River and piers. When Bienville founded New Orleans in 1718, this site was in the middle of the river – an 1800-foot shift has since occurred. Almost as an afterthought to patronize those who wish to gaze at the famous Mississippi, an uncrowded walkway along the river-side of the mall attracts a few from the throngs of numbed shoppers. It's actually a worthwhile way to get oriented and features a number of informative plaques along with views of the crescent and even binoculars to spy on ships and riverboats.

The mall is air-conditioned and full of stores – see the Shopping chapter.

Contemporary Arts Center

This tremendous exhibition and performance space occupies a renovated warehouse. The steel ceiling above the impressive central stairway honors prominent figures in local arts. Among the many acknowledged artists are painter and sculptor Fritz Bultman, visual artist and sculptor Enrique Alferez, architect Charles Rousseve and his wife, Noma, who was the first director of Xavier's

RICHARD CUMMINS

Riverwalk and World Trade Center

Fine Arts Department, and Ellsworth Woodward, the first director of Newcomb's Fine Arts Department.

Dozens of multimedia exhibits appear each year in the gallery spaces. Also featured on the two stages are performances of plays, performance art, dance programs, musical concerts and video screenings. Admission to the Contemporary Arts Center (☎ 528-3800, 900 Camp St) is $3/2 for adults/children, free on Thursday. It's open Tuesday to Saturday 10 am to 5 pm and Sunday 11 am to 5 pm.

Louisiana Children's Museum

This educational museum is like a high-tech kindergarten. Generous corporate sponsors have helped create hands-on exhibits like a supermarket, complete with stocked shelves and check-out registers, and a TV news studio, where young anchors can see themselves on monitors as they forecast a July snowstorm in New Orleans. In the rush to build newer, bigger and better exhibits, the museum has failed to maintain some of the existing displays – 'Mayday!' calls on the tugboat radio go unheard and most kids abandon ship. Overall, however, the nonprofit museum and volunteers have done a good job in providing attractions for everyone from toddlers to 12-year-olds.

The Louisiana Children's Museum (☎ 523-1357, 420 Julia St) is open Tuesday to Saturday 9:30 am to 5:30 pm and Sunday noon to 5:30 pm (also on Monday during the summer months). Children under 16 must be accompanied by an adult. Admission for anyone over a year old costs $5.

Lee Circle

Called Place du Tivoli until it was renamed to honor Confederate General Robert E Lee after the Civil War, Lee Circle has lost some of its earlier cachet. Just a few dozen paces away, an elevated freeway structure disturbs some of the traffic circle's symmetry, and gas stations occupy two of its corners. Nevertheless, the **Robert E Lee monument** at its center, dedicated in 1884, still refuses to turn its back on the North – for that's the direction the statue faces. Also on Lee Circle, **K&B Plaza** is a modish office tower dating to 1963 with an indoor/outdoor sculpture gallery. The outdoor sculptures, featuring Isamu Noguchi's *The Mississippi*, can be viewed anytime; the indoor sections are open Monday to Friday 8:30 am to 4:30 pm.

Confederate Museum

Dedicated to presenting Louisiana life during the Civil War, this museum is housed in gorgeous Memorial Hall, designed by Thomas Sully. Opened to the public in 1891, it's the oldest operating museum in the state. Entering the hall, with its exposed cypress ceiling beams and exhibition cases, is worth the price of admission, but the exhibit itself far exceeds expectations.

There doesn't seem to be an agenda here, apart from a few harsh words (mostly quoting federal officials in Washington, DC) about General Benjamin 'Beast' Butler, the locally reviled head of the Union forces that occupied New Orleans during the war.

Of course, there are rifles and pistols from the war, many of which are strangely beautiful artifacts of the industrial age. But what really makes this museum worth a visit is the endless collection of personal effects that belonged not only to officers and soldiers but to their families back home as well. Knapsacks, playing cards, tobacco pouches and undergarments are fastidiously arranged within the display cabinets. Curious items like Jefferson Davis' slippers and an impressive array of oddly styled hats help to shed light on life during the Civil War.

The Confederate Museum (☎ 523-4522, 929 Camp St), a block from Lee Circle, is open Monday to Saturday 10 am to 4 pm. Admission is $5 ($4 for seniors and children).

ADAM LUTZ

Lee Circle

St Charles Avenue Streetcar Tour

For more than 5 miles, St Charles Ave is a relentless panorama of sybaritic 19th-century mansions, age-old oak trees, slowly moving joggers and antique streetcars. Linking the French Quarter with the Lower Garden District, the Garden District, Uptown and Riverbend, St Charles Ave is longer than most visitors will care to walk. But by hopping aboard the St Charles Ave streetcar – an essential activity while in New Orleans – you can see many of the city's greatest houses and churches while chugging the entire length of the street at a leisurely 10mph. The streetcar costs just $1 each way, and riding it out and back takes about 90 minutes. If you are planning to disembark along the way and get back on, consider

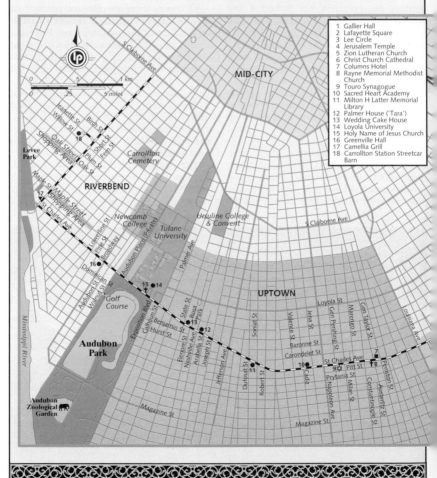

1 Gallier Hall
2 Lafayette Square
3 Lee Circle
4 Jerusalem Temple
5 Zion Lutheran Church
6 Christ Church Cathedral
7 Columns Hotel
8 Rayne Memorial Methodist Church
9 Touro Synagogue
10 Sacred Heart Academy
11 Milton H Latter Memorial Library
12 Palmer House ('Tara')
13 Wedding Cake House
14 Loyola University
15 Holy Name of Jesus Church
16 Greenville Hall
17 Camellia Grill
18 Carrollton Station Streetcar Barn

St Charles Avenue Streetcar Tour

buying a one-day pass ($4). The streetcar is usually jam-packed during the heavy morning and afternoon commute, making those periods less suitable for sightseeing.

Catch the streetcar heading Uptown at the corner of St Charles Ave and Common St. If you want air-conditioning, just pull down the window.

The first landmark you'll see on this tour is the streetcar itself. In fact, the streetcar's entire path – the neutral ground that splits St Charles Ave – is on the National Register of Historic Places. New Orleans makes the claim that this is the world's oldest continuously operating streetcar line, dating back to September 1835, when the New Orleans & Carrollton Railroad Company began running horse-drawn streetcars on St Charles Ave. After the tracks were laid, people began to move into the rural hinterlands upriver from the Vieux Carré and the American sector surrounding Lafayette Square, and in two decades of furious building, the area was transformed from rural countryside to a continuous series of posh suburbs. The streetcars were electrified in 1893, and the classic olive-green cars in use today were built in 1922-4.

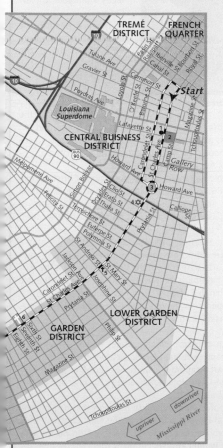

Trundling along, you reach the monumental Greek Revival **Gallier Hall** on the right at No 545. Gallier Hall served as City Hall from its completion in 1853 until 1957. To the left, across from Gallier Hall, is **Lafayette Square**, the focal point of the old American sector.

The streetcar clicks and clacks past several wino hotels that are completely incongruous with St Charles Ave's upscale reputation before reaching **Lee Circle** and skirting the **Robert E Lee monument**. The circle was called Place du Tivoli when the area was laid out in 1807, but it was renamed in 1884 (a time when anti-Reconstructionist sentiments ran extremely high) to honor the Confederate general.

Chugging beneath the freeway overpass, the streetcar enters the Lower Garden District, famous for its streets named after ancient Greek muses. On the right-hand side of the block, between Calliope and Clio (muses of heroic poetry and history) Sts, note the sturdy **Jerusalem Temple**,

St Charles Avenue Streetcar Tour

RICK GERHARTER

Take a seat on the St Charles Ave streetcar

at No 1137, which was built in 1916 and serves as headquarters for a local chapter of the Shriners (whose reputation rests on their penchant for fezzes and tiny cars – an attitude perfectly adaptable to New Orleans).

The first bend in the track occurs at Felicity St, which marked the northern limit of the city of New Orleans until 1852. Nearby, at the corner of St Mary St (on your left), the comely **Zion Lutheran Church** (1871) is a Gothic Revival structure built entirely of wood.

At Jackson Ave, the streetcar begins to pass along the edge of the Garden District. To see what really distinguishes this lovely neighborhood, you have to get off the streetcar and traverse the shady sidewalks between St Charles Ave and Magazine St.

At Sixth St on your right rises the tall Gothic bell tower of the prestigious **Christ Church Cathedral**, an Episcopal church built in 1886. Entombed in the choir aisle is Reverend Leonidas Polk, the first bishop of Louisiana and a general of the Confederate States of America. You leave the Garden District after passing Louisiana Ave, but St Charles Ave itself is just getting warmed up.

Between Peniston and General Taylor, on the right, the grand white columns of the **Columns Hotel** rise above a porch patio where drinks are served into the wee hours. Louis Malle's *Pretty Baby* was filmed in the hotel. Catty-corner from the Columns Hotel is the red-brick **Rayne Memorial Methodist Church**, a landmark built in 1887. Peer through the live oaks for a glimpse of the church's intricate shingled steeple. In a few blocks, after crossing Milan St, the distinctive **Touro Synagogue** appears on the left. The synagogue, noted for its Moorish design and inlaid ornamentation, was dedicated in 1909.

Napoleon Ave, roughly the midway point on the streetcar line, reflects New Orleans' early-19th-century admiration for the French emperor. Nearby street names – Austerlitz, Constantinople, Marengo, Milan and Jena – represent Napoleonic victories.

At Jena St, on the right, stands **Sacred Heart Academy**, a Catholic school for girls established in 1887. The building dates to 1900, and its colonial-revival style is enhanced by distinctly New Orleanian touches like louvered shutters.

At Soniat St, look to the left for the tile-roofed Neo-Italianate mansion that occupies an entire block. It's the **Milton H Latter Memorial Library**, a branch of the New Orleans Public Library system, and was built in 1906 as a private residence. It's worth a stop on the way back. At Arabella St, on your right, stands the **Palmer House**, curiously modeled on Tara, the

St Charles Avenue Streetcar Tour

house in the motion picture *Gone with the Wind*. It was built in 1941, just two years after the blockbuster movie was released.

Past Nashville Ave, to the right, the residences on the Rosa Park cul-de-sac are among the most admired in New Orleans. Just off the corner of Rosa Park is the oft-admired **Wedding Cake House**, 5809 St Charles, a delectable Victorian Colonial Revival home.

Crossing Calhoun St, you see Audubon Park on the left and the campuses of two of the city's universities on the right. The impressive group of red-brick Tudor Gothic buildings are part of the Jesuit **Loyola University**, established in 1904. It's the largest Catholic university in the South. The campus' **McDermott Memorial Church**, dedicated in 1918 and noted for its tall spires, is the only Catholic church along St Charles Ave. Between the two campuses, the spire that belongs to the red-brick,

Stop to bask in the shade at Audubon Park.

Gothic Revival **Holy Name of Jesus Church** is plainly visible in a gap in St Charles Ave's oak trees. **Tulane University** was founded in 1834. Facing St Charles Ave are Tulane's gray-stone Gibson Hall, built in 1894, and Tilton Hall (1902).

Both campuses face **Audubon Park**, named for the famed naturalist. Audubon Park extends about 1½ miles to Magazine St; from Magazine St to the river is the Audubon Zoo and Levee Park, which surrounds the zoo.

Between Broadway and Pine Sts, on the left, **Greenville Hall** (1882) is part of Loyola University. Built in an architectural style dubbed 'steamboat Gothic,' it features twin galleries with carved posts. The crowning cupola contains a statue of St Mary that was leftover from when the building housed St Mary's Dominican College for women.

St Charles Ave ends in an area called the Riverbend, formerly the town of Carrollton. As the streetcar turns onto Carrollton Ave, you can look to the left and see the gentle grassy slope of the Mississippi River levee. Also to the left, you'll soon see the **Camellia Grill**. This is a good place to end your streetcar tour, grab a bit to eat and board a returning car. If you're really into trains, you can stay aboard until Willow St and walk two blocks to have a look at the **Carrollton Station Streetcar Barn**, where the cars rest overnight.

LOWER GARDEN DISTRICT (MAP 5)

While it might be said that this is the Garden District's bedraggled older brother, at one time the Lower Garden District was one of the country's poshest and most elegant suburbs. On its many tree-lined thoroughfares stand countless Greek Revival houses that once were part of a cohesive, classic-style faubourg. Today, the neighborhood's long decline is slowly being reversed, and strolling through the area around Coliseum Square often requires sidestepping contractors and building supplies as homes are being restored.

In the early 19th century, French-born surveyor Barthélémy Lafon drew plans for a community that would be the envy of other classically obsessed planners of his day. Street names honored Greek gods, nymphs and muses, and attractive tree-lined canals along their median strips provided drainage to the river. By the 1830s, the city's elite had built their mansions here, also paying homage to the Greeks with columned galleries looking out over cultivated gardens burgeoning with pecan trees, banana trees, and fish ponds. Gazebos and horse stables further announced that life was good in the area. New Orleans' craze for cast-iron struck the mid-century denizens of the Lower Garden District, who adorned and fenced in their homes with ornate metallic designs, which today lend the area a rustic grace.

However, the neighborhood's glory was short-lived. The wealthy soon moved farther uptown to the newer, more fashionable Garden District, and many of the larger residences of the Lower Garden District were divided into smaller rental units to accommodate immigrants from Germany and Ireland, many of whom were employed on the docks. With the introduction of housing projects and the construction of an entrance to the Mississippi River bridge, the neighborhood rapidly deteriorated. The bridge ramp has since been demolished, reducing the traffic that once marred the neighborhood, and as rents in the French Quarter have risen astronomically high, many boutique shops have moved to Magazine St.

Similarly, an influx of professionals, artists and hipsters seeking fixer-uppers and cheap rents has breathed new life into the area.

Walking Tour

The best way to take in the Lower Garden District is to do a brief walking tour and perhaps some shopping along Magazine St. Strolling the neighborhood's well-shaded streets is only recommended during the daytime.

If you're arriving by streetcar, disembark at Terpsichore St (named for the Greek Muse of dance) and walk one block toward the river. At Prytania and Terpsichore Sts, a small neutral ground creates an open feeling, as was intended in Lafon's original street plan. Turn right on Prytania, then left on Euterpe St, so named for the Greek muse of lyric poetry. Toward the far end of the block on the right, the **John Thornhill House**, 1420 Euterpe St, was built in 1847 and purchased in 1854 by Thornhill, a wealthy cotton factor. Union troops confiscated the house from 1863 to 1866 for use as the headquarters of the Freedmen's Bureau, responsible for establishing the first black school in New Orleans.

Continue to **Coliseum Square**, the focal point of the fashionable Faubourg Annonciation, as this part of the district was known during its heyday. Coliseum Square is a pleasant enough public space, with old oaks offering ample shade, but it doesn't exactly bustle with activity. Rather than linger in the park, bear right on Coliseum St. At No 1729 stands the **Goodrich-Stanley House**, built in 1837 by jeweler William M Goodrich. Goodrich sold the house to the British-born cotton factor Henry Hope Stanley, whose adopted son, Henry Morton Stanley, went on to become famous for finding the missing Scottish missionary, Dr David Livingston. It was Stanley who first uttered the famous question, 'Dr Livingston, I presume?' He was subsequently knighted and founded the Congo Free States. The house originally stood a few blocks away, at 904 Orange St, and was moved to its current spot in 1981.

Continue on Coliseum St across Polymnia St. Behind a handsome wrought-iron fence

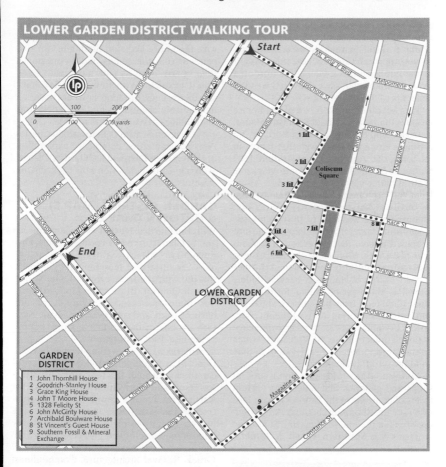

LOWER GARDEN DISTRICT WALKING TOUR

Start

Coliseum
Square

End

LOWER GARDEN
DISTRICT

GARDEN
DISTRICT

1 John Thornhill House
2 Goodrich-Stanley House
3 Grace King House
4 John T Moore House
5 1328 Felicity St
6 John McGinty House
7 Archibald Boulware House
8 St Vincent's Guest House
9 Southern Fossil & Mineral
  Exchange

is the papaya-hued **Grace King House**, 1749 Coliseum St, named for the Louisiana historian and author who lived there from 1905 to 1932. It was built in 1847 by banker Frederick Rodewald and features both Greek Ionic columns on the lower floor and Corinthian columns above.

At Race St, cross Coliseum St, but continue along the brick pathway to Felicity St, whose well-preserved cobbled pavement lends it a more distinctive antiquated feel. Until 1852, the uppermost part of New Orleans ended at Felicity St. Turning the

corner affords a view of the tastefully preserved **John T Moore House**, 1309 Felicity St. The house combines Victorian and Italianate styles and features sweeping balconies with elaborate cast-iron railings. It was built in 1880 by architect James Freret for his family; Moore, whose name the house bears, was Freret's father-in-law and originally owned the property. Opposite, at 1328 Felicity St, is a gorgeous entry door of beveled glass worth inspection (don't stare too hard – it might make the residents uneasy!). Proceed on Felicity St toward the river. Just a few paces away stands the attractive 1870 **John McGinty House**, at 1322 Felicity, a fine example of Italianate masonry architecture. As you approach Camp St, note the scars left in the cobblestones, evidence of uprooted streetcar tracks that once delivered wealthy residents to their front doors.

Turn left on Camp St. A row of fine homes includes the 1854 **Archibald Boulware House**, at 1531 Camp St. Turn right on Race St and continue along the brick wall that fences in the former **St Vincent's Infant Asylum**, 1507 Magazine St. Turn the corner onto Magazine St for a better view of the buildings. A sign from the orphanage days still hangs from the finely styled cast-iron gallery in front. The orphanage was built in 1864 with assistance from federal troops occupying the city. It helped relieve the overcrowded orphanages filled with youngsters of all races who lost their parents to epidemics. A former orphan, Margaret Haughery became widely known as 'the orphans' friend' for donating money and food from her successful bakery, and a statue honoring her is at the intersection of Prytania and Clio Sts. The orphanage is now a guest house, St Vincent's, which offers afternoon teas (see the Places to Stay and Places to Eat chapters).

Continue down Magazine for a look at shops and galleries that reflect the current tastes of denizens of the Lower Garden District (see the Shopping chapter). An intriguing break in the line of Magazine St antique stores is the **Southern Fossil & Mineral**

TOM DOWNS

Grace King House: no Doric columns here

Exchange, 2045 Magazine St. This little shop-museum seems to want to scare people away with the entire skeleton of an alligator suspended from the ceiling and an enormous cave bear raising its paw, along with some 'fossil jewelry.' With items like Tyrannosaurus rex eggs, the shop's owners make an unassailable claim of having 'the oldest stuff on the block.' Everything is for sale.

At Jackson St, turn right toward St Charles Ave. You can either commence exploration of the Garden District (see Garden District Walking Tour, below) or hop back on the streetcar.

GARDEN DISTRICT (MAP 5) & UPTOWN (MAP 6)

With the Garden District as its centerpiece, and St Charles Ave as its primary spine, Uptown New Orleans is a living – and splendid – architectural museum that contrasts sharply with the more crowded, Old World French Quarter. Block upon block of glorious mansions stand as symbols of the bustling trade and enterprise that made New Orleans one of the world's wealthiest cities in the mid-19th century.

Americans began settling farther beyond Canal St as development followed the streetcar tracks through the towns of Lafayette, Jefferson and Carrollton, virtually leaving Barthélémy Lafon's Lower Garden District tract in the dust. These upriver towns, laid out on expansive plantations, were populated almost exclusively by Americans, and the area reflects their wealth and taste for Greek Revival architecture. Commodious street plans allowed for larger, more ostentatious houses and lush gardens. Gradually, all of these towns became part of the city of New Orleans: Lafayette was annexed in 1852, Jefferson in 1870 and Carrollton in 1874.

Garden District Walking Tour

Like the French Quarter, the Garden District is a National Historic District, where architectural preservation ordinances attempt to maintain the character of the area. Its boundaries are roughly those of the former city of Lafayette: St Charles Ave to Magazine St, between Jackson and Louisiana Aves.

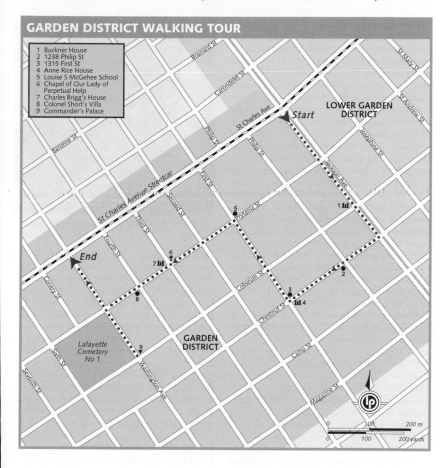

GARDEN DISTRICT WALKING TOUR

1 Buckner House
2 1238 Philip St
3 1315 First St
4 Anne Rice House
5 Louise S McGehee School
6 Chapel of Our Lady of
  Perpetual Help
7 Charles Brigg's House
8 Colonel Short's Villa
9 Commander's Palace

The area of greatest architectural interest is the lower half, below Washington Ave. Ironically, this premier enclave is not particularly safe to walk in at night. Plan to explore the neighborhood during daylight hours.

Begin your walk at Jackson Ave and St Charles Ave, and follow Jackson Ave toward the river. On the corner of Coliseum St is the **Buckner House**, 1410 Jackson St, built in 1856 for cotton merchant Henry S Buckner. The architect was Lewis E Reynolds. With wide galleries on four sides, it is the largest home in the Garden District. If it isn't feeding time

you'll notice that a finely conditioned Dalmatian watchdog complements the stateliness of this mansion. Continue to the corner of Chestnut St and turn right.

At the corner of Philip and Chestnut Sts, the house at **1238 Philip St** was built in 1853 for merchant John Rodenberg. Semioctagonal bay windows rise above a brick wall covered with tropical mandevilla vine on the Chestnut St side of the house, contributing an interesting effect to the Greek Revival structure. This side wing with the bays was added in 1869.

Halfway down the same block of Chestnut St, a rustic **garage** benefits from an elegant decay rarely seen in the Garden District, as crumbling plaster is permitted to expose the underlying brick. The garage is your first view of the estate at **1315 First St**, a glorious Italianate-style house laced with cast-iron ornamentation. The house was designed by architect Samuel Jamison for cotton factor Joseph Carroll.

Before you stray from the corner of Chestnut and First Sts, backtrack a bit to **Anne Rice's house**, at 1329 First St. This attractive home, named 'Rosegate' for the rose motif on the cast-iron fence, doesn't appear in any outward way to be haunted, although it does project some of the renowned occult author's eccentricity. An enormous porcelain dog – reportedly a gift from Anne to her husband, poet Stan Rice – stares whimsically from the 2nd-floor gallery. The Rices graciously open their home to visitors on Monday from 1 to 3 pm; there is no admission charge.

Head up First St towards Prytania St. At 2343 Prytania St, the **Louise S McGehee School** occupies one of the Garden District's most impressive mansions. Built in 1872 – later than other grand mansions in the district – the house combines decorative French Second Empire and classic styles. The architect is unknown, but stylistic clues suggest it may have been James Freret. The building has been home to the all-girls academy since 1929.

Continue on Prytania St, heading toward Washington St. Past Second St, the **Chapel of Our Lady of Perpetual Help**, at No 2521, was designed in 1856 by Henry Howard. It was built for Henry Lonsdale, a merchant who made fortunes in gunnysacks and coffee. A block farther down Prytania St, the lovely **Charles Briggs House**, at No 2605, certainly stands out. Designed by James Gallier in 1849, the house's Gothic-style pointed-arch windows and Elizabethan chimneys are unique in the neighborhood.

On the corner of Fourth and Prytania Sts, **Colonel Short's Villa**, 1448 Fourth St, was home to a Confederate officer. The house was seized by federal authorities during the

Porcelain watchdog of Anne Rice's 'Rosegate'

Civil War, but was returned at war's end to Short, who lived there until his death in 1890. It is an impressive home, designed by architect Henry Howard, and it is distinguished by a cornstalk cast-iron fence that outclasses the more famous cornstalk fence in the French Quarter (fewer layers of paint).

From Colonel Short's Villa, continue to Washington St, where you have several choices: You can explore Lafayette Cemetery No 1 (see below), walk a block on Washington St toward a rewarding lunch at Commander's Palace (see the Places to Eat chapter) or turn right toward St Charles Ave and the streetcar.

Lafayette Cemetery No 1

Established in 1833 by the former City of Lafayette, this cemetery is divided by two intersecting roads that form a cross. You'll notice many German and Irish names on the aboveground graves, testifying that immigrants were devastated by 19th-century yellow fever epidemics. Not far from the entrance is a low tomb containing the remains of an entire family that died of yellow fever. Fraternal organizations and groups like the Jefferson Fire Company No 22 took care of their members and their families in large shared crypts. Some of the wealthier family tombs were built of marble, with elaborate detail rivaling the finest architecture in the district. But most tombs were constructed simply of inexpensive plastered brick. The cemetery filled within decades of opening, before the surrounding neighborhood reached its greatest affluence. By 1872, the prestigious Metairie Cemetery appealed to those with truly extravagant tastes.

An unusual event occurred at Lafayette Cemetery in July 1995, when author Anne Rice, who lives just a few blocks away, staged her own funeral here. She hired a horse-drawn hearse and a brass band to play dirges, and she wore an antique wedding dress as she laid down in a coffin – because, she said, she wanted to experience her funeral *before* she was dead. (The newsworthy stunt coincided with the release of one of Rice's novels, so it wasn't pure frivolity.)

Volunteers from the nonprofit group Save our Cemeteries (☎ 525-3377) offer tours on Monday, Wednesday and Friday at 10:30 am. Tours cost $5, payable at the Washington Ave gate. Proceeds go to restoration efforts. The gates are closed at 2:30 pm – don't get locked in!

In Search of Desire

Desire, the Bywater street that lent its name to the streetcar line made famous by Tennessee Williams' play, *A Streetcar Named Desire*, was not one of Bernard Marigny's inspirations. Named by plantation owner Robert Gautier Montreuil for his daughter, Désirée Montreuil, the street has retained its name (unlike many other downtown streets that had intriguing names). The streetcar, sadly, has been replaced by a bus. Rumor has it, however, that the old Desire streetcar line may make a comeback in the near future.

TOM DOWNS

Audubon Zoological Gardens

Once noted as one of the country's worst zoos, at a time when animals were housed in a rectangle of stately brick buildings near the present entrance, the Audubon Zoo is now among the country's best. This is the heart of the Audubon Institute, which also maintains Woldenberg Park and the Aquarium of the Americas.

The zoo is divided into distinct sections. **Louisiana Swamp** displays the flora and fauna amid a Cajun cultural setting, which shows how the Cajuns harvested Spanish moss for use as furniture stuffing, among other details. The authentic fishing camp comes complete with shrimp trawls, crawfish traps and an oyster dredge. Alligators laze on the muddy bank of the bayou when they're not hibernating during the winter. Year-round in the exhibit, you'll see bobcat (*Lynx rufus floridamus*), red fox (*Vulpes vulpes*), endangered Louisiana black bear (*Urses americanus luteolus*) and the alligator snapping turtle (*Macroclemys temminicki*), a 200-pound giant that wiggles its pink tongue as bait. Human intrusions into the swamp environment are poignantly represented with a *traånasee* cutter, used by fish and game trappers to create access across shallow swamps, and an 'Xmas Tree' oil-well cap, reminding us of the much larger corporate threat to the swamp environment.

The **Audubon Flight Exhibit** is best on quiet days, when you can enter the giant cage to sit and observe the bird species portrayed by ornithologist-artist John James Audubon in *Birds of America*. Of course, there are ducks galore, but you will be mesmerized by the brilliant plumage of species like the scarlet ibis (*Eudocimus ruber*) and glossy ibis (*Plegadis falcmellus*), among others.

Most visitors are awed by the 'magnificent seven' in the **Reptile Encounter**, which displays representatives of the largest snakes in the world – from the king cobra that grows to over 18 feet in length to the green anaconda that reaches 38 feet. Many local species of nonpoisonous and poisonous snakes are also on display.

At **Butterflies in Flight**, you enter a humid greenhouse that is home to thousands of fluttering exotic butterflies, including tropical swallowtails *(Papilioniddae)* and the iridescent morphos *(Morphidae)*. Tropical birds and plants are also on display. It's worth the additional $2 admission cost, but shed any unnecessary clothes before entering.

The Audubon Zoo (☎ 861-2537), on the river-side of Magazine St and Audubon Park, is accessible from the French Quarter via the Zoo Cruise (see below) and the No 11 Magazine bus, or you can take the St Charles Ave streetcar and walk 1½ miles through shady Audubon Park. The zoo is open weekdays from 10 am to 5 pm and until 6 pm on weekends. Zoo admission costs $8.75 for adults, $4.75 for seniors and $4.50 for children. Look for discount coupons in tourist magazines like *Where*.

Zoo Cruise The Audubon Zoo Cruise offers a unique way to see the zoo and the Aquarium of the Americas (see the CBD & Warehouse District section for information on the aquarium). Combined discount

Cities of the Dead

New Orleans has an outstanding set of boneyards. Cemeteries are called 'cities of the dead' because they exhibit all the diversity and style of the surrounding city. In death, as in life, the wealthy mingle with the poor, with just enough elbow room for all to express some – or, in many cases, ample – personal style. Ornate marble tombs rise to the sky like Gothic churches amid rows of inner-city apartments for the dearly departed (in fact, it is possible to rent). Some neglected sections – postmortem ghettoes, if you will – have attracted the attention of preservationists who hope to restore these important emblems of a unique culture.

The vast majority of the graves in New Orleans are aboveground, and while no small amount of grandiosity inspired the more extravagant high-rise tombs, this practice of building up rather than down originated out of necessity. As early New Orleanians discovered, the region's high water table makes for wet digging; getting a buoyant wood coffin 6 feet underground meant first scuttling it to ensure that it would sink. Even then, a heavy rain could easily draw it back up to the surface again, and the dreadful sight of cadavers washing down flooded streets in the young city was not uncommon. So aboveground tombs constructed of brick and surfaced with plaster became the norm – and grandpa stayed put.

Five distinct styles of tombs evolved, although you won't necessarily see examples of all five within a single cemetery. The **wall vaults** that surround many cemeteries are often called 'ovens' because in the summer months they are known to get hot enough to slowly incinerate the bodies within. Once a body is decomposed – after a year and a day, according to a rule of thumb – these vaults can be reopened for the interment of a newly deceased person. **Family tombs** are the most common type of tomb. The cemetery equivalent of two-story, single-family homes, they are privately owned and typically house the remains of several generations. **Stepped tombs**, marked by steps on all sides, lack stable foundations and have a tendency to sink below ground. The stepped tomb is the only one of these five styles that is designed to contain just one body – all the others are intended for multiple burials. You are most likely to see these in St Louis Cemetery No 1, as they were no longer in use when later cemeteries were established. The **coping** is an aboveground burial chamber built of brick and plaster, which is ironically filled with soil to allow an elevated, water-free interment within the earth (yet another phenomenon that invites the expression, 'Only in Louisiana!'). The grandest tombs are the **society tombs**, so called because they were funded by benevolent associations to ensure proper burial for members of a particular community. Many of these majestic

tickets for the riverboat cruise, zoo and aquarium are available.

The boat departs the zoo at 10 am, noon, 2 and 4 pm. It leaves the zoo at 11 am, 1, 3 and 5 pm, departing from the Audubon Landing near the Australian Outback exhibit.

Tulane University

Tulane University (☎ 865-4000) was founded in 1834 as the Medical College of Louisiana in an attempt to control the repeated cholera and yellow fever epidemics. In 1847, the University of Louisiana merged with the school. Paul Tulane's $1 million donation in 1883 initiated significant expansion – plus it immortalized his name. The highly regarded medical school has since moved downtown to Tulane Ave. Tulane's law program is also well respected.

Newt Gingrich, former Speaker of the US House of Representatives, received his PhD in history from Tulane in 1971. The conservative politician has admitted to smoking pot while at Tulane – a response to President

---

Cities of the Dead

monuments are dedicated to particular 19th-century immigrant groups, who pooled funds to take care of their dead. Professions, religious denominations and branches of the military are also commonly represented. The larger society tombs have more than 20 vaults, and as these are reused over time, the population within these monuments can conceivably reach staggering numbers.

What really makes New Orleans' cemeteries visually enthralling is the incredible array of expressive, creative and often strange statuary and ornamentation that adorns many of the crypts. Angels praying with slumped wings and shoulders, grieving mothers tenderly cradling lethargic (perhaps dead) babies, wrought-iron crosses and gates, and stained-glass mosaics all play on light and shadow to create glorious surroundings for the dead. Some cemeteries are rapidly decaying, with broken tablets and loose plaster falling about the tombs, making them decidedly eerie.

Sadly, over the years many statues have been vandalized and even stolen. Some of the more elaborate pieces can fetch thousands of dollars on an underground market. New Orleans police recently exposed a ring of grave robbers, implicating Royal St antique dealers. Through this kind of thoughtless profiteering, the city is being drained of an attribute that should be preserved, treasured and protected.

MASON FLORENCE

There are more than 40 cemeteries in New Orleans. This book highlights just a few of them: St Louis Cemetery No 1 (Map 2), just outside the French Quarter; Lafayette Cemetery No 1 (Map 5), in the Garden District; Metairie Cemetery (Map 9), just west of City Park; and St Roch Cemetery (Map 3), a few blocks toward the lake from the Marigny. See the appropriate neighborhood sections for more information on each of these sections, and see Organized Tours in the Getting Around chapter to find out about informative cemetery tours.

At Tulane University

Clinton's 'didn't inhale' confession – adding that 'it was the wrong thing to do.' Other distinguished alumni include Amy Carter, daughter of former president Jimmy Carter, who enrolled at Tulane for graduate art-history studies.

The **University Center**, across Freret St on McAlister Drive, features a bookstore, ATM and a box office (☎ 861-9283) that sells tickets for sporting and special events. Downstairs there's a bulletin board for information on apartment-rentals, sublets and ride shares. The *Hullabaloo*, the campus newspaper published during the school year, is a good source for campus happenings, like free Friday open-air concerts and work opportunities.

Amistad Research Center The Amistad Research Center (☎ 865-5535) is one of the nation's largest repositories specializing in African American history. Even if you didn't come to New Orleans to study, the rotating exhibits offer insight on ethnic heritage you're not likely to get from any other source. A video of the Amistad adventure is shown for free. The displayed works of art from the Aaron Douglas Collection are another reason to drop by – a few of the works are copied for sale. The archive is in Tilton Hall, 6823 St Charles Ave, and it's open weekdays 8:30 am to 5 pm.

Hogan Jazz Archive This specialized research library is worth visiting if you're seriously into jazz history, although most of its great wealth of material is not on exhibit.

The Storyville Room is fascinating, with its emphasis on Jelly Roll Morton, who played piano in the district's bordellos during the early 20th century. The collection includes stacks of 78rpm recordings, including early sides recorded by the Original Dixieland Jazz Band in 1917, and you can ask to listen to rare tracks if you like. There's also a wealth of oral histories, photos and early concert posters. Curator Bruce Raeburn is a great man to talk to if you come with serious questions about jazz.

The Jazz Archive (☎ 865-5688, 304 Joseph Merrick Jones Hall, 3rd floor), on Freret St, is open weekdays 8:30 am to 5 pm.

Newcomb Art Gallery H Sophie Newcomb College (☎ 865-5565) was founded in 1886 through a gift of Josephine Louise Newcomb in memory of her daughter. It was the first degree-granting women's college in the US to be established as a coordinate division of a men's university. It has its own campus of red-brick buildings facing Broadway, adjacent to the main Tulane campus.

The Newcomb Art Gallery should qualify as a highlight of any tour of the Tulane campus. It features a permanent exhibit of the college's collection, including Newcomb Pottery, rotating exhibits from the university's art collection, nationally recognized traveling exhibits and contemporary student and faculty exhibits. Flanking the gallery entrance are two important Tiffany stained-glass triptychs depicting figurative scenes, 'The Resurrection' and 'The Supper at Emmaus.' The gallery is open weekdays 9 am to 4 pm. Admission is free.

CITY PARK & FAIR GROUNDS (MAP 9)

Members of the 'Esplanade Ridge' neighborhood and fellow residents near Bayou St John are making a brave attempt to restore their district to its former grandeur. Upscale restaurant and shops are now clustered near the corner of Esplanade Ave and Ponce de Leon St. Visitors are naturally attracted to Bayou Metairie and the great live oaks at City Park, site of the New Orleans Museum of Art. Of course, in addition to a regular horse racing season, the Fair Grounds is also the site of the huge springtime New Orleans Jazz & Heritage Festival (see Special Events in the Facts for the Visitor chapter).

Bayou St John Walking Tour

Graced with a variety of residential architectural styles, the placid Bayou St John is a pleasant place to stroll. It's actually the oldest part of New Orleans. French Canadians began settling the area before the founding of New Orleans. Long before that, Native Americans used the waterway to reach a ridge along what is now Esplanade Ave (or Esplanade Ridge), and this portage was the shortest link between Lake Pontchartrain and the Mississippi River. When the explorers Iberville and Bienville learned of this path, they decided it was the ideal place to settle. A canal built by Governor Carondelet later extended the bayou to the edge of the French Quarter, nearly connecting the lake and the river. Navigation ended with the filling of the canal in 1927.

This tour is largely an appreciation of the beautiful houses that line the Bayou St John. None of the following houses are open to the public aside from the Pitot House, which is open Wednesday to Saturday 10 am to 3 pm. It's a good idea to plan your exploration of this neighborhood during these hours in order to go inside this grand old structure. Start this walk at Esplanade Ave and Moss St, which follows the curve of Bayou St John.

The first stop is the **Pitot House**, 1440 Moss St. This site is covered in greater detail later. After visiting the house, follow the levee toward the **Magnolia Bridge**, a restored iron span built around the turn of the 20th century. It is now a pedestrian and bicycle crossing. Keep your eyes peeled for turtles along the water's edge. In early morning, you can often see at least one old-timer working his crab trap in the bayou. Do not cross the bridge (unless you already want to bag this tour).

Our Lady of the Rosary Rectory, 1342 Moss St, was built as the home of Evariste Blanc, probably in 1834. It exhibits a combination of styles characteristic of the region. The high-hipped roof and wraparound gallery, reminiscent of West Indies houses, were actually the preferred styles of the early French Canadians who settled Bayou St John. Classic details suggest this building is of a later period. At the intersection with

Bayou St John

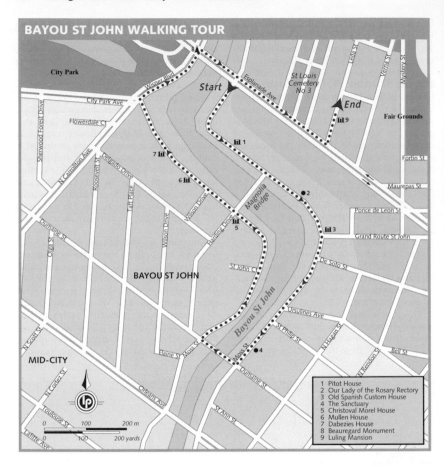

BAYOU ST JOHN WALKING TOUR

City Park

Start

Esplanade Ave.

St Louis Cemetery No 3

End

Fair Grounds

BAYOU ST JOHN

MID-CITY

0   100   200 m
0   100   200 yards

1 Pitot House
2 Our Lady of the Rosary Rectory
3 Old Spanish Custom House
4 The Sanctuary
5 Christoval Morel House
6 Mullen House
7 Dabezies House
8 Beauregard Monument
9 Luling Mansion

Grand Route St John, the **Old Spanish Custom House**, 1300 Moss St, occupies a site that was the plantation of Jean Francois Huchet de Kernion from 1736 to 1771. The present French colonial plantation-style house was probably built after 1807 for Captain Elie Beauregard. It was constructed by Robert Alexander, who borrowed materials from the Old Spanish Custom House, which he demolished while constructing the first US Custom House on Canal St. A bit farther along is **The Sanctuary**, 924 Moss St, built in 1816-22 by Blanc on land originally granted in 1720-1 to French-Canadians. The once-swampy property was later transferred to Don Andrés Almonaster y Roxas, the real-estate speculator who commissioned St Louis Cathedral on Jackson Square.

At Dumaine St, cross the bridge to the other side of Bayou St John, and continue back along the levee toward the Pitot House. A decidedly American influence can be seen in the 1^{1}/2 story Greek Revival design of the **Christoval Morel House**, 1347 Moss St, built in the late 1840s. The whimsical arch supports of the **Mullen House**, 1415 Moss St, are attributed to the ship carpenters employed by Thomas Mullen, who was a partner in the Mullen & Kennedy Shipyard near the Esplanade Bridge in the 1850s. Among the airy California bungalows in the Arts & Crafts style is the notable **Dabezies House**, at 1455 Moss St. Its cobblestones came from Decatur St when that street's bricks were pulled out. Continue along the levee back to Esplanade Ave.

At the Esplanade Bridge, you can see the entrance to City Park, on the left, and the **Beauregard Monument**, dedicated to the French Creole confederate general. Turn right and cross to **St Louis Cemetery No 3**, just a block away. The cemetery was established in 1854 at the site of the old Bayou Cemetery and is worth strolling through for at least a few minutes (longer if you're a cemetery enthusiast). James Gallier Jr designed the striking monument to his mother and father, who were lost at sea. Continue one more block along Esplanade Ave to the largest house in the neighborhood, the **Luling Mansion**, 1438 Leda St. James Gallier Jr and Richard Esterbrook created the Italianate villa design in 1865 for Florence Luling, an Alsatian-born cotton factor. (Luling actually made his fortune selling turpentine to the Yanks during the Civil War.) The villa was sold in 1871 to the Louisiana Jockey Club. Its landscaped gardens once extended from the Fair Grounds Race Track to Esplanade Ave.

City Park

At 1500 acres, City Park is the nation's fifth largest urban park – but relatively little of the area has a true park-like quality. The city acquired the property in 1850 and began improvements in 1896. It is well known for its great live oaks draped with Spanish moss and its bayou lagoons, especially along the narrow strip fronting City Park Ave. Unfortunately, I-610 slices through the park, ruining the solitude and habitat of the central area. The larger, lakeside portion has been reduced to four golf courses plus a riding stable (see Activities, later). Most visitors will only explore the remaining one-third on the river-side of I-610. Even here, nature is almost lost to the accumulation of 'improve-

ments' like redundant stadiums, roads and parking lots, buildings and restaurants, kiddie rides and tennis courts (see Activities) as well as the large New Orleans Museum of Art (see separate heading, below).

From the French Quarter, City Park (☎ 482-4888) is easily reached aboard the No 48 Esplanade bus. Esplanade Ave ends at the park entrance. The park is closed to bicyclists in the evening, but the issue is moot as cyclists will not find that City Park offers a convenient route to the lakeshore.

Botanical Garden This 7-acre garden was built by the WPA and features a showpiece art deco pool and fountain. Both native and exotic plant specimens from tropical and semitropical environments stimulate the sight and smell. Admission to the Botanical Garden (☎ 483-9386) is $3/1 for adults/children. It's open Tuesday through Sunday 10 am to 4:30 pm.

The Last Carousel Carved wooden animals first appeared at City Park in 1906, after a carousel at Audubon Park proved successful. By 1930, New Orleans featured four carousels, but the Great Depression, general deterioration and a growing emphasis on more exciting carnival rides took their toll, leaving the city with its last carousel by 1982. Residents raised $1.2 million to restore the broken animals, fix the squeaky merry-go-round and replace the Wurlitzer organ. The carousel is in **Storyland** (☎ 483-9382), a children's amusement area, open Wednesday

A lion stalks the jungle at City Park.

through Sunday 10 am to 4:30 pm, except during the Christmas holiday season when it's lighted at night from 5 to 10:30 pm. Admission to Storyland costs $1.50 ($3 during Christmas evenings).

Boat Rental Bayou Metairie in City Park is accessible to boats. Canoes and peddle boats are rented at the Casino Building (☎ 483-9371) for $6 to paddle or $8 to peddle. The fishing season begins in March – there's no equipment rental, but cane poles are sold for $4. Daily fishing permits cost $2/1 for adults/children under 16. The shop is open Wednesday to Friday 8:30 am to 5 pm and Saturday and Sunday 7 am to 7 pm.

Dueling Oaks Hot-headed violence is not new to New Orleans. During the 19th century, challenges to Creole honor often led to a meeting behind St Louis Cathedral or at the great oaks on the Allard Plantation near Bayou St John, where both parties could settle the offense with guns during the 19th century. The famous duel between a Baton Rouge newspaper editor who offended Alcée La Branche refutes the notion that the pen is mightier than the sword. After three attempts where the combatants missed each other from 40 yards, the fourth duel felled the editor. Only one of the famous trees still stands near the Museum of Art.

New Orleans Museum of Art
Founded in 1910, the original gift from philanthropist Isaac Delgado continues to grow as the collection of fine art is now valued at more than $200 million and covers three large floors. On the 1st floor are major traveling exhibits, which typically attract crowds and feature associated lectures, films and workshops. A sampler of recent exhibitions included 'Fabergé in America,' 'Andrew Wyeth: the Helga Pictures' and 'Sacred Arts of Haitian Voodoo.'

If you're not here for a special exhibit, you might consider starting with the 3rd-floor permanent exhibits, where pre-Columbian, Native American and African art set the stage for European influences, shown on the 2nd floor.

The New Orleans Museum of Art (☎ 488-2631) is reached from the French Quarter by the No 48 Esplanade bus. You can also get there from the Riverbend area aboard the No 90 Carrollton bus. The Courtyard Cafe offers lunch and snacks from 10:30 am to 4:30 pm. Admission is $6 for adults, $5 for seniors and $3 for children age three to 17. The museum is open Tuesday to Sunday 10 am to 5 pm.

Pitot House
On the banks of Bayou St John sits the Pitot House, a French colonial plantation-style house built in 1799. James Pitot, who was the first mayor of the incorporated city of New Orleans, acquired it in 1810. In 1904, it was purchased by the Missionary Sisters of the Sacred Heart, who used it as a day-care center and girls' orphanage. The sisters were guided by Mother Francis Xavier Cabrini, who in 1946 became the first US citizen canonized as a saint. In 1964, the sisters performed yet another act of charity by donating the house to the Louisiana Landmarks Society, which moved it a short distance to its present site and restored it from floor to ceiling.

Built without corridors, the *en suite* (adjoining) interior rooms allow air to circulate through the louvered shutters on the windows and upstairs back porch. The house features a double-pitched roof and stucco-covered briquette entre poteaux construction. Personalized guided tours cost $3 for adults, $2 for seniors, $1 for children. The Pitot House (☎ 482-0312, 1440 Moss St) is open Wednesday to Saturday 10 am to 3 pm.

Lakeshore Park
Locals cool off, bike, skate or just check each other out for nearly 10 miles along a narrow shoreline strip fronting Lake Pontchartrain. The park extends from the Southern Yacht Club, marked by the lighthouse, to the Inner Harbor Navigation Canal. It's still a long way from Santa Monica, and you shouldn't enter the polluted water, but it beats driving across the mind-numbing Pontchartrain Causeway to see the lake. Near the yacht club are numerous restaurants suitable for lunch, but don't make a special trip for dinner.

ELSEWHERE IN NEW ORLEANS
Metairie Cemetery (Map 9)

Having visited other New Orleans cemeteries doesn't quite prepare you for the over-the-top extravagance and stunning architectural splendor of Metairie Cemetery. Established in 1872 on a former race track (the grounds, you'll notice, still follow the oval layout), Metairie Cemetery is the most American of New Orleans' cities of the dead, and, like the houses of the Garden District, its tombs appear to be attempts at one-upmanship.

Obviously, this is the final resting place of many of New Orleans' most prominent citizens, and some of the cemetery's inhabitants are fairly famous. William Charles Cole Claiborne, Louisiana's first American governor, is here, as is Confederate General PGT Beauregard. Jefferson Davis was laid to rest here, only to be moved to Richmond, Virginia, two years later. Trumpet player Louis Prima occupies a family tomb inscribed with the refrain from his signature song, 'Just a Gigolo' – 'When the end comes they'll know/ I was just a gigolo/Life goes on without me.'

But the real highlight here is architecture. Many of the family tombs and monuments gracing Metairie Cemetery's concentric ovals are stunning, bringing together stone, bronze and stained glass. The statuary here is often elegant, touchingly sad, even sensual. Highlights include the **Brunswig mausoleum**, a pyramid guarded by a sphinx statue, the **Estelle Theleman Hyams monument**, with its stained glass casting a somber blue light over a slumped, despondent angel statue, and the **Moriarty monument**, the reputed 'tallest privately owned monument' in the entire country.

Visitors can drop by the Lakelawn Funeral Home (☎ 486-6331, 5100 Pontchartrain Blvd) and select either the 'Soldier, Statesmen, Patriots, Rebels' or 'Great Families and Captains of Commerce' self-guided tours. You will be given a map and loaned a recorded cassette and tape player (no charge).

Seeing everything on the 150-acre grounds is most easily accomplished by car. The cemetery is on Pontchartrain Blvd at its intersection with Metairie Rd. Admission is free. Tape tours take about an hour, but

Estelle Theleman Hyams monument

stretching this out by getting out of your car for a closer look at the tombs is highly recommended.

Longue Vue House

Longue Vue is an ornate home built in the early 1940s by the late Edith and Edgar Stern – heirs to the Sears & Roebuck fortune and among the leading philanthropists of the 20th century. The gardens include the formal Spanish Court, with trademark fountains modeled after Spain's Alhambra garden by Ellen Biddle Shipman, and a contrasting Wild Garden with a natural forest walk. Visitors also tour the fine-arts gallery, an accredited museum featuring rotating exhibits with such themes as textiles, clocks and Staffordshire pottery.

To get to Longue Vue House (☎ 488-5488, 7 Bamboo Rd), take the Nos 40, 41, 43 or 44 Canal St bus and get off at City Park Ave, which becomes Metairie Rd past the freeway. Either walk about 1 mile along Metairie Rd beside the Metairie Cemetery or wait for a Jefferson Transit Metairie Rd bus. Bamboo Rd is on the left (south) immediately past the bridge over the drainage canal. Motorists can drive toward the lake from the French Quarter on I-10 and take Metairie Rd exit 231. Guided tours last about one hour and cost $7/3 for adults/children ($10/3 around Christmas time). It's open Monday to Saturday 10 am to 4 pm and Sunday 1 to 4:15 pm

Louisiana Nature Center

In eastern New Orleans near the Lake Forest Mall, more than 80 acres of swampy habitat and a small museum introduce the visitor to the local ecology and wildlife. The museum (☎ 246-5672, 5601 Read Blvd) includes both hands-on exhibits for the kids and hands-off displays like live venomous snakes. A large picture window and microphone allow you to see and hear the birds outside. Many of the caged animals were either orphaned or injured and are being tended by the center's staff. One guest, the barred owl (*Strix varia*), frequents the swamps and has a distinctive cry that sounds like 'who cooks for you.'

Immediately outside the museum is a pond inhabited by nutria (see the Flora & Fauna section of the Facts about New Orleans chapter for more on the nutria). Also nearby is an example of a Tchefuncte home and midden (garbage heap). The Tchefuncte people inhabited the bayous from 2000 to 2500 years ago. It is known that these hunter-gatherers ate deer, rabbits, geese, alligators and fish; curiously, however, the rubbish in their middens contains neither crawfish nor crab remains.

More than a mile of raised platform walkway allows visitors to enter the cypress swamp and reach other trails. Plenty of spur trails and convenient benches allow quiet wildlife observation away from crowds. A duckweed-covered pond awaits at the outermost part of the trail. Occasional traffic sounds remind the visitor of the development threat to these readily drained wetlands.

A laser **planetarium** offers light shows that cost $5 and are presented Friday and Saturday at 9, 10:30 pm and midnight, plus 3:30 pm on Saturday and Sunday.

To get there from downtown, board the No 64 Lake Forest bus at the intersection of Canal and Basin Sts (on the lake-side next to the movie theater). It's an express bus that costs $1.25 and follows I-10 before traveling on Lake Forest Blvd to Read Blvd, where you exit and walk one block toward the river to the park entrance at Nature Center Dr. Continue past the tennis courts to the center. Admission costs $4/2 for adults/children.

It's open Tuesday to Friday 9 am to 5 pm, Saturday 10 am to 5 pm and Sunday noon to 5 pm. The gift shop offers a good selection of nature guides.

ACTIVITIES

Bicycling

New Orleans is a great city to bicycle in – it's flat and compact. Just watch out for those mammoth potholes, which can swallow skinny tires. Better yet, hop on a fat-tire mountain bike, and you've got the perfect urban swamp cruiser. For casual bicycling, pedal through City Park and around the lakefront and in a loop around Audubon Park and the riverside Levee Park. See the Getting Around chapter for rental information and for information about touring either on your own or with a group.

Cooking Classes

You are not likely to learn how to make complex French sauces in a short, introductory cooking demonstration. You can learn how to make a few of the one-dish Cajun and Creole meals that are relatively easy to prepare when you're in a hurry. The first two courses below offer entertaining lectures followed by a lunch made up of the dishes you have watched the chefs prepare. If you're in town for a couple of days, you might take both courses; they're not much more expensive than an equivalent lunch. The Hermann-Grima House has cooking demonstrations (see the French Quarter section, earlier in this chapter).

New Orleans School of Cooking The three-hour demonstration features everyday Creole cooking. An introduction to the area's geography and history is woven into the course explaining how Creole cuisine evolved. The menu consists of gumbo, jambalaya, bread pudding and pralines served with a Dixie beer. Classes at the New Orleans School of Cooking (☎ 525-2665, 525 St Louis St) begin daily at 10 am and cost $25. Call ahead to make reservations.

Cookin' Cajun This two-hour demonstration is a bit more rushed than the School of

At the New Orleans School of Cooking, get jambalaya with history and geography on the side.

Cooking course (it leaves out the geography and history lesson), and the menu typically features either gumbo or jambalaya. Cookin' Cajun (☎ 586-8832) is in the Riverwalk Mall, in the Creole Delicacies Gourmet Shop. The cost is $18. Morning courses (10 am) are usually filled by reservations. Walk-in classes are held every day: Monday to Thursday at 1 pm, Friday and Saturday at 10 am and Sunday at 11 am.

Spice, Inc Celebrated chef Susan Spicer (see the Places to Eat chapter) conducts two-hour courses every Tuesday night, sometimes with a high-profile guest instructor. She probably won't teach you how to make gumbo or jambalaya – courses focus on a given theme like vegetables or fish. It's a bit like being in the studio audience of a TV cooking program, except you actually get to try the food and drink wine. It's an experience, but it comes at a price: $40. Spice, Inc (☎ 558-9992, 1051 Annunciation St) is in the CBD, near the bridge pass.

Golf
Only a streetcar ride from downtown, the 18-hole Audubon Park course (Map 6) is open to the public.

City Park offers four 18-hole courses – the North, South, East and West Bayou Oaks courses (Map 9). The recently built Bayou Oaks Clubhouse & Restaurant (☎ 483-9396, 1040 Filmore Ave) serves the two championship courses (East and West) plus the North course. The Bayou Oaks South course straddles the freeway, and its clubhouse (☎ 483-9396) is on Zachary Taylor Dr, on the lake-side of the freeway. Greens fees range from $7 ($5 after 2 pm) at the South course to $17 at the East and West championship courses. All courses are open from dawn until dusk.

A driving range is available at the Learning Center (☎ 483-9394), across from the main Bayou Oaks Clubhouse. A large bucket of balls costs $6. It opens on weekdays at 9 am (8 am on weekends) and closes at 10 pm.

Fishing
To get a nonresident recreational fishing license, you will need to take either cash or a money order to the Louisiana Department of Fish & Wildlife (Map 4; ☎ 568-5636, 1600 Canal St, Suite 310). It's open weekdays 8:15 am to 4:15 pm. Fees for licenses vary depending on the length of trip and whether you add a saltwater stamp; a basic three-day

freshwater license costs $10. All permits expire on June 30 each year.

As for saltwater fishing, Louisiana's commercial live catch leads the nation – an auspicious indication of the sport fishing potential below the Intracoastal Waterway. Freshwater fishing is also appealing, as the warm inland waters are incredibly productive habitats for catfish, sacalait (white perch) and bass.

Casual anglers can try for the catfish and sacalait in Bayou Metairie at City Park. The fishing season begins in March. There's no equipment rental, but cane poles are sold for $4 at the boat rental near the Casino Building in City Park (Map 9). Daily fishing permits cost $2/1. The rental shop is open 8:30 am to 5 pm Wednesday to Friday, 7 am to 7 pm weekends.

Horseback Riding

In Audubon Park, Cascade Stables (☎ 891-2246, 6500 Magazine St) offers pony rides.

City Park Riding Stables (☎ 483-9398, 1001 Filmore Ave), offers English-style rides accompanied by an instructor for $20 per hour if you're with a group or for $25 per half hour if you want private lessons. No unaccompanied riders are allowed. Riders must be over six years old and have hard-soled boots. The stables are open 9 am to 7 pm weekdays and close at 5 pm on weekends.

In-Line Skating

Audubon Park is an ideal skating area. You can circle the park or concentrate on speed near the river in adjacent (across Magazine St) Levee Park, where you are unlikely to crash into other park visitors. Blade Action Sports (☎ 891-7055, 6108 Magazine St) rents skates near the park.

Lakeshore Park (see the City Park & Fair Grounds section, earlier in this chapter) is also a great place to blade, with long, paved trails.

Gyms

The YMCA International Hotel at Lee Circle (Map 4; ☎ 568-9622, 920 St Charles Ave) has complete and reasonably priced facilities, including a swimming pool appropriate for laps. Day use is $8, or $5 if you are staying at a local hotel (show a key).

If you want to rub elbows with real pros, head for the Mackie Shilstone Spa (Map 5; ☎ 566-1212, 2111 St Charles Ave) in the Avenue Plaza Hotel & Spa. When you get off the elevator on the 2nd floor, you are greeted by a life-size autographed photo of New Orleans' native and professional baseball star Will Clark. Shilstone is a personal trainer for many professional athletes. Admission to the gym costs $5 for guests or $9 for visitors.

Tennis

The City Park Tennis Center (Map 9; ☎ 483-9382) offers 36 lighted courts. Both hard and soft courts are available along with locker rooms, racquet rental, a pro shop and lessons from USPTA pros. It's open Monday to Thursday 7 am to 10 pm, and Friday to Sunday 7 am to 7 pm.

Places to Stay

Most visitors to New Orleans stay within easy reach of the French Quarter or inside the Quarter itself. In the upper Quarter and along Canal St, there is a concentration of large hotels with all the conveniences you'd expect from top-end tourist accommodations; the CBD (Central Business District) is where you'll find most convention-oriented hotels. For more traditional Creole charm, consider staying in the lower Quarter or even in the Faubourg Marigny; here, numerous small hotels and guesthouses have been fashioned from old Creole cottages and houses. Many of these have secluded courtyards, where you can escape the heat and the tourist rush. Staying in or near the Quarter generally comes at a price, though some surprising deals can be found. Budget travelers looking for inexpensive accommodations should check out the guesthouses in the Lower Garden District or in the Bywater. From these areas, it can be a long walk to and from the Quarter (not advisable at night), but public transit is available – the Lower Garden District has the advantage of being near the St Charles Ave streetcar line – and cab rides are not too expensive.

Room rates also vary, depending on the time of year, with peaks during Mardi Gras and Jazz Fest – and to a lesser degree around New Year's Eve. Advance reservations are recommended well ahead of time during

---

Reserve Early for Mardi Gras & Other Festivals

When Professor Longhair waxed the Carnival classic 'Go to the Mardi Gras' in 1958, he didn't say anything about New Orleans' 95% occupancy rate or jacked-up nightly rates during the city's signature holiday. You can't blame 'Fess' – he probably never stayed in a New Orleans hotel. However, much as you are encouraged to join in the fun and frivolity of Mardi Gras, Jazz Fest or New Year's, you will first need to make some very businesslike telephone calls.

Get your accommodation squared away well in advance – at least two or three months ahead of time; otherwise, you may be left out in the cold (and it can be cold during Mardi Gras). After staying at the perfect place while attending a festival, many folks make their reservations for the next year as they check out; some plan even further in advance.

Judging by the inflated rates you have to pay during the four nights of Mardi Gras (Saturday to Tuesday), the New Orleans hotel industry has its own interpretation of 'Fat' Tuesday. Room rates are typically double or even triple the off-peak prices. During Jazz Fest, room rates rise nearly as much. Most of the prices listed in this book are rack rates, so a little math will be required to figure out what a given hotel might charge during Mardi Gras.

Be ready to cough up a deposit of at least the cost of one night's stay, or half of the bill or more, and count on a minimum two- or three-night stay. In addition to these minor impediments, many places adopt a two-week to one-month cancellation policy for reservations during special events – don't expect to cancel at the last minute. And don't expect to haggle, either. In the end, you'll be glad you planned ahead, and you'll most certainly be glad you stayed more than one or two nights!

Other holidays that are big in New Orleans, making preplanning and a bigger budget necessary, are New Year's (when the Sugar Bowl adds to an already festive atmosphere) and Halloween.

these periods, whether you plan to bunk at a hostel or stretch out at a classy hotel, where you can expect the rates to be double the norm. Off-season discounts kick in when occupancy rates drop. During the hot, wet and sticky summer months, desperate innkeepers drastically reduce rates at the most costly properties, so you should consider the comfort value of a modern air-conditioned room during those times.

You can often find discounts from the so-called 'rack rate' quoted to guests who arrive without a reservation. Discounts of 10% or more are commonly granted to members of the American Automobile Association (AAA), as well as senior citizens, students, military personnel, government employees and those with some corporate affiliations. Even someone walking in off the street without a reservation can often negotiate a discount if armed with knowledge that occupancy is down; ask your shuttle or taxi driver how business is. Conversely, don't expect a discount at a hotel that is booked for a convention.

Another note: The 800 numbers of the chains are not your best bet for getting a good deal or checking on room availability. These hotlines also can't guarantee a particular room (say, one with a balcony or a view or one that's been remodeled). Lower rates are often quoted at the local numbers.

Additional charges include the 11% room tax plus a $1 per person occupancy tax. You can also add about $14 a day if you choose to park a car at most of the lodgings in the French Quarter or CBD. Charges for movies and telephone calls can also inflate your bill.

Unless you are just passing through, don't scrimp by booking a discounted room near the airport or along one of the highways. Your savings will be lost when you must either pay a taxi fare or exorbitant parking fees to join the fun in the Quarter.

If you arrive in town without reservations, the New Orleans Metropolitan Convention & Visitors Bureau (☎ 566-5011) offers a free accommodations guide, with a list of member businesses, their price ranges and a map. The bureau has an office on Jackson Square in the French Quarter.

CAMPING

A few private campgrounds and RV parks in eastern New Orleans can be reached by public transit from the French Quarter. Four state park campgrounds within a half-hour drive of New Orleans offer well-maintained camping facilities. All have toilets, hot and cold running water, showers, electrical hookups and shaded sites.

The most convenient campground is about 13 miles southeast of New Orleans at *St Bernard Parish State Park* (☎ 682-2101). It's near the Mississippi River and features wooded lagoons, short nature trails and a swimming pool. Jean Lafitte National Historic Park (see the Excursions chapter for details) is nearby. Take Hwy 46 along the east bank of the Mississippi to Bayou Rd and turn right on Hwy 39. The park entrance is within a mile on your left. Campsites are on a first-come, first-served basis and include water and electricity for $12.

Campers can also stay on the west bank of the river at *Bayou Segnette State Park (Map 1;* ☎ 736-7140), which offers 100 reservable campsites with water and electricity for $12. Cabins, which can accommodate eight people, are available for $65, including linens and cookware. The park was built at the confluence of several canals that have partially drained the former swamp, creating a bottomland hardwood environment with good boat access to swamps and bayous all the way to the Gulf Coast. The popular boat launch is open 24 hours. To get there from New Orleans, cross the Greater New Orleans Bridge and follow Business Hwy 90 (Westbank Expressway) upriver about 10 miles to the bayou entrance at Drake Ave, on your left.

On the north shore of Lake Pontchartrain, *Fountainebleau State Park* (☎ 624-4443) offers hundreds of improved, reservable campsites for $12 and unimproved sites for $10. Dense pine and hardwood forests shade the park's interpretive nature trail and most of the campsites, and there is a beach and pool. The park is across the Lake Pontchartrain Causeway ($1 toll) and about 4 miles east on Hwy 190.

The *Fairview-Riverside State Park* (☎ 845-3318) has another north shore campground on the bank of the Tchefuncte River. It offers improved sites for $12 on a first-come, first-served basis. During the 19th century, the site was a lumber camp. Now the river and woodlands are recovering only to be assaulted by encroaching suburban development near the margins of the park. The park is 3 miles west of the Lake Pontchartrain Causeway on Hwy 22.

The closest privately operated RV parks and campgrounds are along the Chef Menteur Hwy (Hwy 90) in eastern New Orleans (east of the Inner Harbor Navigation Canal). The *Jude Travel & Trailer Park* (☎ 241-0632, 7100 Chef Menteur Hwy) offers a pool, hot tub, showers and laundry, along with full hookups starting at $19. The tent sites cost a bit less. The No 66 Chef Menteur Express bus stops near the park.

Also try the *Mardi Gras Campground* (☎ 243-0085, 6050 Chef Menteur Hwy), near I-10 exit 240A, which offers tent sites for $15, or $25 during Jazz Fest.

Upriver from town, almost all the way to the New Orleans International Airport, the *New Orleans West KOA* (☎ 467-1792, 11129 Jefferson Hwy) offers tent sites for $21 and RV sites for $27.

HOSTELS

Three hostels can be reached from the French Quarter on public transit: Two are a block from the St Charles Ave streetcar, and one is in Mid-City near Canal St. They're predominantly used by foreign visitors; local lodgers are discouraged, as are overly extended stays. They all offer a kitchen, baggage storage, heat or air-conditioning depending on the season, and communal areas, where it's easy to make friends. All are also well known to the airport shuttle drivers. The no-curfew policies will no doubt be appreciated by guests intent on making the most of New Orleans' round-the-clock action. Hostel bulletin boards offer a wealth of local information and travel tips.

You don't need to be a member of Hostelling International to stay at HI's *Marquette House* (Map 5; ☎ 523-3014, 2253 Carondelet St, hineworle@aol.com) on the margins of the Garden District. Membership

to the hosteling organization ($25 a year in the USA) can be purchased at the desk and primarily entitles you to access or discounts at a network of hostels. A dorm bed costs $14/17 for members/nonmembers, including tax. Private rooms cost $40 for doubles; larger, four-person rooms cost $66. Sheet rental is an additional $2.25, and the cost for the coin-operated rental lockers will add up if you need to repeatedly get to your things.

The 176-bed facility consists of four undistinguished buildings; the most distinctive building burned a few years ago. For your money, you get the standard metal bunk with foam mattress and a shower shared by as many as 12 guests. There are two laundries nearby (one is in a bar). To get there from Union Passenger Terminal, walk five blocks toward the river on Howard Ave to St Charles Ave and take the uptown streetcar to Jackson Ave and walk northwest one block to Carondelet St; the hostel is half a block to the left.

In the Lower Garden District, the *Longpré Guest House Hostel* (Map 5; ☎ 581-4540, 1726 Prytania St) offers 24 dorm beds in an 1850s Italianate-style house. Though it's no museum showpiece, the Longpré is a comfortable place, with a front porch that is perfect for hanging out. A large kitchen and rear patio are available for eating. There are coin-operated lockers, but less valuable items can be locked in your room. A laundry is across the street. The only real complaint comes from nonsmokers, as smoking is permitted in the communal TV room (drinking is also allowed).

Bunks come with linens for $12, including tax, if you carry a foreign passport, or for $16 if you're a US citizen. Funky private rooms with loft beds run $40. All rates go up during special events, doubling during Mardi Gras. To get to the hostel from the downtown area, take the St Charles Ave streetcar to Euterpe St and walk one block toward the river to Prytania St.

A free-spirit atmosphere flourishes at the *India House Hostel* (Map 8; ☎ 821-1904, 124 S Lopez St), off Canal St in Mid-City. The large aboveground swimming pool and cabaña-like donor behind the two h that serve as dorms definitely add to the ambience. Bunk beds cost $12, including linen and tax. Simple private cabins are available for $30. Guests can use the washer and dryer. To get there from the Union Passenger Terminal, cross Loyola Ave in front of the depot and take any Claiborne Ave bus ($1.10 fare with transfer) to Canal St, where you transfer to any Canal St bus heading toward the lake. Cross Canal St after you get off at Lopez St.

HOTELS, MOTELS, B&BS & GUESTHOUSES

Hotels There are cheap hotels in New Orleans, but they cater to the transient wino crowd and are no fun. If you're really economizing, you'll find the hostels (see above) are a much better bet. That said, there are safe, comfortable hotels charging $40 to $70 for a double room. Mid-range hotels run $70 to $150, and once you get over $150 a night, you're in the 'top end.'

Motels You'll find few 'motor hotels' near the pedestrian and transit-oriented areas of New Orleans. Their major appeal is free parking. Stay away from the cheap rooms along Airline Hwy (where televangelist Jimmy Swaggart was caught with his pants down). They're next to the railroad and are not a good value for most visitors. Near the airport, a number of large, comfortable chain motels advertise rates from $40 to $70.

B&Bs More romantic B&Bs typically offer a small number of rooms with antique furnishings and full breakfasts at rates that range from $70 to $150 and up.

The Louisiana B&B Association (☎ 346-1857), PO Box 4003, Baton Rouge, LA 70821-4003, offers a free illustrated guide to member B&Bs throughout the state. Bed & Breakfast, Inc (☎ 488-4639), PO Box 52257, New Orleans, LA 70152-2257, makes free reservations at selected B&Bs to suit everyone from backpacking students looking for a romantic mini-splurge to the most discriminating travelers. Owner Hazel Boyce will promptly send or fax an illustrated description of the range of available properties.

Guesthouses In New Orleans, we must add 'guesthouses' to encompass the many large historic homes and other structures converted to accommodate guests, often at rates well below the more exclusive B&Bs. Many are convenient to the French Quarter or near City Park and fill the gap normally occupied by motels in more auto-oriented cities. Rooms start below $40 at the larger guesthouses, most of which offer only a continental breakfast or none at all.

French Quarter (Map 2)

Rates in the French Quarter are higher than in the rest of the city; they average about $110. If you can't part with your car, always inquire about hotel parking fees. Public parking garages near the upper margins of the Quarter (eg, 716 Iberville St) charge $11 for 24 hours

It's possible to be too close to the noisy activity in the French Quarter. Guests staying near Bourbon St should not turn in until they are ready to pass out, and even then the early morning trash pickup and street sweeping can wake the dead. Ask about courtyard-facing rooms, which are significantly quieter. You can generally find quietude in the predominantly residential areas of the lower Quarter.

Mid-Range The *Chateau Motor Hotel* (☎ 524-9636, 1001 Chartres St) offers rooms for $79/99 single/double in a quiet part of the Lower Quarter. That price includes a continental breakfast and parking. A few blocks away and a step up in quality is *Le Richelieu* (☎ 529-2492, 800-535-9653, 1234 Chartres St), where handsomely decorated rooms start at $85/100, including parking. The red-brick building was originally a macaroni factory, but extensive construction has turned this into a comfortable, fairly conservative-looking hotel.

The *Gentry House* (☎ 525-4433, 1031 St Ann St) is in a charming Creole cottage just half a block from the Rampart St music clubs. Rooms come with a coffeemaker and refrigerator and cost $65 to $110.

The *Cornstalk Hotel* (☎ 523-1515, 915 Royal St) is famous for the fence out front,

The Cornstalk Hotel's photogenic fence

which is possibly the most photographed fence in the USA. The colorful cornstalks were cast in 1859 and attract a steady stream of admirers. The rooms inside are also attractive, with high ceilings and antique furnishings. Rooms with private bath cost $110/150 single/double but can drop to $75 at off-peak times.

Hotel St Pierre (☎ 524-4401, 800-225-4040, 911 Burgundy St) is a group of historic Creole cottages with interior courtyards and modern furnishings. Room rates start at $110/130 single/double, and suites start at $140 – lower quotes show a willingness to compete during off-peak periods. The same people operate the *Andrew Jackson Hotel* (☎ 561-5881, 800-654-0224, 919 Royal St), with the same rates and a more central location.

The commotion does not typically extend down Bourbon St to the *Lafitte Guest House* (☎ 581-2678, 800-331-7971, 1003 Bourbon St), an elegant, three-story French manor house. There are 14 rooms, with prices starting at $119 ($159 and up for suites). Call ahead for the brochure, which gives a description of each room. Parking costs $10 a night.

The finely restored buildings of the *Hotel Provincial* (☎ 581-4995, 800-535-7922, 1024 Chartres St) contain around 100 high-ceilinged rooms and suites, which open onto interior courtyards. Standard room rates include parking and start at $99, or $139 for suites.

Top End When the venerable *Hotel Monteleone* (☎ 523-3341, 800-535-9595, 214 Royal St) opened in 1907, it was the largest hotel in the French Quarter – and it still is! The narrow streets hardly allow one to stand back to admire its handsome white terracotta exterior. All rooms were renovated in the early 1990s, and rates typically start at $120/140 single/double except during the summer, when all rooms cost $90 (yes, it is air-conditioned). A curious highlight here, even if you're not staying in the hotel, is the Carousel Bar off the main lobby – it actually revolves, but not fast enough to cause your drinks to fly off the bar.

The *Omni Royal Orleans* (☎ 529-5333, 800-843-6664, 621 St Louis St) offers arguably the best furnishings and in-room amenities of any large hotel in town. Rates range from $109 to $319 depending on the room size and the season. Services include a beauty salon and babysitting, and the Omni Royal's rooftop observation deck affords a stunning view.

The *Royal Sonesta* (☎ 586-0300, 800-766-3782, 300 Bourbon St) offers a choice between rooms with balconies overlooking noisy Bourbon St or quiet courtyard-facing rooms. It was built to look old, but with 500 rooms it is oversized for this portion of the Quarter. The rooms start at $145/185 single/double, and balcony suites start at $420. A better bet is the large *Bourbon Orleans Hotel* (☎ 523-2222, 800-521-5338, 717 Orleans Ave), which has rooms with Queen Anne furnishings, a marble bath and two telephones. Rates for standard doubles tend to hover above $100 but can dip as low as $69 and climb up to $159.

Small hotels are really the most suitable accommodations in New Orleans, as they capture the city's historic charms in ways that the modern high-rises don't come close to matching. Considering that, the warm and elegant *Soniat House* (☎ 522-0570, 800-544-8808, 1133 Chartres St) may well be New Orleans' premier hotel. Certainly for Creole-style elegance, this historic lower Quarter establishment has no equal. It's in a meticulously restored 1830 town house with lacy ironwork, beautiful antique furnishings and a romantic courtyard. It probably isn't a great place for children to stay. Rooms cost $160 to $250; suites cost $275 to $495. The parking fee is $14 a night.

Courtyard of the Hotel Provincial, French Quarter

Tremé District (Map 2)

On Esplanade Ave, along the edge of the Tremé, are several reasonably priced places worth considering for their proximity to the Quarter. **Maison Esplanade** (☎ 523-8080, 800-290-4233, 1244 Esplanade Ave) is a historic home with an exterior stairway (the story behind this has something to do with 19th-century taxes on interior stairs) and nine modest, antique-furnished rooms with private bath starting at $50. Also try the **Rathbone Inn** (☎ 947-2100, 800-947-2101, 1227 Esplanade Ave) for inexpensive rooms in another 1850s mansion. **Hotel Storyville** (☎ 948-4800, 1261 Esplanade Ave) is a thoroughly modern lodging, which was built to look old on the outside only. The spotless suites sleep four and cost between $80 and $125, or $150 to $250 with kitchenettes.

Faubourg Marigny & Bywater (Map 3)

The Faubourg Marigny offers a hip, alternative place to stay close to the Quarter. Beyond the Marigny, the low-rent Bywater is showing signs that it is the creative neighborhood to watch. From either neighborhood, it is possible to walk to the Quarter (it's more than a mile from the Lower Bywater to the Lower Quarter), but cabs are recommended after dark.

The **Lion's Inn B&B** (☎ 945-2339, 2517 Chartres St) 'welcomes all sexual persuasions' with four nice rooms in a renovated house. One sleeps four for $100; the others range from $45 to $85.

Closer to the Quarter, the small **Lamothe House** (☎ 947-1161, 800-367-5858, 621 Esplanade Ave) offers 11 antique-crowded rooms starting at $85 in season and requires a two-night minimum stay on weekends. Published rates for standard doubles start at $84 at **The Frenchmen** (☎ 948-2166, 800-831-1781, 417 Frenchmen St), a small, refurbished 1850s Creole house with an interior court and spa. Balcony rooms cost almost $50 more, but you might negotiate an off-peak discount on any of the rooms. The Frenchmen also offers a 24-hour concierge.

If you're not 'of the money,' the **Hotel de la Monnaie** (☎ 947-0009, 405 Esplanade Ave) may be too costly – two-bedroom suites with kitchenettes range from $190 in the off-season to $270 during special events. Yet these can be a good value if occupied by six guests. The hotel also has one-bedroom suites, which sleep four. Behind the Old US Mint, the hotel was built in the 1980s to look old and features interior courts and river views from the top floors.

At the extreme top end is the **Melrose Mansion** (☎ 944-2255, 937 Esplanade Ave), an elegant 1884 Victorian mansion with excellent service and fine antique furnishings. Room rates start around $250. The pampering begins with the stretch limo sent to fetch guests at the airport. The same people operate the nearby **Girod House** (☎ 522-5214, 835 Esplanade Ave), an all suite guesthouse fashioned out of the 1833 Creole home built by the city's first mayor, Nicholas Girod. The rooms are completely modern, with kitchens, and range in price from $145 to $165.

In the lower Bywater, **Mazant Guest House** (☎ 944-2662, 906 Mazant St), at Burgundy St, is an attractive, two-story former

The all-suite Girod House

plantation house with kitchen facilities and 11 guest rooms. Furnishings are mostly antiques, but not fussily so. The Mazant's selling points are its warm, homey charm, extremely reasonable rates and manager Bob Girault's undying enthusiasm for the local music scene (he'll steer you in the right direction). It attracts European guests who often make use of the kitchen and parlor, making this a fairly social place to stay. Most rooms (with shared bath) cost between $30 and $40; ask about rooms that afford more privacy. Free off-street parking is available, and there are bicycles available for guests' use.

The **Bywater B&B** (☎ 944-8438, 1026 Clouet St) is a popular lesbian artist hangout that houses a folk art collection. Three rooms with shared bath cost about $60.

CBD & Warehouse District (Map 4)

Budget The **YMCA International Hotel** (☎ 568-9622, 920 St Charles Ave), at Lee Circle, has spartan rooms with shared bath for $30/36 single/double plus a $5 key deposit. Guests have full use of the gym facilities and swimming pool. The hotel's restaurant, Back to the Garden, offers cheap and healthy breakfasts and lunches (see the Places to Eat chapter).

Next to the elevated freeway (a long walk to the Quarter), **Days Inn** (☎ 586-0110, 800-232-3297, 1630 Canal St) has standard rooms starting at $89.

Mid-Range Near City Hall, **Comfort Inn Downtown** (☎ 586-0100, 800-228-5150, 1315 Gravier St) has basic rooms in a high-rise starting at $59 during the slow season and going up from there. **Comfort Suites** (☎ 524-1140, 800-228-5150, 346 Baronne St) has modern rooms, which normally start at $129 but can drop to $79 or jump to $209 depending on the season. A step up and only two blocks from the Quarter is the **Hampton Inn** (☎ 529-9990, 800-426-7866, 226 Carondelet St), offering free local calls and continental breakfast in modern rooms for $89 to $159.

The **Holiday Inn Select** (☎ 524-1881, 888-524-1881, 881 Convention Center Rd II

built in the 1990s to resemble a 1930s art deco hotel. Rooms typically start at $100 but can go higher (and maybe lower) depending on whether any conventions are booked across the street.

The *Holiday Inn Downtown Superdome* (☎ 581-1600, 800-535-7830, 330 Loyola Ave) is easily recognized by the 18-story-high

---

Convention Hotels

Large high-rise hotels with chain affiliations tend to cluster near Canal St and offer predictable standards at competitive rates. The Hyatt Regency is an outlying hotel adjacent to the Superdome. Typical room rates start at anywhere from $100 to $200 at these establishments.

Doubletree Hotel
    Map 4; ☎ *581-1300, 800-222-8733,*
    300 Canal St

Hilton Riverside Hotel
    Map 4; ☎ *561-0500, 800-445-8667,*
    2 Poydras St

Hotel Inter-Continental
    Map 4; ☎ *525-5566, 800-332-4246,*
    444 St Charles Ave

Hyatt Regency
    Map 4; ☎ *561-1234, 800-233-1234,*
    500 Poydras St

Le Meridien Hotel
    Map 4; ☎ *525-6500, 800-543-4300,*
    614 Canal St

Marriott Hotel
    Map 2; ☎ *581-1000, 800-228-9290,*
    555 Canal St

Radisson Hotel
    Map 4; ☎ *522-4500, 800-333-3333,*
    1500 Canal St

Sheraton Hotel
    Map 4; ☎ *525-2500, 800-325-3535,*
    500 Canal St

Westin Canal Place
    Map 2; ☎ *566-7006, 800-228-3000,*
    100 Iberville St

---

clarinet painted on the side of the building. Basic rooms start at $99 during nonholiday seasons, and executive accommodations are available from $129.

Top End A few hotels in this area rise above the typically overpriced conventioneers' accommodations. In particular, elegant *Le Pavillon* (☎ 581-3111, 800-535-9095, 833 Poydras Ave), opened in 1907, is a large full-service hotel offering plenty of lovely marble in the lobby and plush updated rooms, which start at $115 for a double in the off-peak season. A smaller hotel that also gets high marks is the *Lafayette Hotel* (☎ 524-4441, 600 St Charles Ave), at Girod St. Rooms with a king-size bed start at $145, suites at $265.

With an ornate, block-long lobby and fine dining, the *Fairmont Hotel* (☎ 529-7111, 800-527-4727, 123 Baronne St) was the city's elite establishment when it opened in the 1920s as the Roosevelt Hotel. It has undergone substantial remodeling, and the rooms vary tremendously in size and furnishings; it's a good idea to look at a room before agreeing to take it. Rates usually start around $225 for one or two people and $450 for suites but can drop substantially during slow periods.

With a high tea, fine English paintings and antique European furnishings, the *Windsor Court Hotel* (☎ 523-6000, 800-237-1236, 300 Gravier St) represents the greatest English invasion of New Orleans since General Pakenham's army. It was founded in 1984 by an honorary British consul who felt that New Orleans needed luxurious accommodations with traditional grand service. Rooms start at $250, and suites cost between $310 and $990.

Lower Garden & Garden Districts (Map 5)

Budget Some of the best values for guesthouse lodgings are in the properties run by the *Prytania Inns* (☎ 566-1515, 1415 Prytania St). Note that during Mardi Gras, room rates for all Prytania Inn properties rise over $100 and there's a three-night minimum stay.

Upstairs from the central office is the *Prytania Inn I*, with rooms that come with private baths and furnishings that have seen better days. There's a courtyard and additional rooms in back. Some rooms have kitchens. Be sure to see the room before you accept it, because the quality of the furnishings can vary greatly. Rates start under $29/39 single/double without breakfast. Add $5 for a full breakfast. *Prytania Inn II (2041 Prytania St)* is a few blocks away in a building that looks more impressive from the outside but houses similar rooms at the same rates as Prytania I. Rooms at *Prytania Inn III (2127 Prytania St)* cost the same, but considering the building, with its glorious parlors furnished with faded but stylish antiques, it's one of the bargains of the city. It is housed in one of the town's most stunning Greek Revival 'raised villas,' built in 1857. It's just barely outside the Garden District.

Yet another of the Prytania Inn properties is the large *St Vincent's Guest House (☎ 523-3411, 1507 Magazine St)*, a former orphanage. A courtyard swimming pool offers a welcome respite from New Orleans' all-too-frequent tortuously hot days. Modern rooms start at $49.

Guests like the antique-filled rooms at the *St Charles Guest House (☎ 523-6556, 1748 Prytania St)*. Longtime owner Dennis Hilton offers a few small rooms with shared bath for $45 to $65, while most rooms with private bath cost $75 to $95 for movie-set-like furnishings and continental breakfast. Rates naturally go up for special events.

Mid-Range The *Whitney Inn (☎ 521-8000, 800-379-5322, 1509 St Charles Ave)* is a refurbished 19th-century guesthouse offering antique-furnished rooms, with rates starting at $75, including a continental breakfast. Suites are also available, starting at $135.

The rooms at the modern *Ramada Plaza Hotel (☎ 566-1200, 800-443-4675, 2203 St Charles Ave)*, at Jackson Ave, won't win any interior design contests, but they are clean and comfortable. Rates start at $79/89 single/double during between-holiday lulls and rise by $100 during Mardi Gras. Parking is free.

The *Prytania Park Hotel (☎ 524-0427, 800-862-1984, 1525 Prytania St)* is a modern motel with 49 small but nicely appointed

The Greek Revival Prytania Inn III

TOM DOWNS

rooms alongside a restored 1850s guesthouse with 13 rooms. Published rates start at $100/120 single/double and include a continental breakfast, but discounts are easily obtained when few cars appear in the free parking lot.

At the *Avenue Plaza Hotel & Spa* (☎ 566-1212, 800-535-9575, 2111 St Charles Ave), all rooms have king-size beds – perhaps in hopes of attracting professional athletes to their spa. Standard rooms start at $90; studio suites with kitchens cost around $210.

The *Maison St Charles* (☎ 522-0187, 800-831-1783, 1319 St Charles Ave) is a Quality Inn property with modern rooms starting at $69 single or double.

At the *Josephine Guest House* (☎ 524-6361, 800-779-6361, 1450 Josephine St), at Prytania St, you can't miss the whimsical, large floating cherubs over the entries or the pelican lawn ornament. Rooms in the carefully restored mansion cost $100 to $150 and include breakfast on Wedgwood china.

The 1858 Georgian Revival *Terrell Guest House* (☎ 524-9859, 1441 Magazine St), at Euterpe St, offers impressive antique furnishings and marble fireplaces in the main bedrooms for $150. The 3rd-floor dormer rooms and rear servants' quarters cost $100 to $125. All rooms have private bath and include a full breakfast and cocktails.

Top End When Edith Stern moved from her Longue Vue mansion, she settled into the *Pontchartrain Hotel* (☎ 524-0581, 800-777-6193, 2031 St Charles Ave), at Josephine St, built in 1927. It has been restored to its original splendor and represents a very good value for a full-service hotel. Rooms start at $145 and go up to $400 for luxury suites.

Uptown (Map 6) & Riverbend (Map 7)

Most of the hotels in Uptown are in the upper mid-range and top-end categories. If you're coming for Mardi Gras, staying along St Charles Ave is not a bad plan, since many parades go down this Uptown thoroughfare.

The *Columns Hotel* (☎ 899-9308, 3811 St Charles Ave), at General Taylor, is one of the great establishments of New Orleans, but its reputation doesn't rest solely on its rooms. The downstairs bar and patio is one of the city's most festive gathering spots. On the 2nd and 3rd floors, 20 rooms of various size range from $90 for a smallish double to $175 for the two-room 'Pretty Baby Suite' (named for the Louis Malle film shot here in the 1970s). To absorb the late-night revelry – no doubt at the expense of sleeping! – take a front room on the 2nd floor; room No 16 ($160) has a balcony overlooking the front entry and St Charles Ave.

Just three blocks from the Columns, *Lagniappe Bed & Breakfast* (☎ 800-317-2120, 1925 Peniston St) has very quaint and comfortable rooms, all with private bath and tastefully selected antiques. Double occupancy rates of $125 include full breakfast, off-street parking and – true to the name – numerous extras ranging from fresh flowers and fruit to complimentary beer, wine and soft drinks. The friendly and attentive owners live on site, and they treat their guests to a charming and comfortable stay.

Near Audubon Park in Riverbend, the *Parkview Guest House* (☎ 861-7564, 7004 St Charles Ave) was built in 1884 to impress visitors to the World Cotton Exchange Exposition the following year. Antique furnishings abound in the lounge and rooms. Rooms with shared bath start at $89/99 single/double, and rooms with private bath start at $109/119.

City Park & Fair Grounds (Map 9)

A glorious mansion built in 1859 for the Greek Counsel, the *Benachi Torre House B&B* (☎ 525-7040, 800-308-7040, 2257 Bayou Rd), at Rocheblave St, occupies a tremendous iron-fenced lot, complete with carriage house and original cistern. Handsome, restored rooms cost $85 to $95. Owners Jim Derbes and Cecilia Rau also rehabilitated the nearby *Lagniappe Guest House* (☎ 525-7040, 800-308-7040, 2216 Esplanade Ave), which offers two-room suites starting at $995.

The *House on Bayou Road* (☎ 945-0092, 800-882-2968, 2275 Bayou Rd) is a top-end B&B in a former Creole plantation home surrounded by two acres of land. Rooms in the main house cost $105 to $155 for a double to over $200 for a suite; a private cottage is also offered. Guests may take a cooking course as part of a two- or five-night package.

A bit farther toward the lake is the recently restored **Edgar Degas House B&B** (☎ 821-5009, 2306 Esplanade Ave), an 1854 Italianate-style house where the famed French impressionist lived when visiting his mother's family in 1873. While in New Orleans, Degas painted his brother's wife in the *Portrait of Estelle* (on exhibit in the New Orleans Museum of Art) and his uncle, a cotton factor, in *The Cotton Market in New Orleans*. Garret rooms, once the cramped top-floor servants' quarters, cost $100, and others range from $130 to $200; all have private bath.

The 1834 plantation-style **Duvigneaud House** (☎ 821-5009, 2857 Grand Route St John) offers antique furnishings in B&B suites, which sleep four, for $135. Each unit also has a private courtyard and comfortable porch, as well as a kitchen and laundry.

Mid-City (Map 8)

The Mid-City area, toward the lake from downtown, is where US Hwy 61 is made up of Tulane Ave and Airline Hwy. It's an automobile-dominated street strip where the largest lodging, the city jail (not recommended), contributes to a crummy atmosphere. Postwar motels along this old route tend to be a bit shabby, but a few acceptable accommodations are available along Tulane Ave close to downtown. The No 39 Tulane bus provides frequent service along the route from the CBD stop near Canal St at Elk Place.

One motel with a good reputation is the **Quality Inn Midtown** (☎ 486-5541, 800-228-5151, 3900 Tulane Ave), where rooms start at $45 single or double in the off-season. The

Best Western Patio Motel (☎ 822-0200, 2820 Tulane Ave) offers comfortable and clean rooms starting at $50. Nearby, opposite the Dixie brewery, the **Capri Motel** (☎ 821-9051, 2424 Tulane Ave) has rooms with king beds and art deco fixtures in the bathrooms for $40.

Airport

Hotels near the airport, mostly chains, are a good option for your last night in the city if you have an early flight to catch. The cheapest rooms are available from **Days Inn-Airport** (☎ 469-2531, 1300 Veterans Memorial Blvd) and **Comfort Inn-Airport** (☎ 467-1300, 800-777-7036, 1700 I-10 Service Rd).

La Quinta New Orleans Airport (☎ 466-1401, 800-531-5900, 2610 Williams Blvd) has renovated rooms with king beds for $77 double or $65 with a AAA discount. The **New Orleans Airport Hilton** (☎ 469-5000, 901 Airline Hwy) and **Best Western New Orleans Inn at the Airport** (☎ 464-1644, 1021 Airline Hwy) are literally across the street from the airport. The Hilton is pricey and considered a fine standout hotel, but the Best Western can offer rooms as low as $50 a double. Ask at any of these hotels for discount shuttles to the city.

LONG-TERM RENTALS

Some residents prefer to leave town and rent their homes to visitors when the big events crank up. Such an arrangement can be a good deal for large groups. Check the B&B associations or the classified ads in the Sunday edition of the *Times-Picayune* a few months before the event. Be sure to pinpoint the nearest cross street on a map; homes advertised as 'near the French Quarter' could be either a long taxi ride away or in a dangerous area.

Places to Eat

Don't start a new diet before coming to New Orleans. Why torture yourself? Some people come to this city for the sole purpose of eating. They plan their entire itinerary around their meals, resigning themselves to the reality that they'll be a few pounds heavier when they get home.

New Orleans has rich and unique culinary traditions that run deeper than those of most North American cities. Beginning with the traditions of French cuisine, the chefs and household cooks of New Orleans created and gradually elevated their own style of cooking. Creole cuisine, one of the USA's most distinctive regional cuisines, originated here. Many venerated 19th-century eateries continue to satisfy the local palate – you can still dine at Antoine's, established in 1840, and experience pretty much the same meal that was served more than a century ago.

But New Orleans' reputation as a gastronomic paradise doesn't rest solely on traditions. Many chefs are challenging the city's old culinary habits and winning over loyal followings. Some have pioneered creative culinary approaches to rival the cutting-edge trends of New York, San Francisco and Los Angeles. Asian, Mexican, Indian and European influences are creeping in, sometimes in surprising combinations. But new trends pass muster only if they appeal to the local population, which takes its food rather seriously and isn't easily impressed. The local audience won't go for food unless, above all else, it tastes great.

Creole vs Cajun

Put very simply, Creole food is urban cooking and Cajun food is country cooking. Just the same, New Orleans' indifference to this type of definition may drive visitors bats if they're trying to figure out the difference between the two cuisines. Restaurants advertising Creole cuisine often have similar menus to those calling themselves Cajun. Then there are the growing number of Cajun-

RICHARD CUMMINS

Creole restaurants. And just what does Creole mean these days, anyway?

Gumbo, the region's signature soup, doesn't shed much light on the subject of broad distinctions. Not only is it a mainstay of both Creole and Cajun food, but no two gumbos are alike. As a rule, Creoles use okra as a thickener – 'gombo' is, after all, an African term for okra – while the Cajuns are more likely to use filé (ground sassafras leaves). Ultimately, after tasting a variety of gumbos, you'll have to agree with the locals that the difference between Creole and Cajun cuisines isn't important, as long as it's delicious.

The origins of both Creole and Cajun food are quite similar, as both result from adaptations made by European settlers in the difficult environment of southern Louisiana. Both the Creoles and the Cajuns began with a basic understanding of French cuisine, and both incorporated American Indian knowledge of local ingredients. And, of course, they learned from each other. Consequently, the basic elements of Creole and Cajun cuisine are the same: distinctive *roux* (flour browned with butter), the backbone of so many of the region's dishes; substitutes for wheat flour, such as okra or filé, used as thickening agents; and all the meats, fish, crustaceans and shellfish that are so abundant in southern Louisiana and along the Gulf Coast.

But traditionally there are some significant differences. If it comes from the swamp – alligator meat, frog legs, crawfish – it's probably Cajun in origin. The use of cayenne and other peppers also makes Cajun food hotter and spicier – Cajun country is, in fact, where that ubiquitous American condiment, Tabasco sauce, comes from. And over the years, Cajuns developed a reputation for experimentation, the result being versatile dishes like jambalaya that can accommodate just about any added ingredients. It's on the whole an earthier and, some say, livelier cuisine. Creole cooking is usually described as more refined, milder and more subtle. It has also benefited more from the contributions of African cooks, who introduced okra and the use of rice and yams as staples.

Soul Food

Soul food is black Southern food, and since New Orleans is a Southern city and predominantly black, soul food is naturally as much a part of the local tradition as anything labeled Creole or Cajun. When talking about soul food, we're talking fried chicken, chitterlings (or chitluns), collard greens and corn bread. We're talking ham hocks, poke chops (or maybe you call 'em 'pork chops'), beans, and macaroni and cheese. We're talking a dive, without table service, probably somewhere far from the French Quarter. And we're talking cheap. We aren't talking health food, that's for sure.

There has been a recent trend to make soul food more upscale and refined, much to the chagrin of people who have been eating this type of food all their lives. You can make the same dishes, perhaps with less grease and choicer ingredients, and charge higher prices, but locals will insist, 'It ain't soul food.'

Barbecue is taken pretty seriously here, too, but not in restaurants. Along parade routes and in front of bars in black neighborhoods, you'll sometimes see a customized barbecue cooker, which looks like a converted oil drum, with tantalizing, aromatic smoke puffing from its stovepipe. Jazz trumpeter Kermit Ruffins named his band 'the Barbecue Swingers' as a tribute to his love of barbecue. He often shows up for gigs with a barbecue smoker in the back of his truck, and he'll dish out the 'B-B-Que' to his fans during his set breaks.

Po' Boys & Muffulettas

New Orleans is rightly proud to have introduced two great sandwiches to the world: the po' boy and the muffuletta.

The po' boy is the more conventional of the two. (A more proper pronunciation would be 'poor boy' – but spend a little time in New Orleans, and you'll agree that sounds silly.) In other parts of the country, similar sandwiches are called submarines, heroes or grinders. The po' boy – so-called since the Depression, when you could have a large oyster po' boy for just a quarter – is built on roast beef, ham, fried shrimp, catfish or oysters between slices of New Orleans' soft, spongy brand of French bread. If you like, order it 'dressed,' with lettuce, tomato and mayonnaise. Uptown, it seems that every few blocks there's a store selling po' boys, and there are also a couple of places in the French Quarter where you can get them.

Muffuletta & Dixie

The muffuletta is an unusual New Orleans original. Created in 1906 by Salvatore Lupo, the Sicilian-born proprietor of the Central Grocery on Decatur St, the muffuletta combines ham, salami, provolone and olive relish between slices of flat, round muffuletta bread. The sandwich takes its name from the bread, which is a little like focaccia, but it gets its character from the unique olive relish, made of green and black olives, capers, carrots, garlic, celery, pimentos, bits of cauliflower and olive oil. It is delicious – and a little messy to eat. The Central Grocery (Map 2) is still open for business, and it does a brisk trade in muffulettas. The Progress Grocery Co Inc, two doors down,

The Crème de la Crème of the Crescent City

New Orleans is the city of celebrity chefs. Since Paul Prudhomme's days at Commander's Palace in the 1970s, the Crescent City has always had a media sensation at the vanguard of its restaurant scene, and the resulting national attention has proven to be a boon for the city's foodmongers in general. The nonstop parade seems to work like clockwork – once one chef's star is fading, a new one emerges, ensuring that New Orleans remains a foodie destination. Here's a rundown of big names on the New Orleans restaurant scene.

Paul Prudhomme

Although he's often mistaken for comedian Dom Deluise, Paul Prudhomme is probably the most recognizable chef in America. Not only does he still own one of the city's best-loved restaurants, K-Paul's, on Chartres St, but his TV shows, cookbooks and popular line of Cajun seasonings can be found in millions of homes. He is to Cajun cuisine what Louis Armstrong was to jazz – a virtuoso and ambassador of New Orleans culture – and his celebrity paved the way for later superchefs like Emeril Lagasse. His greatest contribution to American cuisine is the blackening technique, which he perfected with dishes like blackened redfish at K-Paul's.

Susan Spicer

When Susan Spicer opened Bayona in the early 1990s, her nouvelle cuisine definitely went against the grain in traditional New Orleans. Nevertheless, she became one of the city's superchefs for her understated and original cooking, which often displays deft combinations of Asian, European and Indian concepts. As she explains it, her cooking has a lot to do with her upbringing. She's a self-described 'Navy brat' who grew up in many countries, and her mother's home cooking often borrowed international techniques, reflecting a curiosity and adaptability that rubbed off on Susan. She consistently challenges local and international traditions in ways that also demonstrate understanding and respect. 'I try not to innovate just

also serves up an excellent (some say better) version of the sandwich (see French Quarter).

Vegetarian

Vegetarians often express dismay to find an almost universal addition of ham, sausage or seafood to many dishes. But a few restaurants exclusively cater to vegetarians. Chefs at most fine-dining establishments will assemble a collage of meatless appetizers and side dishes, and some actually offer vegetarian entrées.

Part of the problem is that produce is not New Orleans' strength. That may be changing, as strong collaborative links form between chefs and Louisiana growers. The

---

The Crème de la Crème of the Crescent City

for the sake of innovation,' she says, 'and I believe it's important to understand the basic principles of a cuisine before you experiment with it.'

Emeril Lagasse

In terms of media exposure, Emeril Lagasse is currently the hottest chef in America, and he appears intent on riding his fame to the fullest extent. A native of Fall River, Massachusetts (his family is French Canadian and Portuguese), Lagasse (he pronounces his name 'la-**GA**-see') is another Commander's Palace alumnus. He opened his first restaurant, Emeril's, in the Warehouse District in 1990 and has been soaring ever since. At last count, he owned three restaurants in New Orleans (NOLA, Emeril's and Delmonico), along with one in Orlando, Florida, and another in Las Vegas, Nevada, and his Food Channel TV programs are filmed in New York. As his empire steadily expands, Lagasse probably finds himself spending more time on airplanes than he does in the kitchen. While his reputation as a chef is unassailable, his greatest appeal is as an entertainer, and his genius is in self-promotion. As millions of Americans profess, his shtick is irresistible – his trademark '*Bam!*,' which he always yells while adding spices to his cooking, is the most frequently imitated phrase in town – and when visitors come to New Orleans they usually feel an equal affinity for his food.

René Bajeux

Many understandably want to describe Grill Room chef René Bajeux's creative cuisine as 'fusion,' and although few chefs combine Asian, French and contemporary American flavors as successfully as he does, the French native is uncomfortable with such categorization. 'Fusion is confusion,' he says. 'Too many flavors in one dish. What I'm looking for is a simple marriage of flavors. If it's rabbit, I want it to taste like rabbit.' With such a straightforward philosophy, he's nevertheless managed to create a cuisine that's thoroughly original. Since he arrived in 1997, the Grill Room has become what many consider New Orleans' best restaurant.

Anne Kearney

Chef Anne Kearney may well become the next household name out of New Orleans, but her restaurant, Peristyle, remains a modest, romantic little place (it seats only 56), and she proudly describes her food as 'bistro' fare rather than aligning it with more glamorous nouveau and fusion trends. Kearney's career got off to an auspicious start. Since arriving in New Orleans from her native Ohio, she has worked with some high-profile chefs, including the late John Neal (who founded Peristyle) and Emeril Lagasse. In fact, Lagasse helped Kearney reopen Peristyle after Neal's demise – quite a vote of confidence from one of the nation's most popular chefs. She says she learned a lot about the business by working with Lagasse, but in the kitchen Kearney's style is all her own.

World-famous Lucky Dog cart, Bourbon St

increasing interchange means farmers know what chefs are interested in purchasing, and in turn chefs know what farmers are capable of producing during a given season and can plan their menus accordingly. For guests in the city's restaurants, the result is food that's healthier, fresher, tastier and more varied – with more for the vegetarian to savor.

International Cuisines

Italian – not French – is New Orleans' most popular foreign cuisine. During the early 20th century, the riverfront side of the French Quarter was home to a sizable Sicilian community, and there are still a few family restaurants from that era in the neighborhood. You'll often discover that red sauces are endowed with a distinct Louisiana flavor – that's because zesty Creole tomatoes are frequently used instead of Romas. But the Italian influence extends beyond traditional Italian restaurants. Fine-dining establishments may offer northern Italian specialties such as risotto and seafood dishes, which are readily adapted using local ingredients. Pasta is also common in Creole restaurants.

New Orleans has attracted Vietnamese immigrants in great numbers, and most New Orleanians have a favorite place to go for *pho* (beef noodle soup) or nouveau Vietnamese cuisine. The Vietnamese influence is also evident in some of the city's most prominent restaurants, including Emeril Lagasse's NOLA (See the French Quarter section, below). If you are looking for other Asian alternatives to Cajun and Creole food, you can find passable Thai, Indian and Japanese restaurants in the French Quarter and Uptown.

Mexican restaurants are not numerous, but there are some really good places for cheap basics like burritos and tacos. Some of these are actually owned by Central Americans, and their menus may include tasty items like yucca or empanadas.

Southern Breakfast (Grits 101)

If you hear a Southern drawl behind the breakfast counter, a serving of grits is probably forthcoming. Grits are coarsely ground hominy and were introduced to Europeans settlers by the Indians. They are boiled until they have an even, porridge-like consistency, and they taste like whatever they are served with – usually about half a cube of butter. Southerners are rightly particular about their grits – if not prepared properly, they are lumpy or contain hard kernels. If you haven't acquired the taste for them, keep trying! And if you do have a hankering for grits, show up early – they don't keep all day, and a lot of restaurants stop serving them at 10 or 11 am. A standard New Orleans breakfast also includes fried eggs, meat and a fresh biscuit (sometimes with gravy).

In New Orleans, French toast, called *pain perdu* (lost bread) by Francophiles, is another favorite. You can back up any breakfast with chicory coffee.

Desserts

Like any self-respecting Southern city, New Orleans can gratify your need for a good slice of pie, whether it's key lime pie, sweet potato pie or pecan pie. Pecan pie seems to caramelize more completely and taste better when cooked with a little bourbon.

Pecans also regularly turn up in pralines, those concentrated little doses of sugar, butter and evaporated milk. A popular variant has shredded coconut in place of pecans.

After a day or so on the shelf, stale French bread becomes the basis for bread pudding, and every pastry chef in New Orleans has a favorite recipe for it. It's served with a 'hard sauce' ('hard' refers to its alcoholic content), usually rum with butter and sugar.

Drinks

Alcohol Some visitors come to New Orleans with no plan other than to get thoroughly intoxicated and stay that way until it's time to leave. This is a rather sad approach to travel, but New Orleans is ready to accommodate it.

New Orleans considers itself a pioneer in alcoholic beverages (see the 'Cocktails' boxed text in the Entertainment chapter), and the city boasts a number of original mixed drinks. Probably the best known these days is the Hurricane, a rum-based passion-fruit drink invented at Pat O'Brien's. The success of this drink is no doubt to blame for the recent daiquiri craze.

In the past, drinking in New Orleans wasn't such a fruity experience. Several of the city's bars featured drinks made with absinthe before the supposedly insanity-inducing wormwood-based liqueur was outlawed in 1912. Some of these drinks still exist, albeit in name only. You can't get absinthe in any licensed drinking establishment today. The Sazerac, absinthe Suissesse and absinthe frappé now contain Ojen or Pernod instead.

The gin fizz, created about a century ago by a local barkeep named Henry C Ramos, is also a New Orleans tradition. The concoction of gin, cream, lemon juice, sugar and egg whites was a favorite of Governor Huey Long. Mint juleps, although not a New Orleans original, are equally popular in town.

New Orleans' own Dixie beer is drinkable only if chilled till near-frozen. If given a choice between it and Budweiser, go with Bud. Fortunately, the nearby Abita Brewery supplies most New Orleans bars with its passable ambers.

Coffee As the principal Gulf Coast entrepôt (trading center) for coffee beans from Central and South America, coffee roasters in New Orleans have long supplied both local and national markets. In fact, well before computer programmers began swilling espresso coffees and double lattes in Seattle, New Orleans residents were sipping café au lait, made with equal parts of steamed milk and coffee, which is sometimes a blend of coffee beans and chicory. Chicory is a locally grown root plant, related to endive, used to extend coffee. It's typically used in a mixture

A local Dixie fan

TOM DOWNS

of 60% coffee beans to 40% chicory. Almost anywhere you find activity in New Orleans, you will find a café nearby.

FRENCH QUARTER (MAP 2)

Obviously, this is where most visitors to New Orleans eat most of their meals. The French Quarter offers the greatest number and variety of restaurants in town, and some establishments are among the country's most famous eateries. But the Quarter is also the most expensive part of New Orleans in which to dine, and during peak seasons reservations at some of the more popular places can be difficult to get.

Budget

Cafés In the French Market, *Cafe Du Monde* (☎ 581-2914, 800 Decatur St) is a 24-hour New Orleans institution, which hasn't exploited its fame and convenient riverside location opposite Jackson Square by charging astronomical prices or adding new menu selections. Many visitors and locals have weathered sudden showers or drunken escapades under Du Monde's patio awning while

---

Chef Recommendations

The esteemed chefs of New Orleans often prefer to talk about their colleagues' cooking rather than their own. Here are recommendations from a few of the people whose efforts keep New Orleans' culinary reputation strong:

Susan Spicer – 'The Trout Muddy Waters at Uglesich's…just talking about it reminds me it's been too long since I last had it.'

Paul Prudhomme – 'Gabrielle's pork chop stuffed with peppers, served with a root-beer gravy. No kidding – root beer. Also, I like Brigtsen's redfish panfried with Creole sauce.'

René Bajeux – 'Brigtsen's does a rabbit appetizer that I like. I also like Peristyle's foie gras and Commander's Palace's cheesecake.'

---

a server delivers café au lait and an order of beignets (light, square-shaped doughnuts dusted with powdered sugar) for $2.

Everyone from hipsters to burnouts hangs out at *Kaldi's Coffeehouse* (☎ 586-8989, 941 Decatur St), where you can usually find a newspaper in the bin by the door. The former bank building has tables on the mezzanine, affording a view of the action on the streets, and a few computer terminals with Internet connections.

Next to the police station, *Café Beignet* (☎ 524-5530, 334B Royal St) offers a quaint patio setting and serves good small meals over the counter. French-style omelettes stuffed with ham, Belgian waffles and beignets are all a good start to the day, while quiches and sandwiches make up the simple lunch fare (most items are under $6).

Royal Blend (☎ 523-2716, 621 Royal St) has a pleasant garden courtyard in which to sip coffee – an inexpensive opportunity for tourists to venture 'behind the scenes' in the French Quarter.

Start your day with the locals at *Croissant d'Or Patisserie* (☎ 524-4663, 617 Ursulines Ave), between Chartres and Royal Sts. A fluffy individual quiche and one of the extraordinary filled croissants served with juice and coffee costs about $6. Check out the floral ceiling-tile coving.

For a sugar fix, drop by *Southern Candymakers* (☎ 523-5544, 334 Decatur St) and try a coconut praline.

Restaurants The crowded *La Madeleine French Bakery & Café* (☎ 568-9950, 547 St Ann St), on Jackson Square, offers some of the flakiest quiche crusts in town. A crawfish-and-spinach quiche with juice and coffee costs under $8. The French bread, baked in a wood-burning oven, has a crunchy crust, which you don't often find in New Orleans. Nicely seasoned soups, pastas and pizzas round out the lunch and dinner menu, while an assortment of fresh-baked pastries and muffins makes this equally popular for breakfast. There's another branch in the Riverbend.

The *Quarter Scene Restaurant* (☎ 522-6533, 900 Dumaine St), at Dauphine St, has the best late-night menu (until midnight on

Have a café au lait with a light beignet at Café Du Monde

weekdays, 24 hours on weekends). The spicy grilled vegetable plate with rice or pasta and a salad costs $7; add grilled chicken or shrimp for $2 more. This spot has a simple but somewhat formal atmosphere, with large windows, linen napkins, attentive service and kitschy cherubic statues.

The *Clover Grill* (☎ 598-1010, 900 Bourbon St) is a 24-hour diner, which looks much like a '50s joint and serves that kind of food. But the nostalgia stops there. The Clover's disco-caliber sound system booms out dance music, and the boys serving the food are reputed to get pretty frisky at times. But the burgers are seriously good and attract a mixed clientele. (As is so often the case in this part of the Quarter, the later it is, the gayer the Clover gets.)

Deja Vu Bar & Diner (☎ 523-1930, 400 Dauphine St) offers food around the clock at bargain-basement prices. Breakfasts start under $3. For lunch and dinner, the Deja Vu serves both jumbo burgers and garden burgers ($3.50), and red beans and rice ($5).

Po' boys aren't as ubiquitous in the Quarter as they are Uptown, and unfortunately they aren't as good either. But if you're dying

for a sandwich, there's *Johnny's Po-Boys* (☎ 524-8129, 511 St Louis St). Either call for delivery or order take-out and head for the river. Ask to have your sandwich dressed (extra charge) if you want lettuce, tomato and mayonnaise. On a positive note, the potato salad is delicious.

It's usually crowded with tourists, but alert servers at *Café Maspero* (☎ 523-6250, 601 Decatur St) deliver huge sandwiches or red beans and rice for about $5 and offer cold Abita on tap. Without trying very hard, Maspero's has atmosphere, endowed mainly by smoky brick arches, which make its street-level eating rooms feel underground. During the slow season, many locals sneak back in to reclaim an old haunt – a sure indication that the food is still up to snuff.

At *Mama Rosa's* (☎ 523-5546, 616 N Rampart St), you can usually get away from the crowds. This quiet, neighborly pizza joint on the edge of the French Quarter offers good and cheap pies ($10 to $15) and Italian salad ($3), served with tremendous slabs of French bread.

For a muffuletta you have two choices, which are almost side by side on Decatur St between Dumaine and Philip Sts. The *Central Grocery* (☎ 523-1620, 923 Decatur St) is the mother church for the muffuletta. The crazy sandwich was invented here in 1906. The grocery is authentic, but swarms of tourists crowd into its narrow aisles on weekends. A whole muffuletta and a Barq's root beer ($9) is a meal for two. Two doors down, *Progress Grocery Co Inc* (☎ 525-6627, 915 Decatur St) serves up its own variety of muffuletta, which is less oily than those at Central Grocery.

Though there aren't many dives worth going to in the Quarter, there is *Country Flame* (☎ 522-1138, 620 Iberville St), where cheap and substantial Cuban and Mexican dishes and barbecued meats keep the indoor picnic tables crowded. Meats are flavorfully greasy – what do you expect when a charbroiled rib eye costs only $6.50? If that doesn't suit you, stick with the vegetarian fajita served with yucca, guacamole, beans, rice and tortillas ($5).

The *Gumbo Shop* (☎ 525-1486, 630 St Peter St) is not a place locals go for gumbo. It's out-of-towners who eat here (in astonishing numbers), and most of them come away satisfied. The jambalaya ($8) tastes suspiciously similar to the seafood okra gumbo ($6.50), which may be why this place doesn't get much respect from New Orleanians.

Opposite the Old US Mint, *Louisiana Pizza Kitchen* (☎ 522-9500, 95 French Market Place) is a popular chain offering wood-fired individual pizza crusts that resemble toasted pita bread and are topped with a delicious array of ingredients ($6 to $9). Try a Caesar salad and the pizza with garlic, sun-dried tomatoes and feta.

An exclusively vegetarian lunch and dinner spot, *Old Dog New Trick Café* (☎ 522-4569, 307 Exchange Alley) offers dinner entrées like polenta stuffed with black beans and feta ($10) and grilled tofu with peanut-ginger sauce ($9), both served with grilled vegetables. The tasty soups make an inexpensive meal.

Mona Lisa (☎ 522-6746, 1212 Royal St) offers pizzas, pastas and a delicious spinach salad with blue-cheese dressing. Bring your own wine for a budget candlelight dinner.

Coop's Place (☎ 525-9053, 1109 Decatur St) is as much a neighborhood bar as it is a restaurant, and that's a virtue that sets it apart from so many of its tourist-trap neighbors. The darkly lit cavern has a full menu, with jambalaya, fried alligator and burgers. It's also a good place to grab a plate of red beans and rice for around $5 and swill it down with beer off the tap.

Acme Oyster and Seafood House (☎ 522-5973, 724 Iberville St) is a neighborhood standby that's revered by locals and out-of-towners alike. It first opened in 1910, and it retains some of the atmosphere of the old Quarter, but it stands on its reputation for shucking out some of the city's best oysters, along with decent red beans and rice. Be warned – the line of people waiting for a table often spills out onto the sidewalk.

Mid-Range

At chef Emeril Lagasse's *NOLA* (☎ 522-6652, 534 St Louis St), a very fine dining experience can be had at lower prices than at his other restaurants: Emeril's, in the CBD & Warehouse District, and Delmonico, in the Garden District. Lagasse deftly culls local, Asian and Californian traditions for natural, subtle combinations, with hints of intriguing flavors continuously darting over the palate. But the key to NOLA's upstanding reputation is the exemplary standard of the ingredients, especially meats and fruits of the sea. Fresh fish parts neatly under your fork, and roasted filet mignon, cooked rare, is so tender you can almost chew it with your eyebrows. NOLA also scores high for its wood-fired pizzas (a good starter for a group) and its 27-page wine list (with many affordable choices). An energetic staff help make this an exciting place to eat. Lunches range from $13 to $20, and dinner entrées cost between $18 and $25.

Irene's Cuisine (☎ 529-8811, 539 St Philip St) has small, cozy dining rooms that are perfect for quiet conversation. The food straddles the Italian-French border and includes offerings like finely seasoned roasted rosemary chicken ($11), pan-seared rack of lamb with an exquisite port-wine glaze ($17) and flavorful 'duck St Philip' ($17), served with fresh spinach, French mustard and berries. Irene's is open daily from 6 to 10 pm, and reservations are not accepted; long waits are not uncommon.

Olivier's (☎ 525-7734, 204 Decatur St) often goes unnoticed because of its quiet location at the upper reaches of Decatur St, but this place is a rarity: a restaurant serving authentic, inexpensive and excellent Creole food in the French Quarter. The restaurant has been run by the Olivier family for five generations, and it's currently in the capable hands of chef Armand Olivier, who has introduced many elements of contemporary cooking without undermining tradition. Start with the gumbo sampler ($9), an education in local cuisine, which offers a taste of Creole gumbo, filé gumbo and okra gumbo. Then choose among the seafood and meat entrées (shrimp Creole, Creole rabbit, crab cakes, pork medallions), which come with a salad. Main dishes range from $13 to $18. Save room for bourbon pecan pie. (Why so many pastry chefs bother to make pecan pie without bourbon is a mystery, but you can get it in spiked, caramelized glory here.)

Another easily missed spot is the *Secret Garden* (☎ 524-2041, 538 St Philip St). Nothing is particularly memorable about the food or atmosphere, but it's inexpensive and pleasant enough. The menu is suspiciously diverse, offering Creole-inflected pastas ($7 to $10), fish zulu (sautéed with artichoke hearts, pimento and black olives; $13) and down-home standards like red beans and rice ($5). The Secret Garden isn't a bad fall-back plan when the line's too long at Irene's across the street.

Lucky Cheng's (☎ 529-2045, 720 St Louis St) has achieved bicoastal chaindom with an odd formula: Asian drag queen waitresses and 'Asian Creole' dishes. Some complain the service is more saucy than the food, while others insist dishes like blackened yellowfin tuna don't need a gimmick. Dinners cost $17 to $31, but lunch is a bargain at $3 to $8. New Orleans is just the place for this type of joint – whether it catches on in the heartland remains to be seen.

For Indian cuisine amid splendid furnishings, try *Shalimar* (☎ 523-0099, 535 Wilkenson Row), where dinners cost $13 to $20 for mostly traditional tandoori and a few of the more exotic dishes from southern India. Vegetarians can choose from a variety of specialties.

Many local beef eaters agree that *Port of Call* (☎ 523-0120, 838 Esplanade Ave) is the place to go for a burger with a baked potato ($7). This may mean the burgers here are the best in town, or perhaps that New Orleanians are creatures of habit. This basic bar and grill also serves up good steaks ($20).

Top End

New Orleans has several venerable dining establishments dating back well into the 19th century. These places maintain traditions such as requiring jackets and frowning on denim. But not all the places listed in this price category are so traditional.

Antoine's (☎ 581-4422, 713 St Louis St) is New Orleans' oldest restaurant, having been open for business since 1840. The dated charm of its dining rooms (a brightly lit room for nonsmokers and a more ambient smoking section) is well suited for family functions, particularly if older folks are involved. The menu hasn't changed much over the last century, and it exhibits all the 19th-century panache on which Antoine's world renown rests. Dining here is certainly of historical interest, but today the meat and fish dishes are often overburdened by staid sauces and fail to thrill the senses. Even the oysters Rockefeller, Antoine's own invention, lacks spirit. Rumor has it that the regulars are treated to better food than first-timers. As a visitor, you're better off with more straightforward chicken and lamb entrées. A full dinner with wine typically costs $30 to $50 per person. After your meal, you can tour the dining rooms dedicated to old-line Mardi Gras krewes.

Arnaud's (☎ 523-5433, 813 Bienville St) is one of the better places to go for traditional haute Creole cuisine. It was founded in 1918 by 'Count' Arnaud Cazenave, a French immigrant whose extravagant tastes are still evident here. Arnaud's is, in fact, an agglomeration of buildings that take up nearly an entire city block. It's a festive place where locals go for special occasions and tourists go to soak in New Orleans' past. You can choose to sit in the main dining room, much admired for its a stately old-world elegance, or the Richelieu Room, where an acoustic jazz ensemble ($4 music charge) adds class. Arnaud's food sometimes gets a bad rap, probably from people who haven't eaten here in ages. While it isn't the most scintillating dining, the kitchen surely handles its specialties well; they appear in red type on the menu – shrimp Arnaud, oysters Bienville (an original dish), speckled trout meuniére (saved by a rich, gravy-like sauce) and a variety of steaks and fowl dishes. À la carte entrées run $17 to $29. Upstairs, check out the Germaine Wells Mardi Gras Museum of vintage costumes worn by Wells, who was Count Arnaud's daughter and a perennial queen of Mardi Gras balls. Arnaud's is open daily for dinner, weekdays for lunch and Sunday for brunch.

Another New Orleans institution, the **Court of Two Sisters** (☎ 522-7261, *613 Royal St*), has wonderful ambience but disappointing food. The courtyard of this historic building, with a canopy created by a sprawling, 200-year-old wisteria, is a very pleasant setting for alfresco dining. When it rains, patrons are seated in one of several slightly faded (some actually drab) indoor dining rooms. The fare is strictly traditional and, unfortunately, uninspired. Considering the Court's high volume – on a warm Sunday, well over 1000 visitors might eat here – the kitchen staff does a commendable job, but you would expect to eat better for $30 to $50 a head.

Although **Galatoire's** (☎ 525-2021, *209 Bourbon St*) has an egalitarian no-reservation policy, it is a clubby sort of place where the regulars are treated regally and tourists are sometimes dished out surprisingly average food. Local devotees – businesspeople for lunch, families for dinner – so love this classic New Orleans establishment that to die here over a plate of, say, grilled pompano with almonds is considered a *belle mort*, or good death. (Fortunately, this doesn't happen very often.) More customary practices include sitting at the same table every day and establishing a long-term relationship with a particular waiter, which reportedly can make all the difference between a great meal and a less-than-great one. These intricacies aside, dining at Galatoire's can nevertheless be an enchanting experience for the traveler. The building has housed a restaurant since 1830 (it was called Victor's before Jean Galatoire bought it in 1905), and history is palpable in the main dining room. After a late lunch, look around the room as it empties – the people who linger into the afternoon sometimes look like figures from a 19th-century oil painting. Oysters Rockefeller, asparagus salad, chicken *clemenceau* and the to-die-for pompano are good bets off the menu (entrées run $15 to $22). It's open every day but Monday from 11:30 to 9 pm. Expect a long wait outside before being seated, especially for lunch on Friday – many locals start their weekend here.

Brennan's Restaurant (☎ 525-9711, *417 Royal St*) prides itself on having introduced the luxury breakfast to New Orleans. As the story goes, the restaurant's founder, Owen Brennan, cooked up the concept after Frances Parkinson Keyes' novel *Dinner at Antoine's* established that restaurant as 'the' place to go for dinner. Half a century later, breakfast at Brennan's, with its 12 elegant dining rooms and a lovely courtyard, is as firmly established a tradition. Breakfast here is no *petit déjeuner*: It's a virtual gastronomic extravaganza that could start with an 'eye-opener' (if you can imagine downing a Sazerac cocktail before breakfast), followed by a baked apple or turtle soup, any of about 20 egg dishes (eggs Owen, eggs *sardou*, oysters Benedict), and then dessert (bananas Foster is a Brennan's original). This'll set you back about $40. An order of *grillades* and grits ($35) makes a nice addition for the table. If that sounds steep, factor in the savings you'll achieve by skipping lunch! Traditional Creole dinners are served nightly.

Some locals complain that **K-Paul's Louisiana Kitchen** (☎ 596-2530, *416 Chartres St*) has lost its edge in recent years. More to the point, K-Paul's – once renowned for its innovation – just hasn't changed much of late. For the visitor, that's actually a good thing, because although chef Paul Prudhomme is

TOM DOWNS

K-Paul Prudhomme

no longer active in the day-to-day operation of the kitchen, the same food he created here in the 1980s is still available. The kitchen goes out of its way to eschew short-cuts. The blackened twin beef tenders ($30), a signature dish, come with an incredibly rich 'debris' – that's Prudhomme's term for an elaborate gravy, slowly cooked over a two-day period. You can also get gumbo here ($5 a cup), with hot andouille sausages made on the premises, and turtle soup ($5.50), which has a nice flavorful snap to it. Jambalaya ($12 for lunch) is simmered for hours with jalapeños and is hot indeed. Despite its popularity, K-Paul's retains a no-reservations policy downstairs, meaning you can dine here without planning ahead – you just have to wait in line (reservations are required for upstairs tables). For weekday lunches, you might be seated on arrival.

Bayona (☎ 525-4455, 430 Dauphine St) is one of the city's best all-around dining experiences. It's in a charming converted Creole cottage, with several former parlors serving as homey dining rooms. On pleasant-weather days, there's also alfresco dining on the back patio. Chef Susan Spicer's menu is always inventive but rarely shocking – she uses a light hand to ensure that every dish, no matter how imaginative, above all tastes good. (See the 'Crème de la Crème of the Crescent City' boxed text for more on Spicer.) The grilled shrimp with black-bean cake and coriander sauce and the goat-cheese crouton with mushrooms in Madeira cream are elegant starters ($5 to $8). Representative entrées ($9 to $13 for lunch, $17 to $21 for dinner) include a grilled pork chop with savory semolina pudding and sage *jus* and a salmon with *choucroute* and Gewürztraminer sauce. The wine list is extensive and predominantly European, with few choices under $40 a bottle. Bayona is open weekdays for lunch and dinner, Saturday for dinner only.

Ralph Brennan's ***Bacco*** (☎ 522-2426, 310 Chartres St) advertises itself as an Italian *ristorante*, but the food benefits from other Mediterranean nuances and has a decidedly New Orleans flair. Chef Haley Gabel's work is creative and tasteworthy, utilizing wood-burning ovens and quality ingredients to great effect. If you go the fish route (probably red fish, $20 and up), expect freshness and sauces like *beurre blanc* that contribute flavor in subtle ways. For dinner, *lasagne del mare* ($19) comes loaded with shrimp, oysters, crab and either tuna or swordfish. Naturally, with the wood oven, gourmet pizza appetizers are a specialty. Dinner entrées range from $17 to $30. Lunch is less expensive, with a daily lunch special of two courses and dessert for $15 or less. Lunch is available every day but Sunday, when it steps aside for brunch. Dinner is served nightly.

Owned by Cindy Brennan, ***Mr B's Bistro*** (☎ 523-2078, 201 Royal St) is a clubby, attractively designed restaurant that appeals to a variety of tastes. Creole overtones predominate in chef Michelle McCraney's menu. The 'gumbo Ya-Ya' with chicken and andouille is excellent, and the barbecued shrimp, sautéed in a delicious buttery sauce rather than grilled, is a fun and messy dish served with a paper bib to protect your shirt. Lunch specials often include less traditional fare, like blackfin tuna coated in a macadamia nut crust, while dinner entrées tend to be tried and true favorites, like rib eye steak and rack of lamb. Lunch is decidedly less expensive, with main dishes running $11 to $15, while complete dinner plates (sans wine) range from $30 to $40. Mr B's is open for dinner daily and lunch every day but Sunday, when brunch is served.

The **Palace Café** (☎ *523-1661, 605 Canal St*) makes a strong first impression, with a striking interior that combines modern and classic designs. It opened in 1990 in a former music store (Werlein's, a New Orleans institution), and the original tile floors and interior columns have been retained. A new corkscrew staircase is a dramatic centerpiece, which brings the upstairs and downstairs dining rooms together. Businesspeople, conventioneers and office workers seem to have laid claim to the place. The food follows through with modern, nonexperimental approaches to classic Creole standards like catfish pecan meunière ($17). Occasional surprises, such as an herbed gnocchi with wild mushrooms starter ($6) served in a smoky chicken stock, add nice twists to the

menu. Local products predominate. The Palace is open nightly for dinner, weekdays for lunch, weekends for brunch.

Café Sbisa (☎ *522-5565, 1011 Decatur St*) is a Vieux Carré institution (since 1899) that has a reputation for innovative Creole cuisine. The restaurant recently closed briefly and reopened better than ever, with an updated interior and menu. Tasteful restoration of the ancient building, with exposed brick and strikingly decadent art above the long bar, help make this one of New Orleans' most beautiful dining rooms, while New American touches introduced by chef Allan Hegquist spruce up a solid menu, which includes blackened redfish ($19), garlic-and-honey roasted chicken ($14) and pasta jambalaya ($17). Café Sbisa is open nightly for dinner, and Sunday for a nice brunch with a roving 'trad' jazz unit.

Peristyle (☎ *593-9535, 1041 Dumaine St*), at Rampart, is one of the city's more romantic spots for dinner (paradoxically, it has a power-lunching daytime crowd on Friday). Chef Anne Kearney, one of New Orleans' rising stars, treats diners to simple yet refined

TOM DOWNS

Decadent art jazzes up Café Sbisa's bar.

creations in intimate surroundings. Her menu plays on American tastes and French Provençal methods of preparation – it's traditional fare that's sophisticated and attractive. Grilled veal, cooked with the bone, is served in a rich Madeira *jus* atop a bed of polenta ($24), and bass is seared until crispy and served with a lemon and caper *beurre noisette* ($22). In chef Kearney's capable hands, dishes like these make tastebuds sing. Peristyle is open Tuesday to Saturday for dinner and for lunch on Friday.

FAUBOURG MARIGNY & BYWATER (MAP 3)

Restaurants in the Faubourg Marigny neighborhood tend to be a bargain compared to their French Quarter counterparts. They also provide a wide range of cuisine, from budget meat-and-potato dishes and spicy Thai to soul food and fine dining.

Budget

Actually more of an appendage to a bar, *The Harbor* (☎ 947-1819, 2529 Dauphine St) is a soul food restaurant that's uncharacteristically close to the French Quarter. You won't meet many tourists here, though. It's the real deal, with fried chicken and pork chops, mustard greens and white bread dished out unceremoniously over a counter at outrageously low prices. The Harbor is open for lunch only.

Cafe Marigny (☎ 945-4472, 1913 Royal St) is a nice spot to enjoy coffee drinks or to check out the gallery exhibits, but the quiche is a tad overpriced.

Old-fashioned meat-and-potato plates cost about $5 at *Buffa's Bar & Restaurant* (☎ 945-9397, 1001 Esplanade Ave). The quiet, 24-hour *La Péniche* (☎ 943-1460, 1940 Dauphine St), at Touro St, is strictly a late-night spot (well…it's open 24 hours, but it gets interesting late). Surly waiters serve a range of foods, from red beans and rice for under $4 to shrimp and oyster dinners for $13.

A hand-painted sign nailed to a tree on Chartres St as it crosses into the Bywater says 'GOOD FOOD A HEAD.' In these parts, that obviously refers to *Elizabeth's* (☎ 944-9272, 601 Gallier St), at Chartres St, which

The way to Elizabeth's

offers one of the best deals in town for breakfast or lunch. Chef Heidi Trull attacks regional traditions with creative fervor and generosity, and no matter what you order from the unassuming menu, it will exceed expectations in quality and quantity. Lulamae's breakfast po' boy, Trull's original combination of smoked sausage, cheesy scrambled eggs and French bread, is as long as a grown man's forearm. Pancakes and waffles come topped with strawberries, and even the basic breakfast ($3.50) is a standout, with eggs, a slab of meat, a biscuit and 'real' grits (none of that instant stuff from Heidi's kitchen). Lunch specials (around $5) and desserts (at least have a brownie) will satisfy a king and add to your girth.

Mid-Range

Siam Café (☎ 949-1750, 435 Esplanade Ave) is a dim, narrow den where you can order all the Thai standards, including pad Thai ($8). But it rises to greater heights with specialties that include a royal hunter's grill ($13) and a selection of spicy curries, some vegetarian ($7 to $13). The Siam also offers a nice variety of beers to cool your mouth down. It's convenient if you're planning to end up at the Dragon's Den nightclub upstairs.

The popular *Santa Fe* (☎ 944-6854, 801 Frenchman St) is a rare Southwestern restaurant in New Orleans, where a *chile rellenos* dinner costs $10 and grilled tuna goes for $15.

At the original *Praline Connection* (☎ 943-3934, 542 Frenchman St), some righteous (but atypically pricey) soul food makes its way to the table: fried chicken, Creole gumbo, beans and greens. If you come with a group, the Praline Connection platter, with enough fried chicken wings, catfish, shrimp, crawfish and okra to feed a small army, is the way to go. It's all served up with one of New Orleans' coolest waitstaffs (fedoras are de rigueur here).

In the heart of the Bywater, *Bywater Barbeque* (☎ 944-4445, 3162 Dauphine St), at Louisa St, dishes out good spare ribs, chicken and pulled pork in heaping quantities for $11 or less. You won't find better barbecue in this part of town.

Mandich Restaurant (☎ 947-9553, 3200 St Claude Ave), at Louisa St, is a Bywater institution that, according to locals, serves authentic New Orleans cuisine. It certainly evokes earlier times, with painted brick, pebbled linoleum, wood paneling and hearty lunches. The food emerging from the kitchen is arranged high on your plate like a bouffant hairdo and is nothing short of astounding. A lunch comprised of seafood gumbo, crisp catfish topped with smothered crawfish tails, baked oyster platters, and liver and onions is guaranteed to force dinner cancellations. Entrées cost $10 to $17. Mandich is open for lunch Tuesday to Friday and for dinner on Friday and Saturday only.

CBD & WAREHOUSE DISTRICT (MAP 4)

Of course, New Orleans' business district is home to some highly acclaimed and expensive power-lunch (and dinner) establishments, but the CBD and the nearby Warehouse District also have some decent eat-and-run spots as well as a pair of noteworthy greasy spoons.

Budget

Inviting aromas fill the small *Le Petit Paris* (☎ 524-7660, 731 Common St), which offers French pastries, omelettes and delicious individual quiches. Try the 'croissant la Seine,' with crawfish and béchamel sauce. All items are under $4. Unfortunately, it's only open for breakfast and lunch on weekdays. You can order your meal in French if you like.

Susan Spicer's *Spice Inc* (☎ 558-9992, 1051 Annunciation St), in the stylishly converted Cotton Mill building, may be a sign that more upscale things are in store for this neighborhood. Deli items (both premade and made to order), drinks and desserts, all measuring up to chef Spicer's high standards, make this a great place to grab something on the run; most items are around $5. It's open weekdays during lunch and early dinner hours.

On historic Julia Row, *Louisiana Products* (☎ 529-1666, 618 Julia St) has the feel of an old general store, but it's really a deli, with limited seating and inexpensive breakfasts and lunches. If you're staying at the nearby YMCA or headed to the Confederacy Museum, drop in for chicory coffee and an egg on a French roll, or try a sandwich and soup.

Mother's (☎ 523-9656, 401 Poydras St), at Tchoupitoulas St, is famous for its hearty down-home breakfasts, like biscuits, grits, debris (shredded beef) and strong coffee for about $7. Although service is over the counter, everything is cooked to order. Some justifiably complain that prices are a wee bit too high and weekend lines are too long. But you might drop back in later for a quick slice of fresh pie.

The *Hummingbird Grill* (☎ 561-9229, 804 St Charles Ave), near Julia St, is a 24-hour greasy spoon that's surprisingly good, considering it's downstairs from a rather dicey transient hotel. At the faded counter you're likely to rub elbows with some of the city's more down-at-heels characters; the tables are served by a more upbeat waitstaff. Be sure to get here early for fresh biscuits and grits. Standard lunch fare won't fail you either.

In the YMCA, *Back to the Garden Café* (☎ 522-8792, 920 St Charles Ave) offers healthy breakfasts and lunch plates for under $6, along with inexpensive smoothies.

Vic's Kangaroo Café (☎ 524-4329, 636 Tchoupitoulas St) is basically an Australian pub that provides a taste of Down Under by serving savory pies (under $5) until 2 am. Try the chook pie or feta with spinach and tomato.

In the heart of the CBD, the cafeteria-style *New City Diner* (☎ *522-8198, 828 Gravier St)* dishes up full breakfasts for $3 and hot lunch specials for $6. The *Red Eye Grill* (☎ *593-9393, 852 S Peters St)* stays open late and is strictly a place to get a greasy burger and fries.

Mid-Range

Cuban lunch specials like roast pork with black beans (every Wednesday) at *Liborio's* (☎ *581-9680, 322 Magazine St)* get high marks and are sure to please garlic fans. Also try the grilled tuna with sweet plantains for $9. The prices are a bit high, but the business crowd doesn't seem to mind.

The *Praline Connection II* (☎ *523-3973, 907 S Peters St)*, at St Joseph St, is a soul food cabaret geared toward giving conventioneers a taste of New Orleans. This isn't really down-home cooking, as delicious standards like fried chicken and originals like gumbo Zaire are given a more refined treatment. Lunch specials run $4 to $7; dinner entrées are between $9 and $15. The champagne gospel brunch ($24), held every Sunday at 11 am, features David Rhodes and Assurance – bring an appetite and high spirits.

Top End

Emeril's (☎ *528-9393, 800 Tchoupitoulas St)* is the flagship of chef Emeril Lagasse's restaurant empire. The noise level can be deafening. The service can be affected or aloof.

Champagne gospel brunch at the Praline Connection II

The chef is rarely in residence (what with traveling to New York to film his popular cooking shows, *The Essence of Emeril* and *Emeril Live)*. And yet, after nearly 10 years on the scene, Emeril's remains one of New Orleans' signature dining establishments, the kind of restaurant where the Worchestershire sauce is house-made and the scallops were caught on day boats and flown in that morning. Set in a converted warehouse in the city's gallery district, the dining room is as handsome as the food that emerges from the kitchen. Solo diners will want to reserve at the food bar facing the kitchen, while those angling for a special treat should reserve the chef's table in the kitchen, where one of Lagasse's sous chefs will deliver your plates straight from the stove. The kitchen's strengths are best appreciated by ordering the daily specials, though menu mainstays like shrimp-and-andouille cheesecake with Creole mustard-tomato coulis or crawfish-stuffed filet mignon with sauce bordelaise are worth a second look as well. The wine list is eclectic, featuring many sleepers that are well priced. Dinner costs around $40 per person without wine.

In the Windsor Court Hotel, the *Grill Room* (☎ *522-1992, 300 Gravier St)* is consistently rated New Orleans' most luxurious, exciting and cutting-edge culinary institution, particularly since René Bajeux took over in 1997. The dining room, while not stuffy, is characterized by a quiet and conservative luxuriousness. (Some big business deals go down here.) Everything chef Bajeux creates is marked by originality. It doesn't come across as experimental – his dishes are the carefully calculated results of a chef who has mastered his flavors. The lunch prix-fixe menu (about $25) might include Southwest purse of pheasant and goat cheese, wontons of shrimp mousse or soup followed up with either crab cakes with sweet-and-sour Asian vegetables, seared mahi mahi or fig-glazed breast of *moulard* duck and a dessert. Dinner appetizers start at $15, and entrées range from $30 to $40. The chef's tasting menu, comprised of samples of six dishes is clearly designed to titillate gourmands at $70 a head.

The **Bon Ton Café** (☎ 524-3386, 401 Magazine St), at Poydras St, is an old-style Cajun restaurant (with a few Creole dishes). Although the dining room looks a little like a pizza parlor, folks show up dressed to the nines, and at $15 to $25 per person, meals don't come cheap. But this is a consistently good throwback to the days before Cajun food was revolutionized by chefs like Paul Prudhomme. Spices are used in tasteful moderation. Rich gumbo, red fish, shrimp étouffée and a rum-soaked bread pudding are sure to satisfy.

Mike's on the Avenue (☎ 523-1709, 628 St Charles Ave) hasn't lost its cachet since chef Mike Fennelly relocated to San Francisco. Fennelly still co-owns the place and continues to oversee the development of the menu from the West Coast, and his paintings still grace the dining room's eggshell-white walls. With Christian Karcher now in charge of the kitchen, the menu remains eclectic, relying on Asian flavors as well as Louisiana staples like crawfish, shrimp and Creole seasonings. Sushi, featured every night, might include tuna and crawfish *remoulade*. Combinations are always conceptually intriguing and to the taste usually delightful, sometimes disappointing. Entrées run $15 to $26 at dinner and $8 to $15 at lunch. Mike's is open daily for breakfast and dinner, weekdays for lunch.

LOWER GARDEN & GARDEN DISTRICTS (MAP 5)

If you're staying in one of the inexpensive guesthouses along Prytania St and are looking for a laid-back eatery where you can grab a decent, quick bite, the Lower Garden stands ready to accommodate you. Some places along St Charles Ave are particularly esteemed for their 24-hour breakfasts and late-night fixings. The Garden District is good for one thing only – Commander's Palace, one of the most highly acclaimed restaurants in the US.

Budget

Cafés In the Lower Garden District, **Rue de la Course** (☎ 529-1455, 1500 Magazine St), at Race St, is a small but comfortable coffeehouse where you can buy a paper and while away the time over a variety of coffee drinks and baked goods. (There are other branches in the French Quarter and Uptown.) Across the street, **St Vincent's Guesthouse & Tea Room** (☎ 523-2318, 1507 Magazine St) has a daily set tea from noon to 4 pm.

Across from Lafayette Cemetery No 1, The Rink shopping center houses a **PJ's Coffee & Tea** (☎ 899-0335, 2727 Prytania St). The front deck is a good place to have a cup of coffee before or after exploring the Garden District. There's another PJ's at 5432 Magazine St, on a block that's busy with bookstores and restaurants.

Restaurants At 1 am in the 24-hour **Trolley Stop** (☎ 523-0090, 1923 St Charles Ave), you'll find Lower Garden District hipsters as well as gents in cummerbunds with a limo waiting out front. The funky former gas station offers ham and eggs for $4 and baked potatoes for even less. The usual assortment of sandwiches, burgers and such rounds out the menu.

The **Please-U-Restaurant** (☎ 525-9131, 1751 St Charles Ave) is a run-down old counter-and-booths establishment with a basic mission to make its customers happy with cheap, satisfying meals. Whether you order steak and eggs, a soft-shell crab sandwich or a po' boy, you won't spend much more than $5. This spot is open weekdays 6 am to 7 pm and Saturday until 2 pm.

Café Angeli (☎ 524-1414, 1818 Magazine St) is a nice little pizza place amid the Lower Garden District's art galleries. Slices cost under $2.50, and large 'gourmet' pizzas are about $15. Inexpensive pastas and focaccia sandwiches are also on the menu.

Hidden away within a furniture store, the **Café at Halpern's Furnishing Store** (☎ 566-1707, 1600 Prytania St), at Terpsichore St, nevertheless attracts a steady business crowd. People come here for quality, with tasty and healthy lunches costing between $4 and $7. Creative dishes like shrimp primavera, chicken fusilli and chicken oriental keep 'em coming back. There's no sign outside indicating that an eatery exists amid so many unfinished armoires and rocking chairs, but just enter the furniture store and head upstairs. The café is open Monday to Saturday from 11 am to 3 pm.

Even though it's in a fairly neglected central neighborhood, *Uglesich's (☎ 523-8571, 1238 Baronne St)* is justifiably one of New Orleans' cherished institutions (since 1924), drawing suits and blue collars alike to its divey, overcrowded dining room. The food, with its strong seaward leanings, never fails to amaze newcomers, who can't believe such imagination and exemplary quality exist in such unlikely surroundings. (Uglesich could have moved long ago, but its owners want to keep their operation just the way it is.) You can get trout, shrimp and crawfish in any number of ways, and the menus tacked to the walls don't really indicate what a dish will end up like (some favorites aren't on the menu at all). When you order from the counter, engaging your server in conversation will usually result in your ordering the right thing. A raw oyster bar makes eating and running a possibility; otherwise, you'll probably wait half an hour or so for a table. Most items are under $10, though a few nudge toward $15. Uglesich is open for lunch weekdays and every other Saturday (call ahead).

Mid-Range

There's nothing especially memorable about *Cafe Roma (☎ 524-2419, 1901 Sophie Wright Place)* but it's one of the Lower Garden District's nicer restaurants, with linen-covered tables next to tall arched doorways that open to the street. Pizza is the specialty item here, made in traditional and gourmet varieties (with toppings including shrimp and artichokes) for $12 to $18. Pastas, chicken dishes and sandwiches round out the menu.

Igor's Garlic Clove (☎ 522-6602, 2135 St Charles Ave), at Jackson Ave, affiliated with the chain of Igor's laundry-bars around town, offers healthy if unspectacular Cajun, Italian and American standbys. Prices vary from $8 for jambalaya to $18 for steak. It's as much a bar as a restaurant, with a TV and loud music (no laundry – that's next door). The lunch menu is an abridged version of what's available for dinner, at marginally lower prices.

On a treeless block of St Charles Ave, *Little Tokyo (☎ 524-8535, 1612 St Charles Ave)* prepares some of New Orleans' best sushi, along with teriyaki and tempura entrées. It's a friendly and busy place decked out with Japanese-style booths and an adjacent

Uglesich's has been amazing diners since 1924

karaoke bar. Entrées start at $12; if you're eating sushi, the tab can easily add up to over $20 per person.

Semolina (☎ 895-4260, 3242 Magazine St), near Toledo St, was founded by three chefs who call themselves 'The Taste Buds.' That kind of contemporary chumminess, along with consistently creative preparation of international pasta dishes, is the foundation of this chain's popularity. Pasta jambalaya, a play on regional flavors with andouille sausage, tasso and spirelli pasta instead of rice; a straightforward pad Thai with shrimp; and Santa Fe pasta, linguine punched up with caramelized onions, black beans and red-chile purée, all come in large portions for about $10.

Top End

Delmonico (☎ 525-4937, 1300 St Charles Ave) had been around for about 100 years when chef Emeril Lagasse bought it and began restoring it to its former glory in the mid-1990s. Lagasse's trademark flashiness is absent here, and sedate, almost stuffy dining rooms reflect the history of this hallowed establishment. Judging by the place's popularity – last minute reservations? Fo'geddaboudit! – Lagasse's fans seem to have no objections. On a recent visit, however, Delmonico was somewhat disappointing. Mistake No 1 was ordering a Manhattan cocktail, which, it turns out, costs $11. Mistake No 2 was ordering duck, which turned out to be a real piece of work – the chewing outlasted a beautiful sauce, which is always guaranteed to make a frustrated diner want to go '*BAM!*' wit some more o' dem spices. To top it off, the smug waiters couldn't fathom anyone not loving everything they set on the table. Agreed: When the tab exceeds $60 per person, you should have no complaints.

In the heart of the Garden District, Lafayette Cemetery No 1 is a unique sort of purgatory. Its inhabitants must spend eternity so close to one of the USA's great restaurants, and they never get to dine there. Ella Brennan, owner of *Commander's Palace* (☎ 899-8221, 1403 Washington Ave), prides her ability to promote her chefs to stardom. She knows how to work the local and national media, and Paul Prudhomme and Emeril Lagasse are among her alumni. Commander's scores big time for living up to the hype and making its guests feel welcome. The service is impeccable and friendly, the decor tasteful and comfortable, and the food coming out of chef Jamie Shannon's kitchen is uniformly splendorous. The main dining room is warmly lit through windows during lunch, but at night its artificial lighting is a little stale – try to reserve in the upstairs parlor or in the Garden Room, which looks out over Ella's lovely courtyard. (The maitre d' likes to tell an anecdote about the 'Naked Lady Bar' upstairs – some of the statues, apparently too well endowed for contemporary diners, were subjected to breast reduction surgery, he says.) You can even dine in the bustling kitchen, at the chef's table (call well ahead for this). The menu, spelled out in terms that only hint at Shannon's indelible imprint, includes regional soup specialties (turtle soup au sherry, $6) and appetizers (around $9) like shrimp remoulade and tasso shrimp. Entrées (from $22 to $37) are where Commander's really sells itself. The Colorado roast rack of lamb is prepared with a Creole mustard crust and an exquisite muscadine lamb sauce. Make you hungry? This is obviously a major splurge, but Commander's lunch prices are mercifully reduced ($14 to $25). The menu changes frequently, but the favorite dishes usually stick around for a long time. A reservation and a coat are required.

UPTOWN (MAP 6)

You might not think there'd be any reason to venture Uptown for a meal – if so, you've got a second think coming, particularly if you'd like to escape the prices, the crowds and the flash of the Quarter. There are some really great neighborhood dives up this way.

Budget

Locals and medical students from nearby hospitals pack the *Bluebird Café* (☎ 895-7166, 3625 Prytania St), near Antonine St, for satisfying breakfasts that tend to go beyond the traditional eggs and grits; the 'powerhouse eggs' dish contains nutritional yeast, tamari and cheese. This place is also known for its malted pancakes and Belgian waffles. For lunch, sandwiches (burgers, veggie melts and BLTs) are available. You often have to wait to be seated at this popular little place.

In New Orleans, great little eateries pop up where you least expect them. On a residential block near the river, **Domilise's Po-Boys** (☎ 899-9126, 5240 Annunciation St), at Bellecastle St, is a bustling little shack that churns out some of the city's best-loved sandwiches. Order a large fried-shrimp po' boy ($7), prepared by the bustling staff (the place is always busy) and sit at the bar, where a friendly old gent draws frosty mugs of draught Dixie. All in all, a most gratifying experience.

Also near the river, **Frankie & Johnny's** (☎ 899-9146, 321 Arabella St), near Tchoupitoulas St, a friendly neighborhood bar-restaurant, is the perfect place to go with a large group. In the spring, when crawfish are in season, order a platter of the boiled critters and a round of beers for your party before choosing from appetizers like alligator pie and turtle soup and entrées like fried fish. For lunch or dinner, five boisterous guests can easily eat and drink to their hearts' content for under $100, including a 20% tip for lessons on how to eat a crawfish.

Casamento's (☎ 895-9761, 4330 Magazine St), near Napoleon, is where hard-core Uptown oyster fiends go for their fix. Every last detail of the interior, ice box and all, has been impeccably (indeed, surreally) maintained since 1949. Spotless, glowing white-tile floors and walls make Casamento's feel more like a laboratory than a family-owned eatery. The oysters are always the freshest and come raw on the half-shell at just $7.50 a dozen. An Italian-inflected gumbo ($7) and oyster loaf (a sandwich of breaded and fried oysters on 'pan bread'; $10.50 for a large one) also have their faithful followings. Other traditions upheld here include closing during the summer and not accepting credit cards. Otherwise, Casamento's is open every day but Monday for lunch and dinner.

Taqueria Corona (☎ 897-3974, 5932 Magazine St), near Eleonore St, draws a regular crowd of students who appreciate inexpensive Mexican fare. The Salvadoran owners

Pinch da Tail, Suck da Head

Louisiana's official state crustacean is the crawfish, which back home you probably know as crayfish. Cajuns call them *écrevisses*, and many rural folks just call them mudbugs. Peeling and eating their delicate thumb-size tail meat is a Cajun ritual that goes well with drinking beer and telling lies to a crowd around a heaping platter of the miniature swamp lobsters. Some are harvested in the wild; others are farm-raised in rice ponds during the off-season. Local harvests first show up in the spring.

Two keys to tasty crawfish are boiling them live and using a good spicy boil made with red pepper and other seasonings. It takes a 7lb platter to yield about a single pound of tail meat. Real dives even provide tables with a disposal hole in the middle for the wasted head and shell.

A few Cajuns seeking riches search for ways to automate the peeling process; until that happens, the peeling is up to you. First, grab and uncurl the crawfish, snapping the head and body from the tail. Hold the tail with both hands, using your thumb and finger to crack the tail open and pinch out the meat. As an option, you can suck the head to taste the flavorful 'fat' from the orange-colored hepatopancreas organ.

Can I tempt ya?

How Ya Like Dem Ersters?

Hard-core New Orleans oyster bars, like Casamento's Uptown, can be a little intimidating for neophytes. There's a certain cultishness in the way experienced patrons stand before a cold marble bar top as half a dozen oysters (which some locals pronounce 'ersters') are shucked and laid out on the half-shell. With restrained anticipation, often disguised by an air of ritualism, these oyster fiends dash lemon and a spot of hot sauce or a bit of horseradish onto the first of the oysters. They then slurp down the addictive bivalve, pausing to savor that first oyster's saltiness and to summon up a renewed sense of anticipation before turning their attention to the second one, and this behavioral pattern repeats itself until all six half-shells lie empty on the counter. For many New Orleanians, this entire ritual is completed in about the length of time it takes to fill a tank of gas.

Naturally, people who hold oysters in such high esteem have come to attribute certain health-promoting qualities to them. According to one popular myth, eating oysters can increase a person's sex drive and enhance their sexual prowess. The always contrarian Health Department, however, insists that people eating raw shellfish only risk food poisoning. After all, oysters are raised in the shallow bottom of the Gulf, where toxic debris discharged upstream eventually settles and enters the shells. As a test, with your next half dozen order a large glass of water and dip each plump little oyster in the water and swish it around. Afterward, check out the sediment in the glass and consider whether you would drink it.

Oysters also have a variety of ways of insinuating themselves into a leisurely classic New Orleans meal. In some people's minds, seafood gumbo *must* include oysters or be called something else. And the list of appetizers on many of the city's menus generally includes several baked oyster dishes. The most famous local oyster dish, served with a devilish little fork, is oysters Rockefeller, an Antoine's restaurant creation that owes its success as much to an irresistible secret spinach sauce as it does to the well-hidden oysters.

Then, of course, oysters make the classic po' boy. The name, local parlance for 'poor boy,' refers to the cheapness of oysters during the Great Depression. An oyster sandwich cost just 20¢ in those days. In some traditional quarters of the city, you can still order an oyster loaf, which as some people may recall was once known as 'La Mediatrice' – the peacemaker – because bringing one home was considered an effective way for a guilty husband to appease an angry wife. It's composed of oysters dipped in cornmeal, deep fried and served on white toast, and it appears to have gone out of fashion as divorces became more popular.

draw on California and Southwest Mexican styles of cooking and have established a niche in New Orleans for their winning combination of fresh ingredients and zesty sauces. A variety of meat and fish tacos prepared on soft flour tortillas cost around $2 apiece, though you'll probably want to order two. A burrito makes a filling meal for $5.50.

The casual dining room at *Café Atchafala* (☎ *891-5271, 901 Louisiana Ave*) is admirably nondescript, a complement to the down-home Southern cooking that comes

out of the kitchen. It's the kind of place where Southern hospitality and cornbread aren't on the menu, because you get them automatically. Deep South stalwarts, like fried green tomatoes, crab cakes, fried fish and chicken, and stuffed pork chops, appeal to milder palates seeking relief from over-indulgence in Creole spice. Café Atchafala is open for lunch and dinner Monday to Saturday.

A trip to soul food stalwart *Dunbar's* (☎ *899-0734, 4927 Freret St)*, at Upperline St, will set you up with a mess of fried chicken and red beans and rice, plus a slab of cornbread, for $5. The pork chop plate costs $6, the oyster plate $9.50. These are clean and basic soul food digs in a sketchy part of town. If you're not driving or taking a cab, you can get there from the French Quarter by taking the No 15 Freret bus from Canal St and Elks Place to Upperline St.

Mid-Range

Reginelli's (☎ *899-1414, 741 State St)*, at Magazine St, is a suitably creative place for lunch if you've been checking out nearby art galleries and antique shops. Pizzas ($10 to $14) and focaccia sandwiches (around $7) get the contemporary treatment, with ingredients like sun-dried tomatoes, goat and feta cheeses, artichokes and roasted walnuts making frequent appearances on the tables of this casual and upbeat place.

Vaqueros (☎ *891-6441, 4938 Prytania St)*, near Robert St, is an earthy Santa Fe-style restaurant with worn leather tabletops. Tortillas are made on the premises every day, and interpretations of hearty Mexican fare (tacos, fajitas, tamales) are prepared with care. As the crowds jamming into the place testify, New Orleanians are sold on the concept. Lunch platters run from $6 to $8.50; the same choices are marked up by a few dollars at dinner, when additional fish and meat entrées are available.

An undiscovered gem, *Kyoto* (☎ *891-3644, 4920 Prytania St)*, near Robert St, is a pleasant little sushi bar. Individual orders of sushi cost about $3.50. Plan on spending about $20 per person.

Pascal's Manale (☎ *895-4877, 1838 Napoleon Ave)*, at Dryades St, is an old-time establishment (dating to 1913), with walls bedecked with black-and-white photos. Specialties are mostly traditional New Orleans seafood and Italian standards. Pascal's signature dish, called 'barbecue shrimp,' is actually shelled jumbo prawns sautéed in a rich sauce made of butter, garlic and zesty spices. A platter for the table costs $18. The same shrimp can be had in sandwich form ($11) for lunch (weekdays only). Dinner is served nightly.

RIVERBEND (MAP 7)

The Riverbend usually draws visitors for its nightclubs, but it should not be overlooked for its restaurants. There are some real standouts in this part of town.

Budget

A destination in itself, the *Camellia Grill* (☎ *866-9573, 626 S Carrollton Ave)* has enjoyed increasing popularity ever since it opened in 1946. Its secret? It refuses to change with the times. Well-made American short-order fare (the burgers and omelettes stand out) is served by some of the city's snazziest (in black bow ties) and most entertaining waiters. That this is the South, there is no doubt – the Camellia's addictive pecan waffles and pecan pies have made regulars out of people you'd never expect to see in a diner. The Camellia is open until 3 am on Friday and Saturday nights.

Another late-night munchie spot is *Rick's Famous Pancake Cottage* (☎ *822-2630, 1438 S Carrollton Ave)*, where you can get a blintz with blueberries and cream cheese. It's convenient if you're going to a club on Willow St.

Cooter Brown's Tavern & Oyster Bar (☎ *866-9104, 509 S Carrollton Ave)* is a popular place to stop in for oysters on the half shell ($6.50 for six, $9 for a dozen) and sandwiches (like delicate fried catfish for $6.50) that far exceed bar-food standards. While you're here, check out the 'Hall of Foam.' After 8 pm, the place turns into a rowdy college hangout. (See the Entertainment chapter for Cooter's virtues as a bar.)

Bow-tied waiters and beautiful burgers

A quiet neighborhood shopping district and hangout for Tulane students is along Maple St. *Figaro's Pizzerie (☎ 866-0100, 7900 Maple St)* has a covered deck, which is a pleasant place to spend a warm evening watching the street activity. Pizza ($10 to $16) on soft, flavorful crust is the way to go here – the Neapolitan pizzas are particularly tasty – and a pitcher of Abita Amber will make things downright festive. Pasta dishes and specialties like shrimp scampi ($13), while good, are nothing to write home about.

Mid-Range

Jacques-Imo's Café (☎ 861-0886, 8324 Oak St) is just a few doors from the famous Maple Leaf Bar. Not that you need an excuse to dine at this superb New American-Creole restaurant. Outward appearances give the impression it's a dive, but once inside you're led through a kitchen, which bustles with all the energy and industry of a steamship engine room, before being seated in a comfortable closed-in patio dining room. Chef Austin Leslie's fried chicken ($10 with sides) is legendary, and there's genuine creativity in chef Jacques Lionardi's nightly specials ($15), which might include fried trout smothered with jalapeño, pecans and shrimp. Save room for some of the best key lime pie available anywhere. Jacques-Imo's is open for dinner only, and reservations are not accepted.

Zachary's (☎ 865-1559, 8400 Oak St) preserves the environment that traditional Creole cuisine originally came from – home. Lunch and dinner are served in the capacious dining room of an old house, and people come to enjoy a superb gumbo ($6) and subtly seasoned blackened rainbow trout ($10). Considering how delicious everything else is, Zachary's jambalaya is disappointingly dry. The lunch menu includes expertly prepared staples like fried chicken and red beans ($8). The expressions on the faces of your fellow diners will almost certainly illustrate how good food relaxes the soul, and the friendly family running things here completes the sense of comfort. After dinner, you can walk just half a block to see Louisiana music at the Maple Leaf Bar.

Top End

Despite all the critical acclaim that has been heaped upon chef Frank Brigtsen – *Food & Wine's* Southeastern Chef of the Year, New Orleans Chef of the Year – his eponymous restaurant, *Brigtsen's Restaurant (☎ 861-7610, 723 Dante St)*, remains a decidedly family-focused, purposefully unpretentious place where his spouse, Marna Brigtsen, is the hostess and her two sisters lead the team of waitresses. After spending seven years under Paul Prudhomme – first at Commander's Palace and later at K-Paul's – Brigtsen opened his own restaurant in 1986. Set in a converted double shotgun building, the restaurant feels homey and inviting. Service is attentive but never oppressive. Brigtsen terms his cooking 'modern Louisiana cuisine,' and those in search of haute Cajun cuisine will not find a better restaurant in the city. Rabbit and duck are among his specialties. Look for the roast duck with dirty rice and honey-pecan gravy or rabbit tenderloin on a tasso parmesan grits cake with Creole mustard sauce. Dinner will run about $25 per person not including wine.

CITY PARK & FAIR GROUNDS (MAP 9)

Restaurants in the vicinity of the Fair Grounds naturally attract huge crowds for dinner during Jazz Fest. But several places out this way are worth coming to no matter what time of year it is – you can easily combine a meal along Esplanade Ave with a trip to City Park or a stroll along Bayou St John.

Budget

During Jazz Fest, you can enjoy food of all kinds at the many stands in the Fair Grounds. But many music lovers still prefer to head to nearby markets for deli items. Probably the most popular source for a picnic lunch, *Whole Foods Market (☎ 943-1626, 3135 Esplanade Ave)* has quality meats, fresh baked goods and salads. It's just a block from the Fair Grounds. *True Brew (☎ 947-3948, 3133 Ponce de Leon)* is a nouveau coffee hangout – no chicory here.

JOHN ELK III

Mid-Range

Lola's (□ 488-6946, 3312 Esplanade Ave) is an energetic and funky little place serving good, inexpensive Spanish food. Cool, soothing gazpacho ($3) is a good way to start. Elaborate paellas and *fideuas* (an angel-hair pasta variation on the rice-based paella; $10 to $14) are specialties here – they're feasts for the eyes as well as the stomach, and great for sharing. Fish, meats and stews are also good and reasonably priced. Lola's takes no reservations, and lines are almost inevitable. It's BYOB, so get a bottle of wine at Whole Foods across the street and have it uncorked to make the wait more bearable. Lola's is open for dinner only.

Cafe Degas (☎ 945-5635, 3127 Esplanade Ave) is a congenial and romantic little spot that warms the heart with great French bistro fare. Diners are seated in a large enclosed deck featuring a fully grown tree thrusting through the floor and roof, and the casual atmosphere is accentuated by a mildly eccentric waitstaff. Savory meat dishes are Degas' forté, but you can also order a healthy lunch, like salad niçoise with grilled tuna ($8). Lamb shanks ($18) are cooked to perfection with a delicate but assertive Dijon sauce and, natch, are arranged beautifully on the plate. Cafe Degas is open daily for lunch and dinner.

At **Gabrielle** (☎ 948-6233, 3201 Esplanade Ave), chef Greg Sonnier captures the attention of both locals and a national audience with his innovative mixture of Creole and Cajun dishes served in modest surroundings. Dinner entrées cost between $15 and $25. Save room for dessert, as Greg's wife Mary creates outstanding pastries

MID-CITY (MAP 8)

Mid-City is known for its down-to-earth neighborhood eateries and, surprisingly, some of the best Vietnamese food in town. A number of good restaurants are within a block of the intersection of N Carrollton Ave and Canal St – convenient for Mid-City Carnival parade watchers and not so far out of the way if you're in town for Jazz Fest.

Budget

Betsy's Pancake House (☎ 822-0213, 2542 Canal St) is a busy spot offering breakfasts for about $2.50 and lunch specials for $5. **Mandina's** (☎ 182 9179, 3800 Canal St) is a popular local Cajun and Italian restaurant with lunch and dinner for under $12, including the seafood platter. It's a good choice for guests at the nearby hostel.

A little outside of the generally accepted bounds of Mid City, **Cafe Benet** (☎ 822-1376, 3925 Washington Ave), near Broad Ave, offers inexpensive soul food amid a tidy yet stark interior with Formica tables. Try the baked macaroni lunch with three pieces of chicken and a vegetable for $5.

Vegan diners will appreciate **Jack Sprats** (☎ 486-2200, 3240 S Carrollton Ave), where it's the spices that make the dish. Lunch and dinner plates cost between $5 and $8 and include a salad and bread.

Mid-Range

Lemon Grass Cafe (☎ 488-8335, 216 N Carrollton) is the culinary atelier of chef Minh Bui, whose often inspired play on arousing combinations of ingredients and flavors borrows freely from French cuisine as well as the cooking of his own native Vietnam. Entrées ($16 to $20) change frequently so that the freshest ingredients can be used, but may include mirliton (chayote) with shrimp and a buttery French sauce, or ginger chicken and stir-fried vegetables couched in a deep-fried, cracker-like 'bird's nest.' You can also graze on delicious appetizers (around $7), such as summer rolls (with a heavenly peanut sauce), deep-fried oysters and shrimp dumplings. Desserts are also exceptional.

Near Canal St, **Palmers** (☎ 482-3658, 135 N Carrollton Ave) is a basic Caribbean joint with nonexistent decor. It's festive when crowded (during Jazz Fest) but a little sad when things are slow. Still, the food is always alive with flavor. Start with a bowl of Jamaican pepperpot ($3), a chicken-and-potato based broth that gets its intriguing flavor from a blend of peppers, and choose from an irresistible selection of entrées, including a piquant jerk fish, marinated 24 hours and served up in a pool of spicy sauce ($11), and West Indian-style curry chicken with plantains ($8.50). Red Stripe and an odd assortment of rum drinks are available to wash it all down.

Opposite the Lafitte housing project, ***Dooky Chase Restaurant*** (☎ *821-0600, 2301 Orleans Ave)*, at Miro, is a historic gathering place that has gained national renown on the strength of chefs Leah and Dooky Chase Jr's inspired Creole cuisine. Emily and Edward 'Dooky' Chase Sr opened it as a sandwich shop in 1941 – it was then the only restaurant in the neighborhood where blacks could receive table service – and civil rights activists and touring jazz musicians (Duke Ellington, Nat 'King' Cole – the list goes on) frequently gathered here. In the 1970s, the Chases expanded and remodeled the place – they may have gone overboard, as the main dining room has all the atmosphere of a hotel conference room. If you want to soak in the historic vibe, request a table in the more convivial original Gold Room. Entrées run between $10 to $25. In the same building, but through a different entrance, Dook's down-home take-out counter and bar offers fried chicken and gumbo at considerably lower prices. The restaurant is open daily for lunch and dinner.

Entertainment

No matter what, you will be entertained in New Orleans. And it doesn't matter what time of year it is, because this city is justifiably famous for its year-round carnival atmosphere and its nonstop music. Of course, if your idea of entertainment is getting completely blotto on a Bourbon St balcony and baring your breasts or buttocks for all to see, you can do that here, too. Or you can just be a spectator of the endless hedonistic Bourbon St parade.

Your best sources for upcoming performances and reviews are the free monthly entertainment guide *Offbeat* and the weekly *Gambit*. The *Times-Picayune* entertainment section, 'Lagniappe,' is published on Friday. Tune into radio station WWOZ (90.7 FM) for a round-the-clock education on Southern Louisiana music, or call the station's events hotline, the Second Line (☎ 840-4040), for a daily listing of shows. Listings for gay and lesbian bars and dance clubs appear in the biweekly *Impact* and *Ambush* magazines, which also provide an entertainment calendar and list other current events.

TicketMaster (☎ 522-5555) has information on, and sells tickets to, just about any major event in the city. You can reserve tickets over the phone with a credit card and pick them up at the venue or at a TicketMaster outlet. Outlets include Tower Records on Decatur St downtown, Blockbuster Video on N Carrollton Ave in Mid-City and inside the Riverside Market Shopping Center (Map 6) on Tchoupitoulas St in Uptown.

BARS & CLUBS
French Quarter (Map 2)
Live Music The arrival of *House of Blues* (☎ 529-2583, 255 Decatur St) has sparked a music revival in the French Quarter. Some locals grumbled when Dan Akroyd and a pack of out-of-town investors opened the club, but the full calendar of headliner acts (from the hottest local talent to touring bands) and the congenial space have won most of them over. After hours the club turns into a

'In blues we trust'

popular disco. On Sunday morning, HOB's Gospel Brunch will fortify your soul. Tickets for nightly shows cost between $7 (House of Blues All Stars) to $25 (Dr John).

HOB's formula has been so successful that other clubs have tried to follow suit – even New Orleans' own legendary Tipitina's. The recently opened *Tipitina's French Quarter* (☎ 895-8477, 233 N Peters St) doesn't live up to the reputation of the original Uptown 'Tips,' and locals who feel that following House of Blues to the Quarter was beneath the famous nightclub have taken to calling it 'House of Tips.' Tipitina's French Quarter is an awkwardly shaped space, with the stage facing the audience at an odd angle, and it lacks Crescent City atmosphere. But having Tipitina's in the Quarter means more great music in the heart of town, and that's not such a bad thing, is it? (See the Uptown section, later in this chapter, for more on the original Tipitina's.)

Quint Davis' *Storyville District (☎ 410-1000, 125 Bourbon St)* is the best thing to happen on Bourbon St in a long time. The club features outstanding local music day and night in two separate rooms. One Monday lineup included Henry Butler, Kermit Ruffins, Los Hombres Calientes and the Dirty Dozen Brass Band. It's the kind of logistical plate-spinning you'd expect from Jazz Fest organizer Davis. On top of that, the club serves good New Orleans bar food (po' boys, etc) by none other than Ralph Brennan. The clincher: The club never charges a cover. Drinks are, of course, a little on the expensive side.

Levon Helm's Classic American Café (☎ 522-5907, 300 Decatur St) has all the atmosphere of a shopping mall food court. The stage is too high (so people way in back can see) and the 'Classic American' concept doesn't really jibe with New Orleans. But Helm's booking agent seems to have a talent (or at least the budget) for bringing headliners like Irma Thomas for regular gigs; unfortunately, this means she performs less often at her own club, The Lion's Den, which is where you'd really rather see her. Helm's own group, The Band, also plays here regularly.

Those are the big clubs, but not necessarily the best. Out on Rampart St, the smaller, genuinely swanky *Funky Butt on Congo Square (☎ 558-0872, 225 Rampart St)* is a bi-level club with a sexy, Jazz Age atmosphere. There's almost always something interesting going on here – usually jazz, though on occasion a Mardi Gras Indian gang will set the joint on fire. Although the Funky Butt isn't an old establishment, in name it definitely claims a piece of New Orleans history. Owner Richard Rochester says legendary musician Danny Barker suggested he name his club in honor of Buddy Bolden's raunchy 'Funky Butt' theme song. During Bolden's reign as cornet king of New Orleans, the song lent its name to a hall where Bolden often played. The new Funky Butt also stands opposite Congo Square, the throbbing heart of African culture during the mid-19th century.

Nearby, *Donna's Bar & Grill (☎ 596-6914, 800 Rampart St)* is still the premier brass band club in the city, although the scene here isn't as electrifying as it was a few years ago. All the best young musicians used to perform here, and when they weren't booked they'd drop in to jam. Something seems to have caused a dramatic change, because the club has definitely lost some of its vigor. Nevertheless, you can still count on seeing brass bands here every night of the week. Friday night, featuring the Tremé Brass Band and the New Birth Brass Band, is the highlight of the weekly calendar.

Preservation Hall (☎ 522-2841, 726 St Peter St) always pleases large crowds (mostly tourists) with 'trad jazz.' But this New Orleans institution owes its success equally to its picturesque setting in a worn-out hall, which maintains a perfect state of decay, and to the bands, usually comprised of talented grandpas. Barbara Reid and Grayson 'Ken' Mills formed the Society for the Preservation of New Orleans Jazz in 1961, drawing visitors and musicians to the hall. When it's warm enough to leave the window shutters open, you can join the crowd on the sidewalk to listen to the sets. Admission is $5; line up before 8 or after 10 pm.

In some people's minds, the *Palm Court Jazz Cafe (☎ 525-0200, 1204 Decatur St)* is the best club in town for traditional jazz. It lacks the rustic patina of Preservation Hall, but it is roomier and has a bar, and guests can expect chairs and a table. Palm Court has an excellent calendar, too, with local legend Lucien Barbarin performing here regularly.

ANTHONY PIDGEON

Jazz at Preservation Hall

Bourbon Street & the Blathering Boozeoisie

You don't need a guidebook to tell you about Bourbon St, the main stem of New Orleans' round-the-clock tourist bacchanalia. The street's reputation as a haven of delirium precedes itself. Most tourists end up on Bourbon St, and some never seem to find their way out.

Bourbon St is undeniably unique. Where else in America can you find eight historic blocks closed to traffic so tourists and conventioneers can get loaded, spill beer on each other, flash their breasts from cast-iron balconies, yell their heads off, leave trash all over the place and even vomit on the buildings?

New Orleans relies on the tourist dollar, and judging by the nightly scene on Bourbon St, the city effortlessly succeeds in showing visitors a good time. It isn't a bad arrangement between the city and tourists hell-bent on waking up with a major hangover. To New Orleans' credit, Bourbon St has a certain 'Big Easy' panache that's rare among tourist traps. But if you're looking for genuine local color, Bourbon St will only disappoint. Locals rarely go to Bourbon St unless they're regulars at Galatoire's or have jobs in its bars and shops.

Recently, a few savvy investors have begun efforts to shake off Bourbon St's special economic zone status. The 1999 opening of Storyville, a development promoted by Jazz Fest organizer Quint Davis, promises to improve the street's music scene and, it is hoped, to draw local crowds. Storyville offers ersatz atmosphere, but the musical program is the best Bourbon St has seen in decades. Hopefully, other businesses along New Orleans' most famous street will follow suit.

Many visitors are given the mistaken impression from the 'Dedicated to the Preservation of Jazz' banner that *Maison Bourbon* (☎ 522-8818, 641 Bourbon St) is Preservation Hall. You can almost always find a seat to enjoy a Dixieland set for the price of drink. Note that many musicians will abruptly stop playing to berate photographers and video camera-toting auteurs who ignore the signs forbidding photos.

Opposite the Farmer's Market, Jimmy Buffett's *Margaritaville Café* (☎ 592-2560, 1104 Decatur St) may bank primarily on its cheesy Parrothead image, but it also stands on its consistent policy of booking as many

as three performers each day and not charging a cover.

Dance Clubs A key to nearly two centuries of successful entertainment in New Orleans has been live music plus booze. Credit for breaking the mold must go to the large gay nightclubs on lower Bourbon St; these spots rely strictly on DJs for entertainment. Foremost are the twin sentinels of pulsing sounds: *Oz* (☎ 593-9491, 800 Bourbon St) and the *Bourbon Pub* (☎ 529-2107, 801 Bourbon St). Both are open to straights who want to dance nonstop and don't have a problem with guys in G-strings on stage.

A young mixed crowd that is predominantly heterosexual packs the dance floor at the **Gold Mine Saloon** (☎ 586-0745, 705 Dauphine St), which charges a $1 cover. Ask around about other high-energy nightspots and unadvertised all-night rave parties.

Bars You haven't completed the tourist rounds until you've had a 'Hurricane' or mint julep at **Pat O'Brien's** (☎ 525-4823, 800-597-4823, 718 St Peter St). Here, a labyrinthine series of alcoves links Bourbon St and St Peter St with a grand courtyard patio lit by flaming fountains. You can join trendy, young Uptown locals who cruise the scene at this continuous party, and then buy bar souvenirs at the gift shop. A trademark of Pat O'Brien's, the Hurricane is a 29oz concoction of rum, orange juice, pineapple juice and grenadine ($5 plus $2 refundable deposit on the souvenir glass). Don't forget to get your deposit before you leave, unless you want to keep the glass as a souvenir.

Lafitte's Blacksmith Shop (☎ 523-0066, 941 Bourbon St) is a dark and atmospheric haunt with a back room piano bar. Observing the impressionistic images created by tabletop candles – little dabs of light brighten

Cocktails, or Drinking from an Eggcup

New Orleans doesn't just claim to be the drinkingest city in America. It also claims, with great hubris, to have introduced the whole concept of having a drink for the hell of it – that is, having a cocktail. (Obviously, this claim assumes that in earlier, more puritanical times, spirits were drunk like medicine to bolster the constitution or to brace oneself for bad news.) Of course, other cities make similar claims, but you come to expect that sort of thing. What burg doesn't want just a little dash of color stirred into the usual drab history of settlement, growth and industry? But even if cocktails did originate elsewhere, the raconteurs of the Big Easy have more imagination, and they are sticklers when it comes to etymology. So, sorry, pal – New Orleans wins again.

The story begins with the actual inventor of the cocktail, a man named Peychaud, who fled the 18th-century slave uprisings in Santo Domingo. Peychaud settled in New Orleans, where he opened an apothecary on Royal St. (So far, so good – the hero and setting, down to the street, are convincingly established.) Peychaud, we are told, had a penchant for drinking brandy in an eggcup. The concept appealed to the people of New Orleans, and Peychaud began serving drinks in this fashion at his shop. (This is perhaps the weakest link in the story, for we might, at this point, wonder why people were so willing to drink from an eggcup. But read on…) The eggcup, of course, was not called an eggcup in French-speaking New Orleans. It was called a *coquetier*. It was called that until Peychaud's patrons began mispronouncing it. The term evolved – much as Acadian turned into Cajun – from *coquetier* to *cock-tay* to *cocktail*.

In time, the eggcup was disposed of in favor of a regular glass. And other liquors came to be more popular than brandy. In the mid-19th century, a French brandy manufacturer, Sazerac-du-Forge, lent its name to a brandy cocktail, called the Sazerac, that evolved into an absinthe-based drink, which eventually featured whiskey instead of brandy. And today, the Sazerac cocktail includes no absinthe, either. You can order one in just about any New Orleans bar, but don't expect great things from the syrupy beverage.

A sizable portion of the nation's population went hook, line and sinker for the cocktail, which prompted the teetotalling portion of the population to invoke a ban on alcoholic beverages. When Prohibition went into effect in 1919, the entire country was boozing it up, New Orleans style.

Lafitte's Blacksmith Shop

patrons' cheeks and eyes, transforming them into figures in a Toulouse-Lautrec oil painting – is probably all the reason you need to come to this quiet corner on lower Bourbon St. As for the lore of the place, there are plenty of unconfirmed stories about Jean Lafitte and his brother Pierre, New Orleans' legendary pirates. No one knows if they really ran a blacksmith shop as a cover for their illegal trade in slaves, but it makes a good story.

Another ancient bar, **Napoleon House** (☎ 524-9752, 500 Chartres St) dates to 1797. In fact, it's a particularly attractive example of what Walker Percy termed 'vital decay.' By all appearances, its stuccoed walls haven't received so much as a paint job in over two centuries, and the diffuse glow pouring through the open doors and windows in the afternoon illuminates the room's gorgeous patina. The back courtyard is also pleasant, day or night. But would Napoleon himself have appreciated these surroundings? When the deposed emperor was banished to St Helena, a band of loyal New Orleanians, including former mayor Nicholas Girod and the pirate Jean Lafitte, reputedly plotted to

snatch him and set him up in this building's 3rd-floor digs. But Napoleon died before the alleged plan was carried out.

The **Old Absinthe House** (☎ 523-3181, 240 Bourbon St) is one of many bars that served absinthe, the notorious wormwood potion, until it was outlawed in 1914. (Federal agents alleged that absinthe destroyed the central nervous system and drove its enthusiasts mad, and while that hasn't been scientifically proven, it hasn't been disproven either.) This is a historic spot, having opened in 1806, and its attractive bar is graced by an old marble water fountain topped by a bronze statuette of Napoleon Bonaparte. But if you want absinthe today, you'll have to smuggle it into the country – Pernod is the 90-proof stand-in of choice.

Jim Monaghan's **Molly's at the Market** (☎ 525-5169, 1107 Decatur St) is the Irish cultural center of the French Quarter. Monaghan inaugurated the wild St Patrick's Day Parade that starts at Molly's. It's a good place to get a pint of Abita or Guinness and watch TV or grab some pub food to eat in the back courtyard. Molly's attracts a diverse mix of New Orleans characters – it's not just the shamrock crowd. *Fahy's Irish Pub* (☎ 586-9806, 540 Burgundy St) attracts a neighborhood crowd with pool, darts and Guinness.

The *Rawhide Lounge* (☎ 525-8106, 740 Burgundy St) is – surprise! – a gay leather bar.

Tremé District (Map 2)

The Tremé, the historic black neighborhood on the other side of Rampart St from the French Quarter, has always had great little bars where musicians love to perform. In recent history, the Little People's Place was one of those spots, where a show was much more intimate than anything going on Uptown or in the Quarter. At this writing, Little People's Place no longer features live music, but it's worth keeping your ear to the ground to learn if anything has started up there again.

Joe's Cozy Corner (no ☎, 1030 N Robertson St), at Ursulines Ave, has a regular show on Sunday night, featuring Kermit Ruffins & the Barbecue Swingers and the Rebirth Brass Band. The small neighborhood hangout gets extremely crowded, with a mix of older folks, slick inner-city operators and, of late, a greater number of Uptown college students who cab to the Tremé. Because this is a neighborhood gig, musicians from around town are always likely to drop by and sit in. Just across the street, shows are sometimes put on at the *Tremé Music Hall* (☎ 596-6942, 1601 Ursulines Ave).

Faubourg Marigny & Bywater (Map 3)

New Orleans' premier contemporary jazz venue, *Snug Harbor* (☎ 949-0696, 626 Frenchmen St) regularly books headliner talent. There really isn't a bad seat in the place, upstairs or down, and the room's acoustics are unparalleled in town. Performers who regularly appear here include pianist Ellis Marsalis and R&B singer Charmaine Neville.

Cafe Brasil (☎ 947-9386, 2100 Chartres St), at Frenchman St, is a very hip, bohemian space with a colorful Caribbean vibe. The club often features the city's best jazz and brass artists. The large stage is big enough for two ensembles, and it is often called upon to

serve in that regard when the club stages its legendary 'battle of the bands' face-offs. When there's no live music, the space seems too expansive for the smattering of locals sitting at the bar, but this sort of minimalist excess also has its appeal.

Another cool live music venue, *Dream Palace* (☎ 945-2040, 534 Frenchmen St) almost always has something hot going on. The club doesn't feature live music every night, but the bar and its 2nd-floor balcony are worth visiting anytime.

Upstairs from the Siam Café, the *Dragon's Den* (☎ 949-1750, 435 Esplanade Ave) offers a mixed bag of live music with no cover. Don't expect to hear any headliners among the loud rock and R&B groups performing at *Igor's Checkpoint Charlie* (☎ 947-0979, 501 Esplanade Ave), where you can also do your laundry and play pool. There's no cover.

Royal St Inn (☎ 948-7499, 1431 Royal St) is a popular bar, which always seems to be playing Patsy Cline on the jukebox. It offers $2 pints and pool, but the real attraction is the mixed gay and straight crowd that never seems to lose the Mardi Gras spirit.

The *Hi-Ho Lounge* (☎ 947-5344, St Claude Ave), at Marigny St, is fairly friendly, as hip bohemian dives go, but in every other respect it verges on the cliché – fire-sale furniture, cheap booze and a barrage of young eccentrics donning outlandish outfits. It's sort of a slow-moving caboose carrying the would-be avant-garde. The club does have an interesting musical calendar, offering a steady diet of bands that may turn out to be the next big thing.

In increasing numbers, artists and urban pioneers are reviving the Bywater's shotgun houses and Creole cottages, and the neighborhood's wealth of local bars readily accommodates this crowd.

Marigny also has a pair of lesbian discos: *Rubyfruit Jungle* (☎ 947-4000, 640 Frenchmen St) and *Charlene's* (☎ 945-9328, 940 Elysian Fields Ave). Charlene's sometimes features live music.

The *Saturn Bar* (☎ 949-7532, 3067 St Claude Ave) is like an old junk store or garage that happens to have a bar in it. (Be careful

Ernie K-Doe's Mother-in-Law Lounge

'K-Doe, when is your voice *ever* goin' to change?'

Ernie K-Doe frequently stops singing to ask himself this question. If the legendary R&B singer, whose hit 'Mother in Law' was No 1 on the national charts for five weeks in 1961, appears mightily impressed with himself, no one in the room seems to mind. Because, after all, he *is* a living legend. And because everything he says is accompanied by that knowing sparkle in his eye. And because this happens to be K-Doe's own place, the Mother-in-Law Lounge, and nobody comes here thinking K-Doe can't say anything he wants. Many of the place's regulars have known K-Doe all his life.

The longer you stay in K-Doe's Mother-in-Law Lounge, the more it sinks in that you are a guest in this man's home. The self-proclaimed 'Emperor of the Universe' has opened

Ernie K-Doe's Mother-in-Law Lounge

up a piece of his life for his fans to share. Many fans were here in 1995, when K-Doe and his wife, Antoinette, were married in front of the bar. Antoinette is a strong woman with a serious demeanor, but she doesn't lack sentiment. She directs an ambivalent finger toward a curved vinyl booth that's beginning to show its age. 'That's the love seat where we were married, which is why we never take it out.'

Every year in late January, the K-Does renew their vows in a ceremony that draws friends, family, fans and media in jubilant throngs to the Mother-in-Law.

Family photos, record albums and mementos cover the walls. An enlarged photograph of K-Doe's current mother-in-law – Antoinette's mother – overlooks the bar. Appearing relaxed and fairly harmless in a panama hat, she bears no resemblance to the notorious subject of K-Doe's greatest hit.

K-Doe, relaxing behind the bar, quietly sips a soft drink (he's on the wagon), and when the mood strikes him he sings, accompanying whatever is playing on the jukebox. Naturally, many of the irresistibly catchy tunes are his own. 'We knocked 'em dead in New York with this one,' he says as 'A Certain Girl' comes on. Truth be told, he knocked 'em dead everywhere with that one. And although the bar's sound system isn't the best, there's no mistaking that golden voice. It still has the power to shake hips and, occasionally, move souls.

Ernie K-Doe's Mother-in-Law Lounge (☎ 947-1078, *1500 N Claiborne Ave*), at Columbus, is not for everybody. You really have to be a fan of the singer to appreciate the experience. Call before coming, because K-Doe might be performing elsewhere. Take a cab, as this stretch of Claiborne Ave isn't good for public transportation or walking.

not to bump into that Frigidaire on your way in.) Light comes only from two saturnine neon lamps (a surreal touch) and there doesn't seem to be a comfortable seat in the place. The mummy hanging from the ceiling looks like somebody actually dug it up – and some of the characters who spend time here look like they might have done it. All in all, a great bar.

Vaughan's (☎ 947-5562, 800 Lesseps St) on a Thursday night is as good as New Orleans gets. That's the night trumpeter Kermit Ruffins raises the roof. The weekly gig regularly features Ruffins' band, the Barbecue Swingers, and drummer Shannon Powell, an amazing performer. Anyone might show up to sit in – Wynton Marsalis has dropped by, and when pianist Henry Butler shows up, the bar's poor little upright piano darn near explodes. The crowds spill out onto the street, and between sets Kerm often dishes out barbecue from the smoker on the back of his pickup truck. The rest of the week, Vaughan's quietly serves the neighborhood well.

CBD & Warehouse District (Map 4)

Live Music Blues are naturally part of the tradition at *Howlin' Wolf* (☎ 523-2551, 828 S Peters St), but rock bands and other local acts also appear at this first-rate club. Revered blues artist Snooks Eaglin is a regular, and George Porter Jr is a hit whenever he appears.

In the Hilton Riverside Hotel, *Pete Fountain's* (☎ 523-4374, 2 Poydras St) features the famed clarinet player, who first made his mark nationally as a performer on the Lawrence Welk show in the late 1950s. His musical interest began while growing up in New Orleans, playing in the school band and a number of Dixieland bands. Fountain was a sideman in one of Al Hirt's first bands.

Bugsy's (☎ 522-6020, 829 Convention Center Blvd) is a second-tier blues and jazz club with a large dance floor. Nevertheless, it can be an inexpensive nightspot where you're sure to find a seat.

If you can't make it out to Cajun country, *Michaul's* (☎ 522-5517, 840 St Charles Ave),

Emile Vinette at Vaughan's

near the YMCA, offers Cajun music and dance lessons with overpriced Cajun vittles. Another Cajun music and food place is **Mulate's** (☎ 767-4794, 201 Julia St). Don't expect to see famous groups at either of these places.

The **Lion's Den** (☎ 822-4693, 2655 Gravier St) is a neighborhood bar that happens to be owned by Irma Thomas, the 'Soul Queen' of New Orleans. Call to find out if Irma's performing anytime soon. Seeing her sing here before a small crowd is an intimate, unforgettable experience. Sometimes you can drop in to see her band rehearse.

Bars Among the most popular after-work spots is **Vic's Kangaroo Café** (☎ 524-4329, 636 Tchoupitoulas St), where Australian hospitality, hearty beers on tap and cheap food attract a sizable crowd to the bar's narrow confines.

Kabby's Restaurant & Sports Edition (☎ 584-3880), in the Hilton Riverside Hotel on the mezzanine level, can tune into any sports action broadcast in the galaxy. National newspapers are also available in case you missed yesterday's game. All this comes at a price – a glass of domestic beer costs $3.25.

Lower Garden & Garden Districts (Map 5)

With so many young hipsters in the area, you'd think there'd be more interesting places to hang out. With two exceptions, neither music nor chic clubs are found here – just a few budget bars that rely on a local crowd and a captive audience from the nearby backpacker hostels.

Monaco Bob's (☎ 586-1282, 1179 Annunciation St) alternates between a weekly wet T-shirt night and live music, featuring mainly R&B acts in a small club that attracts a hip young crowd; out-of-town bands also sometimes play here. Uptown barhopping trendsetters typically drop in at the **Half Moon** (☎ 522-7313, 1125 St Mary St), at Sophie Wright Place, but you might stay and play at the best pool tables in the area.

Igor's Lounge (☎ 522-2145, 2133 St Charles Ave) is a 24-hour dive bar with a greasy grill, pool tables and washing machines. It's not

worth canceling your return to London for Igor's free red beans and rice on Monday night, nor for the free Sunday barbecue at the **RC Bridge Lounge** (no ☎, 1201 Magazine St), but these extras liven up the joints anyway. Another laundry bar, **Lucky's Lounge** (☎ 523-6538, 1625 St Charles Ave) offers happy hour draft beers for $1.25 from 5 to 7 pm and from midnight to 4 am.

The Bulldog (☎ 891-1516, 3236 Magazine St), at Toledano St, entices beer aficionados, particularly those of the postcollege set, with a wide array of import and domestic microbrews on draft and in bottles.

Uptown (Map 6)

Live Music The legendary **Tipitina's** (☎ 895-8477, 897-3943 for the concert line, 501 Napoleon Ave), at Tchoupitoulas Ave, is recovering from changes wrought by the arrival of House of Blues in the French Quarter. 'Tips,' as locals refer to it, has responded by opening a venue in the French Quarter, and some feel the Uptown location has suffered as the emphasis has been on booking name acts at the newer site. Nevertheless, Uptown Tips is still the 'real' Tips, and it remains a shrine to the great Professor Longhair, whose 1953 hit 'Tipitina' inspired the club's name. And outstanding music from the local talent pool still packs 'em in. Cover charges start at $8.

Most of the time **Le Bon Temps Roulé** (☎ 895-8117, 4801 Magazine St), at Bordeaux St, is just a neighborhood bar – and a good one – with a mostly college and postcollege crowd drawn in by two pool tables and a commendable beer selection. But late at night, blues, zydeco or jazz rocks the joint's little back room. Any time you can catch an extraordinary talent like Henry Butler in such close quarters, don't miss it.

Acoustic performers of just about any genre regularly play at the **Neutral Ground Coffee House** (☎ 891-3381, 5110 Danneel St), at Dufosat St, a nonprofit organization dedicated to keeping live music alive. Most nights showcase three or more performers, and a few nights each month are reserved for nonsmokers. There's never a cover charge.

Bars Suits and gowns abound at the lively *Columns Hotel* (☎ 899-9308, 3811 St Charles Ave), where the Uptown elite gather to celebrate and be seen. Ordinary out-of-town folk won't feel unwelcome, though men might want to don a jacket. Over the clinking glasses filled with mint juleps and gin fizzes, the burbling of the crowd grows louder as the night grows older.

Riverbend (Map 7)

The Riverbend has a healthy nightlife, with a number of clubs that commendably book the best of New Orleans' musical talent. Proximity to Tulane and Loyola means that many Riverbend clubs fill up with party-hearty college kids, who can easily undermine that sultry New Orleans spell.

Live Music The *Maple Leaf Bar* (☎ 866-9359, 8316 Oak St) has a solid musical calendar, and its dimly lit, pressed-tin caverns are the kind of environs you'd expect from a New Orleans club. That's why scenes from the film *Angel Heart*, in which the late great blues man Brownie McGhee starred, were shot here. You can regularly catch performances by local stars like Walter 'Wolfman' Washington, Rockin' Dopsie Jr & the Zydeco Twisters or the Rebirth Brass Band. Slide guitarist John Mooney also plays here often, and on Monday night (no cover) a traditional piano player sets the tone. You can choose to work up a sweat on the small dance floor directly in front of the stage or to relax at the bar in the next room. There's also a nice back patio in which to cool your heels.

Carrollton Station (☎ 865-9190, 8140 Willow St) is only a block from the streetcar line on S Carrollton Ave, opposite the historic streetcar barn with the same name. It features live R&B music on weekends. Just down the street from Carrollton Station, *Jimmy's* (☎ 861-8200, 8200 Willow St) is a worthwhile addition to any Uptown pub crawl, with live music just about every night.

Bars *Cooter Brown's Tavern & Oyster Bar* (☎ 866-9104, 509 S Carrollton Ave), near St Charles Ave, is a student hangout that takes its beer seriously, with over 40 draft brews

and hundreds of international bottled brews. What really makes this place unique in its love of suds is its 'Beersoleum & Hall of Foam' – a gallery of 100 plaster bas-relief statuettes of everybody from Liberace to Chairman Mao, each holding a bottle of beer (Albert Einstein, Mother Theresa and Andy Warhol also appear). This curious, still-growing exhibit is the work of the uniquely talented Scott Connery, a former New Orleanian who now sends additions from his Las Vegas home.

Cooter Brown's Hall of Foam

Upstream from the Riverbend area, beside a levee, sits an advertisement-adorned roadhouse, which probably hit its prime in the 1940s – the *Rivershack Tavern* (☎ 834-4938, 3449 River Rd). The old hand-painted signs were discovered when the asbestos shingles were removed. It's packed with students and bikers every Wednesday night, when all 37 draft beers cost only $1.50 a pint; or you can always contribute to the tacky ashtray collection in exchange for a brew. If you're hungry, the lunch specials are pretty good. Don't miss the clever legs on the bar stools.

Mid-City (Map 8)

One of the more incredible music venues in town is *Mid-City Rock & Bowl* (☎ 482-3133, 4133 S Carrollton Ave). What we have here is a gimmick – live music in an already bustling bowling alley – taken about as far as it can possibly go. The clincher is that owner John Blancher consistently books artists straight out of the American musical book of legends. Watching the likes of blind blues man Snooks Eaglin, soul-singing Ernie K-Doe (self-anointed 'Emperor of the Universe') or zydeco squeeze-box king Boozoo Chavis – all of whom can still rock the house – becomes an unreal experience when you hear the crash of bowling pins between songs. Add to this a perky teenage bar staff and unusual side acts, like a lip-synching black Elvis impersonator, and you begin to get the idea that Blancher (who *looks* fairly normal) is a genius of the absurd. He claims he was on the road to visit a religious shrine when he had an epiphany to buy the bowling alley. With two stages (upstairs and down) and a cast of musical characters you'd never expect to see in this type of setting, Rock & Bowl is a rockin' good time.

Backpacking lodgers at India House are close to the *Dixie Taverne (☎ 822-8268, 3340 Canal St)*, where domestic pitchers of beer cost $3, and women can drink for free each Thursday.

LARGER VENUES

Acts like Madonna or the Rolling Stones, or the blockbuster Essence Festival fill the *Louisiana Superdome (Map 4; ☎ 587-3810, 1500 Poydras St)*, while artists with slightly less pull, such as Bruce Springsteen, are likely to perform at the more intimate *Saenger Performing Arts Center Theatre (Map 2; ☎ 522-5555, 143 N Rampart St)*. Headliners like Paul Simon have performed at the *Kiefer University of New Orleans Lakefront Arena (☎ 286-7222)*.

The city's *Mahalia Jackson Theater of the Performing Arts (Map 2; ☎ 565-7470)*, in Armstrong Park, is dedicated to the powerful late gospel singer, who was born in New Orleans in 1911 and in 1927 moved to Chicago, where her career blossomed. The theater holds many Mardi Gras masquerade balls and other performances.

THEATER

Major touring troupes typically perform at the *Saenger Theatre (Map 2; ☎ 522-5555, 143 N Rampart St)*, where it's worth the admission just to see the fine restoration of the ornate 1927 theater. Student plays are fre-

quently offered at the *UNO Performing Arts Center (☎ 286-7469)* and Tulane University's *Lupin Theatre (Map 7; ☎ 865-5105)*. Most other theater activity picks up after the locals have packed away their Carnival costumes. In addition to the following performing groups, you should also check to see what's playing at the *Contemporary Arts Center (Map 4; ☎ 523-1216, 900 Camp St)*.

Le Petit Théâtre du Vieux Carré (☎ 522-2081, 616 St Peter St) is one of the oldest theater groups in the country. The troupe offers particularly Southern fare like *Steel Magnolias*, as well as special children's programming such as classics from Rudyard Kipling and others.

Founded in 1986, *Southern Repertory Theatre (☎ 861-8163, 333 Canal Place, 3rd floor)* performs classically Southern plays that deal with relationships, crisis and humor in a 150-seat theater.

Theatre Marigny (☎ 944-2653, 616 Frenchmen St) offers works that often portray humorous local themes, including *Where Y'at*, about a working-class 'y'at' family from the West Bank. At times, the Marigny's bohemian cast and audience interact in a familiar manner reminiscent of audience-participation scenes in the campy *Rocky Horror Picture Show*.

True Brew Theatre (☎ 522-2907, 200 Julia St), in the Warehouse District, is an added feature of the popular coffee shop. The group performs seasonal classics like Dickens' *Christmas Carol* along with its own works, such as *And the Ball and All*, which pokes fun at former Mardi Gras parade queens.

Also check the playlist at *Theater 13 (☎ 524-3090, 333 St Charles Ave)*, on the 13th floor of the Masonic Temple Building.

Comedy improvisation is featured every Saturday night at *Movie Pitchers (☎ 488-8881, 3941 Bienville St)*.

CLASSICAL MUSIC

New Orleans' concertgoers are justifiably proud of the *Louisiana Philharmonic Orchestra (☎ 523-6530)*, led by music director Klaus Peter Seibel. When the New Orleans Symphony financially collapsed in 1990, the musicians invested their own money to create one of only two musician-owned symphonies in the world. From September through May, the symphony performs at the richly ornamented Orpheum Theater (Map 4; 129 University Place), downtown. Tickets cost between $11 and $36. A special concert series at nearby plantations is extremely popular and costs only $7.

CINEMAS

IMAX stands for 'image maximum' films shown on a 74-foot by 54-foot screen at the *Entergy IMAX Theatre (Map 2; ☎ 581-4629)*, at the foot of Canal St near the Aquarium of the Americas (see the Things to See & Do chapter). Films like *The Living Sea* and *Antarctica* are guaranteed to capture your attention. Shows begin on the hour between 10 am and 8 pm. Admission costs $6.50 for adults, $4.50 for children.

For first-run art and mainstream movies, try the *Canal Place Cinemas (☎ 581-5400, 333 Canal Place)*, on the 3rd floor, which offers review clippings at the counter. The Uptown *Prytania Theatre (☎ 895-4518, 5339 Prytania St)* is another venue with a similar approach.

In Mid-City, *Movie Pitchers (☎ 488-8881, 3941 Bienville Ave)* plays films that wouldn't otherwise get exposure in New Orleans. *Zeitgeist Theatre Experiments (☎ 524-0064, 740 O'Keefe St)*, across from the main post office, is a 'multi-use venue of arts exhibition of all disciplines,' with decidedly avant-garde film and documentary offerings. Patrons at the Dog Days film program were encouraged to bring their mutts to the show. Sounds like a real howl!

RIVERBOAT JAZZ

You can dine and dance ($39) or just dance ($18) to live jazz aboard the *Creole Queen (Map 5; ☎ 524-0814, 800-445-4109)* as she cruises the Mississippi River. You should board at the Canal St Wharf at 7 pm for the boat's 8 pm departure.

FREE & OUTDOOR EVENTS

There are always *street performers* passing the hat at Jackson Square, from solo performers echoing saxophone sounds off the

French Quarter street musicians

front of the St Louis Cathedral to complete brass bands. Some may be youths that get together to jam away from the marching band, while others are between jobs. When a visitor asked an accordionist of an accomplished washtub band who the band was, he responded, 'Tired & Hungry.' Mimes, tarot card readers, artists and other street performers are also part of the passing show.

Sounds of a sousaphone and brass instruments are like an open invitation to join the party. You must be spontaneous to tag along with a second line as a brass band moves down the street – if you hesitate or insist on taking snapshots you'll miss all the fun.

SPECTATOR SPORTS

With the exception of sports, New Orleans residents tend to be participants rather than spectators. So, naturally, they bring their boisterous attitudes to cheer horses and players alike. Perhaps the most emblematic and traditional sport in New Orleans is horse racing. Gone is the New Orleans Jazz professional basketball team, now the saintly but misnamed Utah Jazz. Tickets to all *Louisiana Superdome (Map 4; ☎ 733-0255, 1500 Poydras St)* events are available through TicketMaster.

Horse Racing

Buried in the infield at the *Fair Grounds Race Track (Map 9; ☎ 944-5515, 1751 Gentilly Blvd)* are derby winners from an era when

New Orleans was one of the premier tracks in the country. Opened in 1872, the Fair Grounds is the third-oldest track in the nation – the handsome gatehouse entryway was designed by James Gallier in 1859 for an agricultural fair, and the stands were rebuilt following a disastrous fire in 1993. The racing season runs November to March on Wednesday through Sunday, with a 1:30 pm post time.

Football

The 60,000-seat *Louisiana Superdome* (see above) is home to the National Football League's New Orleans Saints. Barring postseason play, the Saints play nine home games from August through December. Tickets cost $22 to $50. Seats are generally available.

Baseball

With 72 home games from April to September, you can catch the minor league New Orleans Zephyrs (☎ 282-6777) baseball team on almost any week of the summer season. *Zephyr Field* (☎ 734-5155, 6000 Airline Hwy), at the junction with Dickory Ave, opened in 1997. Games between the Zephyrs (a Milwaukee Brewers affiliate) and other AAA clubs in the Southern League are always played in cool evening comfort – the first pitch is at 7:05 pm, except on Sunday, when games begin at 6:05 pm. General admission costs $5, or you can splurge for reserved seats at $7 for adults, $6 for seniors and $5 for children.

College Sports

College football, basketball and baseball games get plenty of attention; local teams tend to rank highly nationwide and contribute stars to the professional ranks. Attending college games is inexpensive (plus refreshments are usually very cheap), and you can often get a glimpse of the nation's up-and-coming players.

The Tulane Green Wave plays NCAA Division I football at the Superdome. The best and most exciting Tulane game is a battle with long-standing rival Louisiana State University (LSU) from Baton Rouge.

The hottest football ticket is the New Year's Sugar Bowl contest, featuring the Southeastern Conference champions. Out-of-town fans keep the demand high for Superdome tickets, which cost $60 to $100.

The University of New Orleans Privateers basketball team is quite good; games are played at the UNO Kiefer Lakefront Arena (☎ 280-6100). At Tulane, women's and men's games are played at the small but very lively Avron B Fogelman Arena (☎ 865-5000) on campus.

Tulane and UNO baseball games are worth a lazy afternoon. Tulane plays on campus, while UNO games take place in the larger, lakefront Privateer Park. In late February, baseball teams from Louisiana face off against Mississippi teams in the Winn-Dixie Showdown, a three-day series of triple-headers in the Superdome. Admission for an entire day of baseball is $6.

Shopping

JOHN ELK III

Creole condiments

Visitors in search of the most apropos New Orleans' souvenir are going to have to face some hard decisions. The city has a culture and traditions all its own, and many shops are devoted to selling items that have no market elsewhere – the obvious case in point being the multitude of emporiums trading in Mardi Gras accessories.

But perhaps Mardi Gras accessories don't interest you. Naturally, New Orleans is also a great city in which to hunt down local music recordings (whether you like CDs, LPs or 45s), as well as rare posters and photographs of musicians past and present. Lovers of art, antiques, antiquarian books and vintage clothing will also delight in bountiful shopping strips like Royal and Magazine Sts. Then, of course, there are the oddball tourist items sold at the French Market, including shellacked alligator heads and pepper sauces hot enough to make smoke come out of your ears. Customary shopping of the mall variety

can also be done here, but you won't find it exceptional unless you're coming from the boondocks.

Most shops are open Monday through Saturday from 10 or 11 am (no matter how early the sign might indicate) to 5 or 6 pm. Bookstores are an exception: Many are open daily, and booksellers tend to sleep in and keep later hours in the evening. Of course, most tourist-oriented shops are also open daily – on Sunday the Flea Market in particular is a hive of activity.

For foreign visitors, US prices are competitive with those anywhere in the world, especially for cameras, electronics, computer equipment and clothes. Merchants participating in the Louisiana Tax Free Shopping (LTFS) program provide tax refund vouchers to passport carriers at the time of purchase, as in the European VAT refund program (see Taxes & Refunds in the Facts for the Visitor chapter for more information).

WHAT TO BUY
Art

New Orleans is one of the most unself-consciously creative cities in the world, as you'd have to expect from a city that devotes several months of the year preparing for a masquerade party. Creative energy flows unchecked in New Orleans, which proves itself to be very hospitable to artistic types. In perusing the city's galleries, you are likely to run across some very unconventional material by local artists.

To get a quick feel for the range of offerings along Royal St, head for the one-block stretch between St Louis and Toulouse Sts. On one side of the street, the six-floor gallery of Kurt E Schon (Map 2; ☎ 524-5462, 523 Royal St) purveys fine 19th-century paintings, such as the series of Wagner operas by Ferdinand Leeke offered for more than half a million dollars. Across the street is Barrister's Gallery (Map 2; ☎ 525-2767, 526 Royal St), where a bizarre collection includes such tasteless but amusing works as 'The Last Flight,' artist GK's painting of rock stars killed in plane crashes, and 'Death Row Show' by mass-murderer John Wayne Gacy.

Two blocks toward Canal St, A Gallery of Fine Photography (Map 2; ☎ 568-1313, 313 Royal St) offers historical prints such as William Henry Jackson's early-20th-century views of New Orleans or the Depression-era work of Fonville Winan. The gallery also regularly features the work of Herman Leonard, the great photographer of jazz artists, and music documentarian Michael P Smith, who has been capturing images of the city's music and culture since the early 1970s. Don't miss the stunning exhibits upstairs.

In the up-and-coming Bywater, the rustic Porché West Gallery (Map 3; no phone, 3218 Dauphine St, porche@communique.net) is the shop/studio of photographer Christopher Porché West. Pathos defines his black-and-white images of the people of New Orleans, and his photos of Mardi Gras Indians are

---

Mardi Gras Accoutrements

When it comes to big-business holidays in New Orleans, Mardi Gras outclasses Christmas by far – what is known as 'the holidays' throughout the rest of the USA is a mere warm-up here. A shopping excursion in January or February can help shed a little light on the subject.

Go to the eye-popping, supermarket-sized Jefferson Variety (☎ 834-5222, 239 Iris Ave), in Jefferson, where the nonstop *ca-ching* of cash registers is certainly music to the proprietor's ears, as New Orleanians fork over several months' income for bags filled with 'throws' (trinkets) and other items manufactured specifically for Mardi Gras. Then you might begin to understand just how vital Carnival is to New Orleans.

The local yellow pages has a sizable 'Carnival Supplies' section, which lists numerous emporiums trading in throws, costume accessories and festive decorations for the home. These tend to be in outlying parts of town and in the suburbs, but if you've caught Mardi Gras fever you'll want to make a shopping excursion.

The smallish French Quarter branch of Accent Annex (☎ 592-9886, 633 Toulouse St) will probably satisfy the needs of most tourists. It's a good, relatively unscary starting place, as is Mardi Gras Center (Map 2; ☎ 524-4384, 831 Chartres St).

The Zulu Social Aid & Pleasure Club operates a small souvenir gift shop (Map 8; ☎ 822-1559, 7220 N Broad Ave), at Orleans Ave, where you can pick up T-shirts emblazoned with the famous Zulu warrior logo, along with Zulu's hefty medallions and beads.

Used-clothing stores are a good place to start assembling Carnival habiliments. All you need is a wig or hat, face paint, glitter and enough imagination to ensure that it's all brought together in a suitably gaudy fashion. (See the Vintage Clothing section for store recommendations.)

among the best. Presentation is one of Porché West's strengths – he has an eye for beauty in old, decaying objects and finds a place for these in his gallery (ancient electric lamp fixtures lie on the floor awaiting a future designation, and faded wooden shutters elegantly frame an enlarged photo). Porché West keeps somewhat odd hours, but you're most likely to catch him in the afternoon.

In the Warehouse District, anchored by the nearby Contemporary Arts Center, at 900 Camp St (see the Things to See & Do chapter), artists have created a vibrant community of galleries on Julia St between Commerce and Baronne Sts. Drop by any gallery to pick up a comprehensive guide.

One of the nearby galleries that shouldn't be missed is the 628 Gallery (Map 4; ☎ 529-3306, 628 Baronne St), where Young Artists/Young Aspirations (YA/YA), founded by painter Jana Napoli, is an exemplary arts program that works with at-risk teens. Sponsors like Swatch, the UN General Assembly and film director Spike Lee have commissioned the teens of YA/YA to apply their creative talents.

Another studio with a focus on youth is the New Orleans School of Glassworks (☎ 529-7277, 727 Magazine St). The school's gallery sells the artisans' wares at reasonable prices.

Antiques & Interesting Junk

New Orleans rewards the shopper who appreciates that a surprising number of things just get better with age, including old chairs, ashtrays, toys and ceramic statuettes, which once upon a time were prizes at the county fair. And even if you're looking for those things that don't get better with age (plaid polyester clothing and love seats in plaid polyester upholstery come to mind), you're still in luck.

When it comes to home furnishings, New Orleanians pride themselves on having exquisite taste. A peek inside an opulent Garden District mansion generally reveals greater extravagance within than without, while Creole cottages in the Bywater are often decked out with a panache that far exceeds expectation. It follows that the local

market for antiques is not particularly accommodating to the bargain hunter.

You'll find antique shops and art galleries scattered all along Magazine St, but a few clusters really stand out. Below Jackson Ave, Aaron's Antique Mall (Map 5; ☎ 523-0630, 2214 Magazine St) is a virtual gold mine, with the occasional blockbuster bargain. If you're mining for that distinctly New Orleanian curio or objet d'art, this is a good place to start, and it's only one – and the largest – of half a dozen emporiums of vintage odds and ends lining the block between St Andrew and Josephine Sts.

Jean Bragg Antiques (Map 2; ☎ 895-7375, 3901 Magazine St), at General Taylor St, is a good source for the Arts & Crafts-style Newcomb pottery, which originated at New Orleans' own Newcomb College. French provincial furnishings are emphasized across the street at Wirthmore Antiques (Map 2; ☎ 899-3811, 3900 Magazine St).

An area worth checking is the few blocks between Louisiana and Napoleon Aves. Another, smaller cluster above Napoleon Ave includes Hilderbrand Gallery (☎ 895-3312, 4524 Magazine St), with 19th-century paintings, and Modell's Restoration (Map 2; ☎ 895-5267, 4600 Magazine St), which sells antique lamps.

In Mid-City, African American art and literature are featured at the Community Book Center & Neighborhood Gallery (Map 8; ☎ 822-2665, 219 N Broad Ave). In addition to exhibition space dedicated to local artists, the gallery also includes an area for performing arts events like storytelling, African dancing, music and poetry.

Vintage Clothing

When it comes to used clothing, this town ain't too shabby. However, if you're looking for outrageous stuff around Mardi Gras, you're likely to find that the stores have been picked clean.

In the Lower Garden District, Mariposa (Map 5; ☎ 523-3037, 2038 Magazine St), near Jackson Ave, is always worth a gander, though the shop's prices sometimes defy logic: Ordinary Arrow shirts are overpriced, while nicer items can occasionally be found for a bargain. On the same block, Jim Smiley Fine Vintage Clothing (Map 5; ☎ 528-9449, 2001 Magazine St) is a great little shop dealing in very well-preserved garments, as well as laces, linens and textiles.

Farther uptown, Fiesta (Map 5; ☎ 895-7877, 3322 Magazine St) can usually be counted on for sporty duds.

Coins

Coin shops tend to carry everything from Confederate currency to Mardi Gras doubloons and old musket balls. The Coin Vault at the US Mint (Map 2; ☎ 523-6468, 400 Esplanade Ave) has a knowledgeable staff. For a wide selection of coins and other collectibles, like political campaign buttons, try James H Cohen & Sons (☎ 522-3305, 437 Royal St). The Civil War Store (☎ 522-3328, 212 Chartres St) is a small shop that sells Confederate currency and old 'Dix' bills.

Books

With so many local authors and academics, it's only natural that book lovers will find plenty of good independent bookstores. Most of the stores selling used books also carry a small stock of new titles and guides about New Orleans.

General Books In the French Quarter, Bookstar (Map 2; ☎ 523-6411, 414 N Peters St) is a large chain outlet with a wide variety of new books and magazines. Bookstar features a sizable collection of works by local authors. Next door, Tower Records (☎ 529-4411, 408 N Peters St) has magazines, underground comics and obscure publications.

In the CBD, DeVille Books (Map 4; ☎ 525-1486, 344 Carondelet St) also mixes a few fine used volumes with new offerings, Lonely Planet travel guides and maps.

Among mostly new titles, the Garden District Bookshop (Map 5; ☎ 895-2266, 2727 Prytania St), in The Rink, offers a select collection of first editions and books on the region.

Beaucoup Books (Map 6; ☎ 895-2663, 5414 Magazine St) offers a good New Orleans selection plus a large stock of foreign language books, travel guides and fiction.

At the Maple Street Bookstore (Map 7; ☎ 866-4916, 7523 Maple St), shopkeeper Rhonda Kellog Faust advocates for the anti-racism group ERACE and is a storehouse of local knowledge. The business, which includes a children's bookstore, was founded by her mother and aunt more than 30 years ago. In the Riverbend, there's Little Professor Books (Map 7; ☎ 866-7646, 1000 S Carrollton Ave).

Specialty Books Both a bookstore and a literary attraction, Faulkner House (Map 2; ☎ 524-2940, 624 Pirate's Alley) offers a good selection of new titles and first editions, with a particularly strong collection of books by local and Southern authors. Of course, William Faulkner is a staple, and a literary group works out of the shop (see the French Quarter section in the Things to See & Do chapter).

A small collection of new and used books on the region's history and politics is available in the gift shop of the Historic New Orleans Collection (Map 2; ☎ 598-7147, 533 Royal St).

For books written by or for African Americans, head to Vera Walker's Community Book Center (Map 8; ☎ 822-2665, 217 N Broad St). The Uptown Square Book Shop (☎ 865-8310, 200 Broadway), in the Uptown Square Mall, specializes in African American literary fiction.

Voodoo and occult works are available from Starling Books (☎ 595-6777, 1022 Royal St). Books on Native Americans are featured at Vision Quest (☎ 523-0920, 1034 Royal St).

Old Children's Books (☎ 525-3655, 734 Royal St) offers well-preserved antique books for children – not books for perpetual adolescents.

Antiquarian & Used Books New Orleans offers bibliophiles a variety of stores with small- to medium-sized collections around the French Quarter and Uptown. Most offer an up-to-date listing of other local secondhand bookstores compiled by Russell Desmond, owner of Arcadian Books & Art Prints (Map 2; ☎ 523-4138, 714 Orleans St).

Desmond speaks French fluently and is a wonderful, yet cynical, ambassador to New Orleans.

Among the French Quarter stores with good general offerings, you will find two floors of used books at Beckham's Book Store (☎ 522-9875, 228 Decatur St). Nearby, another two-story shop, Crescent City Books (☎ 524-4997, 204 Chartres St) offers a variety of used works at reasonable prices plus a few new titles. In the far reaches of the lower Quarter, Kaboom Books (Map 2; ☎ 529-5780, 901 Barracks St) is a worthwhile store to visit for its large and varied collection. Also try Dauphine Street Books (☎ 529-2333, 410 Dauphine St). To peruse either the general interest books or New Orleans material at Librairie Books (☎ 525-4837, 823 Chartres St), you must be able to tolerate a smoke-filled room.

Larger collections are shelved at the Uptown shop of George Herget (Map 6; ☎ 891-5595, 3109 Magazine St) and at Great Acquisitions Book Service (Map 7; ☎ 861-8707, 8120 Hampson St), in the Riverbend.

Music

A multitude of independent record stores serve the discriminating local audience. Most of these are also good sources for information about Louisiana music. You can shop for new and used CDs at Louisiana Music Factory (Map 2; ☎ 523-1094, 225 N Peters St), a great shop specializing in regional music. The listening stations are a great way to familiarize yourself with local artists before you plunk down the dough for a CD. Upstairs is a small collection of used LPs, and there's also a nice selection of T-shirts that you won't find elsewhere. Nearby, Magic Bus (Map 2; ☎ 522-0530, 527 Conti St) mostly sells used albums, but the used CD bins are worth a look.

After visiting the jazz exhibit at the Old US Mint (Map 2; ☎ 568-6968, 400 Esplanade Ave), scan the collection of CDs and tapes offered in the museum's ground floor gift shop. Nearby is Jazzology/Audiofile Records (☎ 525-1776, 1206 Decatur St).

The museum-like collection of historic rock posters and album covers at Record Ron's Stuff (☎ 522-2239, 239 Chartres St) is just the tip of the iceberg. His main store, Record Ron's (☎ 524-9444, 1129 Decatur St), is filled with a large, pricey collection of Louisiana recordings (mainly LPs).

Uptown also has a few worthwhile record stores. Jim Russell Rare Records (Map 5; ☎ 522-2602, 1837 Magazine St) is not the huge emporium it once was, but it's still probably the best shop in New Orleans for used 45s. The used LPs have mostly given way to CDs, with an uneven selection available at frequent discounts.

Underground Sounds (Map 5; ☎ 897-9030, 735 Octavia St), near Magazine St, and Mushroom (☎ 866-6065, 1037 Broadway) serve the university area's music needs and also sell tickets to shows at Tipitina's (see the Entertainment chapter).

Kitchen Goods & Cookbooks

The most popular cookbooks tend to be the collected Cajun recipes from groups like the Lafayette Junior League – not exactly gourmet stuff, but you'll learn the regional basics, such as how to use the 'Holy Trinity' (onion, celery and peppers). Of course, most celebrated New Orleans chefs offer cookbooks of their own. And you must make enough room in your luggage to take home a sampler of hot sauces.

Try the Farmer's Market (see the French Market, below) for spices, hot sauces, kitchen tools and cookbooks. Nearby, the hyperbusy Central Grocery (Map 2; ☎ 523-1620, 923 Decatur St) offers cooking ingredients typically found in Louisiana kitchens: Zatarain's Creole Seasoning and Crab Boil (even Chef Emeril uses it), McIlhenny Tabasco or Crystal hot sauce, chicory coffee and filé, for making filé gumbo.

In the Warehouse District, the small Louisiana Products (Map 4; ☎ 529-1666, 618 Julia St) is a down-home spot where you can find a selection of everyday foods and ingredients at prices that are not inflated for tourist budgets.

Creole Delicacies Gourmet Shop (☎ 525-9508, 533 St Ann St) sells utensils and cookbooks – also try the Riverwalk Mall location (☎ 523-6425), where there's a Cajun cooking class (see Activities in the Things to See & Do chapter). Another shop with cooking tools and cookbooks, also affiliated with cooking instruction, is Bayou Country General Store (Map 2; ☎ 523-3113, 600 Decatur St), in the Jackson Brewery Mall.

Pralines

A natural use of the abundant Louisiana sugar crop is to mix it with some butter and pecans to make pralines. Freshness really counts. A local favorite for a sugar fix is Southern Candy Makers (☎ 523-5544, 334 Decatur St). Loretta's (Map 2; ☎ 529-6170), in the Farmer's Market, also has a loyal following. For pralines Uptown, stop by Tee Eva's (☎ 899-8350, 4430 Magazine St), near Napoleon Ave.

Crawfish

If you really have a thing for crawfish and they're hard to come in your hometown, it might make sense to buy some in New Orleans and ship them back home. (Weird as it may sound, out-of-state crawfish fiends do this all the time.) Fisherman Seafood (Map 5; ☎ 897-9907, 3301 Magazine St), at Toledano St, will pack and ship to anywhere in the USA.

Voodoo & Occult

Maybe you're not feeling well – some gris-gris worn in a sachet will make you feel better. (For yellow fever and malaria, the Yoruba voodoo practitioners used the most powerful gris-gris, High John the Conqueror, or *Iopomea purga*.) Dried frog gris-gris is useful if you want to practice a little black magic on a bad neighbor. Or maybe you just need some love potion No 9. For potions, take your pick from Rev Zombie's Voodoo Shop (☎ 897-2030, 723 St Peter St), where you'll also find a large selection of books on the occult; the Witch's Closet (☎ 593-9222, 521 St Philip St) or the Voodoo Museum (Map 2; ☎ 523-7685, 724 Dumaine St).

Voodoo shop, St Peter St, French Quarter

Alligator Stuff

As a souvenir from your trip to New Orleans, you can purchase a polyurethaned alligator head – something to toss into the trunk of the car, where it will probably add new meaning to the expression, 'Heads will roll.' This is how New Orleans caters to tourists – in suitable eccentric fashion. The trade in alligator heads really should not be encouraged – if the things catch on, it could conceivably spell the end for the species. Although the alligator has made a comeback from near extinction, poachers could readily decimate the population again if demand rose. Hides from legally harvested gators are fashioned into high-value products, which can be seen at Wehmeier's Belt Shop (☎ 525-2758, 719 Toulouse St). The preserved heads are sold at the Flea Market.

Is it carry-on or carrion?

Adult Toys

Forget to pack your handcuffs or other sex toys? The Gay Mart (Map 2; ☎ 523-6005, 808 N Rampart St) is the place to go for adult toys, jewelry, leather items and novelties. Send a postcard that is certain to raise a few postal workers' eyebrows from Postmark New Orleans (☎ 529-2052, 631 Toulouse St).

WHERE TO SHOP
French Market (Map 2)

The French Market houses a vibrant Flea Market filled with bargains on everything from music CDs to crafts, along with a Farmer's Market emphasizing local foodstuffs and cooking supplies.

For more than 200 years, New Orleans trade has focused on the high ground beside the levee. Native Americans conducted the earliest commerce by offering hides to Europeans, and French colonials followed with an open-air market. The Spanish built the first structure in 1791 to house butchers and regulate the often abused sale of food, but it was destroyed by hurricane and fire; the site is now a parking lot between Cafe Du Monde and the levee. In 1813, the city surveyor, Jacques Tanesse, designed a replacement, the Halle des Boucheries (Butcher's Market).

John James Audubon, who frequented the French Market to buy specimens in 1821, described the market as the 'dirtiest place in all the cities of the United States.' But it wasn't until more than a century later that the WPA extensively renovated the city-managed French Market from St Ann St to Barracks St. In 1975, further renovations and new construction began in order to house visitors centers and commercial enterprises unrelated to original market activity, which was relegated to the Farmer's Market.

Cafés have occupied the Butcher's Market building since 1860. Cafe du Monde, the market's oldest tenant, sells loads of its packaged chicory blend coffee and boxed beignet mix to visitors (see the Places to Eat chapter). It never closes. A rare public rest room is in Building II near the Red Store.

Farmer's Market In 1937 the WPA built the Farmer's Market sheds, on Ursulines St between St Peter St and French Market Place, to serve as the main wholesale produce terminal for the 18 existing municipal markets throughout the city. At the time, New Orleans operated more municipal markets than any city in the country. These neighborhood markets are now closed or privately owned. The handsome St Roch Market, 2381 St Claude St, still stands, and is one of the best spots for crawfish during the spring, but the municipal price control system is gone.

Only a vestige of the former market activity remains at the Farmer's Market, where large freezer trucks have replaced the small trucks of farmers. Still, you might occasionally see a beat-up pickup on sagging springs heading from the market to sell a load of fresh produce on the streets of the Tremé District. (Many restaurateurs and residents now rely on the Saturday morning Green Market in the Warehouse District at Girod and Magazine Sts – where real farmers sell to those out 'makin' groceries.')

Merchants in the Farmer's Market offer fresh fruits and vegetables, including mangos, papaya, green beans, bananas, plantains, peaches, strawberries, watermelon, apples, pecans and cold drinks. In addition, there are lots of kitchen supplies, spices (including a large selection of hot sauces), garlic and chili strings, and cookbooks for the tourist trade. The Farmer's Market is open 24 hours a day.

Flea Market Bottom-fishing shoppers can pick up some unique southern Louisiana

products here any day of the week. Sure, there is a motley assortment of T-shirt and sunglasses vendors, but you will also find authentic African art, well-priced hand-crafted sterling silver jewelry, inexpensive Chinese-made Mardi Gras masks and dolls, musical tapes and CDs of dubious origin, and enough preserved alligator heads to populate a swamp. (Alligator poaching is a problem, but it's the hides, and to a lesser degree the meat, that have value – not the smelly heads. We are told that most of these are byproducts of legitimate game control sanctioned by the Louisiana Department of Wildlife. See Fauna in the Facts about New Orleans chapter for more information.)

Royal Street (Map 2)
Along Royal St, the finest arts are offered by galleries built on the early Creole and American settlers' tradition of art appreciation. Many regard Royal St as the 'Main Street' of the French Quarter. For a walking tour, see the Things to See & Do chapter.

Along Royal St from Iberville to St Ann Sts, visitors will find the most distinguished galleries and specialty shops. These establishments and restaurants inhabit buildings that have been prominent commercial addresses since before the Louisiana Purchase. At an early date, a secondary commercial and retail corridor evolved one block toward the river along upper Chartres St. The narrow Exchange Place, between Royal and Chartres Sts, is another historic commercial zone, which now harbors galleries and restaurants.

More recently, clothing boutiques and other small shops have extended the Royal St shopping area into the lower Quarter to St Philip St. Many shops are gay- and lesbian-owned, like Billy Bob's Chinese Laundry (☎ 524-5578, 927 Royal St) or The Shop of the Two Sisters (☎ 524-6213, 838 Royal St). Portions of Royal St are closed to automobiles during daytime shopping hours.

Jackson Brewery Mall (Map 2)
You have to wonder about a brewery that couldn't survive in New Orleans. Now the Jackson Brewery (☎ 566-7245, 600 Decatur St) has been redeveloped into a small

shopping mall best known for its convenient ATM and public rest rooms. The Bayou Country General Store (☎ 523-3313) sells cooking supplies and cookbooks. The mall is open Sunday to Thursday 10 am to 9 pm and until 10 pm on Friday and Saturday.

Canal Street (Map 2)

Beginning in the 1830s, businesses began a gradual shift from the Creole French Quarter to Canal St and the American sector above it. Though the street was never a canal, its broad neutral ground separated the Creole and American sectors. Now this neutral ground is a bus corridor. Mingling with the multitude of tax-free camera shops and drugstores are a few remnants from the days when shopping downtown was popular with the elite.

Upscale men's clothes are available at Rubenstein Bros (☎ 581-6666, 102 St Charles Ave), where each customer gets personalized service immediately after entering the two-story haberdashery – the shop can afford it by selling designer shirts for $200. It's worth going out of your way just to window-shop at Alders (☎ 523-5292, 722 Canal St), where jewelry, crystal, porcelain and silver displays catch the eye.

Canal Place Shopping Centre If you get invited to a masquerade ball and didn't happen to pack a gown or tuxedo in your backpack, just head over to the Saks Fifth Avenue store in the fashionable air-conditioned Canal Place Centre, 333 Canal St at N Peters St. It's a five-block walk from either the St Charles Ave streetcar or the Riverfront streetcar.

Featured at the mall entrance is LA Showcase (☎ 558-0054), offering eclectic, locally crafted furnishings, reminding us that the locals don't typically hire designers. Craftspeople operate the nonprofit cooperative RHINO (Right Here In New Orleans), on the lower level, showcasing the fanciful work of more than 70 artists. The 2nd-level RHINO shop, Fyberspace (☎ 523-7945), features handcrafted fabrics and wearable art. Other popular shops include Chanel, Laura Ashley, Brooks Brothers and Coach.

Canal Place Shopping Centre

A multiplex cinema and a performing arts theater are on the 3rd floor (see the Entertainment chapter).

Riverwalk Mall (Map 4)

Low attendance and huge losses accompanied the 1984 New Orleans World's Fair – a fair best known for killing plans for other US expositions. Though the exposition was supposed to help redevelop the Warehouse District and give the tourist industry a shot in the arm, the Riverwalk Mall (☎ 522-1555), on the riverfront upriver from the aquarium, is the primary result of this massive boondoggle.

It seems ironic that the French Quarter sidewalks were also repaved for fairgoers, because the Riverwalk Mall provides a sanitized alternative to the Quarter's shops and restaurants. In fact, many Quarter shops have outlets in the mall or its food court – perhaps to keep the cash flowing during heavy rain. The mall lacks an anchor store but does have branches of Banana Republic, Sharper Image and other mall favorites. Many stores have shorter operating hours than the mall, which is open 10 am to 9 pm Monday to Thursday, until 10 pm Friday and Saturday, and until 7 pm on Sunday. If you don't want to walk there, take the Riverfront streetcar.

The 'riverwalk' is a narrow sidewalk on the side of the mall (see CBD & Warehouse District in the Things to See & Do chapter).

New Orleans Centre (Map 4)

Adjoining the Superdome at LaSalle St and Poydras Ave, the air-conditioned New Orleans Centre (☎ 568-0000) is yet another downtown shopping emporium with Lord & Taylor and Macy's department stores and a wide selection of favorite mall shops, as well as a food court. There aren't any unique stores to recommend here.

Uptown & Garden District

A small group of upscale shops, including a bookstore and coffee shop, are housed in The Rink (Map 5), opposite Lafayette Cemetery No 1 at Prytania and Washington Sts in the heart of the Garden District.

Along the length of Magazine St, there are many antique shops and galleries. Travelers in search of an odd old piece of New Orleans will find particularly good concentrations of stores between St Andrew and Josephine Sts and between Eighth and Ninth Sts. The No 11 Magazine bus makes a loop from Decatur St at the edge of the French Quarter to Audubon Park.

The Riverside Market Shopping Center (Map 6), at Jefferson Ave and Tchoupitoulas St, is a modern surprise that primarily serves the locals' grocery, video rental, liquor and drugstore needs. The No 10 Tchoupitoulas bus goes there from downtown.

Riverbend (Map 7)

An interesting area here is the fashionable shops and restaurants fronting a small square on Dublin St near S Carrollton Ave where it meets St Charles Ave. To get there, take the St Charles Ave streetcar to the Riverbend near Camellia Grill.

Celebrated jewelry designer Migon Faget's boutique (☎ 865-7361, 710 Dublin St), behind the Winn-Dixie supermarket, is only one block from the streetcar line. Faget is a Newcomb College alumnus who carries on the Newcomb art tradition with highly regarded jewelry designs – some of which are specifically created for the alumnae association.

Student-oriented shopping is centered on Maple St, which is also accessible by the St Charles Ave streetcar line. Here bookstores, coffee shops and restaurants make for a happening district.

On the river-side of S Carrollton, Oak St is an older neighborhood commercial zone intersecting the streetcar line. It is reasonably compact for pedestrian strolls and offers a few interesting businesses, such as a vibrant fresh fish market, along with a few restaurants and the stellar Maple Leaf Bar (see the Entertainment chapter). At the foot of Broadway St at River Rd, Uptown Square is a faded mall that has seen better days.

Excursions

New Orleans is a beguiling – and exhausting – city. When you reach the point that you can't face another plate of shrimp *rémoulade*, and the thought of one more Sazerac cocktail sets your stomach to churning, head for the hinterlands. Browse through the quaint antique stores across Lake Pontchartrain on the North Shore in Covington. Paddle a canoe through the swamp at the Jean Lafitte National Historic Park. Come face to face with a gator on a boat tour led by Alligator Annie. Get a glimpse of antebellum opulence along the River Road. Learn of Louisiana's peculiar political past and present at the state capital, Baton Rouge. Spend the night on a houseboat anchored in your own private patch of swamp. Or sample a taste of Cajun cooking at a cinder-block roadhouse, where the beer is ice cold and the boiled crawfish are so spicy you'll break a sweat.

NORTH SHORE

There was a time, not long past, when the northern shore of Lake Pontchartrain was a resort destination for New Orleans residents, who came – first by boat, then train and finally, in 1956 with the completion of the 24-mile causeway, by car – to enjoy the cool lake breezes and calm restful atmosphere. Today these North Shore communities are less resort destinations than they are bedroom communities for New Orleans.

Of the towns on the North Shore, the jewels are undoubtedly Covington and Abita Springs, with Hammond, Madisonville and Slidell having little to offer beyond comparatively economical overnight accommodations. Mandeville is the site of a lovely state park and campgrounds, as well as a trio of good restaurants. The St Tammany Parish Tourist & Convention Commission (☎ 504-892-0520, 68099 Hwy 59, Mandeville, LA 70471) is located off I-12 at exit 65.

Fontainebleau State Park

What a gem! The 2700-acre park sprawls along the north shore of Lake Pontchartrain in **Mandeville**. It has nature trails, the ruins of a plantation brickyard and sugar mill, a sandy beach, a swimming pool (open in summer), a campground and lots of picnic areas. It's bordered by Lake Pontchartrain, Bayou Cane and Bayou Castine, making it an excellent spot for bird and wildlife watching. The Tammany Trace (see separate heading) passes through here.

The ***campground*** has well-spaced, shaded sites with picnic tables and grills. Some sites have clean bathhouses and restrooms and a public phone. Standard sites cost $10, while those with extras are $12. For groups, there's a separate camping area and a lodge that sleeps nine to 13 people ($90).

To get to Fontainebleau (☎ 504-624-4443, 888-677-3668) from I-12, take exit 65, go south 3½ miles and turn left onto Hwy 190; then go 2½ miles and turn right. From New Orleans, take the Lake Pontchartrain Causeway and exit at Hwy 190 east; continue 5 miles to the entrance.

Tammany Trace

An old railroad track was converted into this 32-mile trail. So far 9 miles have been paved – from Mandeville to Abita Springs, including a section through Fontainebleau State Park – for **biking**, **hiking** and **in-line skating**. An unpaved equestrian trail parallels the trace.

Abita Springs

North of Mandeville, along Hwy 59, is the bucolic little burg of Abita Springs, once popular in the late 1800s as a spot to take in what were thought to be curative waters. Today, the springwater still flows from a **fountain** in the center of the village, but the real attraction is the **Abita Brewery** (☎ 504-893-3143, 21084 Hwy 36), just a mile or so west of town. Abita was the first microbrewery in the Southeast, and its popular Turbo Dog, Purple Haze and Amber beers are top sellers throughout the state. Housed in a jumble of prefabricated metal and block buildings, with an overgrown auto-repair shop at its core, the brewery is not picturesque, but the personalized tours are charming and idiosyncratic – proof positive that beer making is not just the province of multinational conglomerates. And, as an added bonus, tours begin and end in the employees' break room, where a variety of beers – and a nonalcoholic root beer – are always on tap, and you are urged to help yourself. Tours of the brewery are free and offered at 1 and 3 pm on Saturday, and 3 pm on Sunday. Other times may be arranged by appointment. On your way home, you may want to stop off at the Abita Brew Pub (see Places to Eat) for a more formal tasting of their brews.

Covington

Founded in 1816, Covington was a port city of some import on the Bogue Falaya River and emerged as the seat of government for St Tammany Parish in 1819. In the ensuing years, the city served as a center of commerce for North Shore communities until 1956, when the causeway was completed across Lake Ponchatrain. Covington then became a bedroom community for nearby New Orleans.

Mamou – Capitol of Cajun Music, Citadel of Hedonism

Tanté Sue, a grandmotherly-looking woman, her face framed by a halo of gray curls, is taking healthy swigs from a bottle of cinnamon-flavored schnapps, squeezing her chest in time to the music as if playing an anthropomorphic accordion. A gaggle of middle-aged couples waltz a wide arc around the band, moving about the dance floor with unstudied ease. A clutch of college kids on a day trip from Baton Rouge gather in the corner to gawk, their hands wrapped tight around cans of Budweiser. Not an uncommon sight for Louisiana, you say? Check the clock. It's only 9:30 on a Saturday morning, and **Fred's Lounge** (☎ 318-468-5411) is at full tilt.

It's like this every Saturday at Fred's, a brick, corner bar on the main drag, 6th Street, in the little town of Mamou. And for those lucky enough to squeeze through the front door, it may well be the best free entertainment to be had in Louisiana. From 9 am to 1 pm each Saturday, Wayne Thibodaux and Cajun Fever broadcast live from the bar over KVPI 92.5 FM, playing loping accordion and drum-fueled waltzes.

After Tanté Sue shoos the last customer away, lots of folks move down the street to one of the other bars, which, inspired by the success of Fred's, have begun offering live music on Saturday afternoon. But the cognoscenti claim a stool at the bar of the **Hotel Cazan** (☎ 318-468-7187), an aging deco building that opened in the early 1900s as a bank before being converted to a bar in the late 1940s. If the proprietor fancies you, he'll take the time to show you the bullet holes riddling the massive mahogany bar and the spots where the old tellers' windows once were. There is a pool table in back and rooms for rent upstairs, most of which cost around $20 a night and are a study in austerity, and – in all fairness – may well be unclean. But for $20 what do you expect?

If you've worked up an appetite dancing, your best bet is to try **Ortego's Meat Market** (☎ 318-468-3746), around the corner on South St, where they make a good, lightly-spiced boudin sausage. Locals vouch for their tasso (spicy, smoked pork or beef) as well. And if you really want to make friends at Fred's, you'll stop off here first to purchase a few pounds of boudin for the crowd.

To get to Mamou, take I-10 west to Baton Rouge, then Hwy 190 west through Opelousas to Eunice. Turn north on Hwy 13 to Mamou. Total travel time: two to 2½ hours.

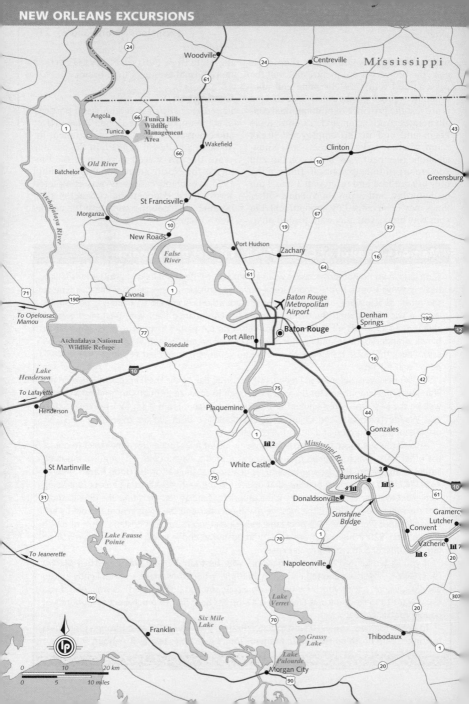

1 Middendorf's
2 Nottoway Plantation
3 Cajun Village
4 Houmas House
5 Tezcuco Plantation,
   African American Museum
6 Oak Alley Plantation
7 Laura Plantation
8 Hwy 641 Bridge
9 San Francisco Plantation
10 Destrehan Plantation
11 Barataria Preserve

Goin' to the Zydeco

Opelousas is the epicenter of Louisiana zydeco club culture. Sure, numerous New Orleans clubs feature zydeco bands each week – from Rosie Ledet and the Zydeco Playboys to Boozoo Chavis – but don't fool yourself. You haven't really experienced this music 'til you've made the trek to Slim's Y-Ki-Ki or Richard's Club, two of the most venerable live-music venues in the state. These are the kinds of bars where if you clap at the close of a song to show your appreciation you're immediately branded an interloper, for in the clubs of southwest Louisiana, if you like the music you dance.

Both **Slim's Y-Ki-Ki** (☎ 318-942-9980, Hwy 167 N) and **Richard's Club** (☎ 318-543-6596, Hwy 190 W) are highly recommended, family-run bars that welcome outlanders with open arms. Though it might be best to call ahead, you can almost be assured that most any Saturday night one, if not both, of these wobbly wood-frame buildings will be featuring local acts of international renown.

If you're in need of a bit of sustenance before a long night of dancing and drinking, seek out the **Palace Café** (☎ 318-942-2142, Hwy 190), a downtown institution, in business since 1954, and justifiably famous for its onion rings and fried chicken. And the atmosphere – a throwback to the day they threw open the doors – can't be beat. Lunch and dinner run about $5 to $8.

Accommodations range from the cheap and funky **Yambilee Courts Motel** (☎ 318-942-9762, Hwy 190 W), where the rooms are but $35 for singles and $38 for doubles, to the comparatively upscale **Quality Inn** (☎ 318-948-9500), Hwy 190 at I-49, which has all the accustomed amenities, including an outdoor pool, and singles/doubles for $60/$65.

Opelousas is 70 miles west of New Orleans by way of I-10 and then 45 miles northwest of Baton Rouge by way of Hwy 190. Total travel time is from 1 1/2 to two hours.

Long the haunt of artists and writers, Covington was home to the revered 20th-century author Walker Percy, whose novels examining what he termed the 'modern malaise' – *The Moviegoer, Lancelot, Love in the Ruins* – won wide acclaim. Today, the quaint little town is enjoying a renaissance, as artists and writers are joined by entrepreneurs in remaking the brick storefronts in the downtown area into a shop and gallery district reminiscent of New Orleans' Magazine St corridor. Along Columbia St and, to a lesser degree, Lee and Boston Sts, are a delightful selection of antique shops, modern-art galleries and furnishing stores worthy of an afternoon of ambling about.

Places to Stay

Though intended as a day-trip destination, the North Shore is so close to New Orleans that you may want to consider staying here when New Orleans hotels are booked to the brim, or when your budget calls out for relief. For camping, see Fontainebleau State Park. For motels, the Hwy 190 corridor leading north from I-10 offers the most choices at the widest range of prices. No matter if you stay in Mandeville or Abita Springs, all North Shore attractions are just a 10- or 15-minute drive from one another. And New Orleans is a 35-minute drive away.

Abita Springs There are a couple of B&Bs downtown, the most appealing of which is *Trail's End Bed & Breakfast* (☎ 504-867-9899, 71648 Maple St), a charming Victorian cottage close to the Tammany Trace and well within walking distance of two popular restaurants and the town springs. Rates are $75/85 a single/double, with a $20 weekend supplement. Breakfast at the Abita Springs Café (see Places to Eat) is included.

Covington The *Mt Vernon Motel* (☎ 504-892-1041, 1110 N Hwy 190) is a spiffy little 30-room property, which was recently renovated. Though the desk clerk can be gruff, the rates are right: $35 for one bed (one or two people), $45 for two beds. Better yet, just a mile or so north along Hwy 21 on the edge of Covington, is the **Green Springs Motel** (☎ 504-892-4686, 72533 Hwy 21), a simple, single-story brick motel tucked into a neighborhood of beautiful homes. Rates are $35/45, and there is a nice pool (open summers only).

Closer to the interstate are a number of chain motels, the choicest of which is *Best Western Northpark Inn* (☎ 504-892-2601, 625 N Hwy 190). Among the amenities are a better-than-average continental breakfast, a heated outdoor pool and an adjoining restaurant, Dakota (see Places to Eat), which rivals many New Orleans spots for elegant, sophisticated food. Rates are $60/70.

Places to Eat

Many of the restaurants that line Hwy 190 claim a Mandeville address but are in fact as close to Covington. In Mandeville proper, an eclectic trio of restaurants offers good and greasy po' boys, home-cooking favorites and one of the finest Chinese restaurants in the South.

Mandeville The local favorite for breakfast, *Mande's Restaurant* (☎ 504-626-9047, 340 N Causeway) serves bounteous platters of grits and eggs ($4) along with plate lunches ($6), which are rib-sticking if not inspired. It is open seven days a week from 7 am until 6 pm. Just west of town and open for lunch and dinner every day but Sunday is *Rag's Po-Boys* (☎ 504-845-3327, 4960 Hwy 22), purveyor of the best po' boys in town. Get your roast beef sandwich ($4) 'dressed' (with mayo, lettuce, tomatoes and a dab of mustard) and eat it quickly before the gravy soaks through the loaf.

Trey Yuen (☎ 504-626-4476, 600 Causeway Blvd) is a revelation: a well-appointed, even fashionable, Chinese restaurant serving inventive cuisine. Among the perennial favorites are pot stickers, shrimp in a cloud and a spicy-rich lobster in black-bean sauce.

Lunch will cost $10 plus, dinner $20 plus. Trey Yuen is open for dinner daily from 6 to 10 pm and lunch Wednesday through Friday and Sunday.

Abita Springs At the *Abita Brew Pub* (☎ 504-892-5837, 72011 Holly St) you can gaze at the vats full of beer while savoring seafood, salads, sandwiches and steaks. Try the blackened shrimp and avocado salad ($8) or the seafood muffuletta ($8). The brew sampler ($4.50) features five 4oz glasses of different beers. It opens daily at 11 am and closes at 9 pm Monday through Thursday, at 10 pm Friday and Saturday, and at 8 pm on Sunday.

Better yet is the *Abita Springs Café* (☎ 504-867-9950, 22132 Level St), open from 8 am to 2 pm every day but Monday. Try the seafood omelette ($6), a po' boy ($5) or a daily soup like crawfish and corn ($3 a cup).

For haute cuisine in a refined setting, *Artesia* (☎ 504-892-1662, 21516 Hwy 36) is the choice. Recently voted one of the best new restaurants in greater New Orleans, this subdued restaurant, set in a restored Victorian home, serves dinner Wednesday through Saturday. Dishes like medallion of monkfish with a black-truffle crust ($24) and quail over a bed of smoked porcini mushrooms and whipped potatoes ($18) draw a crowd from New Orleans as well as the surrounding suburbs. Lunch, served Wednesday through Friday, can be had for $10 to $15.

Covington Open daily from 8 am to 5:30 pm, *Coffee Rani* (☎ 504-893-6158, 226 Lee Lane) is the spot for pastries and sandwiches. The café exhibits work by local artists, and the staff are a font of information on what's doing in town.

Judice's (☎ 504-892-0708, 421 E Gibson St) is a bright sunny restaurant, just off Columbia St. Lunch offerings include a shrimp salad with spicy pecans ($7), but the best meal here is breakfast, when a heaping bowl of stone-ground grits swimming in a rich sauce of roast beef debris and gravy costs but $1.50, and a full breakfast is just $4. They're open every day but Monday for breakfast and lunch, and dinner is served on Friday and Saturday from 5 to 10 pm.

On Boston St you will find two outposts of New Orleans' favorites – the purposefully funky *Acme Oyster Bar* (☎ 504-898-0667) and *Rue de la Course* (☎ 504-893-5553), a pleasant, well-appointed coffeehouse. *Etoile* (☎ 504-892-4578, 407 N Columbia St) is a wine bar and restaurant connected to a retail wine shop. Daily risotto specials and innovative sandwiches are the draws at this vibrantly funky restaurant. Lunch costs $7 to $10, dinner $12 to $15. Etoile is open Monday through Saturday from 11 am until 7 pm.

Adjoining the Best Western Northpark Inn, *Dakota* (☎ 504-892-3712, 628 N Hwy 190) may well be the best restaurant on the North Shore. At dinner, try the sweet-potato nachos with ground lamb in a tomato-currant chutney topped with Roquefort cheese ($7) for an appetizer, and the vanilla-and maple-cured duck atop risotto with grilled asparagus ($18) for an entrée. Dakota has an excellent wine list and an attentive but not overbearing staff. It's open for lunch weekdays, dinner Monday through Saturday, and brunch on Sunday.

Entertainment

Most locals head to New Orleans for a night on the town, but, like in most of southern Louisiana, you can count on restaurants having an adjacent bar that is more than an afterthought. For live entertainment, try the *Abita Brew Pub*, in Abita Springs, or *Etoile*, in Covington (see Places to Eat), though your best bet is Covington's *Columbia St Tap Room* (☎ 504-898-0899, 434 N Columbia St), a boisterous barroom, which hosts rock and blues acts most Thursday through Saturday nights. It stays open until 2 am on the weekends.

Getting There & Away

A car or motorbike is almost essential for exploring the North Shore. The most direct access from New Orleans is via the Lake Pontchartrain Causeway. However, if the thought of a 24-mile-long trip across Lake Pontchartrain on a four-lane ribbon of concrete is not enticing, take I-10 west to I-55 north toward Hammond, or I-10 east toward

Slidell and then I-12 west; the Slidell detour should add another 25 or so minutes of driving time, the Hammond route, maybe an extra 35.

SOUTHWARD TO THE SWAMP

Below New Orleans, the Mississippi River flows 90 miles to the bird's foot-shaped delta, where river pilots board ships entering from the gulf. Rather than drive for hours to Venice, the farthest downstream point accessible by automobile, you can satisfy the same desire to travel to the end of the road at Barataria Preserve, Lafitte or Westwego, each less than an hour's drive from New Orleans. For those in search of a wetlands adventure, the Barataria Preserve beckons. In the little fishing village of Lafitte, about 10 or so miles south of Barataria down Hwy 45, you will find a wonderful country inn and two great seafood shacks in a setting more reminiscent of the Mosquito Coast than suburban New Orleans. A bit further west of the Hwy 45 turnoff, but more easily accessible, is the little town of Westwego, home to one of the state's premier swamp tours.

Barataria Preserve

The Barataria Preserve, a unit of southern Louisiana's Jean Lafitte National Historic Park is set in an area originally settled by Isleños (Canary Islanders) in 1779. It offers hiking and canoe trips into the swamp and a good introduction to the wetlands environment. It is not a pristine wilderness, as canals and other structures offer evidence of human activities, yet wild animals and plants are abundant. Even a brief walk on the boardwalks that wend their way through the swamp will yield sightings of gators and egrets aplenty.

The best place to start is the National Park Service Visitors Center (☎ 504-589-2330, Hwy 3134), 1 mile west of Hwy 45, where you can pick up a map of the 8 miles of hiking trails and 9 miles of dedicated canoe routes, which are all closed to motorized boats. A 25-minute introductory nature film, *Jambalaya: A Delta Almanac*, is also shown at the center, which is open daily from 9 am to 5 pm.

Trails in the preserve are open daily 7 am to 5 pm, with extended hours during daylight-saving time. Ranger-led walks around Bayou Coquille are offered daily at 2 pm. Other activities require reservations, including a guided canoe trek, which meets Sunday at 8:30 am. On evenings around a full moon, moonlight canoe treks are offered.

Earl's Bar (☎ *504-689-3271*), at the corner of Hwy 45 and Hwy 3134, rents canoes for use in the preserve; $25 gets you a canoe seating up to three people plus a drop-off and pick-up service in the preserve. A welcoming bar frequented mostly by locals, Earl's has dirt-cheap ice-cold beer and is open from 9 am until dusk.

You can also rent canoes ($15 for two hours) on the Bayou de Familles just outside the park at *Bayou Barn* (☎ *504-689-2663*), a pleasantly funky restaurant compound of tin-topped weather-beaten buildings on the opposite side of the intersection. Cajun or zydeco bands play to lively local crowds at the dances ($3) held here every Sunday from noon to 6 pm; add the Cajun buffet and the price is $10. Bayou Barn is closed on Monday.

Upscale dining at *Restaurant de Familles* (☎ *504-689-7834*), behind Bayou Barn, is a reward for a day of hiking or paddling. The cathedral-ceilinged dining room, which overlooks the bayou, features Cajun-tinged seafood lunches and dinners for $7 to $15. The soft-shell crabs (in season) smothered in a sauce of butter, artichokes and mushrooms are especially good. The restaurant also boasts a bar and lounge. It's closed on Monday.

Lafitte

After you cross the high-rise bridge and double back onto Hwy 45 heading south, you will first come to the little town of **Jean Lafitte**. Quaint and remote though it may be, it has nothing on the little fishing village of Lafitte, some 8 more miles down the road. Soon the road narrows and you can almost feel the swamplands closing in around you. Due to frequent flooding, even the mobile homes down this way are set on stilts, and the Spanish moss hangs heavy – like green streamers tossed pell-mell onto the boughs of the live oak trees. This is a land remote, a land apart – once the province of the pirate Jean Lafitte and now home to a hardy camp of commercial fishers. Around these parts, 90% of the locals still make their living from the waters, and life owes its design to the patterns of the seasons and the sea. Though there are no typical tourist attractions to

Baby alligator

visit, the abundant waterside funk is worthy of a few hours of wandering.

At **Cochiara's Marina** (☎ 504-689-3701), on the left coming into town and hard by the Goose Bayou Bridge, you can buy a fan belt for your car, Miracle-Gro for your garden and a cold beer from the bar. 'Folks around here like to tell their wife they're going to the hardware store,' says the proprietor, his face creased by a sly smile. 'Where else can you go shopping and catch a buzz?'

Farther south along the ever-narrowing roadway, you pass the turnoff for the Victorian Inn (see Places to Sleep), Lafitte's de-facto tourism office, where the innkeepers will help you secure reservations for swamp tours and the like. A mile or so farther south

is **Boutte's Restaurant** (☎ 504-689-7978), a comfortable local joint with a great rooftop deck overlooking the Intracoastal Waterway. A half-shrimp, half-oyster po' boy costs just $4.50 and is sure to satisfy. Turtle soup at $3 a cup is damn near perfect. Steaks and chicken are also available, but why would you want to order them when the fishing boats dock just a block or two away? **Boutte's** is open from 11 am to 10 pm every day but Monday.

Cattycorner from Boutte's and directly south of Jan's Restaurant is the home of **folk artist JP Scott**, who has constructed a fleet of ships with the detritus he salvaged from around town. Though most of his vessels have been sold to museums and galleries,

Drinks on the Tickfaw & Catfish at the Roadhouse of Your Dreams

West of I-55 and south of I-12, just 10 miles or so beyond Ponchatoula on Hwy 22, is the little town of **Springfield**, epicenter of an odd waterborne phenomenon. Arrayed along the Tickfaw River, which runs parallel to I-55 south from Mississippi and into Louisiana before pouring forth into Lake Maurepas and finally Lake Ponchatrain, are a collection of bars, many of which are accessible only by boat. Rather than being little dives, these bars are behemoths, sprawling out over the water, offering ample deck space for sunning and ample bar space for quaffing cocktails.

Among those that are accessible by car is **Tin Lizzies** (☎ 504-695-6787, 29592 Hwy 22), open Friday to Sunday only and closed during the late fall and winter. From a perch on the deck, you can watch cigarette boats ply the waters and you may be able to hitch a ride to one of the bars, like the **Prop Stop**, which is only accessible by water.

During the spring and summer, **boat parades** and **poker runs** are infrequently held – the latter is a floating game of five card stud, where the players are dealt one card at each bar they stop in, and the winning hand is announced around dusk. For those in search of an adventure, these hinterland hideaways promise drinking and debauchery, far from the maddening tourist milieu.

Many of the bars on the river offer decent to good food, but for a great meal, head to **Middendorf's** (☎ 504-386-6666), at exit 15 off I-55, a gussied-up roadhouse hard by Lake Maurepas. In business since 1934, Middendorf's is famous for its thin-cut catfish fillets ($7 for an ample small order served with green-onion flecked hushpuppies and forgettable fries), cooked to a crisp – fried so crisp in fact that they resemble more of a fish-flavored potato chip than a traditional fillet. That said, they are delicious, as is the oyster stew ($4.50) and the Italian salad ($5), an oily morass of lettuce, olives and parmesan cheese. But the real treat to behold is the timeless wood-paneled interior, where waitresses with beehive hairdos trundle back and forth bearing platters piled high with deftly fried seafood and icy beers. Middendorf's is open 10:30 am to 9 pm or so every day but Monday.

you can still catch a glimpse of a few of his works from the road.

Continuing south down Hwy 45, just before the road ends, you will see the turnoff for **Voleo's Seafood** (☎ 504-689-3889), a ramshackle building fronted by a German-inspired beer garden. Local favorites include seafood-stuffed eggplant and trout topped with a crawfish and cream sauce for about $10 or so. At press time the restaurant was undergoing renovations that might transform it into the nicest restaurant in town. But then again, all is relative, here at land's end.

Places to Stay Only 45 minutes from the French Quarter, these unconventional accommodations can also serve as a base for exploring New Orleans to the north and the Cajun Wetlands to the west. **Cochiara's Marina** (☎ 504-689-3701), at Goose Bayou Bridge, rents out scruffy motel rooms bordering on the bayou for $55 and up. Though the rooms lack charm, they are in a nice spot right on the waterfront.

On the southern side of the bridge, the **Victoria Inn** (☎ 504-689-4757), on Hwy 45, offers 14 rooms in two West Indies-style plantation homes surrounded by gardens. And just over the levee looms a lake, known locally as 'The Pen,' complete with a private dock available to inn guests. The rooms can be a bit cramped for the price, but the innkeepers are welcoming and extremely knowledgeable about the area, and the surroundings are sure to please guests in search of a respite from cookie-cutter motels.

Westwego

At Highway 90 and Louisiana Ave is a site you're not likely to see outside Louisiana, a huge **open-air fish market** – 20 little shacks clustered in a horseshoe fashion around a gravel parking lot – selling fresh-off-the-boat shrimp, crawfish, crabs and such at rock-bottom prices; at last pass, large shrimp were selling for around $2.50 a pound. It's the perfect spot to pick up a sack or two of live crawfish for boiling later or to just take a gander at the bounty of the sea. The fish market is open daily from around dawn until dusk.

Make the turn south onto Louisiana St, and a block later the pavement gives way to dirt, and soon you are pulling up in front of the charmingly ramshackle home of Chacahoula Swamp Tours (☎ 504-436-2640, 422 Louisiana St). This family-owned business, run by Jerry Dupre, his wife and two daughters, offers a far more intimate **swamp experience** than larger operators. Boats seat about 12, rather than 50, and the narration is not amplified. Instead, you float along amid the stillness of the swamps and bayous as Captain Jerry points out the flora and fauna, and coaxes an alligator to the side of the boat for the viewing pleasure of his passengers. Most tours last two hours and are a bargain at $22 per person, including a lunch of a chicken-and-sausage gumbo thickened with okra, which comes with with potato salad, French bread and bread pudding with whiskey sauce. For an extra $16, the Dupre family will pick up passengers from New Orleans hotels.

Places to Eat Still hungry? The Westwego area is home to two outstanding restaurants, each perched at the opposite end of the scale of affordability. **Mo's Pizza** (☎ 504-341-9650, 1112 Ave H) is just a mile or so east of Louisiana St off Hwy 90. Here you will find one of the metropolitan area's best muffulettas ($4) as well as wonderful pizzas, sausage rolls, po' boys and spaghetti with meatballs, all served at ridiculously low prices in a scruffy setting (where the jukebox seems to rattle and hum incessantly to a heavy bass beat). Draft beer is $4 a pitcher. Mo's is open every day but Sunday from 10 am to 10 pm.

Mosca's (☎ 504-436-9942, 4137 Hwy 90), is another 3 miles west in Waggman. Once a hangout for mafiosos (the original chef is said to have worked for Al Capone), it's now a favorite of slumming suburbanites and New Orleans swells, who make the trip to this dilapidated roadhouse for Italian oysters ($25), drowning in oil and garlic, and a crab salad ($11) fat with lump meat that everyone seems to love. Portions are huge – a single entrée easily feeds two – and the wine list is reasonable if uninspired. Mosca's is open Tuesday through Saturday from 5 to 10 pm. No credit cards are accepted.

Getting There & Away

From New Orleans, motorists heading to the Barataria Preserve should take Business Hwy 90 across the Greater New Orleans Bridge to the Westbank Expressway and turn south on Barataria Blvd (Hwy 45) to Hwy 3134, which leads to the national park entrance. The trip takes about 30 minutes.

To reach Lafitte, continue south on Hwy 45 past the turnoff for the park. You will take a switchback turn on a high-rise bridge and then pass through the town of Jean Lafitte before reaching land's end at Lafitte. Total travel time is 45 minutes or so.

Just 30 minutes from New Orleans, Westwego is just off the Westbank Expressway (Hwy 90), west of Marrero.

CAJUN WETLANDS

In 1755, le Grande Derangement, the British expulsion of the rural French settlers from Acadia, created a homeless population of Acadians who searched for decades for a place to settle. In 1785, seven boatloads of exiles arrived at New Orleans. By the early 19th century, some 3000 to 4000 Acadians, or Cajuns, had arrived in Louisiana to occupy the swamplands southwest of New Orleans. Here they eked out a living based upon fishing and trapping and developed a culture substantially different from the Cajuns who settled farther inland in the prairie region, where animal husbandry and farming were the primary vocations. Early German peasant farmers also produced crops for the New Orleans market in the vicinity of Thibodaux. Isleños arrived about 1780 on the upper Bayou Lafourche. By 1800, Acadians and Americans extended down the bayou to Thibodaux. Today the entire polyglot mix has a tendency to proudly call themselves Cajuns. The largest towns in the area are Thibodaux and Houma.

Thibodaux

Positioned at the confluence of Bayou Lafourche and Bayou Terrebonne, Thibodaux (pronounced **ti**-buh-dough) was, at the time when water travel was preeminent, the most important town between New Orleans and Bayou Teche. It has been the Lafourche

Parish seat since 1820. The copper-domed **courthouse**, at the corner of 2nd and Green Sts, was built in 1855 and remains a testament to Thibodaux's glory days. Today, the town is home to a population of approximately 15,000. Stop by the Thibodaux Chamber of Commerce (☎ 504-446-1187, 1048 E Canal St) for maps and information on local events.

The **Wetlands Cajun Cultural Center** (☎ 504-448-1375, 314 St Mary St) is a spacious museum and gallery operated by the National Park Service (NPS). Exhibits cover virtually every aspect of Cajun life in the wetlands, from music to the environmental impacts of trapping and oil exploration. Visitors learn about 'the time of shame,' from 1916 to 1968, when the Louisiana Board of Education discouraged speakers of Cajun-French. Cajun musicians jam on Monday evenings from 5:30 to 7 pm. The center opens daily at 9 am, but closing times vary: Tuesday to Thursday at 6 pm, Friday to Sunday at 5 pm and Monday at 7 pm.

About 2 miles east of town on Hwy 308 down Bayou Lafourche, **Laurel Valley Village** (☎ 504-446-7456), established in 1785, is one of the best-preserved assemblages of plantation slave structures in the state. Hard by the highway, a nonprofit group operates the General Store, which houses numerous displays about the now-abandoned settlement. You'll also find pirogues (provided by Nicholls State University in Thibodaux), vintage farm equipment and livestock. Behind the store, row crops are still farmed, and about a half-mile off the blacktop on Laurel Valley Rd are 70 surviving slave quarters – tumble-down tar-paper shacks, which seem to sway in the slightest breeze. They can be viewed from the road, but a $5 donation should be enough to get a volunteer at the store to take you on a tour. The General Store is open Tuesday to Friday 10 am to 4 pm and weekends from noon to 4 pm.

Places to Eat & Drink Eating well in Thibodaux is a challenge. At breakfast, try *Rob's Donuts* (☎ *504-447-4080*), at the corner of St Mary and Tiger Sts, for praline-stuffed pastries (two for $1) oozing with pecans and syrup. Rob's is open from 2 am

Houseboat Heaven in Henderson

One of the most distinctive overnight experiences you can find anywhere is a night aboard a houseboat in the Atchafalaya Basin. Doug Sebatier and his wife, Diane, run Houseboat Adventures (☎ 318-821-5898) and will 'push you out' from their landing in Henderson into a protected cove for a stay aboard a comfortably cozy, modern houseboat, which sleeps four to six in futons or twin bunks. The boats are equipped with generators to power the TV, VCR, lights and air-conditioning. Or you can skip the noise and go natural, with candles for light, the breeze off the water for cooling and the sounds of the birds, bugs and frogs (and maybe even an alligator's roar in mating season) for entertainment. Boats have two-burner ranges and some have mini-refrigerators. All have porch swings for rocking away the afternoon.

Bring your own food and drinking water, as well as an ice chest if you plan on drinking more than a 12 pack of beer or soft drinks over the course of your stay. Judging from guest-book accounts, beer drinking is a favorite pastime. A flashlight will also come in handy, as will insect repellent, and of course pack your fishing gear. The Sebatiers provide linens and towels, dishware, candles, matches and simple generator-operating lessons. They'll even throw in a pirogue or motorized skiff so you can row around or motor back and forth to shore and nearby restaurants.

Advance reservations are essential. The peak rate, from March to October, is $145 a night (two-night minimum on weekends) plus a $25 towing fee. Discounts are available off-season and for three or more nights. Henderson is about 40 miles west of Baton Rouge, just off I-10.

to 1 pm daily. For lunch and dinner, most locals crowd into *Politz's* (☎ *504-448-0944, 100 Landry St)*, at the corner of St Mary St, to get a heaping plate of corn-flour crusted fried seafood or a broiled catfish dinner for about $11. It is open for lunch and dinner Monday through Saturday until 9 pm.

But to eat really well, you'll have to do a bit of work, first stopping off at one of the Rouse's Grocery Stores (there are numerous locations dotting the town) for a few picnic fixings – some potato salad, French bread, mustard and, for dessert, one of their famous *tarte à la bouille* (a custard pie with a lattice-crust top) – and then head south on Highway 24 toward Schriever. At about the 3-mile mark, you will see *Bourgeois Meat Market* (☎ *504-447-7128, 519 Schriever Hwy)*, one of the few remaining markets that operates its own slaughter house. Open since 1891, this is one of the best spots to sample links of *boudin blanc, boudin rouge* and andouille sausages. Now find a shady spot, slap a link of andouille on that French bread, smear

it with mustard, heft a spoonful of potato salad to your plate and you have the makings of a fine lunch. Their beef jerky is celebrated as the smokehouse equivalent of shrunken sirloin.

To hear Cajun music head to *Dawn's Lounge* (☎ *504-448-2559, 1302 St Patrick Hwy)*, on the extreme northern edge of town. On the way to Dawn's, stop off at *Gros Place* (☎ *504-446-6623, 710 St Patrick St)*, a popular spot set in an old service station, where locals gather to shoot pool and quaff beer after beer. It's open daily from 9 am until around midnight. Stop by on a Friday evening and you're likely to get a chance to sample some deep-fried turkey, which the proprietor cooks for the crowd.

Getting There & Away Thibodaux is 60 miles west of New Orleans, best reached by taking I-10 to the I-310 crossing of the Mississippi River, and then following Hwy 90 to Hwy 1, which parallels Bayou Lafourche for 17 miles to Thibodaux.

Houma

Named for the Houma tribe of Native Americans, who were displaced in the middle years of the 19th century by the Acadians, this town of 30,000 is the economic hub of the Wetlands region. Driving into town, up and over the many bridges that crisscross the numerous bodies of water wending their way through the city center – Bayou Black, Little Bayou Black, the Intracoastal Waterway and Bayou Terrebonne – you come to appreciate Houma's self-styled moniker, Venice of America. That said, the city itself offers little of interest to visitors, save functioning as a way station for travelers on their way to the docks just west of town, from where two of the area's best swamp tours depart. The local tourist commission operates a visitor center (☎ 504-868-2732), on Hwy 90 at St Charles St, west of town.

Swamp Tours Locals vouch for the following two operators as being the best. Alligator Annie Miller's Swamp Tours (☎ 504-879-3934), on Hwy 90, 8 miles west of Houma, is the grand dame of swamp-tour proprietors. Annie has been feeding chicken drumsticks to the gator babies for so long that they're now trained to respond to the sound of her approaching motor and rise from the muck to take a bite. No matter if you take advantage of the moment as a photo opportunity or plunge headlong for the opposite side of the boat, it's all great fun. She charges adults $15 and children $10.

Ten miles west of Houma, Cajun Man's Swamp Cruise (☎ 504-868-4625), on Hwy 90, is run by Black Guidry, who serenades his passengers with a bit of accordion music, piloting them through a scenic slice of swamp, his trusty dog Gator Bait at his side. He charges $15.

Both tours last two hours and are offered year-round on schedules that vary according to season. Call for reservations. Should both be previously booked, check with the folks at the Bayou Delight Restaurant (see Places to Eat & Drink) for alternate suggestions. The restaurant seems to serve as a sort of de facto clubhouse for swamp-tour operators.

Places to Eat & Drink The *A-Bear's Café* (☎ 504-872-6306, 809 Bayou Black Dr) looks and feels like an old country store. Though it caters to the tourist trade, you'll find a good measure of locals inside, tucking into plates of red beans and rice, po' boys and plate lunch specials, topped off with a slice of icebox pie, all for about $10. And on most Friday nights, there's a live Cajun band. It's open Monday to Thursday 7 am to 5 pm, Friday until 10 pm and Saturday until 2 pm. *Dula & Edwin's Cajun Restaurant* (☎ 504-876-0271, 2821 Bayou Blue Rd) is the local favorite for boiled crabs and crawfish, tinged with a trace of heat ($10). The *Bayou Delight Restaurant* (☎ 504-876-4879), on Hwy 90 about 7 miles west of Houma, may display shellacked alligator snouts in the showcase by the register, but don't let that dissuade you; it's not really a tourist trap – not if you order well. Start with homemade onion rings ($2), followed by a plate of white beans and rice with fried catfish ($9). Most Friday and Saturday nights, they have live Cajun or country music. It's open seven days a week from 11 am to 10 pm.

Getting There & Away

Houma is 60 miles west of New Orleans. Take I-10 west to I-310, cross the Mississippi River and follow Hwy 90 south into town. Thibodaux is just 20 miles northwest of Houma by way of Hwy 20.

RIVER ROAD RAMBLE

Elaborate plantation homes line the banks of the Mississippi River between New Orleans and Baton Rouge along the 'River Road.' Here, relatively simple French Creole plantation homes, like those found at Vacherie, stand in stark contrast with the Greek Revival mansions built by American settlers after the Louisiana Purchase in 1803.

No matter the architectural style on the River Road, the stories of plantation slave society get short shrift. Instead, the emphasis is on the glory of days past, when black men and women of bondage labored at the behest of white masters. Save for the ascendant but struggling African American Museum at Tezcuco Plantation and Laura Plantation tours, you will get a feel for what life was like for the master and missus, but rarely will you catch a glimpse of life back of the big house, where slaves made the bricks, raised the roofs, tended the fires and worked the fields. Instead, expect costumed guides leading interior tours of 45 to 60 minutes, which focus on the lovely architecture, ornate gardens and genteel lifestyle of antebellum Louisiana. Most have a gift shop, enormous moss-draped live oaks and daily open hours of 9 or 10 am to 4 or 5 pm. Admission usually includes a guided tour of the main house and self-guided tours of the grounds.

To understand the area, you must know a bit about agriculture. Throughout the time of French colonial stewardship, rice and indigo were the principal plantation crops. But, in 1795, with the introduction of the open-kettle process, which enabled sugar to be reduced to more easily transportable crystals, the agricultural economy was transformed. Sugar cane planting expanded exponentially during the antebellum period – as did slave ownership. Financial success led to the proliferation of grand plantation homes for which River Road is now known. On the eve of the Civil War in 1861, Louisiana had 1200 plantations producing 95% of the sugar in the US.

Following the war, less than 200 plantations remained. Blacks and whites alike left the plantations in droves, heading north and west, in search of jobs. Today, many of the grand homes are open to the public, though the setting is far different than it was. Where once stretched mile after mile of cane fields, now sit myriad chemical plants and refineries, belching forth sulfurous clouds of smoke morning, noon and night – suffocating the surrounding countryside in a wet blanket of industrial fog. It's a truly surreal juxtaposition of old and new, of beauty and the beast.

Orientation

Looking at a map, the East Bank is the area above the Mississippi River, while the West Bank is the area below the river. 'Downriver' means to be headed southeastward, as the river flows toward New Orleans. 'Upriver' means northwestward, against the river's flow, toward Baton Rouge. River Road is a

Women hoeing (Mississippi Delta, late 1930s)

name given, not to one particular road, but to the various routes that follow the sinuous levees. As an example, traveling upriver on the east bank, River Road will show up on a map as Hwy 48, then Hwy 44 and then Hwy 942, yet few of the towns you pass through will display any signage to indicate the change in highway numbers. Sound confusing? It isn't. Just keep the river in sight, and should you stop to ask directions, remember the difference between upriver and downriver, East Bank and West Bank.

Along the East Bank

Only 12 miles from New Orleans International Airport, **Destrehan Plantation** (☎ 504-764-9315, 13034 Hwy 48), downriver from I-310, is the oldest plantation home remaining in the lower Mississippi Valley. Indigo was the principal crop in 1787 when Antoine Robert Robin DeLongy hired a mulatto builder to construct the original French colonial-style mansion, using *bousillage* (mud- and straw-filled) walls supported by cypress timbers. The house features a distinctive African-style hipped roof – no doubt a tip of the hat to the builder's ancestry. When DeLongy's daughter, Celeste, married Jean Noel Destrehan, they added the present Greek Revival facade. It's open daily from 9:30 am to 4 pm. Tours by costumed guides cost $6 for adults, $3 for teens, $2 for children.

The stunning 'steamboat Gothic' **San Francisco Plantation** (☎ 504-535-2341), on Hwy 44, 20 miles upriver from I-310, is on a

San Francisco Plantation

1700-acre site purchased in 1830 by Edmond B Marmillion from Elisee Rillieux, a free person of color. With $100,000 and 100 slaves, Marmillion's son, Valsin, built a grand sugar plantation. Today, only the architectural confection of a house and metal-domed cisterns remain. The surrounding fields where sugar cane once grew now sprout smokestacks. It's open daily from 10 am to 4 pm. Tours of the ornately furnished interior cost $7 for adults, $4 for teens and $2.75 for children.

One mile upriver from the Sunshine Toll Bridge, **Tezcuco Plantation** (☎ 225-562-3929, 3138 Hwy 44), a Greek Revival raised cottage, is no more grand than any number of grand homes downriver in New Orleans. But the onsite **African American Museum & Gallery** (☎ 504-562-7703) is worth a detour. Started by Kathe Hambrick (a local African American woman who, after visiting Tezcuco several years ago, decided that someone needed to tell the story of the slaves), this humble museum displays a wonderful collection of photos, musical instruments, clothing, masks, tools and other relics of African American plantation society. Exhibits change every six months. It's open weekends 1 to 5 pm, weekdays by appointment. Admission is $3.

Upriver from Tezuco is a succession of three plantation homes worthy of a peek from the road. **Houmas House** (☎ 225-473-7841, 40136 Hwy 942), 4 miles upriver from the Sunshine Bridge, was named for the Native American tribe that once inhabited the area. It offers a postcard image of the great Greek Revival plantation home long associated with Louisiana. The original structure, built in the 1790s, now forms the back end of the main house, built in 1840. It's open for tours from 10 am to 5 pm (to 4 pm in winter). Admission is $7 for adults, $5 for teens and $3.50 for children over six.

Upriver another 2 and 3 miles are two private antebellum homes: **Bocage Plantation House**, built in 1801 and remodeled in 1840, and the **Hermitage Plantation House**, built in 1812 by Marius Bringier, a Haitian builder responsible for many of the region's homes, including Whitehall, Tezcuco and Bocage.

Its impressive Tuscan brick columns were added in 1838.

The Ascension Parish Tourist Center (☎ 225-675-6550), in the purposefully quaint **Cajun Village**, at the intersection of Hwys 22 and 70 near I-10 exit 182, offers state and local maps and information. Also on premises is Linda Black's Southern Tangent Gallery (☎ 504-675-6550), featuring works by more than 100 self-taught artists, including color-saturated images painted by Alvin Batiste of nearby Donaldsonville (see Along the West Bank), as well as the Coffee House (see Places to Eat).

Places to Eat For the widest variety of choices and best prices, cross the Sunshine Bridge to the little town of Donaldsonville (see Along the West Bank). That said, there are a number of convenient East Bank eateries worth a try.

Don's Market (☎ 504-536-2275, 388 Central Ave), in Reserve, is the place to pack a picnic lunch. Try their housemade hogshead cheese and andouille sausage. It's open Monday to Saturday 7 am to 7 pm and Sunday 8 am to noon. *Airline Motors Restaurant* (☎ 504-652-9181, 221 E Airline (Hwy 61)), in La Place, is a rough-edged art deco palace of a restaurant, embellished with enough glass blocks, chrome and neon to send you reeling. Grab a seat at the counter and take it all in while enjoying a cup of surprisingly good chicken andouille gumbo ($3) or a BLT. It never closes.

The *Coffee House* (☎ 225-473-8236), in Cajun Village, at the intersection of Hwys 70 and 22, serves a heaping plate of crusty brown, powdered-sugar crowned beignets for $1. Skip the rest of the menu. Four miles farther down Hwy 22 is *Tut's Place* (☎ 225-675-8629, 3408 Hwy 70), a no-frills local favorite of a bar where the welcome is warm and the beers are cold. Most Fridays somebody's in the kitchen cooking for 'the hell of it.' It opens at 6 am daily and closes 'late,' says proprietor Mama Tut.

A local favorite for 40-plus years is *Hymel's Seafood* (☎ 504-562-7031, 8740 Hwy 44), 4 miles downriver from the Sunshine Bridge. This former filling station now

serves a fine platter of soft shell crab ($8) as well as turtle sauce piquant ($7) and weekday lunch specials for around $5. It's open for lunch weekdays and dinner Thursday to 9 pm, Friday and Saturday to 10 pm and Sunday to 8 pm. The *Cabin Restaurant* (☎ 225-473-3007), at the corner of Hwys 44 and 22, 2 miles from the River Rd, is set in a collection of slave dwellings and other dependencies rescued from the demolished Monroe, Welham and Helvetia plantations. The interior walls are papered with old newspapers in the same manner that slaves once insulated the rough-sawn walls of their cabins. Besides po' boys you can get dishes like red beans and rice with sausage for about $5, or an omelette filled with crawfish étouffée ($7). Broiled or fried seafood plates cost around $10. Though the restaurant is geared toward serving the tourist crowds, the food is actually pretty good. It opens daily at 11 am and closes at 6 pm on Sunday, 3 pm on Monday and 9 pm the rest of the week.

Along the West Bank

At Vacherie, **Laura Plantation** (☎ 504-265-7690, 2247 Hwy 18) is a comparatively unassuming West Indies-style plantation home, built in 1805 by Guillaume Duparc and named for his granddaughter, Laura Locoul. Rather than a pristine showplace, Laura is a work in progress, an ongoing historical experiment, wherein visitors are invited to imagine life as it existed for both slave and master. Here, thanks to the ongoing restoration efforts that give you a carpenter's-eye view of repairs, you will come to understand how these monstrous homes were constructed, and what back-breaking labor was required for their upkeep. Tours give equal weight to the grand architecture and mundane ephemera like period clothing and even toiletries. It's open daily. Guided tours cost $5 for adults, $3.50 for children.

Just upriver of Laura Plantation, **Oak Alley Plantation** (☎ 504-265-2151, 3645 Hwy 18) features the most dramatic approach of all the plantations: a quarter-mile canopy of majestic live oaks running from the River Road to the house. The 28 trees, 14 on each side of the driveway, predate the house by

100 years. More symmetry awaits at the plantation house, which is built in Greek Revival style: 28 columns, each 8 feet in diameter, frame the scene. Tours are offered daily from 9 am to 5 pm. Admission costs $7 for adults, $4 for teens, $2 for children.

Donaldsonville is – surprise! – not a plantation, but a pleasant little town with a surprising collection of good restaurants (see Places to Eat). It's also home to the **Historic Donaldsonville Museum** (☎ 225-746-0004), at the corner of Railroad and Mississippi Sts, a charming paean to small-town life set in a majestic white masonry building that was once home to the Lemann Department Store – at the time of its closing, it was the oldest family-owned department store in the state. It's open Tuesday, Thursday and Saturday from 10 am to 4 pm. But the premier attraction in town, indeed one of the premier attractions on the River Road, is **Rossie's Custom Framing** (☎ 225-473-8536, 510 Railroad Ave), where the works of **folk artist Alvin Batiste** are on display. His depictions of life in his hometown will take your breath away. And the prices are more than reasonable, with most pieces in the $50 to $200 range. Most days, he sets his easel up in the shop's window, so he can watch the street life passing by. Hours vary, but afternoons are the best time to catch him in.

For sheer size, **Nottoway Plantation** (☎ 225-545-2730), 2 miles north of White Castle on Hwy 1, which was built between 1849 and 1859 by Virginian sugar planter John Hampton Randolph, is the finest on the river. The largest plantation house in the South, it has 64 rooms covering 53,000 square feet. Guides don't wear costumes and deliver no drama, yet the tours are rich in personal history. The house has original furnishings and period pieces. Wide galleries with rocking chairs are accessible to visitors who wish to sit and gaze out upon the river. Tours run daily 9 am to 5 pm. Entry is $8 adults, $3 children.

Places to Eat For those on a River Road ramble, **Donaldsonville** is by far the best place to stop for a meal. Set at the base of the Sunshine Bridge, it is an easy drive from most attractions.

First & Last Chance Café (☎ 225-473-8236, 812 Railroad St) is a relic of the time when this trackside joint was the only place

Oak Alley Plantation

MICHAEL GIRARD

to grab a drink on the rail trip from New Orleans to Baton Rouge. Great burgers ($2.50) and toothsome steaks smothered in garlic sauce ($15 and up) are the best bets. It's open every day but Sunday 9 am to midnight.

Set in an old grocery store, **Railroad Café** (☎ *225-474-8513, 212 Railroad Ave*) is the spot for an oyster po' boy. The cooks care here, going so far as to ask whether you want your oysters fried 'soft, medium or crisp?' Po' boys and plate lunches run $5 to $7. Hours are Monday to Wednesday 10 am to 2 pm, Thursday to Saturday 10 am to 7:30 pm.

Ruggiero's (☎ *225-473-8476, 206 Railroad Ave*) is a creaky old bar and restaurant serving a wide range of foods, the best of which are the garlicky shrimp and pasta dishes ($12). It's open for lunch Tuesday through Friday 11 am to 1 pm and for dinner Tuesday through Saturday 5 to 9 pm. **Lafitte's Landing at Bittersweet Plantation** (☎ *225-473-1232*), on Railroad St, may well be the best haute cuisine restaurant between New Orleans and Lafayette. Though the restaurant is not as grand as the original Lafitte's Landing (it burned in 1998), the chef, John Folse, has won a large following for his inventive Cajun-influenced cuisine.

Alternately, in Vacherie, **B&C Seafood Market & Cajun Deli** (☎ *225-265-8356, 2155 Hwy 18*) is convenient to Laura Plantation, and if you stick to fried seafood po' boys, you'll eat well here for around $7. It's open weekdays 9 am to 5:30 pm and Saturday from 9 am until 6:30 pm.

Getting There & Away

Travel times between destinations vary widely, depending upon whether you drive the interstate most of the way or prefer to take to the winding roads that hug the levee. It's best to budget the better part of a day for your trip, especially if you want to view more than one plantation. But don't despair if you're still on the road at 6 pm and have 8 pm dinner reservations back in New Orleans. Even the distant upriver plantations are not much more than a one-hour drive from the city via I-10.

Between New Orleans and Baton Rouge, I-10 provides motorists with the quickest

Music room at Nottoway Plantation

RICHARD CUMMINS

access to the winding river levee roads. Alternately, parallel to I-10, Hwy 61, once the primary artery north, offers a glimpse of the US roadside past. Ferries still outnumber bridges across the Mississippi River. A few motorists and all bicyclists use the state-operated ferries ($1 toll traveling westward, free eastward) to cross the river. Traveling upriver from New Orleans, you will come upon the following bridges in succession: the Huey Long Bridge (Hwy 90); I-310, which connects with Hwy 90, farther upriver; the recently opened Grammercy-Wallace Bridge (Hwy 641); and the Sunshine Toll Bridge (Hwy 70) at Donaldsonville.

BATON ROUGE

This Mississippi River town is the home of the state's two largest universities – Louisiana State University (LSU) and Southern University – as well as the nation's tallest capitol, the fifth-largest port and the second-largest petrochemical industry. That's what defines Baton Rouge physically and economically

BATON ROUGE

To St Francisville

To Baton Rouge Metropolitan Airport, Hwy 19, Hwy 61, Southern University

BUS 61 BUS 190

Capitol Lake

Arsenal Park

Capitol Access Rd

Spanishtown Park

Spanish Town Rd

North St

Main St

Laurel St

Florida Blvd

Convention St

North Blvd

America St

Louisiana St

Government St

Europe St

South Blvd

Julia St

Terrace Ave

Oklahoma St

Mississippi River

River Rd

Riverside Mall

Lafayette St

Third St

Civic Center

To Port Allen

To Farr Park

River Rd

Nicholson Drive

Highland Rd

Main St

Magnolia Cemetery

Convention St

North Blvd

Plank Rd

N 21st St

N Acadian Thruway

110

67

BUS 61 BUS 190

73

Thomas H Delpit Drive

Edward Robinson Sr Drive

City Park

City Park Lake

Perkins Rd

To I-12, Rural Life Museum & Windrush Gardens, Denham Springs

10

Acadian Thruway

427

Ferndale Ave

Glendale Ave

Perkins Rd

Mansfield Ave

Stanford Ave

Cloverdale Ave

Morning Glory Ave

University Lake

E Washington St

E Polk St

E Buchanan St

E State St
E Chimes St

Dairymple Drive

Louisiana State University

30

10

0   300   600 m
0   300   600 yards

Without question, though, politics have shaped the city's culture since Baton Rouge became the state capital in 1849. You won't want to plan your vacation around Baton Rouge (population 250,000), but for those interested in Louisiana's peculiar and picaresque political history, the city is worthy of an afternoon of exploring.

Oh, in case you were wondering, the city's name, which translates from the French as 'red stick,' is said to derive from a Native American practice of painting cypress poles with blood to mark off the boundaries of hunting territories.

Orientation

The new and old state capitols, casinos and a riverfront entertainment complex are downtown off I-110, just north of I-10. LSU is in the southwest quadrant of the city, off I-10. The neighboring streets are home to parks, inexpensive restaurants, nightclubs, movie theaters and shops. Highland Rd is the main college thoroughfare.

Things to See

Huey P Long, a flamboyant and charismatic populist politician, served as governor of Louisiana from 1928 to 1932, entering the US Senate late in 1932. At the height of his power, he had a virtual stranglehold on the state. With a promise to 'sock it to the rich fat cats,' Long – known as 'the Kingfish' – won the undying faith of the working men and women of Louisiana, on whose behalf he embarked upon a massive series of publicworks programs, like the building of hospitals, schools and highways throughout the rural parishes. But, along with such good works came a good measure of graft and not a small measure of megalomania. His handiwork can be seen throughout the city, most famously at the state capitol building.

Louisiana State Capitol Among Long's more brazen acts was the building of an art deco capitol (☎ 225-342-7317) in 1931 – at a cost of more than $5 million during the height of the Depression and against the will of the state legislature. It would prove to be his most visible legacy, and the scene of his

denouement. Today, the 34-story skyscraper, a towering palace of marble, is a beauty to behold.

In the lobby, what isn't covered with bronze friezes or sculpted metal panels is painted with murals or plastered with gold leaf. Behind the bank of elevators, a small display of mementos sits next to the bullet-pocked marble wall where he was gunned down in 1935, at the time when he was considering a run for the presidency. On the 27th floor there is an **observation tower** offering sweeping views of the city, as well as a wonderful vantage point from which to watch the barges chugging by on the river.

The Baton Rouge Visitor Information Center (☎ 225-383-1825) here is open daily 8 am until 4:30 pm, and there is a *cafeteria* in the basement offering the best breakfasts and lunches that government money can subsidize. Outside, facing the capitol, is a massive bronze sculpture of Long, his left hand resting on a marble replica of the capitol as if it were a scepter. His body is buried beneath. The inscription on the sculpture boasts that he was 'an unconquered friend of the poor who dreamed of the day when the wealth of the land would be spread among the people.'

A few blocks away is the **Old State Capitol** (☎ 225-342-0500, 100 North Blvd). The 150-year-old imposing Gothic structure sits on a bluff overlooking the Mississippi River and now serves as the Center for Political & Governmental History. Don't let that discourage you: Louisiana's often-scandalous political history provides an entertaining insight into its culture. There's a 20-minute film bolstered by interactive exhibits, the best of which allows you to stand at a lectern, call up a speech by Huey Long or, say a more recent governor like Edwin Edwards, and then watch and listen as the performance is projected on a screen in front of you while the text scrolls by on a teleprompter set to your left. (If Edwards' name does not spring to mind, he is the criminally suspect former governor who once remarked that he would never be indicted, unless he was 'caught in bed with a live boy or a dead girl.' It's open Tuesday to Saturday 10 am to

4 pm, Sunday noon to 4 pm. It costs $4 for adults, $3 for seniors and veterans, $2 for students.

Southwest of downtown is the **Rural Life Museum** (☎ 225-765-2437, 4600 Essen Lane), set on the site of the former Windrush Plantation and operated by LSU. Instead of the opulent image of plantation life presented at many plantation homes, the focus here is on everyday life in the 19th century. You will find a superlative collection of rural buildings typically found on sugar plantations, including slave cottages, a commissary, shotgun-style and dogtrot houses, an overseer's home and a sugar house with a 'Jamaica train' of open kettles. There's also a functioning blacksmith shop open to visitors. But the oddest – and most compelling – 'attraction' is the controversial sculpture known as 'Uncle Jack,' a tribute to the 'good darkies of Louisiana,' originally cast in 1927 and now on display at the museum's entrance (see boxed text). The museum is open daily 8:30 am to 5 pm, and admission is $5 adults, $4 seniors, $3 children. You may view the sculpture without paying the entrance fee.

JOHN ELK III

Baton Rouge from atop the capitol

Places to Eat

Downtown The best bet for eating lunch downtown is *Poor Boy Loyd's* (☎ 225-387-2271, 205 Florida St). The walls are chock-ablock with political memorabilia, and the chicken and dumplings ($5), not to mention the po' boys, are renowned. It's open weekdays from 7 am to 2 pm.

Near Downtown A neighborhood joint, *Phil's Oyster Bar* (☎ 225-924-3045, 5162 Government St) has a bar on one side of the room, booths on the other. The oyster shuckers keep up a steady banter as they slide dozen after dozen across the bar to waiting customers. Try the oyster loaves as well. Lunch or dinner runs $8 to $10. *Arzi's Café* (☎ 225-927-2111, 5219 Government St) may well be one of the few Louisiana places outside New Orleans where you can eat a purely vegetarian meal and be assured that you're eating as well as the omnivores around you. Falafel, baba ganoush, spanakopita and dolmas are offered; the best deal being an appetizer assortment to share for $18. Lamb, beef and chicken dishes are also on the menu. Lunch or dinner will cost about $10 and up. *Fleur-De-Lis Cocktail Lounge* (☎ 225-924-2904, 5655 Government St) is a funky Baton Rouge favorite that's been in business since the 1940s. The Pepto Bismo-pink exterior and art decotinged interior are a kick, and the 'Roman' pizzas are tasty to boot. It's open Tuesday through Saturday from 10 am to 10 pm.

Near LSU Across the tracks from LSU, *Silver Moon* (☎ 755-2553, 5142 Oleson St), off Nicholson Drive, serves monstrous portions of some of the best Creole soul food in the state at ridiculously low prices (around $5). This tiny lunchroom turns out salty, near-perfect white beans and rice, smothered pork chops and turnip greens by the bowlful. Fridays only, jambalaya is offered and it's so good they always run out early. It's open Monday through Saturday from 11 am to 4 pm or so.

The closest spot to the Rural Life Museum, *Louisiana Pizza Kitchen* (☎ 504-763-9100, 7951 One Calais Ave) serves new-wave pizzas, including a roasted chicken version

Uncle Jack: A Vestige of Louisiana's Paternalistic Past

Most visitors to the Rural Life Museum do not make much of the sculpture of the kindly gentleman, his head bowed, his hat tipped in a gesture of respect, or maybe resignation. Known to folks around these parts as 'Uncle Jack,' the sculpture was originally erected in 1927 at the behest of Jack Bryan of Natchitoches and intended as a tribute to 'the arduous and faithful service of the good darkies of Louisiana.'

During the Civil Rights Movement, the sculpture was torn from its base and tossed in a patch of weeds beside a lake in the same town. By 1974, the Rural Life Museum in Baton Rouge acquired the sculpture, with the promise that they would maintain it properly. Today, the sculpture stands at the entrance to the museum grounds, with no attempt at explanation or contextual grounding, a sad and curious reminder of our paternalistic past.

topped with a black-bean purée, cilantro, slivers of jalapeño pepper and sliced fresh tomatoes ($8). Try the pastas, too. It's open Sunday through Thursday from 11 am to 10 pm, Friday and Saturday from 11 am to 11 pm. *Juban's Restaurant (☎ 225-346-8422, 3739 Perkins Rd)*, at S Arcadian Thruway, though set in a shopping strip, serves sophisticated nouveau Creole foods. Among the best lunch bets is the crawfish cannelloni ($11). Dinner prices are slightly higher. It's open weekdays 11:30 am to 2 pm and 6 to 10 pm, Saturday 6 to 10 pm.

Getting There & Away

Traveling from New Orleans I-12 merges into I-10 on the eastern periphery of Baton Rouge, at which point I-10 continues westward toward Lafayette. I-110 veers north to downtown Baton Rouge, continuing on to connect with Hwy 61, leading north to St Francisville.

Glossary

Acadia – East Canadian region between the St Lawrence River and the Atlantic Ocean and including New Brunswick and part of Maine; it was settled by the French between 1632 and 1713

andouille – French sausage made with tripe; the Creole version is ground pork in casings made from smoked pig intestines, also known as chitterlings

arpent – a French unit of measurement equal to 0.85 acres

banquette – a diminutive form of 'banc,' meaning bench, applied to the early wooden boardwalks; it's sometimes used today to refer to sidewalks

batture – a sedimentary deposit on the inward side of a river bend or other sluggish sections on the river side of the levee crest; often covered with a tangled mass of trees and shrubs

bayou – a natural canal of sluggish and marshy water that is a tributary of the main river channel

beignet – a deep-fried pastry that is New Orleans' version of the doughnut; it's typically covered with powdered sugar but there are also savory variations

boudin – Cajun sausage filled with pork, pork liver and rice

bousillage – the mud and Spanish moss mixture sometimes used as a wall filler in *colombage* construction

briquette entre poteaux – similar to English half-timber construction, but using bricks to fill the intervening wall space between posts

café au lait – mixture of coffee and steamed milk

Cajun – a corruption of Acadian; Louisianans descended from French-speaking colonists exiled from *Acadia* in the 18th century; may also apply to other rural settlers that live amid Cajuns

carpetbagger – a derogatory name given to itinerant financial or political opportunists, particularly Northerners in the reconstructed South, who moved in with their possessions in heavy cloth satchels; their Southern accomplices were branded as scalawags

Chantilly – a dessert topping of whipped cream sweetened with sugar and possibly a liqueur

chenier – a beach ridge formed above swamp deposits, typically covered with live oaks (from the French 'chène,' meaning oak)

chicken-fried – a breaded and deep-fat fried piece of meat, usually steak or pork chops, served with gravy

chicory – a plant related to endive; Creole coffee is a blend of roasted coffee beans (60%) and chicory root (40%)

Code Noir – the 'Black Code' adopted by the French administration in 1724 that regulated the treatment and rights of free people of color and slaves; free people of color were accorded the rights of full citizenship except that they could not vote, hold public office or marry a white person

colombage – a type of construction using heavy timbers (horizontal, vertical and diagonal) with mortise and tenon joints

corvée – French for forced, as in slave or statute labor; plantation owners were expected to provide corvée to maintain levees or public roads adjacent to their land

Creole – a term first coined in the early 18th century to describe children born of French immigrants in Louisiana and, later, the children of the slaves of these immigrants; after the Civil War the term came to encompass the free Creoles of color; these days persons descended from any of the above cultures are regarded as Creole

CSA – Confederate States of America

dirty rice – rice fried with small quantities of giblets or ground pork, along with green onions, peppers and celery

dressed – a 'dressed' po' boy sandwich comes with a mayonnaise, mustard, lettuce and tomato

entresol – the mezzanine-like area of low rooms between the ground floor and the 1st floor; in many French Quarter buildings the entresol was used for storage

étouffée – a spicy tomato-based stew that typically includes either crawfish, shrimp or chicken and is served with rice

fais-do-do – a Cajun house dance

filé – ground sassafras leaves used to thicken sauces; a Native American contribution to Louisiana cuisine

frottoir – a metal rubbing-board used for percussion, especially in *zydeco* music

gallery – a balcony or roofed promenade

gens de couleur libre – free people of color during the antebellum period; after the Civil War they were known as Creoles of color

go-cup – a plastic container provided for bar patrons so that they can transfer an alcoholic beverage from a bottle or glass as they leave; in New Orleans it is legal to drink alcoholic beverages in the streets; however, it's illegal to carry an open glass container

grand dérangement – the great dispersal of Acadians that followed the 18th-century colonial wars between England and France; about 10,000 Acadians were deported from Nova Scotia by the English in 1755

gris-gris – magical objects having curative, protective or evil powers; used in voodoo

grits – coarsely ground hominy prepared as a mush and served throughout the South; it picks up the flavor of whatever is ladled over it, often butter or gravy

gumbo – traditionally an African soup thickened with okra and containing seafood or chicken; Cajun gumbos substitute *filé* powder for okra

hushpuppy – a bread substitute made from deep-fried dough balls of cornmeal and onion and served with many Southern meals; folklore suggests the name comes from a cook who quieted a howling dog by tossing one to the animal

icebox pie -a cold, often creamy, pie

jambalaya – a one-dish meal of rice cooked with onions, peppers, celery, ham and sausage

KKK – Ku Klux Klan; an organization founded in 1866 that espouses white supremacy; although outlawed by the Federal government in 1870, it has secretly conducted a campaign of violence against blacks and others whom they accuse of betraying the white race

lagniappe – a small gift from a merchant or resident; literally, a 'little something extra'

levee – a raised embankment that protects a river from flooding

meunière – an cooking style where food, usually fish, is seasoned, coated lightly with flour and pan-fried in butter; it's served with a lemon-butter sauce

mirliton – an indigenous pear-shaped vegetable with a hard shell that is cooked like squash and stuffed with either ham or shrimp and spicy dressing; it's known as chayote in Spanish-speaking parts of the world

muffuletta – an enormous sandwich of ham, hard salami, provolone and olive salad piled onto a round loaf of Italian bread liberally sprinkled with olive oil and vinegar

mulatto – a person of mixed black and white ancestry

NPS – National Park Service

neutral ground – a median; the Canal St median served as a neutral meeting space dividing the Creole and American communities

picayune – something of little value

pirogue – a dugout canoe that was traditionally carved by burning the center of a log and scraping out the embers; modern pirogues are shallow-draft vessels that can be made from plywood

placage – a system where free women of color lived as concubines and raised families under the protection of white men

po' boy – a submarine-style sandwich served on fresh French bread; fried oysters, soft-shell crabs, catfish and deli meats are offered as fillings

praline – a dessert treat made from pecans, sugar and butter

quadroon – a person who is one-quarter black; the term was used to refer to light-skinned free women of color in the 18th and 19th centuries

R&B – abbreviation of rhythm & blues; a musical style developed by African Americans that combines blues and jazz

red beans and rice –a spicy bean stew with peppers, many seasonings and a hunk of salt pork or *tasso*; often served over white rice with *andouille* sausage

rémoulade – a mayonnaise-based sauce with a variety of ingredients such as pickles, herbs, capers and mustard; crawfish or shrimp rémoulade is often a cold noodle salad

réveillon – a traditional Creole Christmas Eve dinner

roux – a mixture of flour and oil or butter that is heated slowly until it browns and used as a thickener in Cajun soups and sauces

second line – the partying group that follows parading musicians

swamp – a permanently waterlogged area that often supports trees

tasso – highly spiced cured pork or beef that's smoked for two days; small quantities are used to flavor many dishes

Vieux Carré – the original walled city of New Orleans bounded by Canal St, N Rampart St, Esplanade Ave and the Mississippi River; French for 'old square'

y'at – a term applying to those with heavy New Orleans accents; these people say the greeting, 'Where y'at?' using a very broad 'a'

zydeco – fast, syncopated Creole dance music influenced by Cajun, Afro-American and Afro-Caribbean cultures; it is often a combination of R&B and Cajun with French lyrics; bands typically feature guitar, accordion and *frottoir*

Acknowledgments

THANKS

Many thanks to the travelers who used the last edition and wrote to us with helpful hints, useful advice and anecdotes: Graeme Bell, Bart Berggren, Daniel Brotchie, Suzanne Bundy, Anna Campbell, Francette Cerulli, Angela Crowley, Margaret Cuthbert, David Deephouse, Ingo Friese, Sven Gustafsson, Ian Henderson, Jeff Hester, Lisa Johnson, Mary Latham, Ryan Lopez, Jill Ludwig, Linda Lyon, Tamia Marg, Sumi Osada & Brigitte Hunziker, Allan Parker, Tom Ridout, Tanya Schmalfuss, Cathy Stewart, Anat Zohar.

LONELY PLANET

Guides by Region

Lonely Planet is known worldwide for publishing practical, reliable and no-nonsense travel information in our guides and on our Web site. The Lonely Planet list covers just about every accessible part of the world. Currently there are ten series: travel guides, shoestring guides, walking guides, city guides, phrasebooks, audio packs, city maps, travel atlases, diving and snorkeling guides and travel literature.

AFRICA Africa – the South • Africa on a shoestring • Arabic (Egyptian) phrasebook • Arabic (Moroccan) phrasebook • Cairo • Cape Town • Central Africa • East Africa • Egypt • Egypt travel atlas • Ethiopian (Amharic) phrasebook • The Gambia & Senegal • Kenya • Kenya travel atlas • Malawi, Mozambique & Zambia • Morocco • North Africa • South Africa, Lesotho & Swaziland • South Africa, Lesotho & Swaziland travel atlas • Swahili phrasebook • Trekking in East Africa • Tunisia • West Africa • Zimbabwe, Botswana & Namibia • Zimbabwe, Botswana & Namibia travel atlas
Travel Literature: The Rainbird: A Central African Journey • Songs to an African Sunset: A Zimbabwean Story • Mali Blues: Traveling to an African Beat

AUSTRALIA & THE PACIFIC Australia • Australian phrasebook • Bushwalking in Australia • Bushwalking in Papua New Guinea • Fiji • Fijian phrasebook • Islands of Australia's Great Barrier Reef • Melbourne • Micronesia • New Caledonia • New South Wales & the ACT • New Zealand • Northern Territory • Outback Australia • Papua New Guinea • Papua New Guinea (Pidgin) phrasebook • Queensland • Rarotonga & the Cook Islands • Samoa • Solomon Islands • South Australia • Sydney • Tahiti & French Polynesia • Tasmania • Tonga • Tramping in New Zealand • Vanuatu • Victoria • Western Australia
Travel Literature: Islands in the Clouds • Sean & David's Long Drive

CENTRAL AMERICA & THE CARIBBEAN Bahamas and Turks & Caicos • Bermuda • Central America on a shoestring • Costa Rica • Cuba • Dominican Republic & Haiti • Eastern Caribbean • Guatemala, Belize & Yucatán: La Ruta Maya • Jamaica • Mexico • Mexico City • Panama • Puerto Rico
Travel Literature: Green Dreams: Travels in Central America

EUROPE Amsterdam • Andalucía • Austria • Baltic States phrasebook • Berlin • Britain • Central Europe • Central Europe phrasebook • Czech & Slovak Republics • Denmark • Dublin • Eastern Europe • Eastern Europe phrasebook • Edinburgh • Estonia, Latvia & Lithuania • Europe • Finland • France • French phrasebook • Germany • German phrasebook • Greece • Greek phrasebook • Hungary • Iceland, Greenland & the Faroe Islands • Ireland • Italian phrasebook • Italy • Lisbon • London • Mediterranean Europe • Mediterranean Europe phrasebook • Paris • Poland • Portugal • Portugal travel atlas • Prague • Romania & Moldova • Russia, Ukraine & Belarus • Russian phrasebook • Scandinavian & Baltic Europe • Scandinavian Europe phrasebook • Scotland • Slovenia • Spain • Spanish phrasebook • St Petersburg • Switzerland • Trekking in Spain • Ukrainian phrasebook • Vienna • Walking in Britain • Walking in Italy • Walking in Switzerland • Western Europe • Western Europe phrasebook
Travel Literature: The Olive Grove: Travels in Greece

INDIAN SUBCONTINENT Bangladesh • Bengali phrasebook • Bhutan • Delhi • Goa • Hindi/Urdu phrasebook • India • India & Bangladesh travel atlas • Indian Himalaya • Karakoram Highway • Nepal • Nepali phrasebook • Pakistan • Rajasthan • South India • Sri Lanka • Sri Lanka phrasebook • Trekking in the Indian Himalaya • Trekking in the Karakoram & Hindukush • Trekking in the Nepal Himalaya
Travel Literature: In Rajasthan • Shopping for Buddhas

LONELY PLANET

Mail Order

Lonely Planet products are distributed worldwide. They are also available by mail order from Lonely Planet, so if you have difficulty finding a title please write to us. North and South American residents should write to 150 Linden St, Oakland, CA 94607, USA; European and African residents should write to 10a Spring Place, London NW5 3BH, UK; and residents of other countries to PO Box 617, Hawthorn, Victoria 3122, Australia.

ISLANDS OF THE INDIAN OCEAN Madagascar & Comoros • Maldives • Mauritius, Réunion & Seychelles

MIDDLE EAST & CENTRAL ASIA Arab Gulf States • Central Asia • Central Asia phrasebook • Iran • Israel & the Palestinian Territories • Israel & the Palestinian Territories travel atlas • Istanbul • Jerusalem • Jordan & Syria • Jordan, Syria & Lebanon travel atlas • Lebanon • Middle East on a shoestring • Turkey • Turkish phrasebook • Turkey travel atlas • Yemen
Travel Literature: The Gates of Damascus • Kingdom of the Film Stars: Journey into Jordan

NORTH AMERICA Alaska • Backpacking in Alaska • Baja California • California & Nevada • Canada • Chicago • Deep South • Florida • Hawaii • Honolulu • Los Angeles • Miami • New England USA • New Orleans • New York City • New York, New Jersey & Pennsylvania • Pacific Northwest USA • Rocky Mountain States • San Francisco • Seattle • Southwest USA • Texas • USA • USA phrasebook • Vancouver • Washington, DC & the Capital Region
Travel Literature: Drive Thru America

NORTH-EAST ASIA Beijing • Cantonese phrasebook • China • Hong Kong • Hong Kong, Macau & Guangzhou • Japan • Japanese phrasebook • Japanese audio pack • Korea • Korean phrasebook • Kyoto • Mandarin phrasebook • Mongolia • Mongolian phrasebook • North-East Asia on a shoestring • Seoul • South-West China • Taiwan • Tibet • Tibetan phrasebook • Tokyo
Travel Literature: Lost Japan

SOUTH AMERICA Argentina, Uruguay & Paraguay • Bolivia • Brazil • Brazilian phrasebook • Buenos Aires • Chile & Easter Island • Chile & Easter Island travel atlas • Colombia • Ecuador & the Galapagos Islands • Latin American Spanish phrasebook • Peru • Quechua phrasebook • Rio de Janeiro • South America on a shoestring • Trekking in the Patagonian Andes • Venezuela
Travel Literature: Full Circle: A South American Journey

SOUTH-EAST ASIA Bali & Lombok • Bangkok • Burmese phrasebook • Cambodia • Hill Tribes phrasebook • Ho Chi Minh City • Indonesia • Indonesian phrasebook • Indonesian audio pack • Jakarta • Java • Laos • Lao phrasebook • Laos travel atlas • Malay phrasebook • Malaysia, Singapore & Brunei • Myanmar (Burma) • Philippines • Pilipino (Tagalog) phrasebook • Singapore • South-East Asia on a shoestring • South-East Asia phrasebook • Thailand • Thailand's Islands & Beaches • Thailand travel atlas • Thai phrasebook • Thai audio pack • Vietnam • Vietnamese phrasebook • Vietnam travel atlas

ALSO AVAILABLE: Antarctica • Brief Encounters: Stories of Love, Sex & Travel • Chasing Rickshaws • Not the Only Planet: Travel Stories from Science Fiction • Travel with Children • Traveller's Tales

Index

Canal Place Shopping Centre 214
Canal St 49, 132, 133, 214
canoeing 60, 152, 222-3
Carnival. *See* Mardi Gras and Carnival
carriage rides 110
car travel
  to/from airport 104
  alcohol and 70-1
  driver's license 54
  to/from New Orleans 102
  within New Orleans 106-7
  parking 106-7
  renting 107
CBD. *See* Central Business District
cemeteries 146-7
  books about 62
  Lafayette Cemetery No 1 144-5
  Metairie Cemetery 153
  St Louis Cemetery No 1 122-3
  St Louis Cemetery No 3 151
  St Roch Cemetery 131-2
  tours 110
  websites 60
Central Business District (CBD) 49, 132-5, **Map 4**
  accommodations 163-4
  bars 200-1
  restaurants 182-4
  safety issues 69
Chamani, Miriam 110, 123, 126
Chapel of Our Lady of Perpetual Help 144
Charles, Bobby 42
Chickasaw Indians 13
children 66-7, 134-5
Choctaw Indians 13, 16, 118
Chopin, Kate 31-2
Christ Church Cathedral 138
cinemas 204. *See also* films
City Park 49, 148-52, **Map 9**
  accommodations 166-7

Bold indicates maps.

carousel 151-2
  restaurants 190-1
  safety issues 69
civil rights movement 19, 61
Civil War 18
classical music 203-4
climate 22, 23
clothing 48, 208-9
clubs. *See* bars
Code Noir 15, 19
Codrescu, Andrei 33, 34
coffee 173-4
Coliseum Square 140
Colonel Short's Villa 144
Columns Hotel 130, 166
Commander's Palace 174, 186
Confederate Museum 135
Connick, Harry, Jr 45, 85, 90, 121
consulates 53
Contemporary Arts Center 134
cookbooks 210-1
cooking classes 154-5
Coolbone 45
Cooter Brown's Tavern & Oyster Bar 202
Cornstalk Hotel 115, 160-1
costs 56-7
Covington 217, 220, 221-2
craps 131
crawfish 187, 211
Crawford, Davell 47
credit cards 56
Creoles 14, 16, 19, 61, 80-1, 168-9
crime 69-70
cultural centers 68-9, 226
Custom House 129
customs 54
cycling. *See* bicycling

D

Dabezies House 151
dance clubs 195-6
Davis, Quint 194, 195
debit cards 56
Degas, Edgar 133, 167
Delmonico 171, 186
demographics 29-30
DePouilly, JNB 119, 130

De Soto, Hernando 13-4
Destrehan Plantation 230
Dillard University 68
Dirty Dozen Brass Band 45, 46
disabled travelers 66
'Dixie,' origin of 56
documents 51, 54
dollar sign, origin of 55
Domino, Fats 22, 42
Donaldsonville 232
Dorsey, Lee 42
drinks 70-1, 173-4, 196.
  See also bars
driving. *See* car travel
Dr John (conjurer) 124-5
Dr John (musician) 43-4, 46, 60
Duke, David 29, 62

E

Eaglin, Snooks 41, 200, 203
ecology 22-6
economy 29
Edwards, Edwin 29, 62, 235
1850 House 119-21
eKno communication card 58
electricity 64
email 59
embassies 52-3
employment 76
entertainment 193-205
  bars 193-203, 217, 220, 222, 224
  cinemas 204
  classical music 203-4
  dance clubs 195-6
  guides 193
  larger venues 203
  live music 193-4, 200-2
  outside New Orleans 217, 220, 222
  riverboat jazz 204
  spectator sports 204-5
  street performers 204
  theater 203
  tickets 193
  websites 59
environment 22-6, 61-2
Ernie K-Doe's Mother-in-Law Lounge 199

Boxed Text

Bold indicates maps.

New Orleans Map Section

ADAM LUTZ

MAP 1 NEW ORLEANS

To Mandeville,
Covington

*Lake
Pontchartrain*

Lake Pontchartrain Causeway (toll)

Linear Park Bike Path

W Esplanade Ave

Williams Blvd

Bonnabel Blvd

10

Veterans Memorial Blvd

10

New Orleans
International Airport

Airport Access Rd

David Drive

Clearview Pkwy

Causeway Blvd

Metairie Rd

Metairie

61

49

Williams Blvd

Airline Hwy

Airline Hwy

61

48

Jefferson Hwy

Earhart Expwy

Central Ave

90

Mississippi River

18

River Levee Bike Path

Hickory Ave

48

90

River Rd

River Rd

48

River Rd

541

Colonial Club Drive

River Rd

Jefferson Parish
Orleans Parish

RIVERBEN
MAP 7

River Rd

River Rd

90

Bridge City

18

**Audubon
Park**

18

90

4th St

Lapalco Blvd

BUS
90

**Bayou
Segnette
State Park**

Drake Ave

Westwego

Cataouatche Canal

*Lake
Cataouatche*

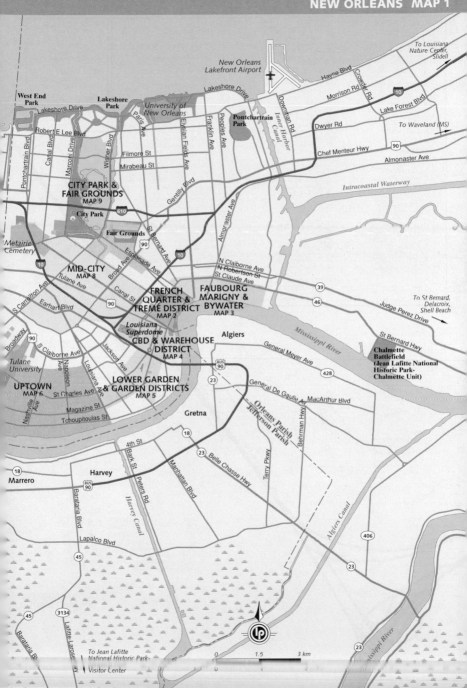

MAP 2 FRENCH QUARTER & TREMÉ DISTRICT

FRENCH QUARTER

PLACES TO STAY
10 Le Richelieu
16 Hotel St Pierre
17 Gentry House
21 Lafitte Guest House
24 Soniat House
36 Cornstalk Hotel
37 Andrew Jackson Hotel
39 Chateau Motor Hotel
41 Hotel Provincial
62 Bourbon Orleans Hotel
92 Royal Sonesta
94 Omni Royal Orleans
114 Hotel Monteleone
115 Holiday Inn
119 Marriot Hotel
124 Westin Canal Place

PLACES TO EAT
8 Port of Call
9 Mona Lisa
11 Peristyle
19 Quarter Scene Restaurant (QSR)
26 Croissant d'Or Patisserie
29 Louisiana Pizza Kitchen
32 Mama Rosa's
34 Clover Grill
40 Irene's Cuisine
44 Coop's Place
53 Secret Garden
54 Kaldi's Coffeehouse
55 Café Sbisa
65 La Madeleine French Bakery & Cafe
68 Progress Grocery Co
69 Central Grocery
70 Royal Blend
71 Court of Two Sisters
72 Gumbo Shop
77 Café du Monde
78 Bayona
79 Déjà Vu Bar & Diner
81 Lucky Cheng's
82 Antoine's
86 Shalimar
87 Café Maspero
91 Arnaud's
93 Brennan's Restaurant
98 K-Paul's Louisiana Kitchen
99 NOLA
100 Johnny's Po-Boys
101 Café Beignet
103 Old Dog New Trick Café
104 Bacco
109 Southern Candymakers
110 Galatoire's
112 Acme Oyster & Seafood House
113 Mr B's Bistro
116 Country Flame
118 Palace Café
122 Olivier's

BARS & CLUBS
15 Donna's Bar & Grill
20 Lafitte's Blacksmith Shop
28 Palm Court Jazz Cafe
31 Funky Butt on Congo Square
33 Rawhide 2010
43 Molly's at the Market
45 Margaritaville Café
47 Gold Mine Saloon
49 Bourbon Pub
50 Oz
57 Fahy's Irish Pub
58 Maison Bourbon
59 Preservation Hall
60 Pat O'Brien's
95 Napoleon House
111 Storyville District
117 Levon Helm's Classic American
120 House of Blues
123 Tipitina's French Quarter

OTHER
7 Kaboom Books
12 Hula Mae's Laundry
13 Voodoo Spiritual Temple
14 Gay Mart
18 Get Me Outta Here Travel
22 Royal Pharmacy
23 Gallier House Museum
25 Vision Quest
27 Beauregard-Keyes House
30 Flea Market
35 Historic Voodoo Museum
38 French Quarter Postal Emporium
42 Ursaline Convent
46 Farmer's Market
48 Marie Laveau's House of Voodoo
51 Royal Mail Sevice
52 Madame John's Legacy
61 Arcadian Books & Art Prints
63 Presbytère
64 Mardi Gras Center
66 New Orleans Welcome Center
67 French Quarter Bicycles
73 Faulkner House Bookshop
74 St Louis Cathedral
75 Cabildo
76 Jackson Monument
80 Hermann-Grima House
83 Kurt E Schon Gallery
84 Historic New Orleans Collection (Court of Two Lions)
85 Barrister's Gallery
90 Post Office
96 Maspero's Exchange
97 ATM
102 A Gallery of Fine Photography
105 Magic Bus
106 NPS Visitor Center
107 Bookstar
108 ATM
121 Louisiana Music Factory
125 Entergy IMAX Theatre

TREMÉ DISTRICT

PLACES TO STAY
1 Maison Esplanade Guest House
2 Hotel Storyville
3 Rathbone Inn

BARS & CLUBS
4 Tremé Music Hall
5 Joe's Cozy Corner

OTHER
6 St Augustine's Church
56 Mortuary Chapel
88 Budget Car Rental
89 Saenger Theater

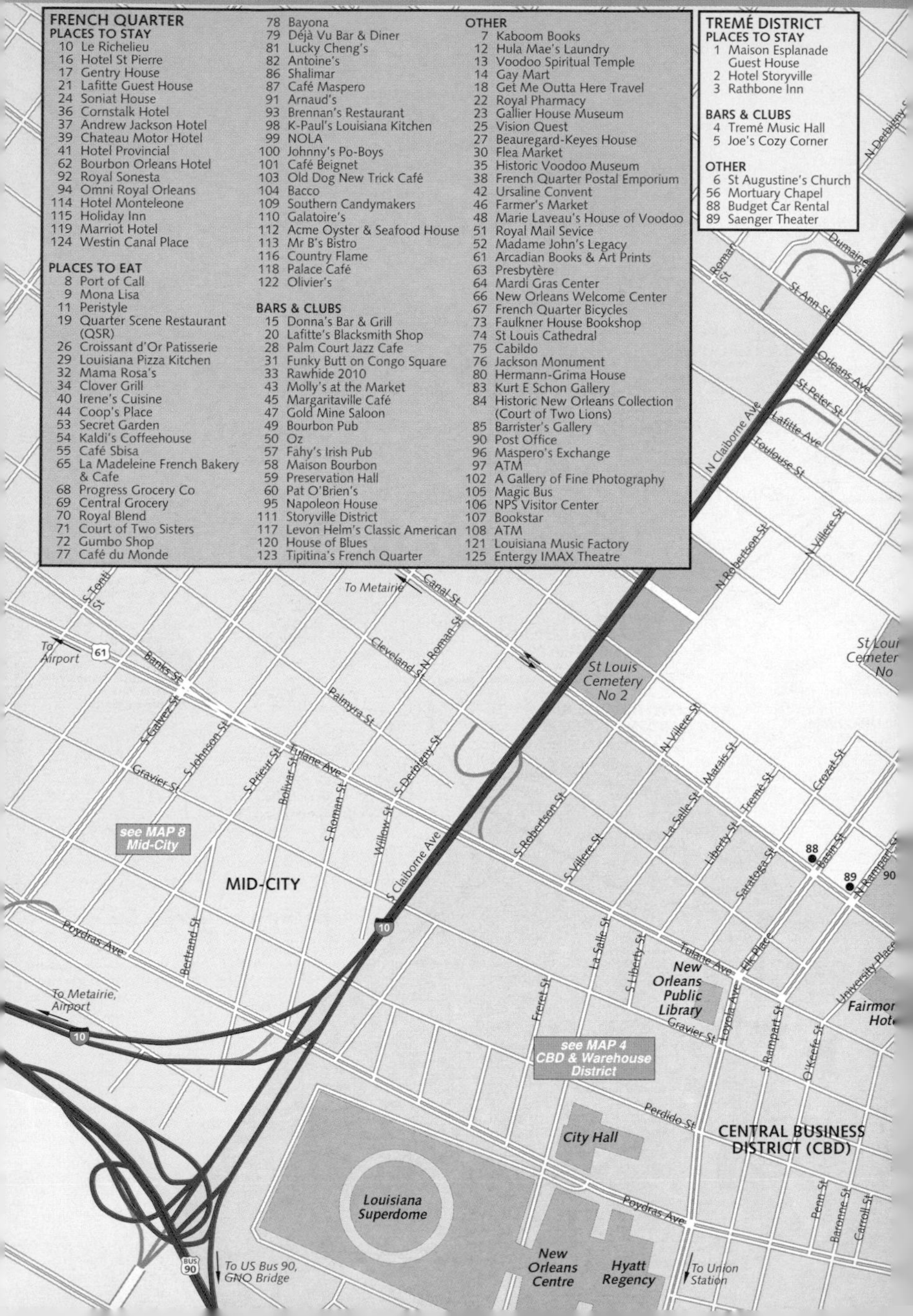

N Derbigny St
Dumaine St
Roman St
St Ann St
Orleans Ave
St Peter St
Lafitte Ave
Toulouse St
N Claiborne Ave
N Villere St
N Robertson St
To Metairie
Canal St
S Tonti St
To Airport
61
Banks St
Cleveland St
N Roman St
Palmyra St
St Louis Cemetery No 2
St Louis Cemetery No
S Galvez St
S Johnson St
S Prieur St
Tulane Ave
Bolivar St
S Derbigny St
Gravier St
S Roman St
Willow St
S Claiborne Ave
S Robertson St
S Villere St
La Salle St
Marais St
Tremé St
Liberty St
Saratoga St
Crozat St
Basin St
N Rampart St
88
89
90
see MAP 8 Mid-City
MID-CITY
10
Poydras Ave
Bertrand St
La Salle St
S Liberty St
Tulane Ave
Elk Place
New Orleans Public Library
University Place
Fairmont Hotel
To Metairie, Airport
Freret St
Gravier St
Loyola Ave
S Rampart St
O'Keefe St
see MAP 4 CBD & Warehouse District
Perdido St
City Hall
CENTRAL BUSINESS DISTRICT (CBD)
Louisiana Superdome
Poydras Ave
Penn St
Baronne St
Carroll St
BUS 90
To US Bus 90, GNO Bridge
New Orleans Centre
Hyatt Regency
To Union Station

To I-610

To UNO,
The Lakefront

Morris St

Columbus St

Kerlerec St

Esplanade Ave

Burgundy St

Dauphine St

**FAUBOURG
MARIGNY**

Royal St

Chartres St

Decatur St

N Rampart St

N Robertson St

N Villere St

Marais St

Treme St

N Claiborne Ave

Bayou Rd

N Claiborne Ave

St Philip St

TREMÉ DISTRICT

St Claude St

Barracks St

Burgundy St

Governor Nicholls St

Ursulines Ave

St Philip St

Orleans Ave

St Ann St

Dumaine St

FRENCH QUARTER

Dauphine St

Bourbon St

Royal St

Chartres St

Decatur St

see MAP 3
Faubourg
Marigny
& Bywater

**Old
US Mint**

N Peters St

Riverfront Streetcar

**Mahalia
Jackson
Theatre**

**Louis
Armstrong
Park**

Louis
Armstrong
Statue

**Municipal
Auditorium**

Park
Entrance

Congo
Square

St Peter St

Toulouse St

St Louis St

Conti St

Bienville St

Iberville St

Bourbon St

Dauphine St

Burgundy St

French Market pl

French
Market

Antoine Alley
Pirates Alley
Ped Mall
Madison St
Wilkinson St

Moonwalk

**Jackson
Square**

Pontalba Apartments

**Jackson
Brewery**

Mississippi River

downriver

ALGIERS

upriver

**Supreme
Court**

Dauphine St

Bourbon St

Royal St

Exchange pl
Chartres St

Decatur St

Clinton St
Clay St

French St
Iberville St

Canal St

Common St

Magazine St

Camp St

St Charles Ave Streetcar

Union St

Perdido St

Magdalen St

Ferry to Algiers

*John James
Audubon
(Riverboat
Zoo Cruise)*

**Woldenberg
Park**

**Canal Place
Shopping
Centre**

*Aquarium of
the Americas*

To Convention
Center

Canal St Ferry

0   150   300 m

0   150   300 yards

MAP 3 FAUBOURG MARIGNY & BYWATER

To UNO,
The Lakefront

To I-610

N Rocheblave St

N Tonti St

N Miro St

N Galvez St

N Johnson St

N Prieur St

St Roch Park

N Roman St

St Roch
Cemetery

N Derbigny St

N Claiborne Ave

N Robertson St

N Villere St

Urquhart St

Marais St

Marigny St

Mandeville St

Spain St

St Roch Ave

Music St

Arts St

Painters St

Almonaster Ave

Franklin Ave

Port St

St Ferdinand St

to MAP 9
City Park &
Fair Grounds

St Claude Ave

St Bernard Ave

Columbus St

St Anthony Ave

Pauger St

Touro St

Frenchmen St

Tristan Fields Ave

N Rampart St

Burgundy St

Dauphine St

Royal St

Chartres St

Decatur St

N Peters St

FAUBOURG
MARIGNY

Marias St

Treme St

St Claude Ave

Kerlerec St

TREMÉ
DISTRICT

N Robertson St

N Villere St

N Rampart St

Barracks St

Dauphine St

Esplanade Ave

Bourbon St

Royal St

Chartres St

Decatur St

French Market Place

N Peters St

see MAP 2
French Quarter
& Tremé District

Governor Nicholls St

Ursulines Ave

FRENCH QUARTER

Burgundy St

St Philip St

Dumaine St

St Ann St

Orleans Ave

French
Market

Riverfront Streetcar

Moonwalk

Old
US Mint

Washington
Square
Park

46

1

7

6

4

5

12

13

14

15

16

17

18

19

20

21

22

23

24

25

26

27

28

8

Mississippi River

upriver

FAUBOURG MARIGNY
PLACES TO STAY
5 Melrose Mansion
12 Girod House
22 Lamothe House
25 The Frenchmen
27 Hotel de la Monnaie
28 Lion's Inn

PLACES TO EAT
4 Buffa's
6 La Peniche
7 Santa Fe
8 The Harbor
13 Café Marigny
20 Praline Connection
26 Siam Café

BARS & CLUBS
1 Hi-Ho Lounge
15 Royal Street Inn
16 Rubyfruit Jungle
17 Snug Harbor
21 Cafe Brasil
23 Dream Palace
24 Igor's Checkpoint Charlie
26 Dragon's Den

OTHER
6 Marigny Laundromat
14 Royal Laundry
18 Theatre Marigny
19 Faubourg Marigny Book Store

BYWATER
PLACES TO STAY
11 Mazant Guest House

PLACES TO EAT
3 Mandich Restaurant
10 Bywater Barbecue
29 Elizabeth's

BARS & CLUBS
2 Saturn Bar
30 Vaughan's

OTHER
9 Porché West Gallery

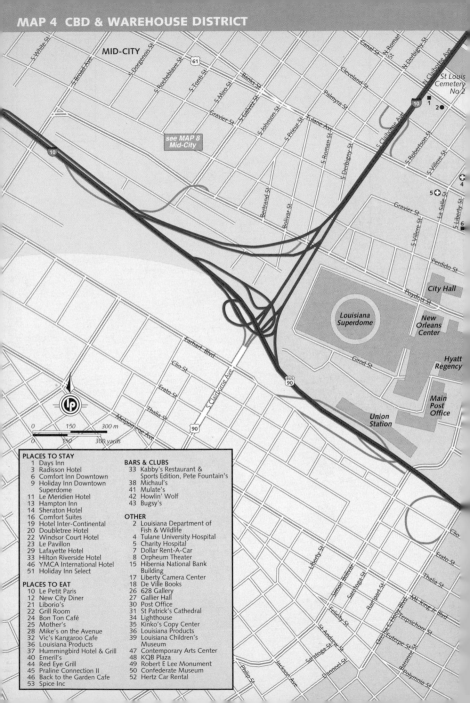

MAP 4 CBD & WAREHOUSE DISTRICT

MID-CITY

61

10

see MAP 8
Mid-City

10

St Louis
Cemetery
No 2

1

2

4

5

6

Gravier St

Perdido St

City Hall

New
Orleans
Center

Louisiana
Superdome

Poydras St

Hyatt
Regency

Girod St

BUS
90

Main
Post
Office

Union
Station

Earhart Blvd

Clio St

Erato St

Thalia St

Melpomene Ave

90

0   150   300 m
0   150   300 yards

Clio St

Erato St

Thalia St

PLACES TO STAY
1   Days Inn
3   Radisson Hotel
6   Comfort Inn Downtown
9   Holiday Inn Downtown
    Superdome
11 Le Meridien Hotel
13 Hampton Inn
14 Sheraton Hotel
16 Comfort Suites
19 Hotel Inter-Continental
20 Doubletree Hotel
22 Windsor Court Hotel
23 Le Pavillon
29 Lafayette Hotel
33 Hilton Riverside Hotel
46 YMCA International Hotel
51 Holiday Inn Select

PLACES TO EAT
10 Le Petit Paris
12 New City Diner
21 Liborio's
22 Grill Room
24 Bon Ton Café
25 Mother's
28 Mike's on the Avenue
32 Vic's Kangaroo Cafe
36 Louisiana Products
37 Hummingbird Hotel & Grill
40 Emeril's
44 Red Eye Grill
45 Praline Connection II
46 Back to the Garden Cafe
53 Spice Inc

BARS & CLUBS
33 Kabby's Restaurant &
    Sports Edition, Pete Fountain's
38 Michaul's
41 Mulate's
42 Howlin' Wolf
43 Bugsy's

OTHER
2   Louisiana Department of
    Fish & Wildlife
4   Tulane University Hospital
5   Charity Hospital
7   Dollar Rent-A-Car
8   Orpheum Theater
15 Hibernia National Bank
    Building
17 Liberty Camera Center
18 De Ville Books
26 628 Gallery
27 Gallier Hall
30 Post Office
31 St Patrick's Cathedral
34 Lighthouse
35 Kinko's Copy Center
36 Louisiana Products
39 Louisiana Children's
    Museum
47 Contemporary Arts Center
48 KQB Plaza
49 Robert E Lee Monument
50 Confederate Museum
52 Hertz Car Rental

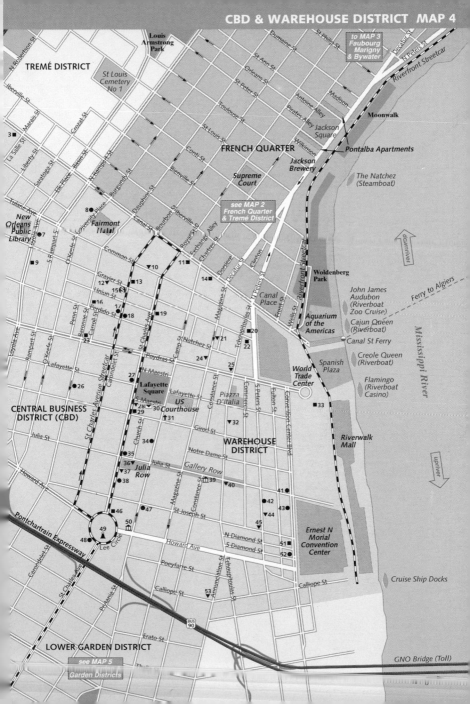

TREMÉ DISTRICT

Louis Armstrong Park

St Louis Cemetery No 1

N Robertson St
Iberville St
Marais St
La Salle St
Liberty St
Treme St
Elk Place
N Rampart St
Burgundy St
Dauphine St
Bourbon St

FRENCH QUARTER

Dumaine St
St Philip St
St Ann St
Orleans St
St Peter St
Toulouse St
St Louis St
Cont St
Bienville St
Iberville St
Canal St

Antoine Alley
Pirates Alley
Madison
Wilkinson

Jackson Square

Moonwalk

Pontalba Apartments

Supreme Court

Jackson Brewery

The Natchez (Steamboat)

see MAP 2 French Quarter & Treme District

to MAP 3 Faubourg Marigny & Bywater

Decatur St
N Peters St
Riverfront Streetcar

downriver

New Orleans Public Library

Fairmont Hotel

3 ■
8 ▲
7 ●
9 ■

O'Keefe St
S Rampart St
Baronne St
Carondelet St
St Charles Ave
Common St
Gravier St
Union St
Perdido St

Royal St
Chartres St
Exchange Alley
Dorsiere St
Decatur St
N Peters St
Wells St
Ernest St

Woldenberg Park

Canal Place

Aquarium of the Americas

John James Audubon (Riverboat Zoo Cruise)

Cajun Queen (Riverboat)

Canal St Ferry

Creole Queen (Riverboat)

Flamingo (Riverboat Casino)

Ferry to Algiers

Mississippi River

▼10
11 ■
12▼
13 ●
15●●
16■
17●
1●
18
19 ■
14 ■

Spanish Plaza

World Trade Center

CENTRAL BUSINESS DISTRICT (CBD)

26 ●

27 ●
Lafayette Square

28▼
29
30
31 ✝
US Courthouse

Lafayette St
S Maestri
N Maestri
Church St
Camp St
Magazine St
Constance St
Tchoupitoulas St

Piazza D'Italia

Poydras St
Natchez St
▼21
22 ▼
20 ■
25 ●
24 ▼
▼32

WAREHOUSE DISTRICT

■ 33

Riverwalk Mall

34 ●
35 ●
36▼
37 ▼
38 ●

Julia Row

Girod St
Notre Dame St
Gallery Row
39 ▲
▼40
41 ●
42 ●
43 ●
▼44
45 ▼

Ernest N Morial Convention Center

Loyola Ave
Rampart St
O'Keefe St
Lafayette St

Penn St
Baronne St
Carroll St
23 ●

St Charles Avenue Streetcar
Carondelet St
S Maestri

Julia St
Howard Ave

46 ■
50
47 ●
48 ●
49 ▲
Lee Circle

St Joseph St
N Diamond St
S Diamond St
51 ●
52 ●

Pontchartrain Expressway

Howard Ave
Poeyfarre St
Calliope St

Cruise Ship Docks

upriver

LOWER GARDEN DISTRICT

St Charles Ave
Carondelet St
Prytania St

53 ●

BUS 90

Erato St

see MAP 5 Garden Districts

GNO Bridge (Toll)

MAP 5 LOWER GARDEN & GARDEN DISTRICTS

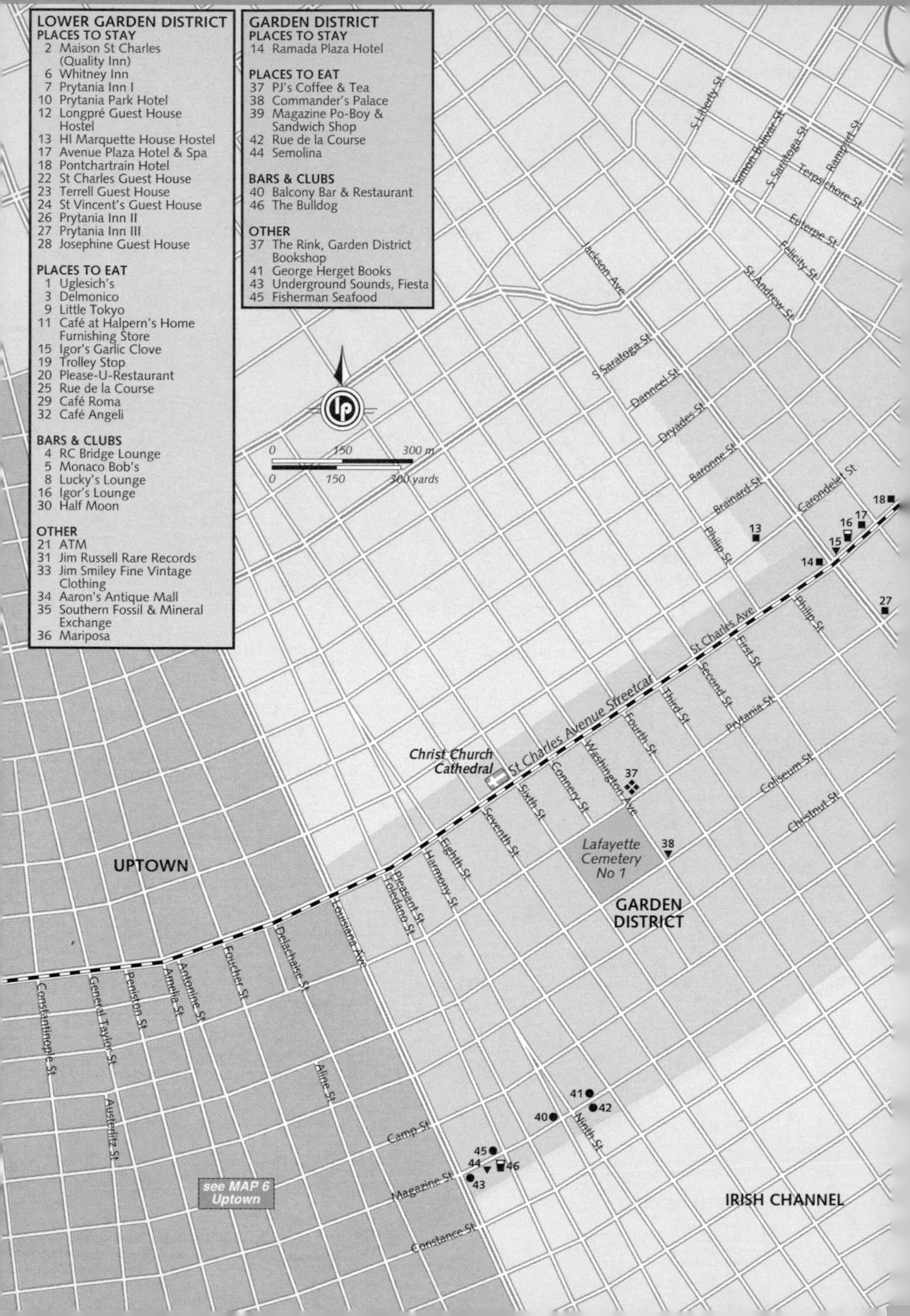
LOWER GARDEN DISTRICT
PLACES TO STAY
2 Maison St Charles (Quality Inn)
6 Whitney Inn
7 Prytania Inn I
10 Prytania Park Hotel
12 Longpré Guest House Hostel
13 HI Marquette House Hostel
17 Avenue Plaza Hotel & Spa
18 Pontchartrain Hotel
22 St Charles Guest House
23 Terrell Guest House
24 St Vincent's Guest House
26 Prytania Inn II
27 Prytania Inn III
28 Josephine Guest House
PLACES TO EAT
1 Uglesich's
3 Delmonico
9 Little Tokyo
11 Café at Halpern's Home Furnishing Store
15 Igor's Garlic Clove
19 Trolley Stop
20 Please-U-Restaurant
25 Rue de la Course
29 Café Roma
32 Café Angeli
BARS & CLUBS
4 RC Bridge Lounge
5 Monaco Bob's
8 Lucky's Lounge
16 Igor's Lounge
30 Half Moon
OTHER
21 ATM
31 Jim Russell Rare Records
33 Jim Smiley Fine Vintage Clothing
34 Aaron's Antique Mall
35 Southern Fossil & Mineral Exchange
36 Mariposa
GARDEN DISTRICT
PLACES TO STAY
14 Ramada Plaza Hotel
PLACES TO EAT
37 PJ's Coffee & Tea
38 Commander's Palace
39 Magazine Po-Boy & Sandwich Shop
42 Rue de la Course
44 Semolina
BARS & CLUBS
40 Balcony Bar & Restaurant
46 The Bulldog
OTHER
37 The Rink, Garden District Bookshop
41 George Herget Books
43 Underground Sounds, Fiesta
45 Fisherman Seafood
0 150 300 m
0 150 300 yards
S Liberty St
Simon Bolivar St
S Saratoga St
Rampart St
Terpsichore St
Euterpe St
Felicity St
St Andrew St
Jackson Ave
S Saratoga St
Danneel St
Dryades St
Baronne St
Brainard St
Carondelet St
Philip St
St Charles Ave
First St
Second St
Third St
Fourth St
Prytania St
Coliseum St
Chestnut St
St Charles Avenue Streetcar
Christ Church Cathedral
Washington Ave
Commery St
Sixth St
Seventh St
Eighth St
Harmony St
Pleasant St
Toledano St
Louisiana Ave
Delachaise St
Foucher St
Antonine St
Amelia St
Peniston St
General Taylor St
Constantinople St
Austerlitz St
Aline St
Lafayette Cemetery No 1
GARDEN DISTRICT
UPTOWN
IRISH CHANNEL
Camp St
Magazine St
Constance St
Ninth St
see MAP 6 Uptown

To I-10

St-Joseph St

CENTRAL BUSINESS DISTRICT (CBD)

S Clio St

H Erato St

Howard Ave

N Diamond St

S Diamond St

Ernest N Morial Convention Center

Riverfront Mall

Lee Circle

Poeyfarre St

Thalia St

▼1

Poeyfarre St

Calliope St

Annunciation St

Tchoupitoulas St

see MAP 4 CBD & Warehouse District

Cruise Ship Docks

Pontchartrain Expressway

Mt King Jr Blvd

Carondelet St

St Charles Ave

2■
3

4
Erato St

BUS 90

5☐

I-90

GNO Bridge (Toll)

6■

7■
Prytania St

LOWER GARDEN DISTRICT

Thalia St

To Algiers

8■
▼9

10■

11

Melpomene St

Polymnia St

■12

Terpsichore St

Terpsichore St

Camp St

20▼
19
▼
§
21

■22

Coliseum St

Magazine St

23■

Constance St

Annunciation St

Euterpe St

Coliseum Square

Urania St
Felicity St

24■
25

Race St

S Peters St

St Mary St

St Andrew St

Orange St

Annunciation Center

26■

Josephine St

28■

Richard St

Annunciation St

Chippewa St

St Thomas St

Religieus St

Tchoupitoulas St

Jackson Ave

29▼
30
●31
▼32

Sophie Wright Place

Market St

Camp St

33●
●34

35●
●36

St James St

Magazine St

Constance St

▼39

Laurel St

Annunciation St

Chippewa St

St Thomas St

Mississippi River

downriver

upriver

Ferry to Gretna

GRETNA

MAP 6 UPTOWN

Leveev Park

Bike Path

S Carrollton Ave

RIVERBEND

see MAP 7
Riverbend

Willow St

Plum St

Oak St

Zimple St

Freret St

Burthe St

Maple St

Hampson St

Newcomb
College

Audubon Blvd

McAlister Place

Tulane
University

Ursuline College
& Convent

Short St

Peres St

Burdette St

Adams St

Hillary St

Cherokee St

Leake Ave

Pearl St

Millaudon St

Lowerline St

Pine St

Dominican St

Broadway

Benjamin St

Hurst St

Garfield St

Pitt St

St Charles Ave

Audubon St

Walnut St

Newcomb Blvd

Audubon Place (Private)

Loyola
University

Calhoun Ave

Palmer Ave

State St

Nashville Ave

Joseph St

Octavia St

Golf
Course

St Charles Avenue Streetcar

Audubon Park

West Ave

International Drive

Benjamin St

Hurst St

Garfield St

Pitt St

Prytania St

Perrier St

Webster St

State St

Eleonore St

Nashville Ave

Arabella St

Joseph St

Octavia St

Jefferson Ave

Leontine St

Valmont St

2

Zoo Ave

North St

South St

Coliseum St

Chestnut St

Camp St

Magazine St

Constance St

Patton St

Laurel St

Annunciation St

Tchoupitoulas St

Belfast St

16 17 ▼

18 ■
● 19

28 ▼

Audubon Zoological
Garden

Exposition Blvd

Calhoun St

Henry Clay St

Natatorium Drive

Arboretum Drive

Rivera Drive

Park Drive

Riverview Drive

Bike Path

▼ 26

❖ 27

uuriver

Mississippi River

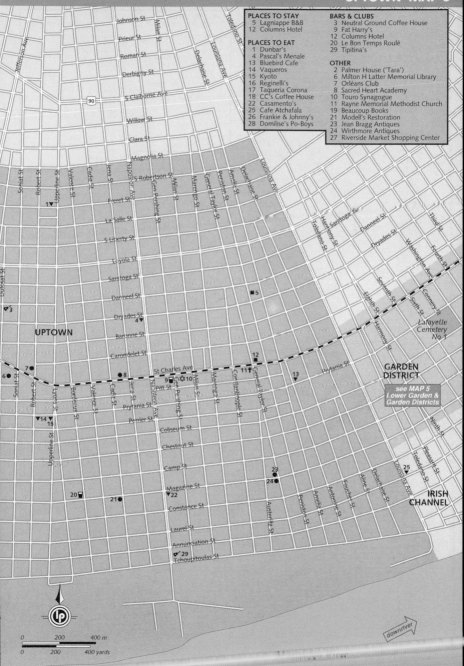

PLACES TO STAY
5 Lagniappe B&B
12 Columns Hotel

PLACES TO EAT
1 Dunbar's
4 Pascal's Menale
13 Bluebird Cafe
14 Vaqueros
15 Kyoto
16 Reginelli's
17 Taqueria Corona
18 CC's Coffee House
22 Casamento's
25 Cafe Atchafala
26 Frankie & Johnny's
28 Domilise's Po-Boys

BARS & CLUBS
3 Neutral Ground Coffee House
9 Fat Harry's
12 Columns Hotel
20 Le Bon Temps Roulé
29 Tipitina's

OTHER
2 Palmer House ('Tara')
6 Milton H Latter Memorial Library
7 Orléans Club
8 Sacred Heart Academy
10 Touro Synagogue
11 Rayne Memorial Methodist Church
19 Beaucoup Books
21 Modell's Restoration
23 Jean Bragg Antiques
24 Wirthmore Antiques
27 Riverside Market Shopping Center

UPTOWN

GARDEN
DISTRICT

see MAP 5
Lower Garden &
Garden Districts

Lafayette
Cemetery
No 1

IRISH
CHANNEL

downriver

0   200   400 m
0   200   400 yards

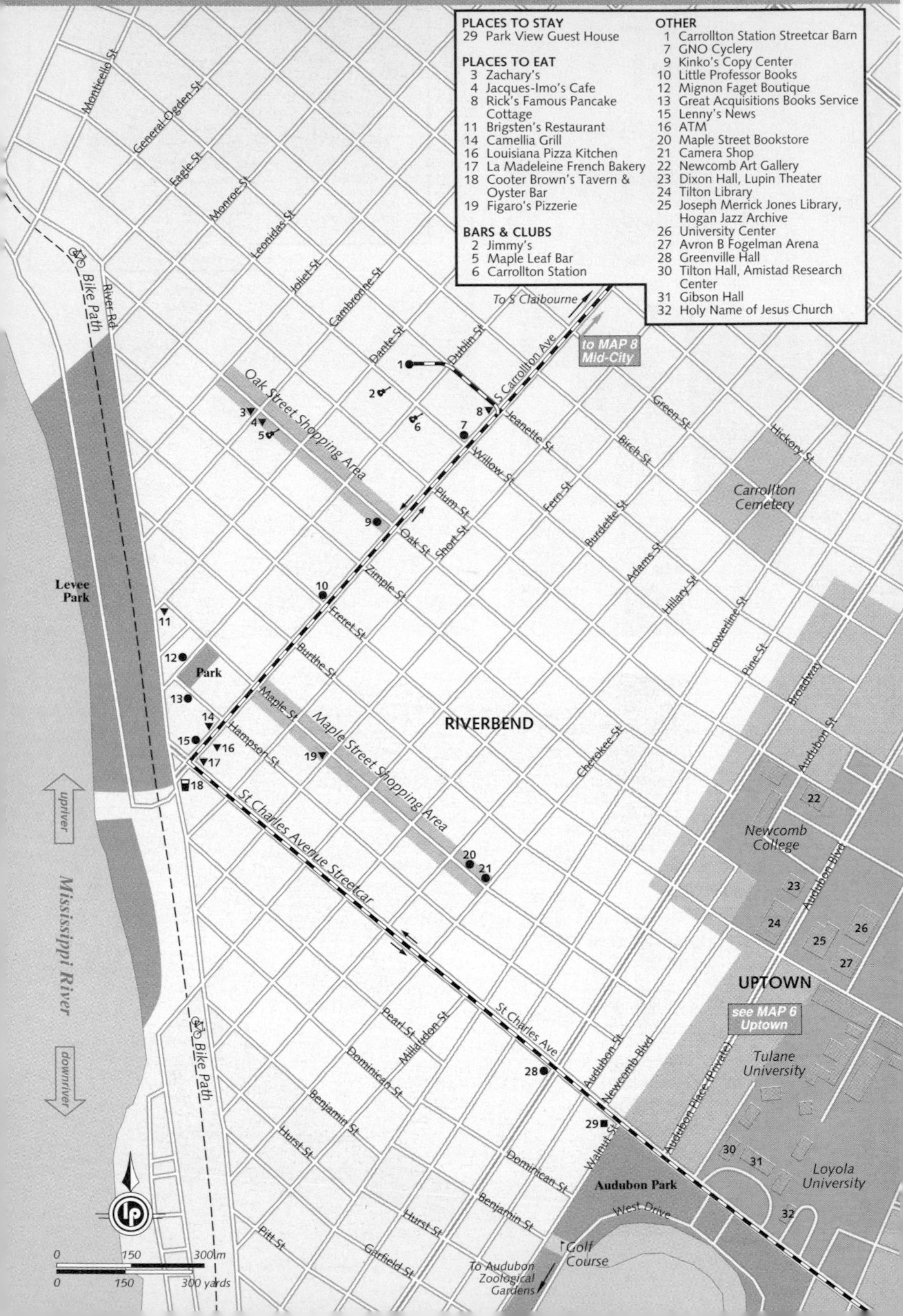

MAP 7 RIVERBEND

RIVERBEND MAP 7

PLACES TO STAY
29 Park View Guest House

PLACES TO EAT
3 Zachary's
4 Jacques-Imo's Cafe
8 Rick's Famous Pancake Cottage
11 Brigsten's Restaurant
14 Camellia Grill
16 Louisiana Pizza Kitchen
17 La Madeleine French Bakery
18 Cooter Brown's Tavern & Oyster Bar
19 Figaro's Pizzerie

BARS & CLUBS
2 Jimmy's
5 Maple Leaf Bar
6 Carrollton Station

OTHER
1 Carrollton Station Streetcar Barn
7 GNO Cyclery
9 Kinko's Copy Center
10 Little Professor Books
12 Mignon Faget Boutique
13 Great Acquisitions Books Service
15 Lenny's News
16 ATM
20 Maple Street Bookstore
21 Camera Shop
22 Newcomb Art Gallery
23 Dixon Hall, Lupin Theater
24 Tilton Library
25 Joseph Merrick Jones Library, Hogan Jazz Archive
26 University Center
27 Avron B Fogelman Arena
28 Greenville Hall
30 Tilton Hall, Amistad Research Center
31 Gibson Hall
32 Holy Name of Jesus Church

To S Claiborne

to MAP 8
Mid-City

Montcello St

General Ogden St

Eagle St

Monroe St

Leonidas St

Joliet St

Cambronne St

Dante St

Dublin St

S Carrollton Ave

Jeannette St

Green St

Hickory St

Oak Street Shopping Area

Willow St

Birch St

Fern St

Carrollton Cemetery

Plum St

Burdette St

Short St

Oak St

Adams St

Zimple St

Hillary St

Lowerline St

Freret St

Pine St

Burthe St

Levee Park

Maple St

Park

Hampson St

Maple Street Shopping Area

Cherokee St

RIVERBEND

Broadway

Audubon Blvd

Newcomb College

Audubon Blvd

St Charles Avenue Streetcar

UPTOWN

see MAP 6
Uptown

Mississippi River

Pearl St

Millaudon St

St Charles Ave

Dominican St

Newcomb Blvd

Audubon Place Private

Tulane University

Benjamin St

Walnut St

Hurst St

Dominican St

Loyola University

Audubon Park

Hurst St

Benjamin St

West Drive

Golf Course

Pitt St

Garfield St

To Audubon Zoological Gardens

River Rd

Bike Path

uptriver

downriver

Bike Path

0   150   300lm
0   150   300 yards

New Orleans blues

MAP 8 MID-CITY

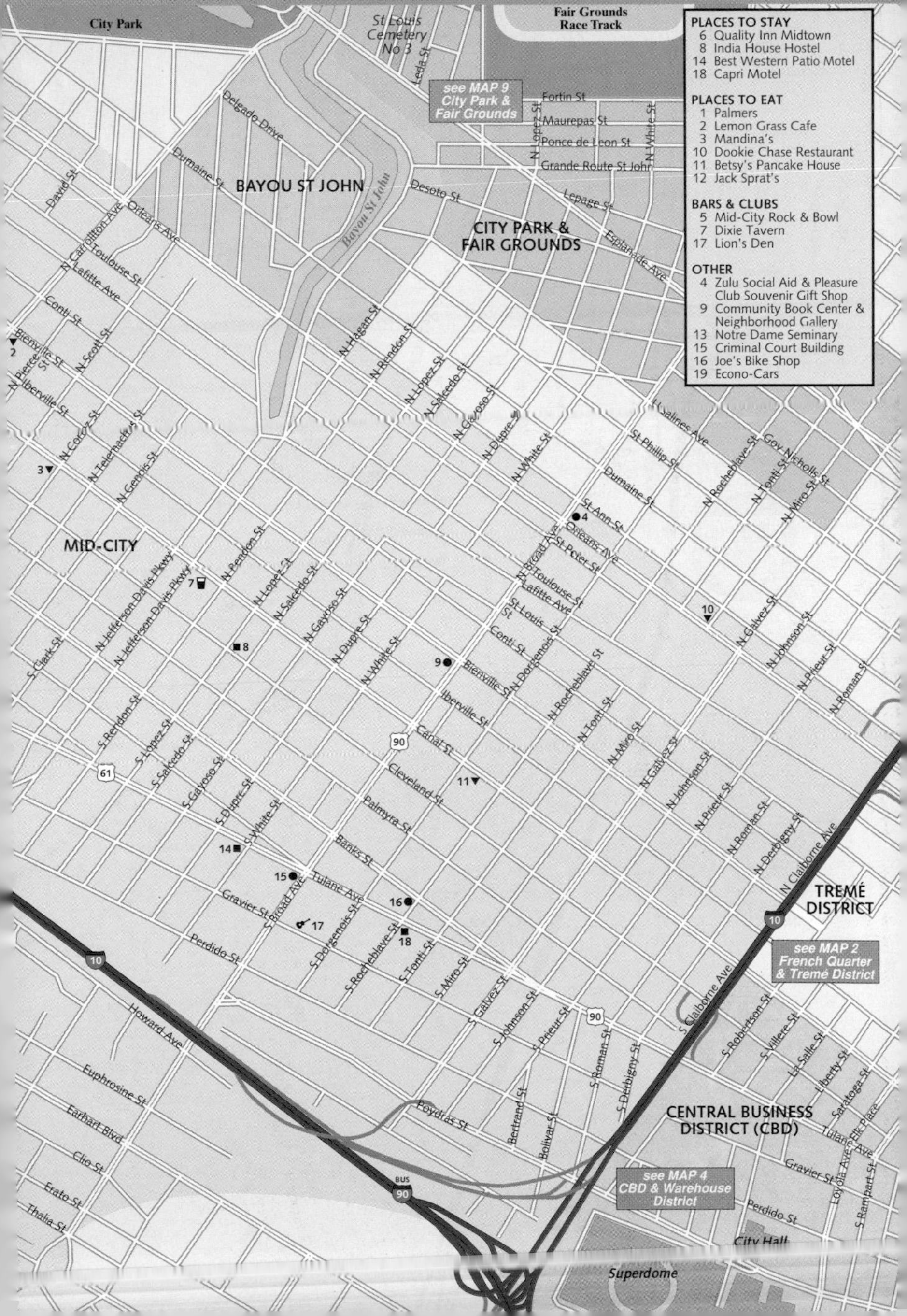

PLACES TO STAY
6 Quality Inn Midtown
8 India House Hostel
14 Best Western Patio Motel
18 Capri Motel
PLACES TO EAT
1 Palmers
2 Lemon Grass Cafe
3 Mandina's
10 Dookie Chase Restaurant
11 Betsy's Pancake House
12 Jack Sprat's
BARS & CLUBS
5 Mid-City Rock & Bowl
7 Dixie Tavern
17 Lion's Den
OTHER
4 Zulu Social Aid & Pleasure Club Souvenir Gift Shop
9 Community Book Center & Neighborhood Gallery
13 Notre Dame Seminary
15 Criminal Court Building
16 Joe's Bike Shop
19 Econo-Cars
City Park
St Louis Cemetery No 3
Fair Grounds Race Track
see MAP 9 City Park & Fair Grounds
BAYOU ST JOHN
Bayou St John
CITY PARK & FAIR GROUNDS
MID-CITY
TREMÉ DISTRICT
see MAP 2 French Quarter & Tremé District
CENTRAL BUSINESS DISTRICT (CBD)
see MAP 4 CBD & Warehouse District
City Hall
Superdome
Delgado Drive
Dumaine St
Desoto St
Fortin St
Maurepas St
Ponce de Leon St
Grande Route St John
Lepage St
Esplanade Ave
Orleans Ave
N Carrollton Ave
Toulouse St
Lafitte Ave
Conti St
Bienville St
Iberville St
Canal St
Cleveland St
Palmyra St
Banks St
Tulane Ave
Gravier St
Perdido St
Howard Ave
Euphrosine St
Earhart Blvd
Clio St
Erato St
Thalia St
Poydras St
N Claiborne Ave
S Claiborne Ave
N Jefferson Davis Pkwy
N Broad Ave
S Broad Ave
St Ann St
St Peter St
St Louis St
St Phillip St
Gov Nicholls St
Loyola Ave
Elk Place
S Rampart St
Saratoga St
Liberty St
La Salle St
S Villere St
S Robertson St
Bertrand St
Bolivar St
S Derbigny St
S Roman St
S Prieur St
S Johnson St
S Galvez St
S Miro St
S Tonti St
S Rocheblave St
S Dorgenois St
S White St
S Dupre St
S Gayoso St
S Salcedo St
S Lopez St
S Rendon St
S Clark St
N Roman St
N Prieur St
N Johnson St
N Galvez St
N Miro St
N Tonti St
N Rocheblave St
N Dorgenois St
N White St
N Dupre St
N Gayoso St
N Salcedo St
N Lopez St
N Rendon St
N Hagan St
N Genois St
N Telemachus St
N Cortez St
N Scott St
N Pierce St
David St
N Derbigny St
Leda St
90
61
10
BUS 90

MAP 9 CITY PARK & FAIR GROUNDS

16th St
14th St
12th St
10th St

Ringold St
To Lakeshore Park
French St
Germain St
Germain St
Canal Blvd
Vicksburg St
Memphis St
General Diaz St
Marshall Foch St
Argonne Blvd
Central Hale St
Orleans Ave

Bellaire Drive
Fleur de Lis Drive
Pontchartrain Blvd
West End Blvd
Catina St
Milne Blvd
Colbert St
Louisville St
Louri-Fourteenth St

Veterans Memorial Blvd
Cedar St
Polk St
Polk St
Harney St
W Harney St
Sharon St
W Brooks St
Brooks St
Brooks St
Kenilworth St
Kenilworth St

Sylvia Drive
Marcia Drive

610

To Metairie,
Kenner,
New Orleans
International
Airport

Florida Blvd
Florida Blvd
Milne Blvd
Rosemary St
Woodlawn St
Hawthorne Place
Canal Blvd
Ada Place
Charles Place
Jamel Place
N Park Place
N W Park Place
F F Park Place
Mid Park Place
Central Park Pl
S Park Pl

Homedale St
Homedale St
Pontalba St
Catina St
West End Blvd
Mound Ave
Hidalgo St
Navarre St
Hawthorne Place
Louque St
Vicksburg St
Voisin St
General Diaz St
Greenwood St
Weiblen Place
Virginia Ct
Marshall Foch St
Orleans Ave
Orleans Ave

Tad
Gormley
Stadium

Roosevelt Mall
Roosevelt Mall
Magnolia Drive

Stadium Drive
• 1
Victory Ave
• 3
Dreyfous A.

Lakelawn Park
& Mausoleum

Delgado
Community
College

Metairie
Cemetery

10

St Patrick
Cemetery

Holt
Cemetery

Rosedale Dr.

• 7

Canal Blvd
City Park Ave
Virginia

Helena St
N Anthony St
N Bernadotte St
N St Patrick St
N Olympia St
N Murat St
N Olympia St
N Murat St

Metairie Rd

To Longue
Vue House

Congregation
Gates of Prayer
Cemetery

N Bernadotte St
S St Patrick St
S Olympia St
S Murat St
S Alexander St
N Alexander St
N Murat St
N Hennessy St
N Solomon St
David St
N Carrollton Ave

see MAP 8
Mid-City

Toulouse
Lafitte Ave
N Pierc.
Bienville St
Iberville St

MID-CITY

lp

Quinct St
Heaton St
Pear St
Marks St
Peach St
S Bernadotte St
S Olympia St
S Murat St
S Alexander St
S Hennessy St
S Solomon St
Banks St
Palmyra St
Station Ave
Cleveland St
Canal St
S Carrollton Ave
S Scott St
S Pierce St
S Custer St

0   200   400 m
0   200   400 yards

Livingston
Live Oak St
Cherry St
Mistletoe St
Hamilton-Dixon St
Baudin St
D'Hennecourt St
Ulloa St

Tulane Ave

To Lakeshore Park,
Lake Pontchartrain

Park Island Drive

Diagonal Drive

Mandolin St

Marconi Drive

Harrison Ave

Senate St

Lemurville St

Caton St

Foy St

Cadillac St

Buchanan St

Milton St

Alfred St

St Denis St

Encampment St

Imperial Drive

Sere St

Bayou Oaks South
Golf Course

Zachary Taylor Drive

City Park

Bayou St John

Gibson St

Hamburg St

Paris Ave

Sere St

Lafreniere St

Pleasure St

Gentilly Blvd

Florida Ave

Tunica St

Roger Williams St

DeSaix Blvd

Treasure St

Abundance St

CITY PARK & FAIR GROUNDS

Fredericks Drive

Trafalgar St

Derby Place

Castiglione St

Belfort Ave

Agriculture St

St Bernard Ave

Rohrer Ave

Gaynos St

Paris Ave

Bruxelles St

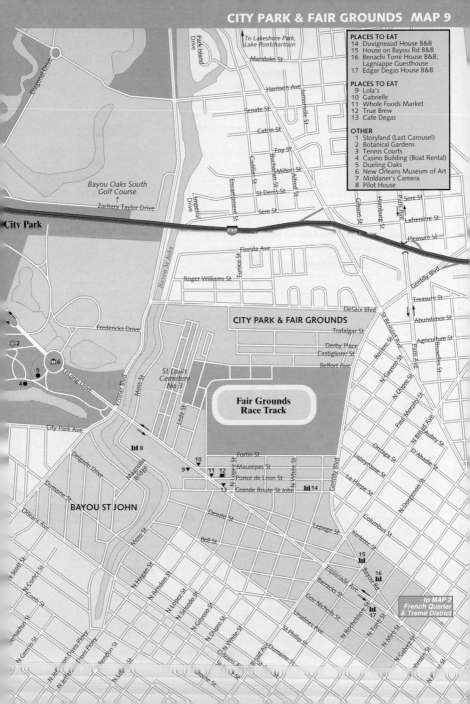

St Louis
Cemetery
No 3

Moss St

Lelong Drive

Esplanade Ave

**Fair Grounds
Race Track**

N D'Hpie St

Paul Morphy St

N Broad St

N Tonti St

Aubry St

D'Abadie St

City Park Ave

Leda St

Fortin St

Maurepas St

Lopez St

Ursulines Ave

N White St

Onzaga St

Lapeyrouse St

La Harpe St

N Dorgenois St

8

Delgado Drive

Magnolia Bridge

10

9

11 12

Ponce de Leon St

13

Grande Route St John

14

Columbus St

Durmaine Ave

BAYOU ST JOHN

Desoto St

Bell St

Lepage St

Kerlerec St

Orleans Ave

N Scott St

N Cortez St

N Conti St

Moss St

N Rendon St

N Salcedo St

N Galvez St

N Dorgenois St

Esplanade Ave

Barracks St

N Rocheblave St

N Tonti St

N Miro St

N Galvez St

15

16

17

Gov Nicholls St

Ursulines Ave

St Philip St

N Prieur St

Orleans Ave

Dumaine St

Morse St

N Johnson St

Davis Pkwy

N Lope St

Rendon St

*to MAP 2
French Quarter
& Tremé District*

MAP LEGEND

BOUNDARIES

- ·· ·— ·— ·— · International
- ··· —·· —·· — State
- ·— — — — — Parish

HYDROGRAPHY

- Water
- Coastline
- Beach
- River, Waterfall
- Swamp, Spring

ROUTES & TRANSPORT

- Freeway
- Toll Freeway
- Primary Road
- Secondary Road
- Tertiary Road
- Unpaved Road
- Pedestrian Mall
- Trail, Bike Trail
- Ferry Route
- Railway, Train Station
- St Charles Avenue Streetcar

ROUTE SHIELDS

- (10) Interstate   (61) State Highway
- (190) US Highway

AREA FEATURES

- Park, Garden
- Ecological Reserve
- Cemetery
- Building
- Plaza
- Golf Course

MAP SYMBOLS

✈ Airfield		⚓ Mission
✈ Airport		⚑ Monument
∴ Archaeological Site, Ruins		☪ Mosque
⑤ Bank		▲ Mountain
Baseball Diamond		🏛 Museum
Beach		Observatory
Border Crossing		← One-Way Street
Bus Depot, Bus Stop		Park
Cathedral		Ⓟ Parking
Cave		)(Pass
† Church		Picnic Area
Dive Site		★ Police Station
Embassy		Pool
Ferry Terminal		Post Office
Foot Bridge		❶ Public Toilets
Garden		Shopping Mall
Gas Station		🏛 Stately Home
✚ Hospital, Clinic		☆ Synagogue
❶ Information		Trailhead
Live Music		Winery
☀ Lookout		🐘 Zoo

- ✪ NATIONAL CAPITAL
- ◉ State, Provincial Capital
- ● LARGE CITY
- ● Medium City
- ● Small City
- ● Town, Village
- ○ Point of Interest
- ■ Place to Stay
- ⛺ Campground
- ⛽ RV Park
- ▼ Place to Eat
- ☕ Bar (Place to Drink)
- ☕ Café

Note: Not all symbols displayed above appear in this book.

LONELY PLANET OFFICES

Australia
PO Box 617, Hawthorn 3122, Victoria
☎ 03 9819 1877 fax 03 9819 6459
email talk2us@lonelyplanet.com.au

USA
150 Linden Street, Oakland, California 94607
☎ 510 893 8555, TOLL FREE 800 275 8555
fax 510 893 8572
email info@lonelyplanet.com

UK
10A Spring Place, London NW5 3BH
☎ 020 7428 4800 fax 020 7428 4828
email go@lonelyplanet.co.uk

France
1 rue du Dahomey, 75011 Paris
☎ 01 55 25 33 00 fax 01 55 25 33 01
email bip@lonelyplanet.fr
3615 lonelyplanet *(1,29 F TTC/min)*

World Wide Web: www.lonelyplanet.com *or* AOL keyword: lp
Lonely Planet Images: lpi@lonelyplanet.com.au